House of Penance

HOUSE OF

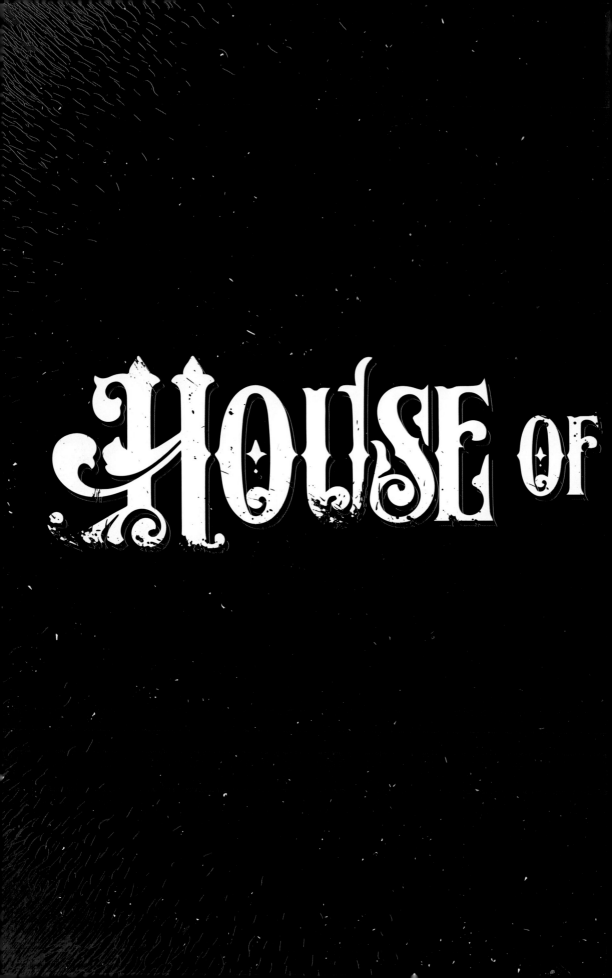

PENANCE

story and words by
PETER J. TOMASI

art by
IAN BERTRAM

colors by
DAVE STEWART

letters by
NATE PIEKOS OF BLAMBOT®

cover art and chapter breaks by
IAN BERTRAM with **DAVE STEWART**

DARK HORSE BOOKS

president & publisher **MIKE RICHARDSON**

editor **DANIEL CHABON**

assistant editor **CARDNER CLARK**

designer **SARAH TERRY**

digital art technician **CHRISTINA McKENZIE**

HOUSE OF PENANCE

Published by Dark Horse Books
A division of Dark Horse Comics, Inc.
10956 SE Main Street, Milwaukie, OR 97222 | DarkHorse.com

To find a comics shop in your area, call the Comic Shop Locator Service toll-free at 1-888-266-4226.
International Licensing: (503) 905-2377

First edition: January 2017 | ISBN 978-1-50670-033-5

1 3 5 7 9 10 8 6 4 2
Printed in China

Library of Congress Cataloging-in-Publication Data

Names: Tomasi, Peter, author. | Bertram, Ian (Comic book artist), artist. |
    Stewart, Dave, colorist, artist. | Piekos, Nate, letterer.
Title: House of penance / written by Peter J. Tomasi ; art by Ian Bertram ;
    colors by Dave Stewart ; letters by Nate Piekos of Blambot ; cover art and
    chapter breaks by Ian Bertram with Dave Stewart.
Description: First edition. | Milwaukie, OR : Dark Horse Books, 2017.
Identifiers: LCCN 2016032628 | ISBN 9781506700335 (paperback)
Subjects: LCSH: Graphic novels. | BISAC: COMICS & GRAPHIC NOVELS / Horror.
Classification: LCC PN6727.T63 H68 2017 | DDC 741.5/973--dc23
LC record available at https://lccn.loc.gov/2016032628

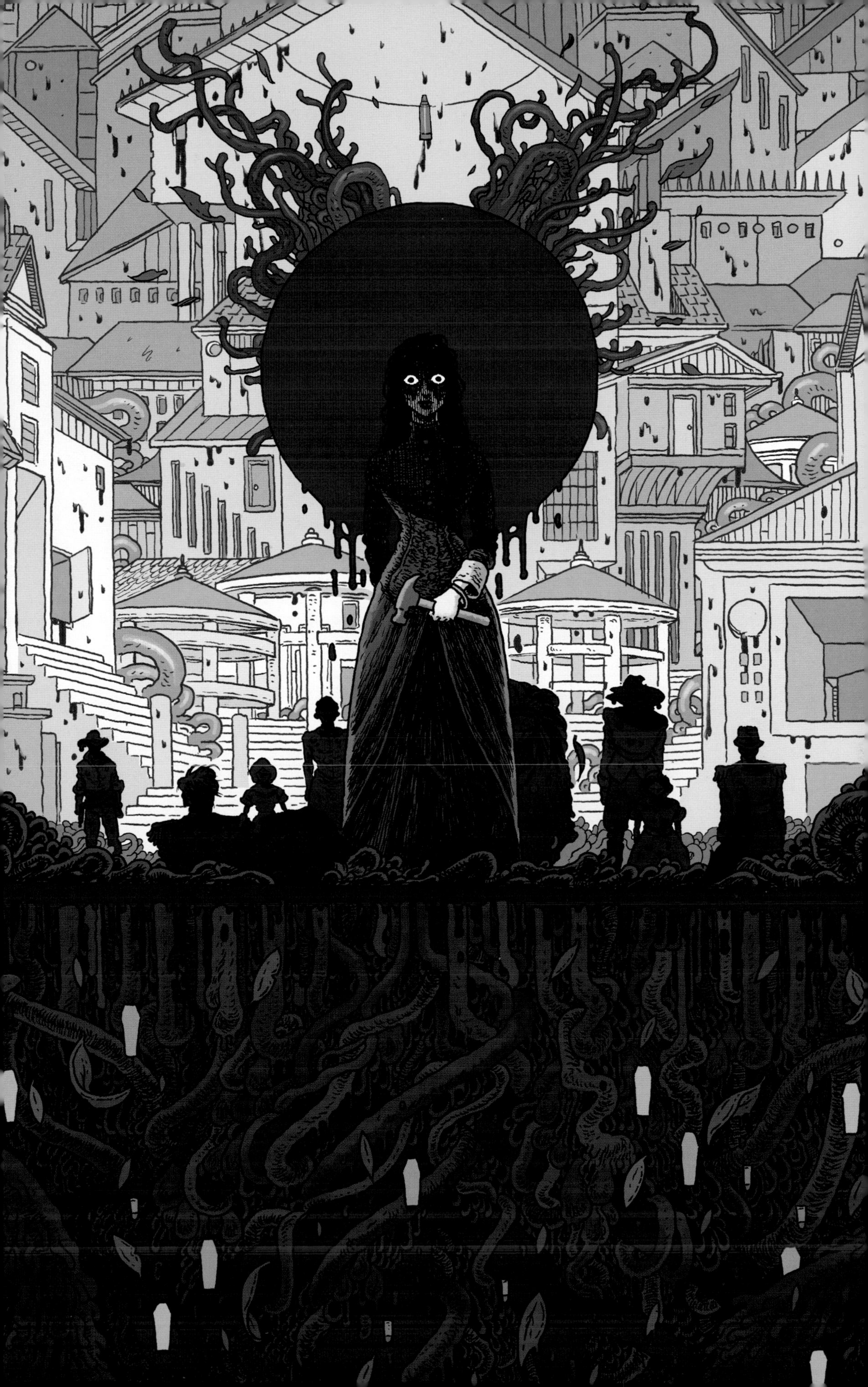

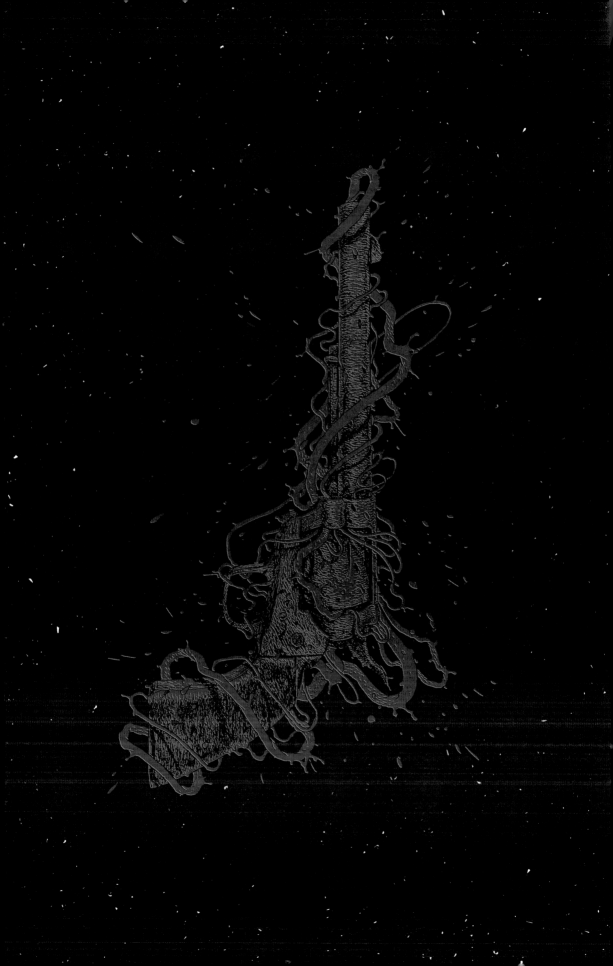

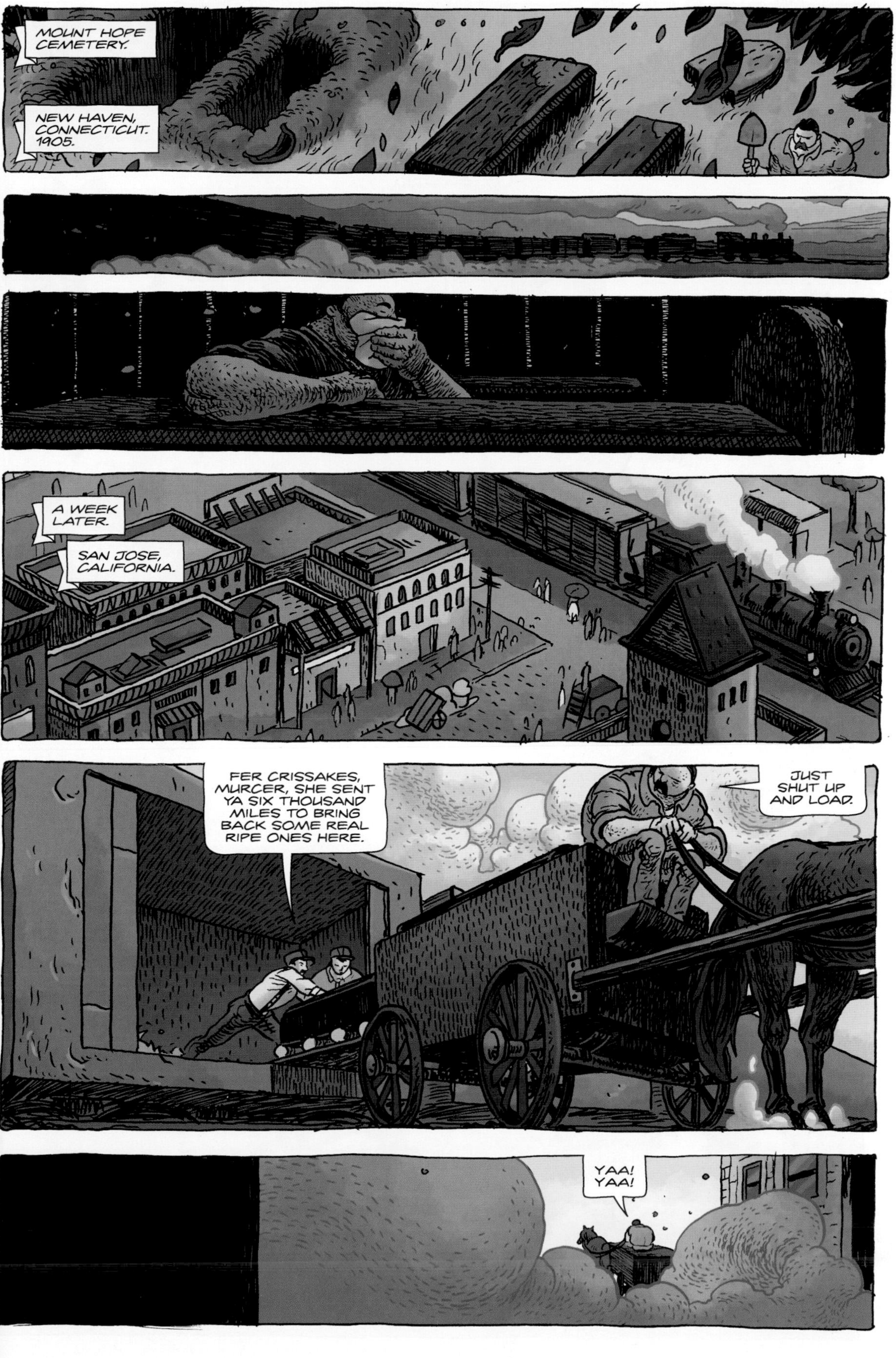
MOUNT HOPE CEMETERY.
NEW HAVEN, CONNECTICUT. 1905.
A WEEK LATER.
SAN JOSE, CALIFORNIA.
FER CRISSAKES, MURCER, SHE SENT YA SIX THOUSAND MILES TO BRING BACK SOME REAL RIPE ONES HERE.
JUST SHUT UP AND LOAD.
YAA! YAA!

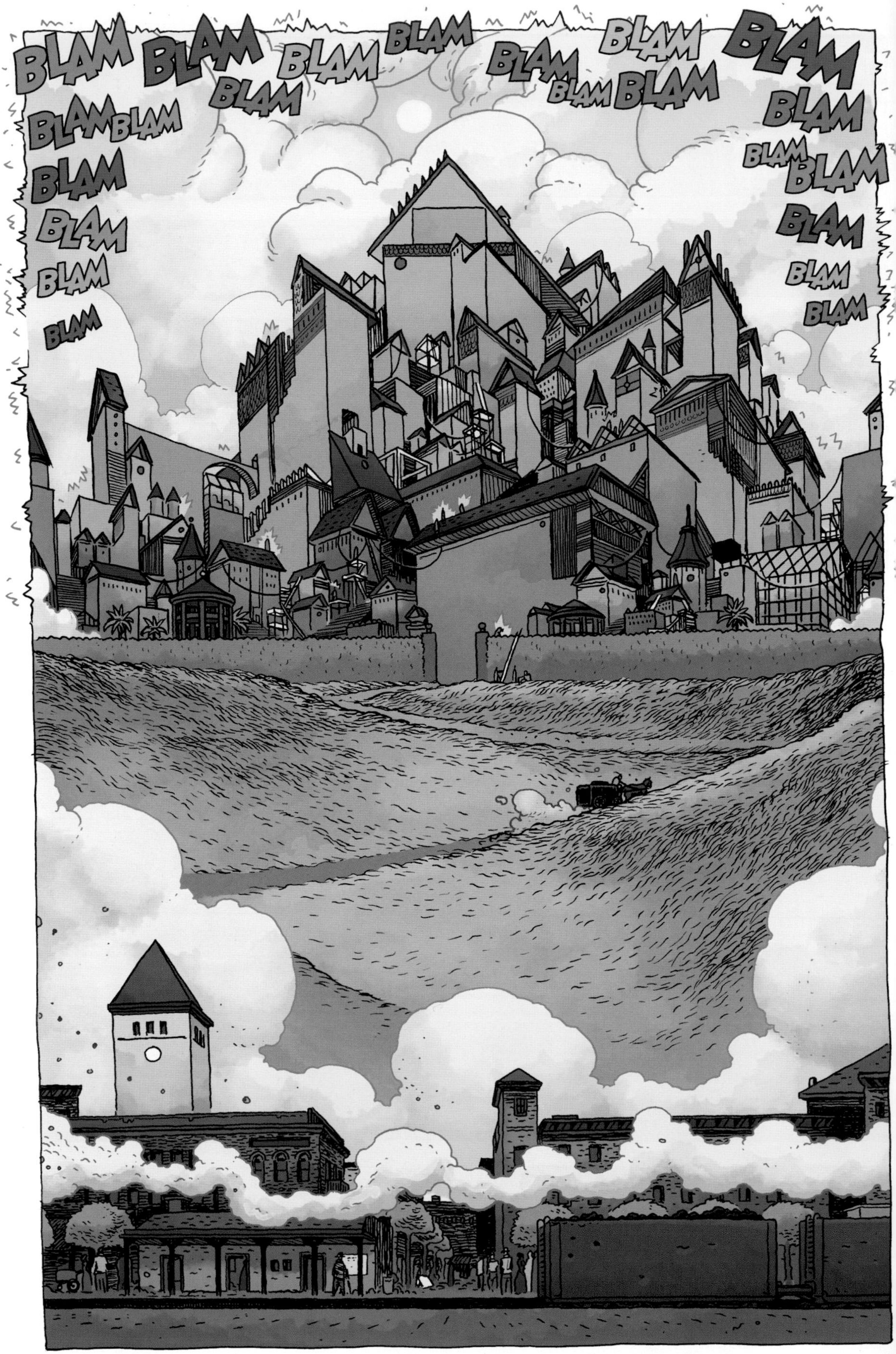
BLAM
BLAM
BLAM
BLAM
BLAM
BLAM BLAM
BLAM
BLAM
BLAM
BLAM
BLAM
BLAM
BLAM
BLAM
BLAM BLAM
BLAM
BLAM BLAM
BLAM
BLAM
BLAM

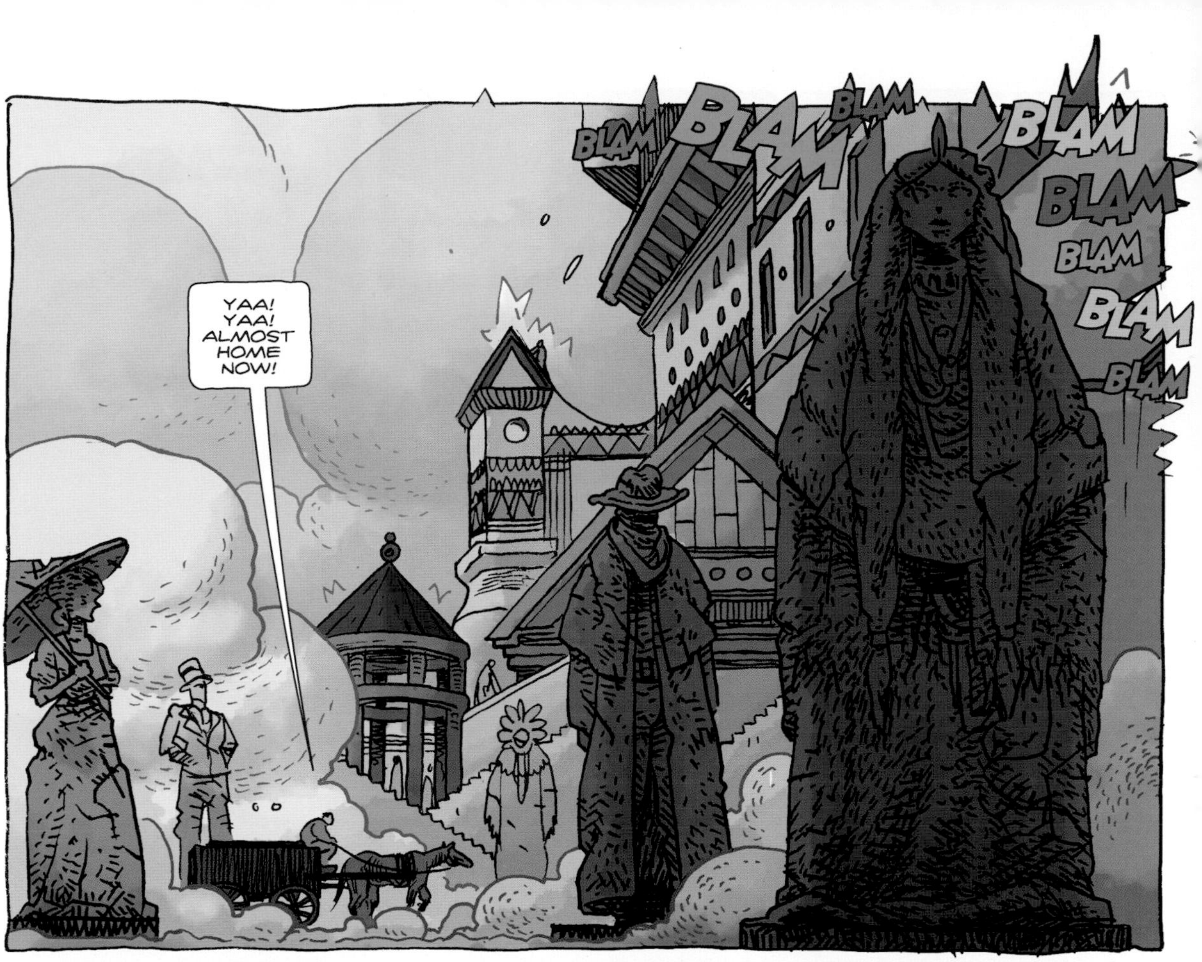
BLAM BLAM BLAM BLAM
YAA! YAA! ALMOST HOME NOW!
BLAM
BLAM
BLAM
BLAM
BLAM

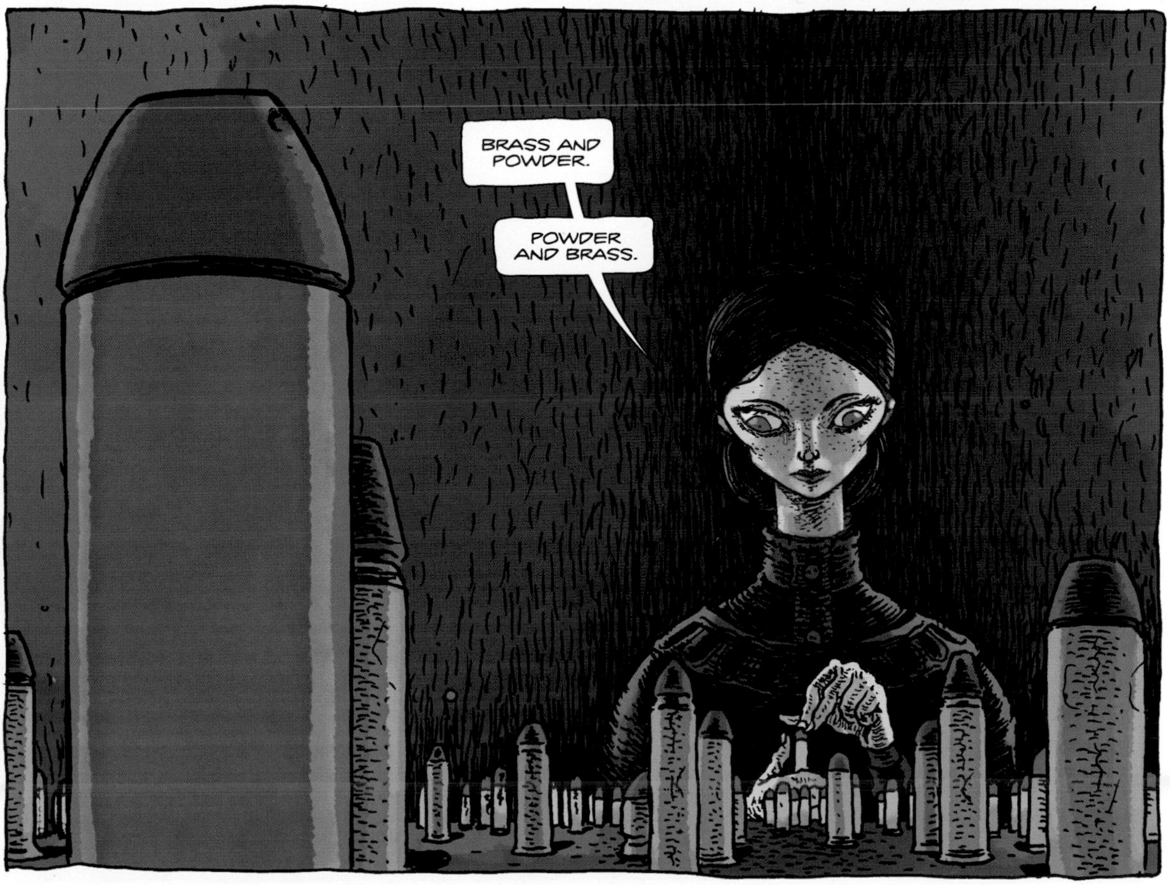
BRASS AND POWDER.
POWDER AND BRASS.

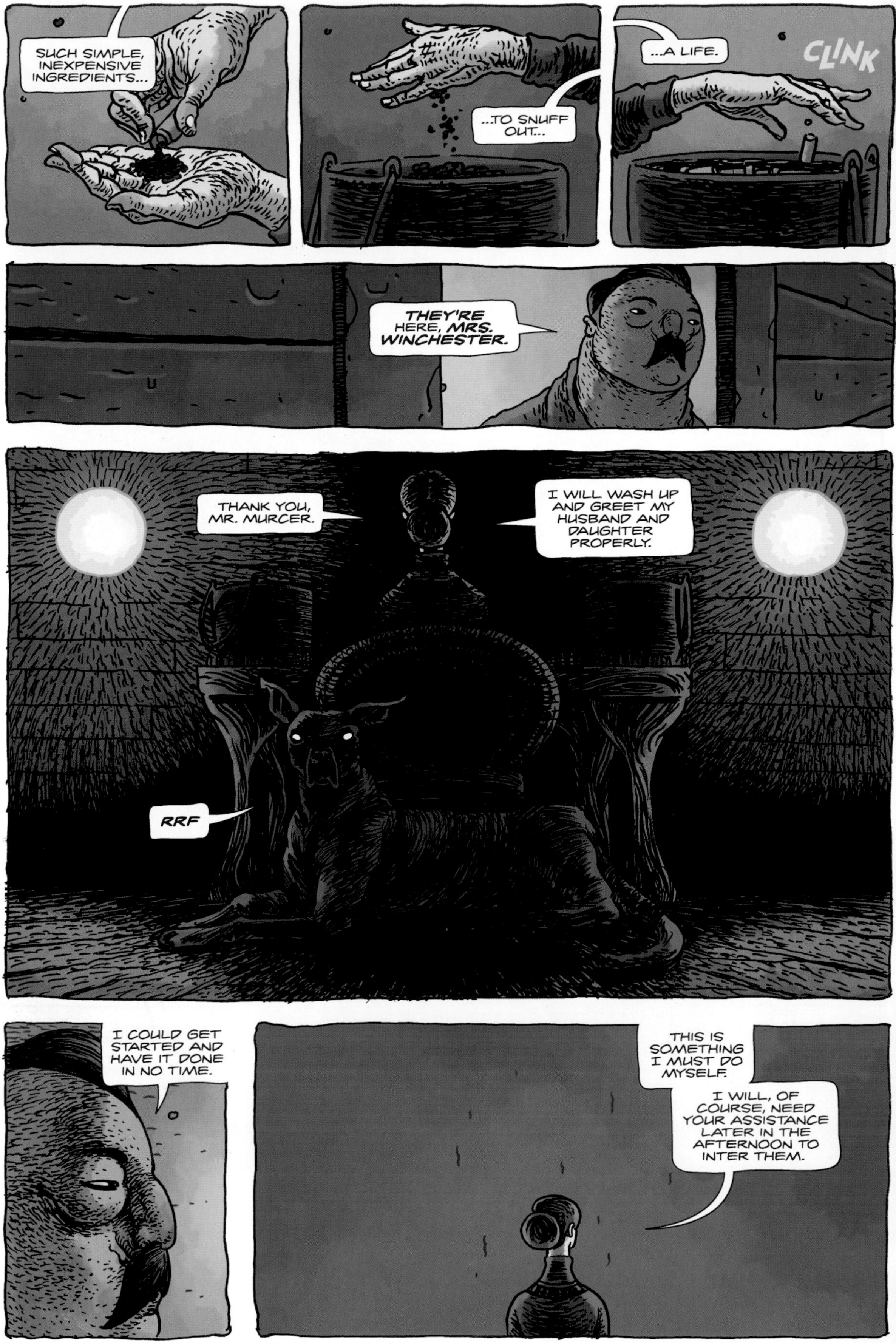
SUCH SIMPLE, INEXPENSIVE INGREDIENTS...
...TO SNUFF OUT...
...A LIFE.
CLINK
THEY'RE HERE, MRS. WINCHESTER.
THANK YOU, MR. MURCER.
I WILL WASH UP AND GREET MY HUSBAND AND DAUGHTER PROPERLY.
RRF
I COULD GET STARTED AND HAVE IT DONE IN NO TIME.
THIS IS SOMETHING I MUST DO MYSELF.
I WILL, OF COURSE, NEED YOUR ASSISTANCE LATER IN THE AFTERNOON TO INTER THEM.

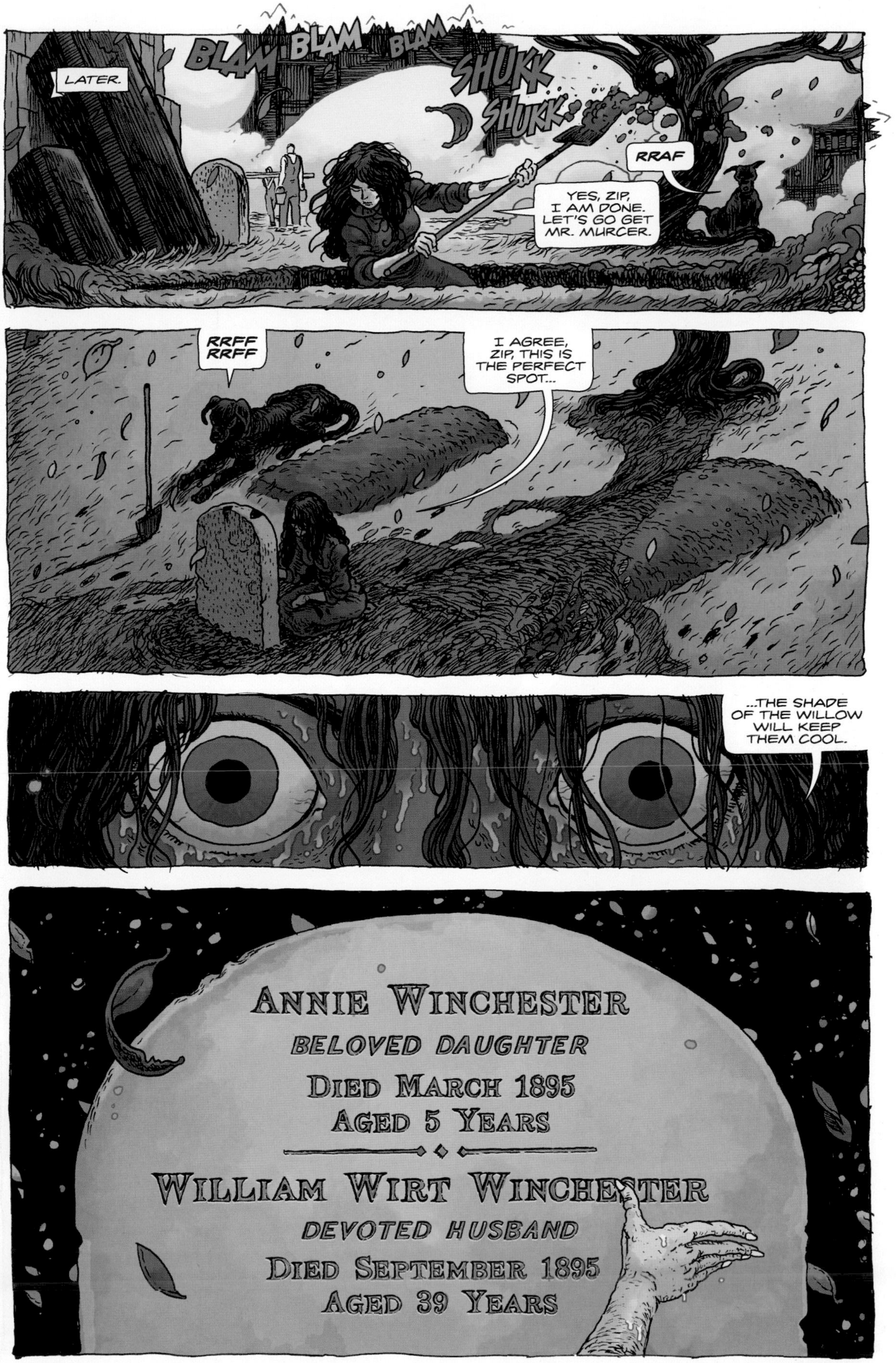
LATER.
BLAM BLAM BLAM
SHUKK SHUKK
RRAF
YES, ZIP, I AM DONE. LET'S GO GET MR. MURCER.
RRFF RRFF
I AGREE, ZIP, THIS IS THE PERFECT SPOT...
...THE SHADE OF THE WILLOW WILL KEEP THEM COOL.
ANNIE WINCHESTER
BELOVED DAUGHTER
DIED MARCH 1895
AGED 5 YEARS
WILLIAM WIRT WINCHESTER
DEVOTED HUSBAND
DIED SEPTEMBER 1895
AGED 39 YEARS

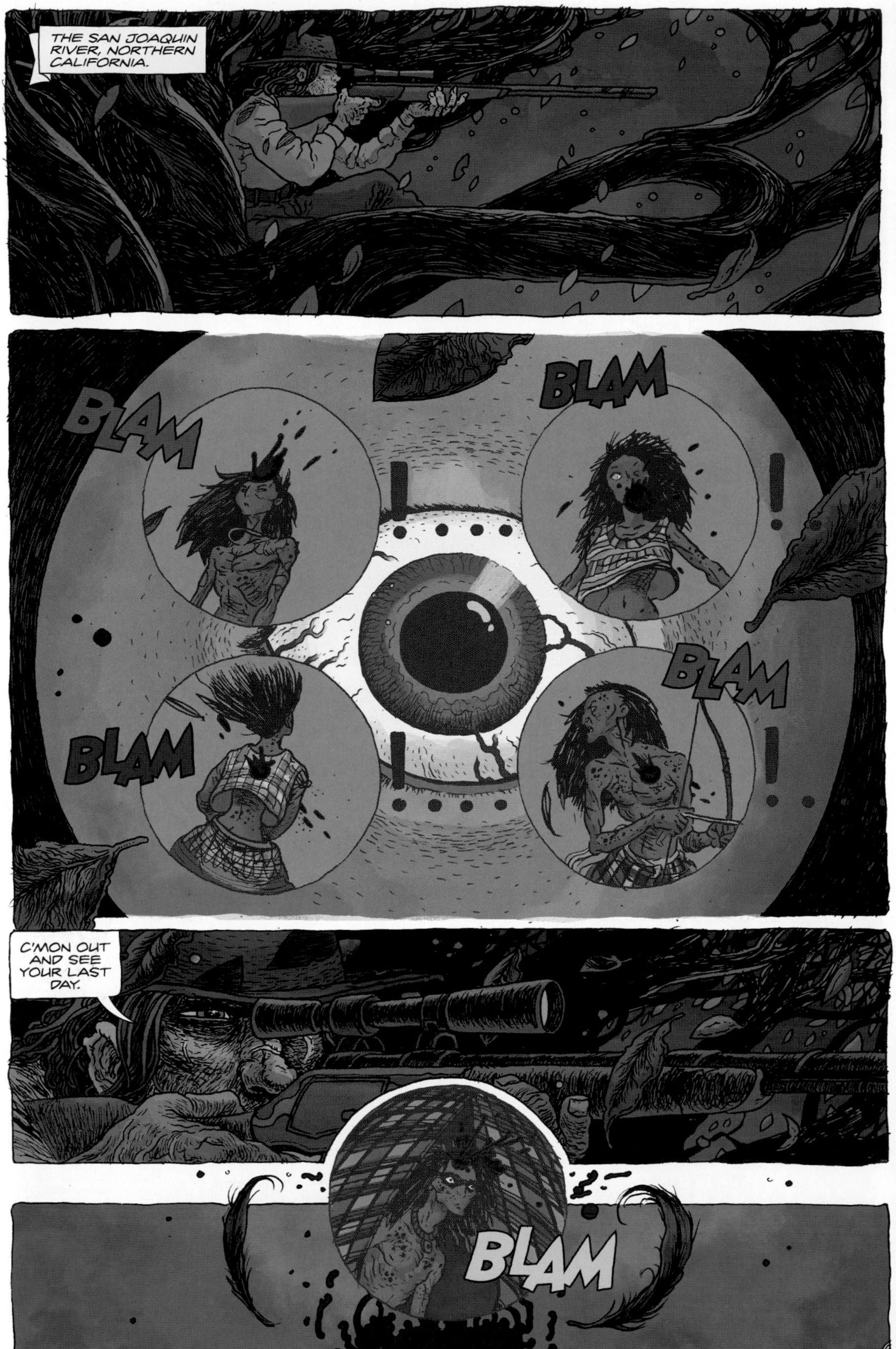
THE SAN JOAQUIN RIVER, NORTHERN CALIFORNIA.
BLAM
BLAM
BLAM
BLAM
C'MON OUT AND SEE YOUR LAST DAY.
BLAM

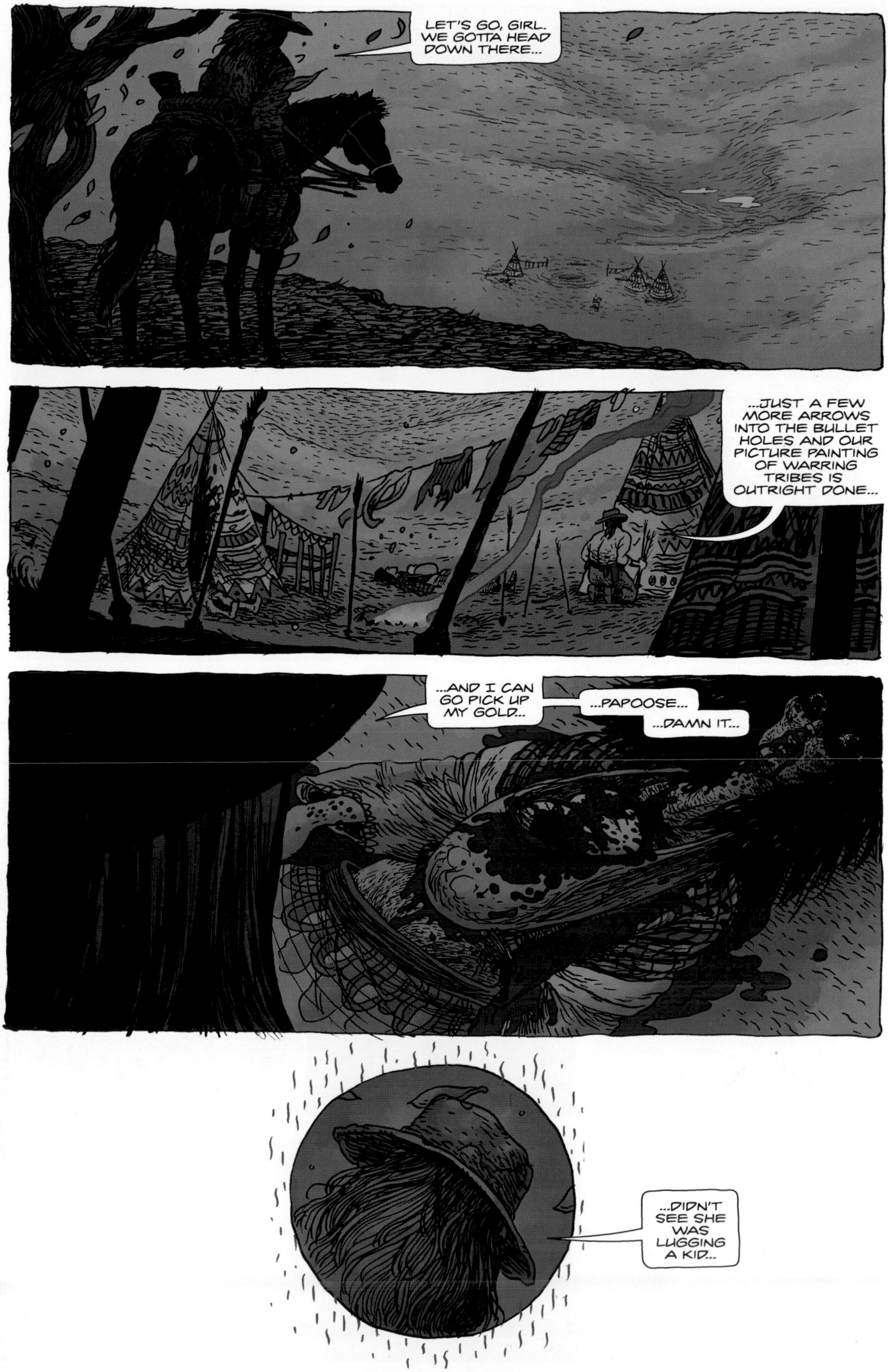
LET'S GO, GIRL. WE GOTTA HEAD DOWN THERE...
...JUST A FEW MORE ARROWS INTO THE BULLET HOLES AND OUR PICTURE PAINTING OF WARRING TRIBES IS OUTRIGHT DONE...
...AND I CAN GO PICK UP MY GOLD...
...PAPOOSE...
...DAMN IT...
...DIDN'T SEE SHE WAS LUGGING A KID...

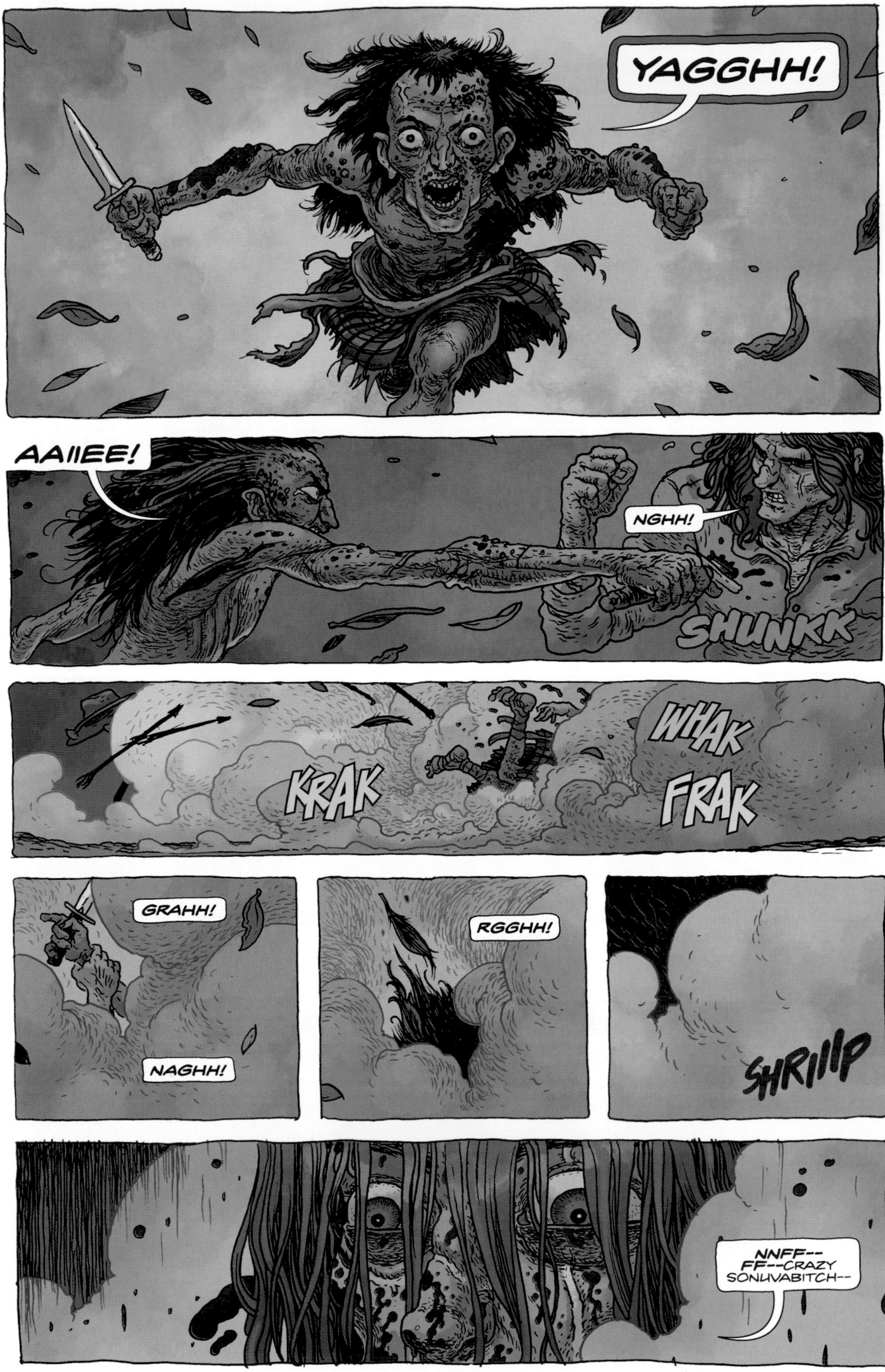
YAGGHH!
AAIIEE!
NGHH!
SHUNKK
WHAK
KRAK
FRAK
GRAHH!
NAGHH!
RGGHH!
SHRIIIP
NNFF-- FF--CRAZY SONUVABITCH--

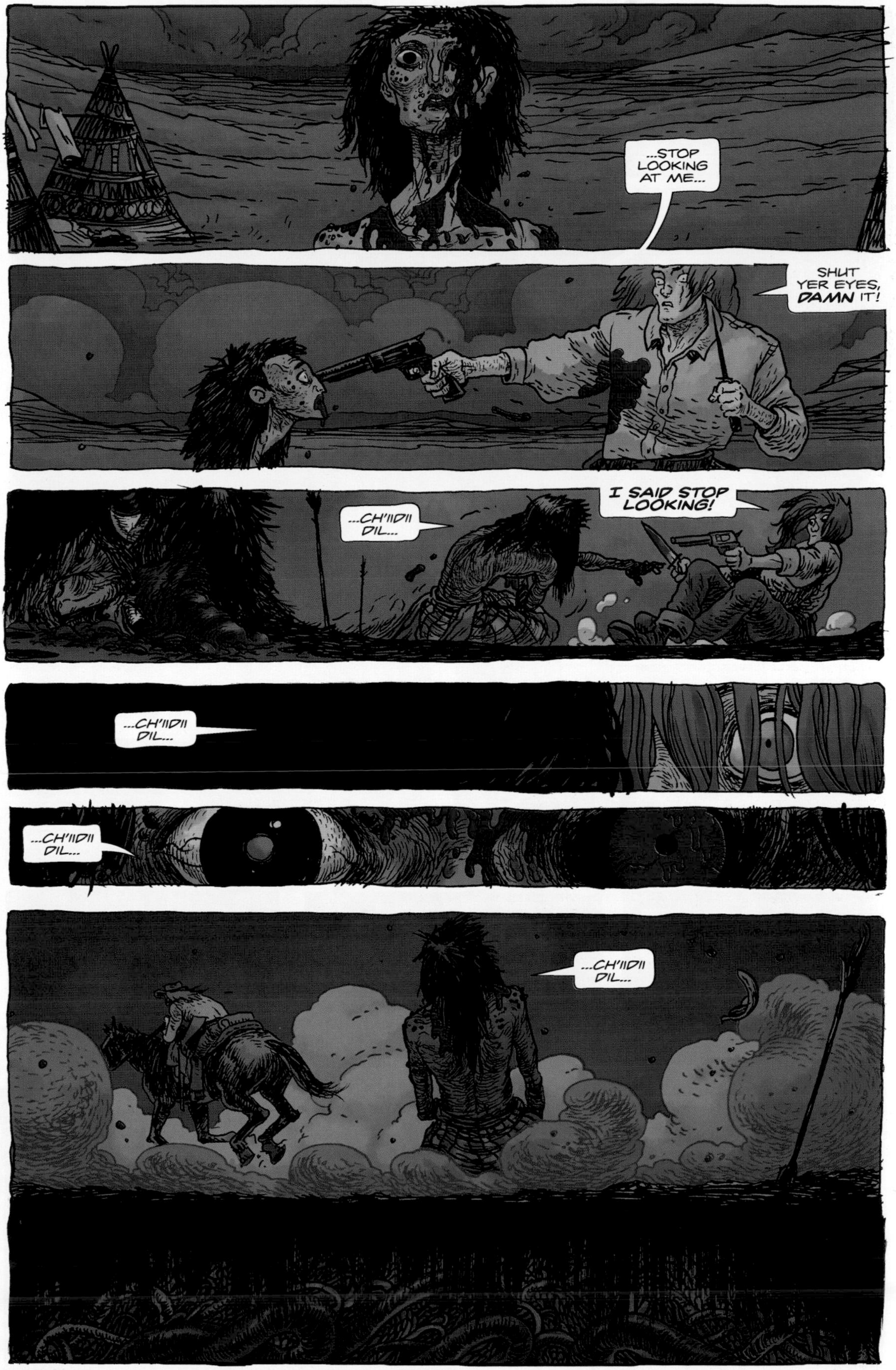
...STOP LOOKING AT ME...
SHUT YER EYES, DAMN IT!
...CH'IIDII DIL...
I SAID STOP LOOKING!
...CH'IIDII DIL...
...CH'IIDII DIL...
...CH'IIDII DIL...

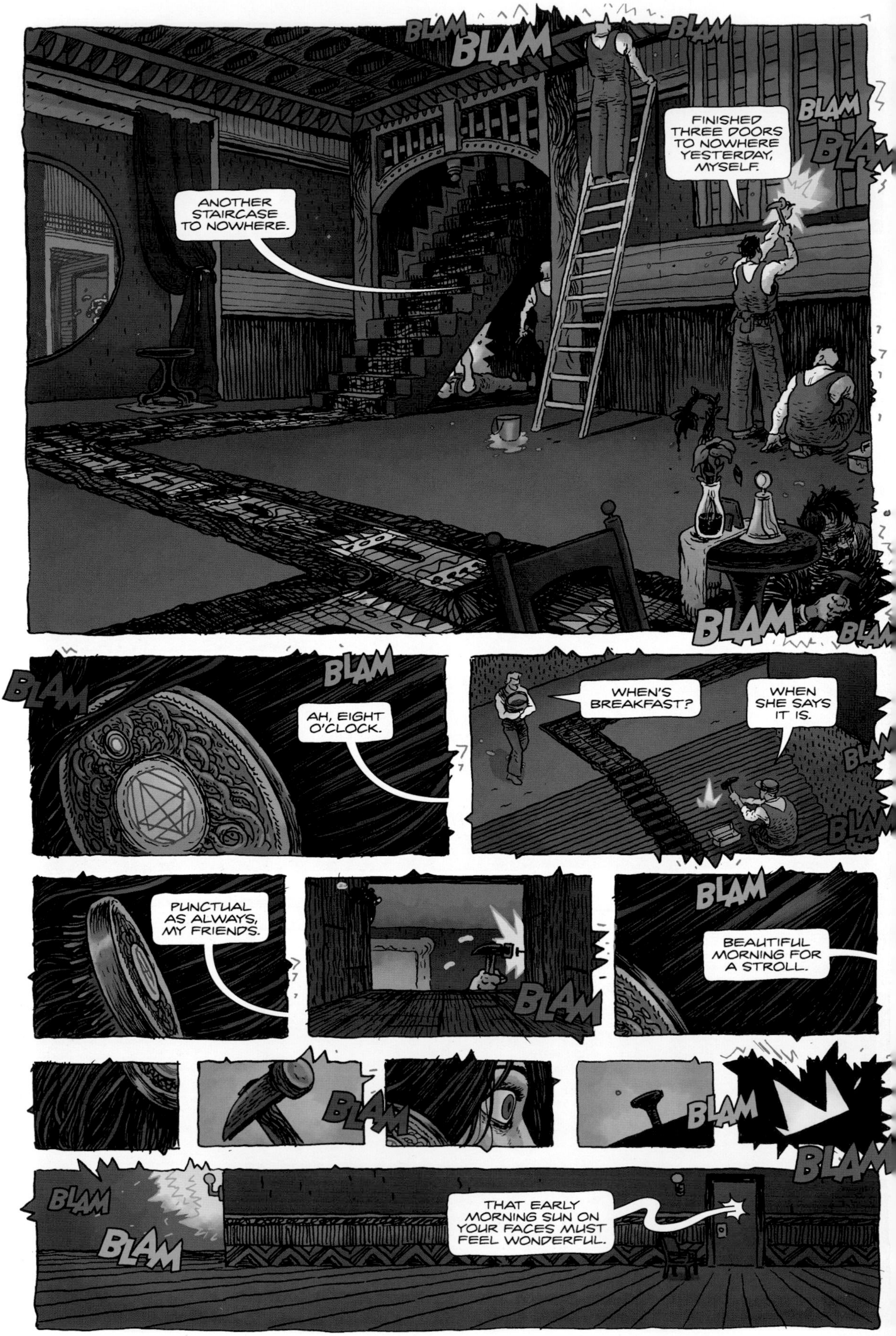
BLAM
BLAM
BLAM
BLAM
BLAM
ANOTHER STAIRCASE TO NOWHERE.
FINISHED THREE DOORS TO NOWHERE YESTERDAY, MYSELF.
BLAM
BLAM
BLAM
BLAM
AH, EIGHT O'CLOCK.
WHEN'S BREAKFAST?
WHEN SHE SAYS IT IS.
PUNCTUAL AS ALWAYS, MY FRIENDS.
BLAM
BLAM
BEAUTIFUL MORNING FOR A STROLL.
BLAM
BLAM
BLAM
BLAM
BLAM
THAT EARLY MORNING SUN ON YOUR FACES MUST FEEL WONDERFUL.

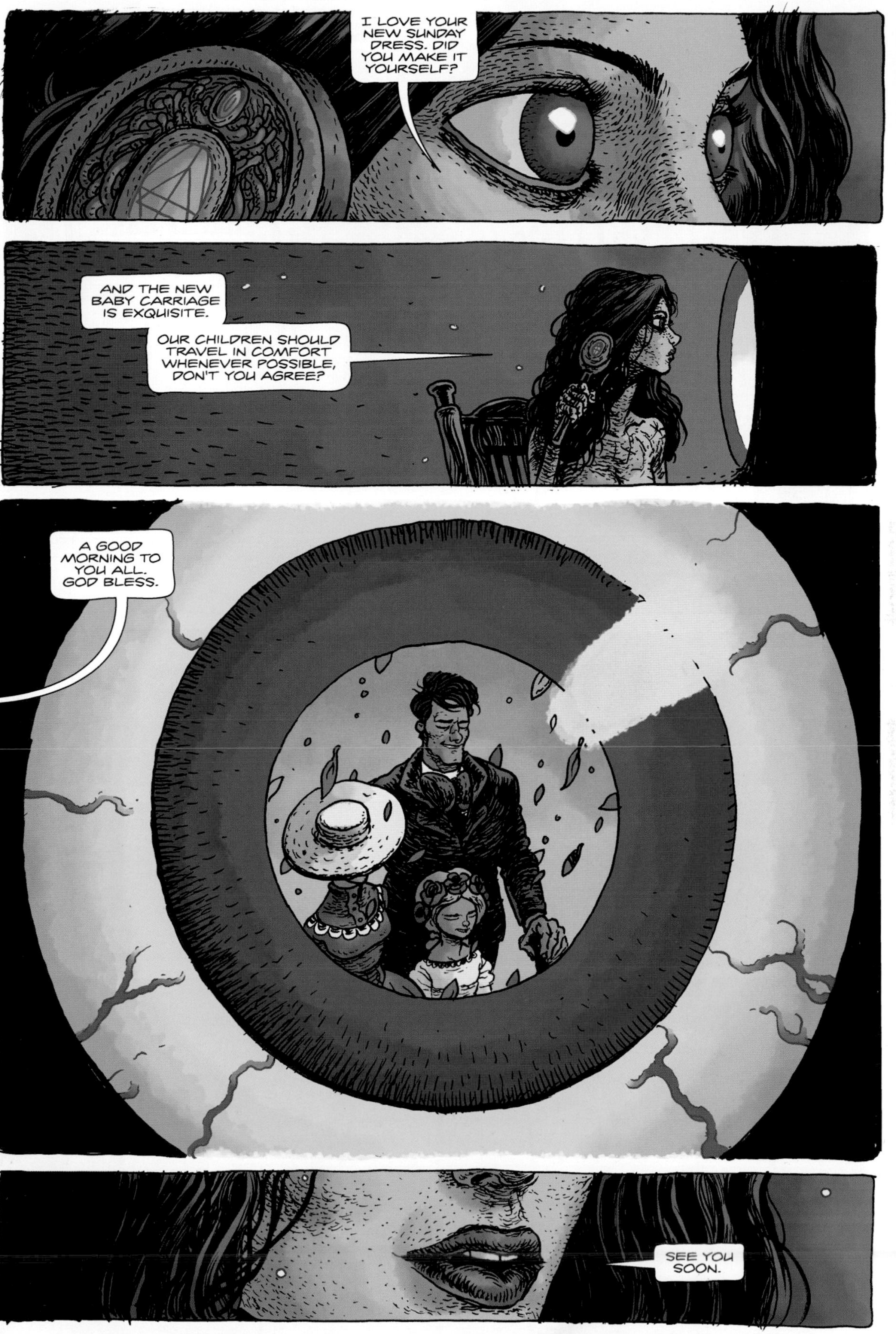
I LOVE YOUR NEW SUNDAY DRESS. DID YOU MAKE IT YOURSELF?
AND THE NEW BABY CARRIAGE IS EXQUISITE.
OUR CHILDREN SHOULD TRAVEL IN COMFORT WHENEVER POSSIBLE, DON'T YOU AGREE?
A GOOD MORNING TO YOU ALL. GOD BLESS.
SEE YOU SOON.

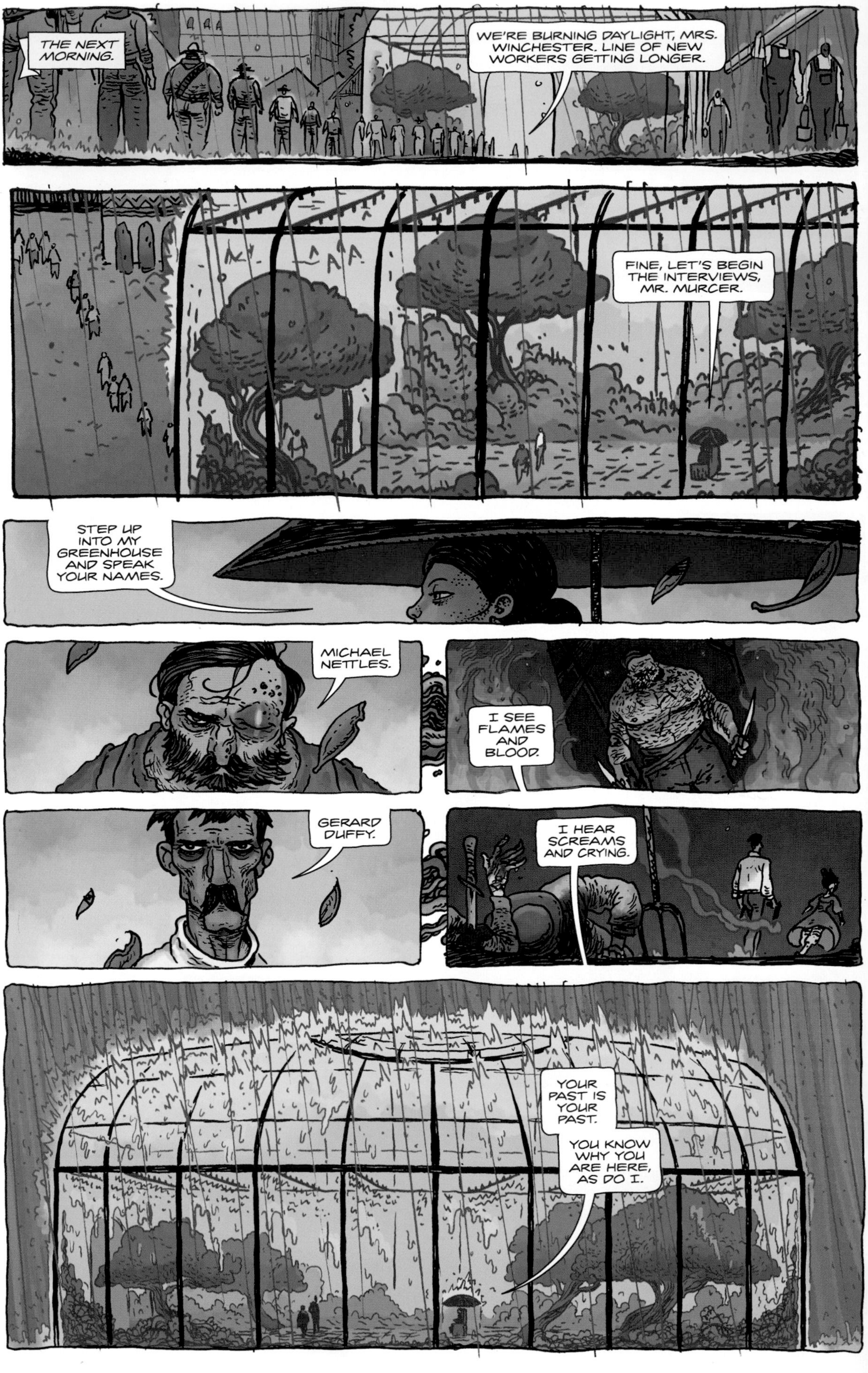
THE NEXT MORNING.
WE'RE BURNING DAYLIGHT, MRS. WINCHESTER. LINE OF NEW WORKERS GETTING LONGER.
FINE, LET'S BEGIN THE INTERVIEWS, MR. MURCER.
STEP UP INTO MY GREENHOUSE AND SPEAK YOUR NAMES.
MICHAEL NETTLES.
I SEE FLAMES AND BLOOD.
GERARD DUFFY.
I HEAR SCREAMS AND CRYING.
YOUR PAST IS YOUR PAST.
YOU KNOW WHY YOU ARE HERE, AS DO I.

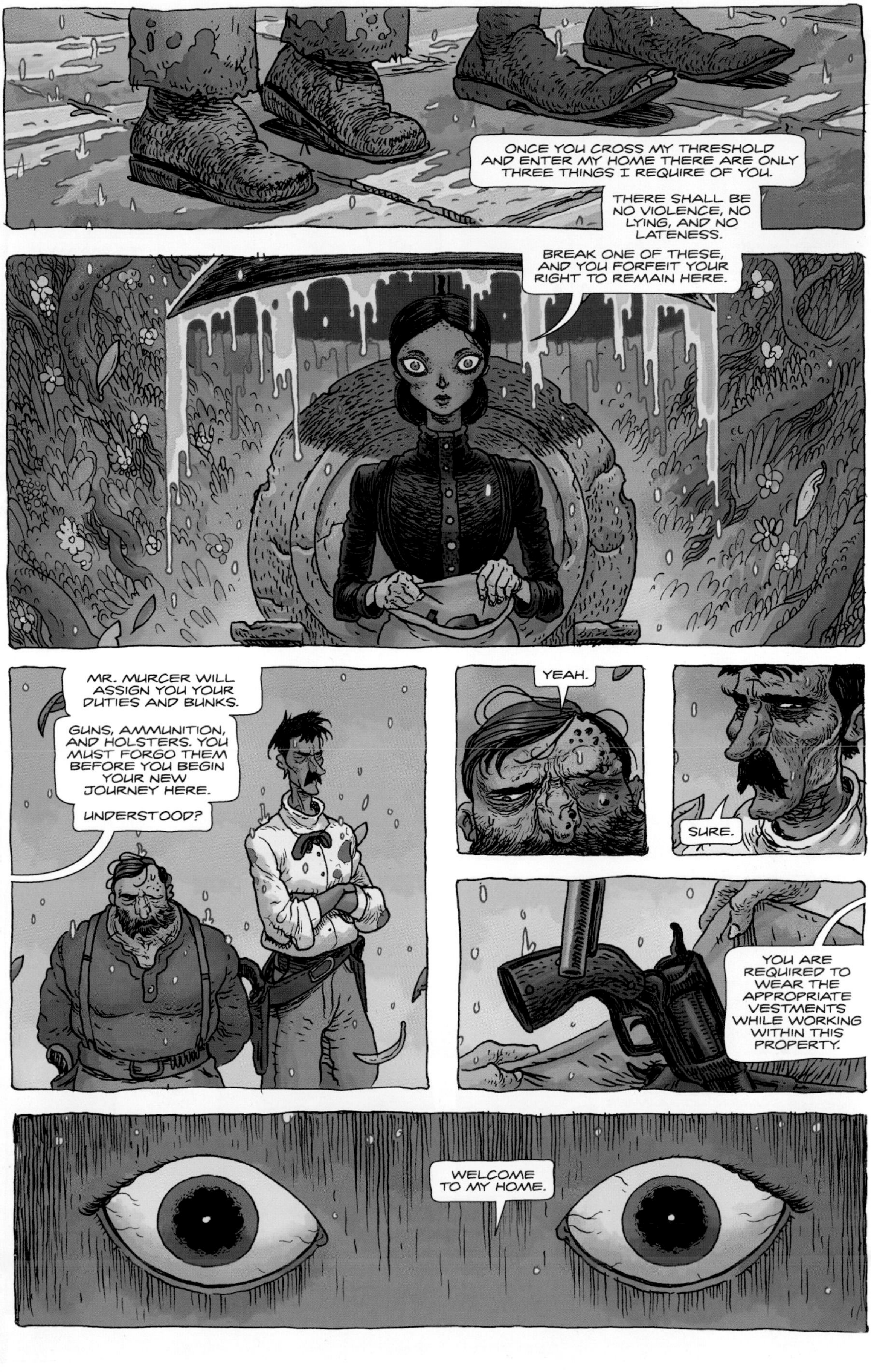
ONCE YOU CROSS MY THRESHOLD AND ENTER MY HOME THERE ARE ONLY THREE THINGS I REQUIRE OF YOU.
THERE SHALL BE NO VIOLENCE, NO LYING, AND NO LATENESS.
BREAK ONE OF THESE, AND YOU FORFEIT YOUR RIGHT TO REMAIN HERE.
MR. MURCER WILL ASSIGN YOU YOUR DUTIES AND BUNKS.
GUNS, AMMUNITION, AND HOLSTERS. YOU MUST FORGO THEM BEFORE YOU BEGIN YOUR NEW JOURNEY HERE.
UNDERSTOOD?
YEAH.
SURE.
YOU ARE REQUIRED TO WEAR THE APPROPRIATE VESTMENTS WHILE WORKING WITHIN THIS PROPERTY.
WELCOME TO MY HOME.

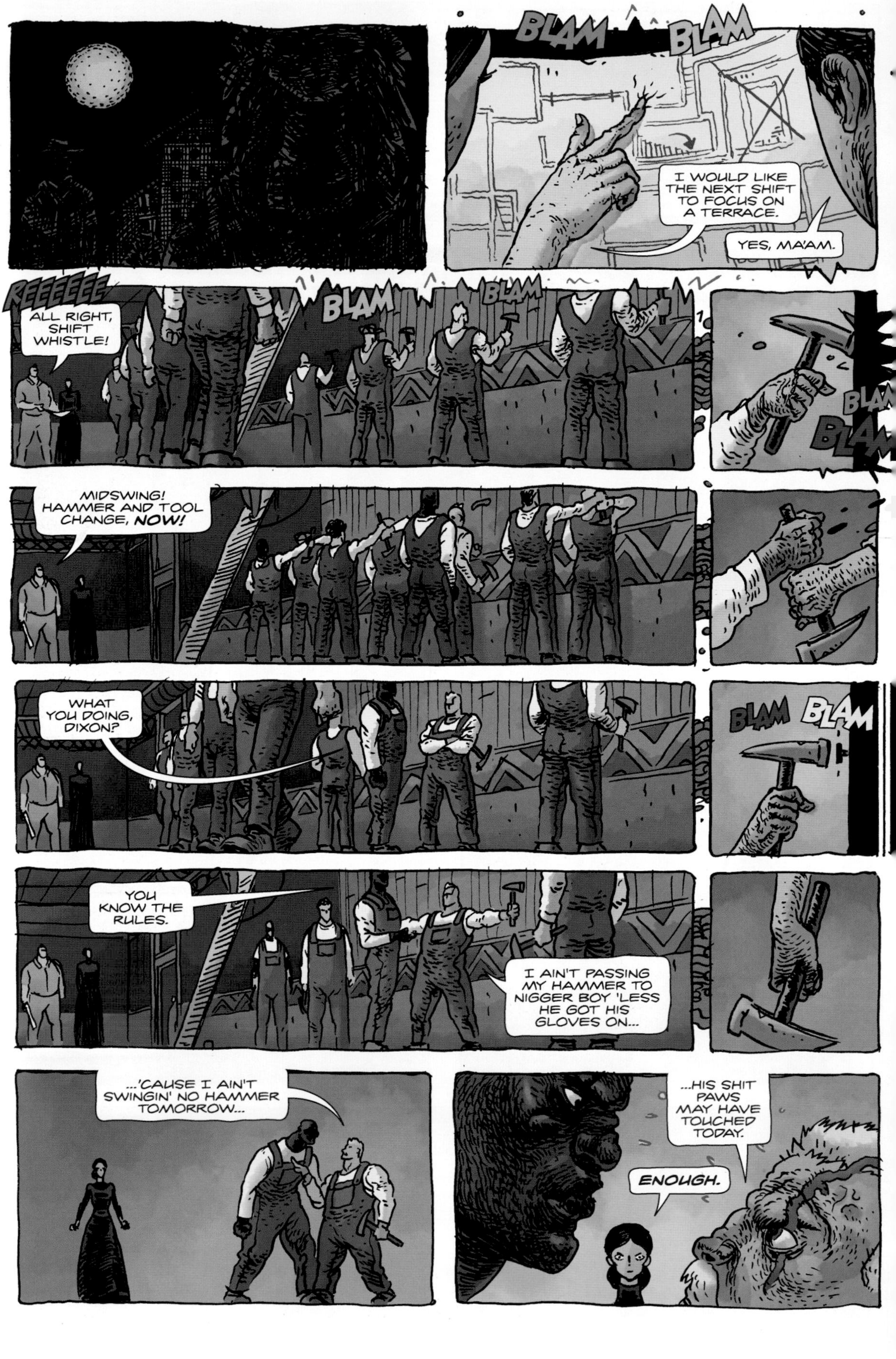
BLAM
BLAM
I WOULD LIKE THE NEXT SHIFT TO FOCUS ON A TERRACE.
YES, MA'AM.
REEEEEEE
ALL RIGHT, SHIFT WHISTLE!
BLAM
BLAM
MIDSWING! HAMMER AND TOOL CHANGE, **NOW!**
WHAT YOU DOING, DIXON?
BLAM
BLAM
YOU KNOW THE RULES.
I AIN'T PASSING MY HAMMER TO NIGGER BOY 'LESS HE GOT HIS GLOVES ON...
...'CAUSE I AIN'T SWINGIN' NO HAMMER TOMORROW...
...HIS SHIT PAWS MAY HAVE TOUCHED TODAY.
ENOUGH.

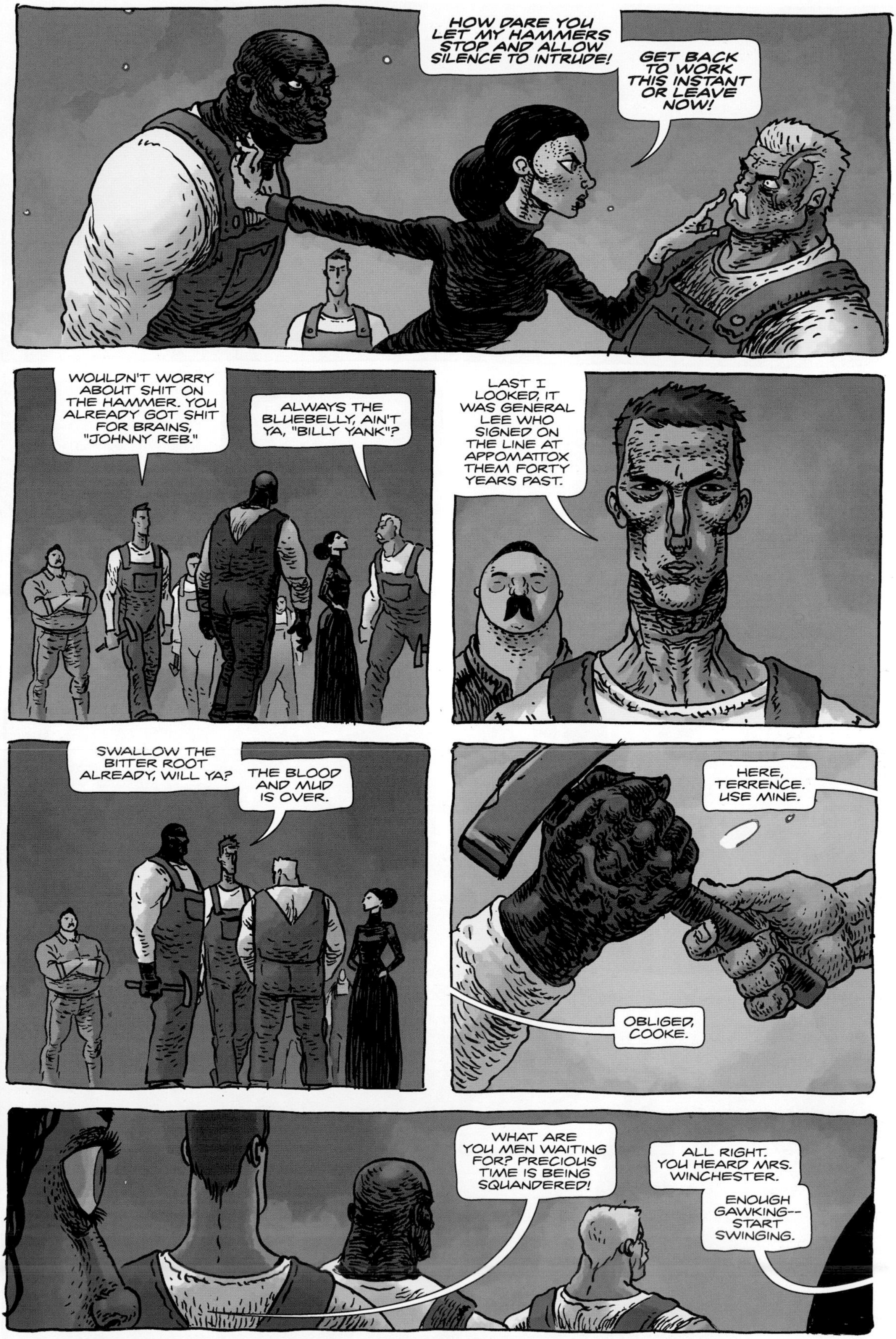
HOW DARE YOU LET MY HAMMERS STOP AND ALLOW SILENCE TO INTRUDE!
GET BACK TO WORK THIS INSTANT OR LEAVE NOW!
WOULDN'T WORRY ABOUT SHIT ON THE HAMMER. YOU ALREADY GOT SHIT FOR BRAINS, "JOHNNY REB."
ALWAYS THE BLUEBELLY, AIN'T YA, "BILLY YANK"?
LAST I LOOKED, IT WAS GENERAL LEE WHO SIGNED ON THE LINE AT APPOMATTOX THEM FORTY YEARS PAST.
SWALLOW THE BITTER ROOT ALREADY, WILL YA?
THE BLOOD AND MUD IS OVER.
HERE, TERRENCE. USE MINE.
OBLIGED, COOKE.
WHAT ARE YOU MEN WAITING FOR? PRECIOUS TIME IS BEING SQUANDERED!
ALL RIGHT. YOU HEARD MRS. WINCHESTER.
ENOUGH GAWKING-- START SWINGING.

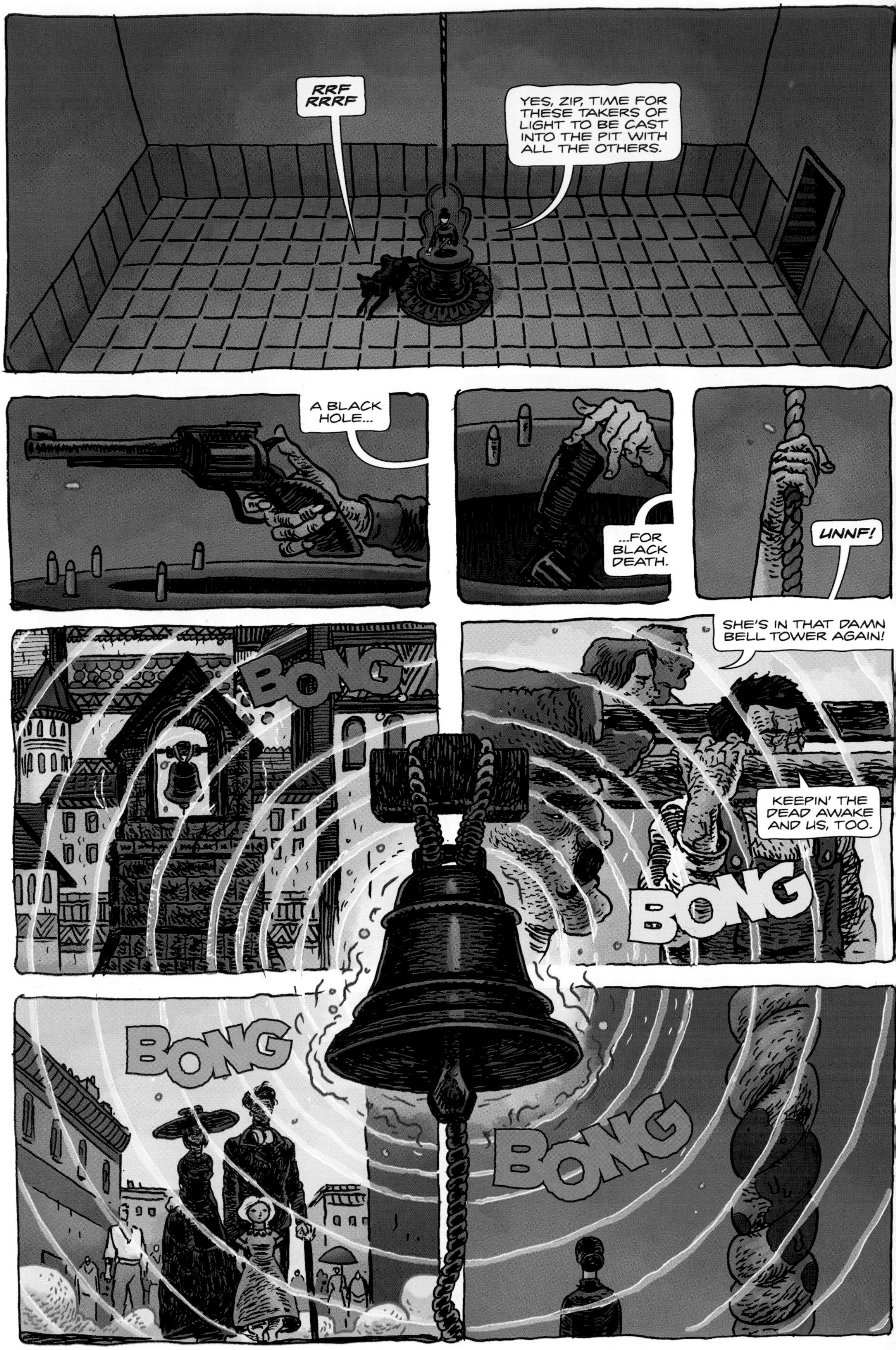
RRF RRRF
YES, ZIP, TIME FOR THESE TAKERS OF LIGHT TO BE CAST INTO THE PIT WITH ALL THE OTHERS.
A BLACK HOLE...
...FOR BLACK DEATH.
UNNF!
BONG
SHE'S IN THAT DAMN BELL TOWER AGAIN!
KEEPIN' THE DEAD AWAKE AND US, TOO.
BONG
BONG
BONG

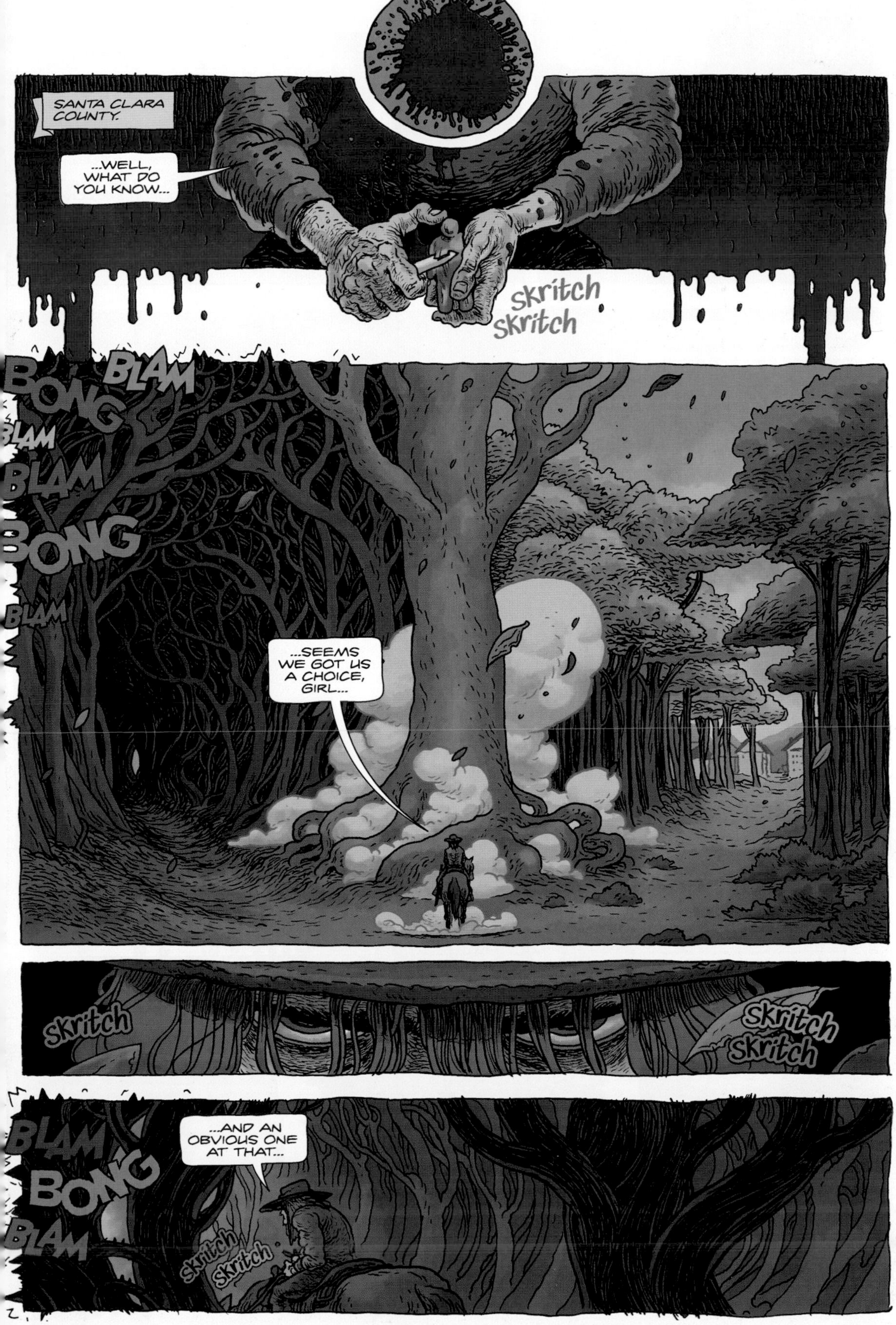
SANTA CLARA COUNTY.
...WELL, WHAT DO YOU KNOW...
SKRITCH SKRITCH
BLAM BONG BLAM BLAM BONG BLAM
...SEEMS WE GOT US A CHOICE, GIRL...
SKRITCH
SKRITCH SKRITCH
BLAM BONG BLAM
...AND AN OBVIOUS ONE AT THAT...
SKRITCH SKRITCH

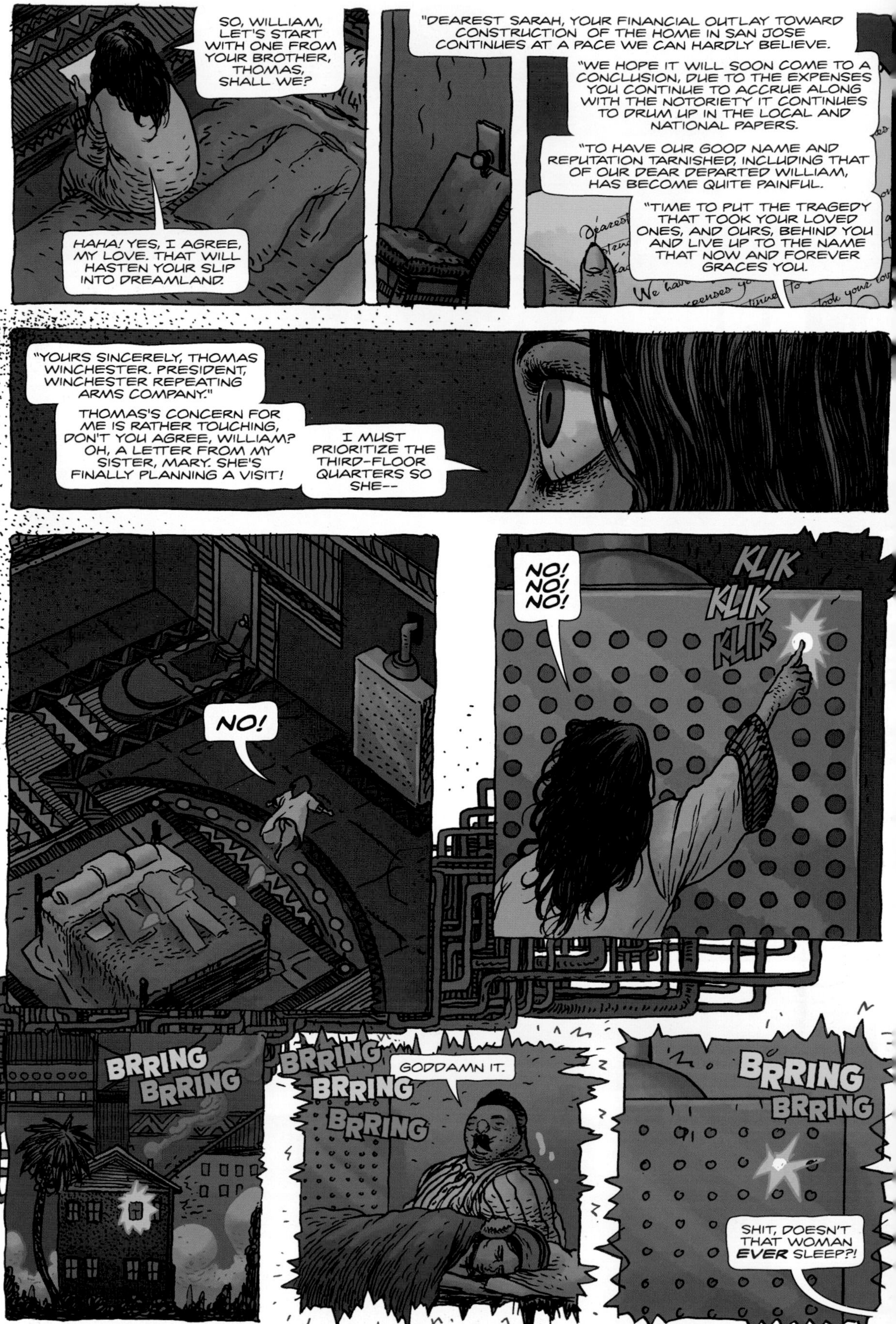

SO, WILLIAM, LET'S START WITH ONE FROM YOUR BROTHER, THOMAS, SHALL WE?
HAHA! YES, I AGREE, MY LOVE. THAT WILL HASTEN YOUR SLIP INTO DREAMLAND.
"DEAREST SARAH, YOUR FINANCIAL OUTLAY TOWARD CONSTRUCTION OF THE HOME IN SAN JOSE CONTINUES AT A PACE WE CAN HARDLY BELIEVE.
"WE HOPE IT WILL SOON COME TO A CONCLUSION, DUE TO THE EXPENSES YOU CONTINUE TO ACCRUE ALONG WITH THE NOTORIETY IT CONTINUES TO DRUM UP IN THE LOCAL AND NATIONAL PAPERS.
"TO HAVE OUR GOOD NAME AND REPUTATION TARNISHED, INCLUDING THAT OF OUR DEAR DEPARTED WILLIAM, HAS BECOME QUITE PAINFUL.
"TIME TO PUT THE TRAGEDY THAT TOOK YOUR LOVED ONES, AND OURS, BEHIND YOU AND LIVE UP TO THE NAME THAT NOW AND FOREVER GRACES YOU.
"YOURS SINCERELY, THOMAS WINCHESTER. PRESIDENT, WINCHESTER REPEATING ARMS COMPANY."
THOMAS'S CONCERN FOR ME IS RATHER TOUCHING, DON'T YOU AGREE, WILLIAM? OH, A LETTER FROM MY SISTER, MARY. SHE'S FINALLY PLANNING A VISIT!
I MUST PRIORITIZE THE THIRD-FLOOR QUARTERS SO SHE--
NO!
NO! NO! NO!
KLIK KLIK KLIK
BRRING BRRING
BRRING BRRING BRRING
GODDAMN IT.
BRRING BRRING
SHIT, DOESN'T THAT WOMAN EVER SLEEP?!

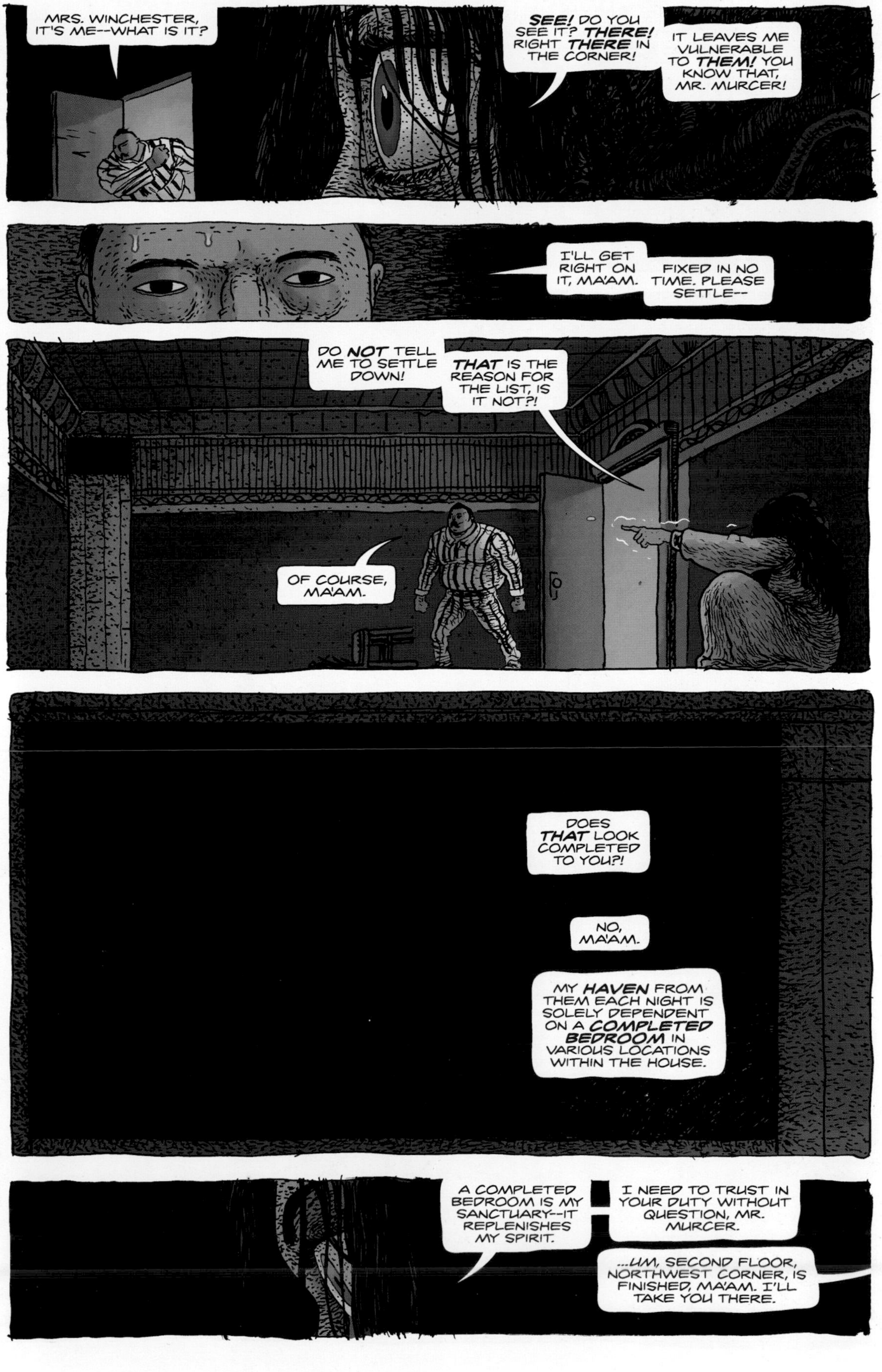
MRS. WINCHESTER, IT'S ME--WHAT IS IT?
SEE! DO YOU SEE IT? THERE! RIGHT THERE IN THE CORNER!
IT LEAVES ME VULNERABLE TO THEM! YOU KNOW THAT, MR. MURCER!
I'LL GET RIGHT ON IT, MA'AM.
FIXED IN NO TIME. PLEASE SETTLE--
DO NOT TELL ME TO SETTLE DOWN!
THAT IS THE REASON FOR THE LIST, IS IT NOT?!
OF COURSE, MA'AM.
DOES THAT LOOK COMPLETED TO YOU?!
NO, MA'AM.
MY HAVEN FROM THEM EACH NIGHT IS SOLELY DEPENDENT ON A COMPLETED BEDROOM IN VARIOUS LOCATIONS WITHIN THE HOUSE.
A COMPLETED BEDROOM IS MY SANCTUARY--IT REPLENISHES MY SPIRIT.
I NEED TO TRUST IN YOUR DUTY WITHOUT QUESTION, MR. MURCER.
...UM, SECOND FLOOR, NORTHWEST CORNER, IS FINISHED, MA'AM. I'LL TAKE YOU THERE.

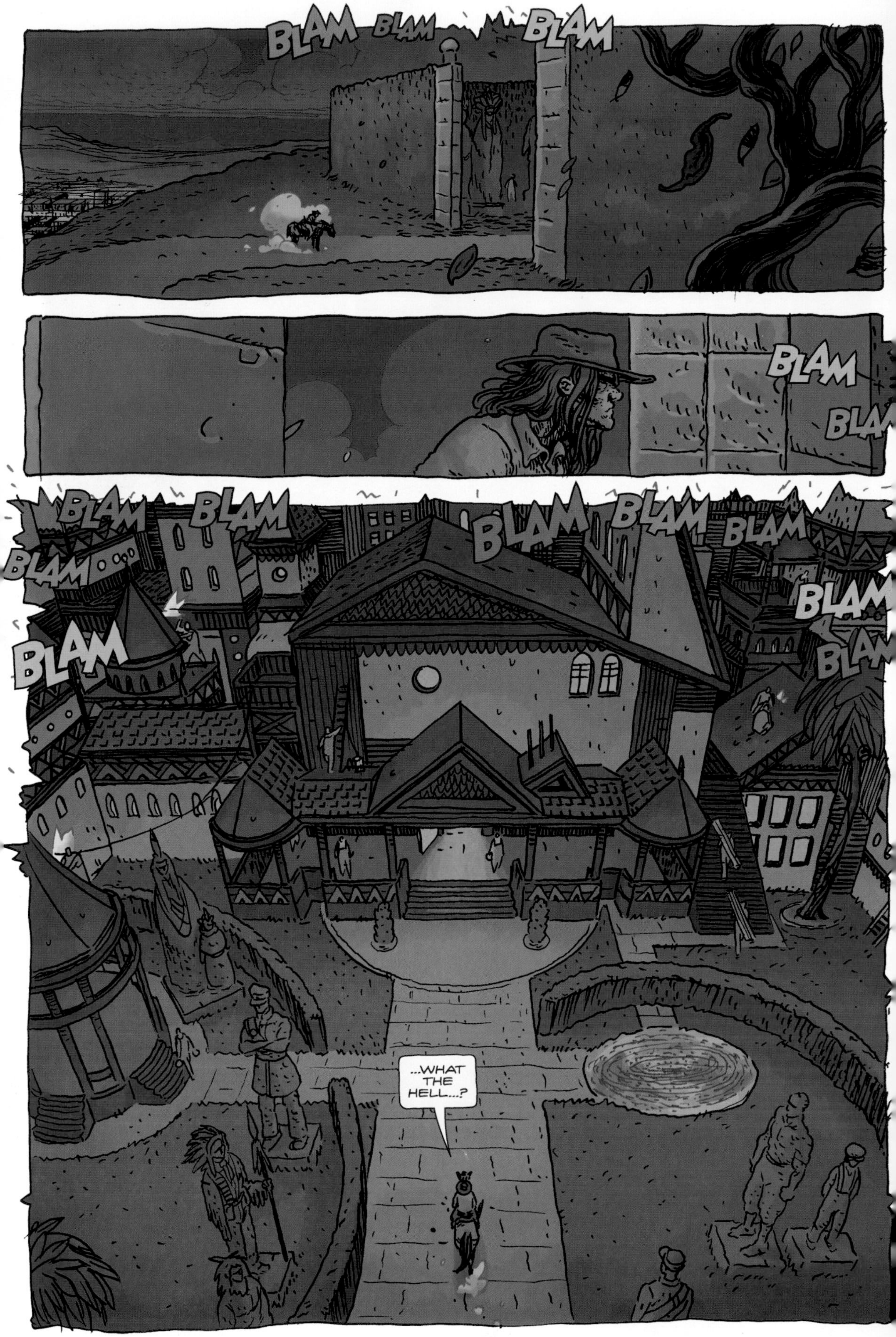
BLAM BLAM BLAM
BLAM
BLAM
BLAM BLAM BLAM BLAM BLAM BLAM BLAM BLAM
...WHAT THE HELL...?

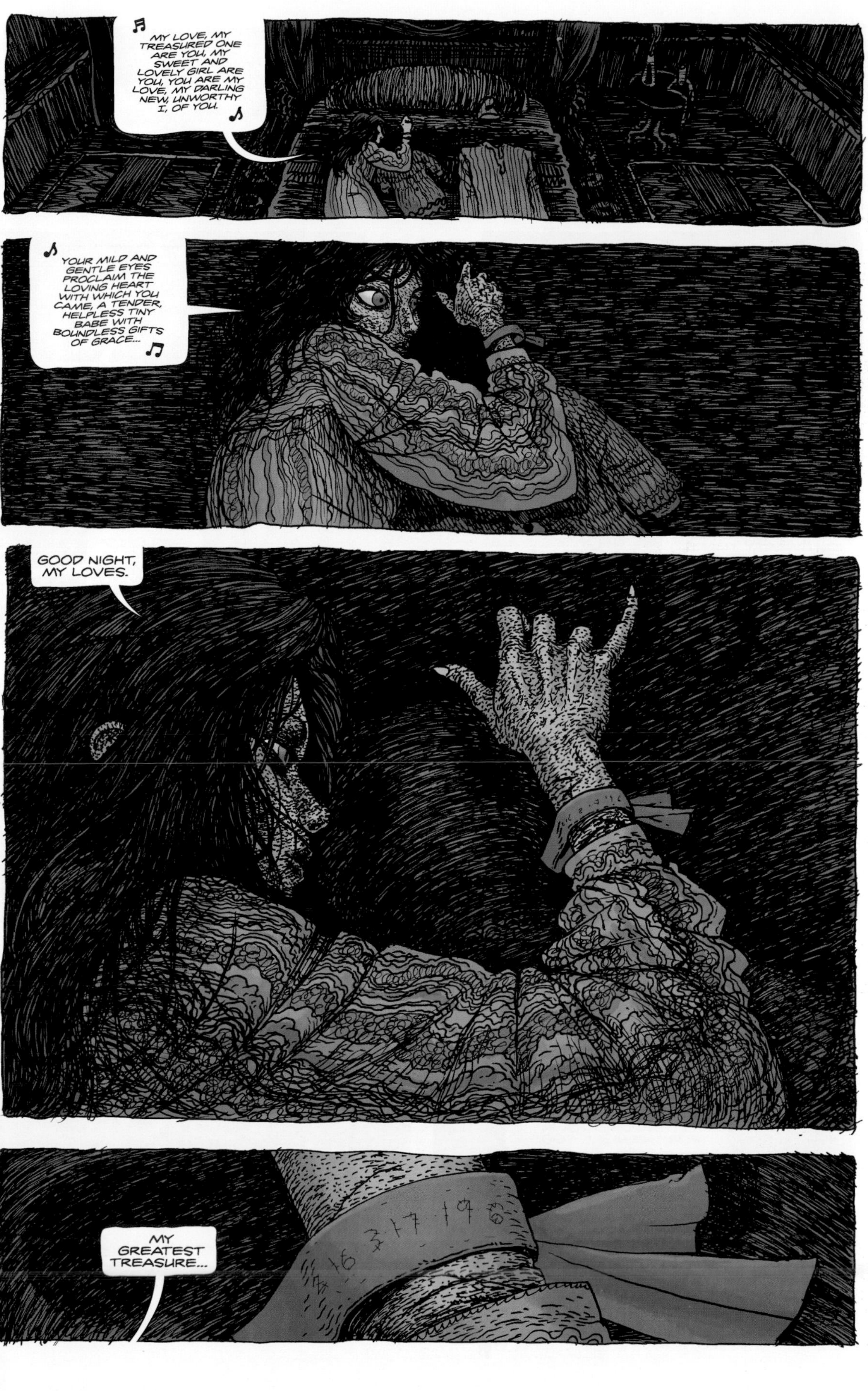
MY LOVE, MY TREASURED ONE ARE YOU, MY SWEET AND LOVELY GIRL ARE YOU, YOU ARE MY LOVE, MY DARLING NEW, UNWORTHY I, OF YOU.
YOUR MILD AND GENTLE EYES PROCLAIM THE LOVING HEART WITH WHICH YOU CAME, A TENDER, HELPLESS TINY BABE WITH BOUNDLESS GIFTS OF GRACE...
GOOD NIGHT, MY LOVES.
MY GREATEST TREASURE...

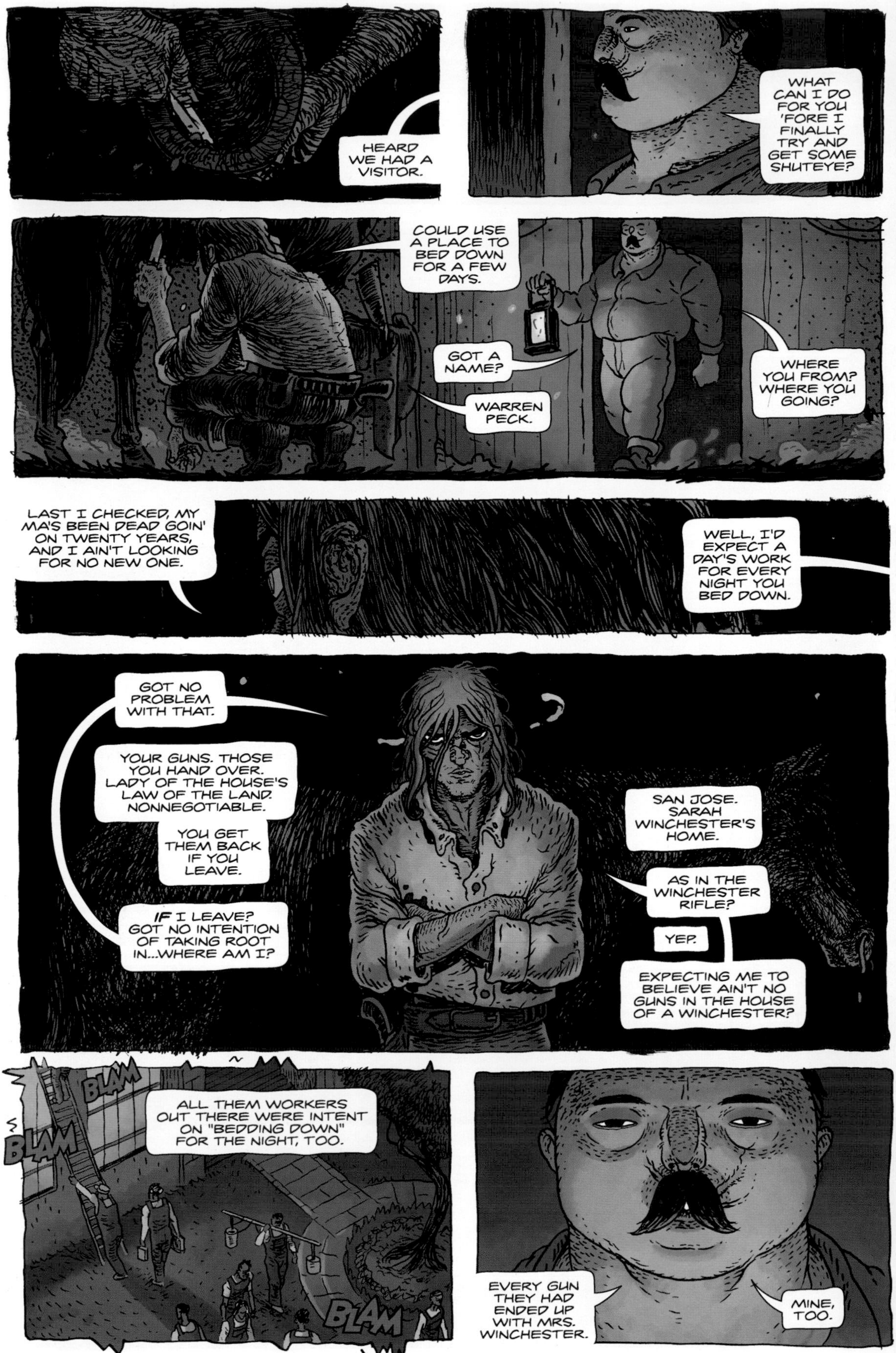
HEARD WE HAD A VISITOR.
WHAT CAN I DO FOR YOU 'FORE I FINALLY TRY AND GET SOME SHUTEYE?
COULD USE A PLACE TO BED DOWN FOR A FEW DAYS.
GOT A NAME?
WARREN PECK.
WHERE YOU FROM? WHERE YOU GOING?
LAST I CHECKED, MY MA'S BEEN DEAD GOIN' ON TWENTY YEARS, AND I AIN'T LOOKING FOR NO NEW ONE.
WELL, I'D EXPECT A DAY'S WORK FOR EVERY NIGHT YOU BED DOWN.
GOT NO PROBLEM WITH THAT.
YOUR GUNS. THOSE YOU HAND OVER. LADY OF THE HOUSE'S LAW OF THE LAND. NONNEGOTIABLE.
YOU GET THEM BACK IF YOU LEAVE.
IF I LEAVE? GOT NO INTENTION OF TAKING ROOT IN...WHERE AM I?
SAN JOSE. SARAH WINCHESTER'S HOME.
AS IN THE WINCHESTER RIFLE?
YEP.
EXPECTING ME TO BELIEVE AIN'T NO GUNS IN THE HOUSE OF A WINCHESTER?
BLAM
BLAM
ALL THEM WORKERS OUT THERE WERE INTENT ON "BEDDING DOWN" FOR THE NIGHT, TOO.
BLAM
EVERY GUN THEY HAD ENDED UP WITH MRS. WINCHESTER.
MINE, TOO.

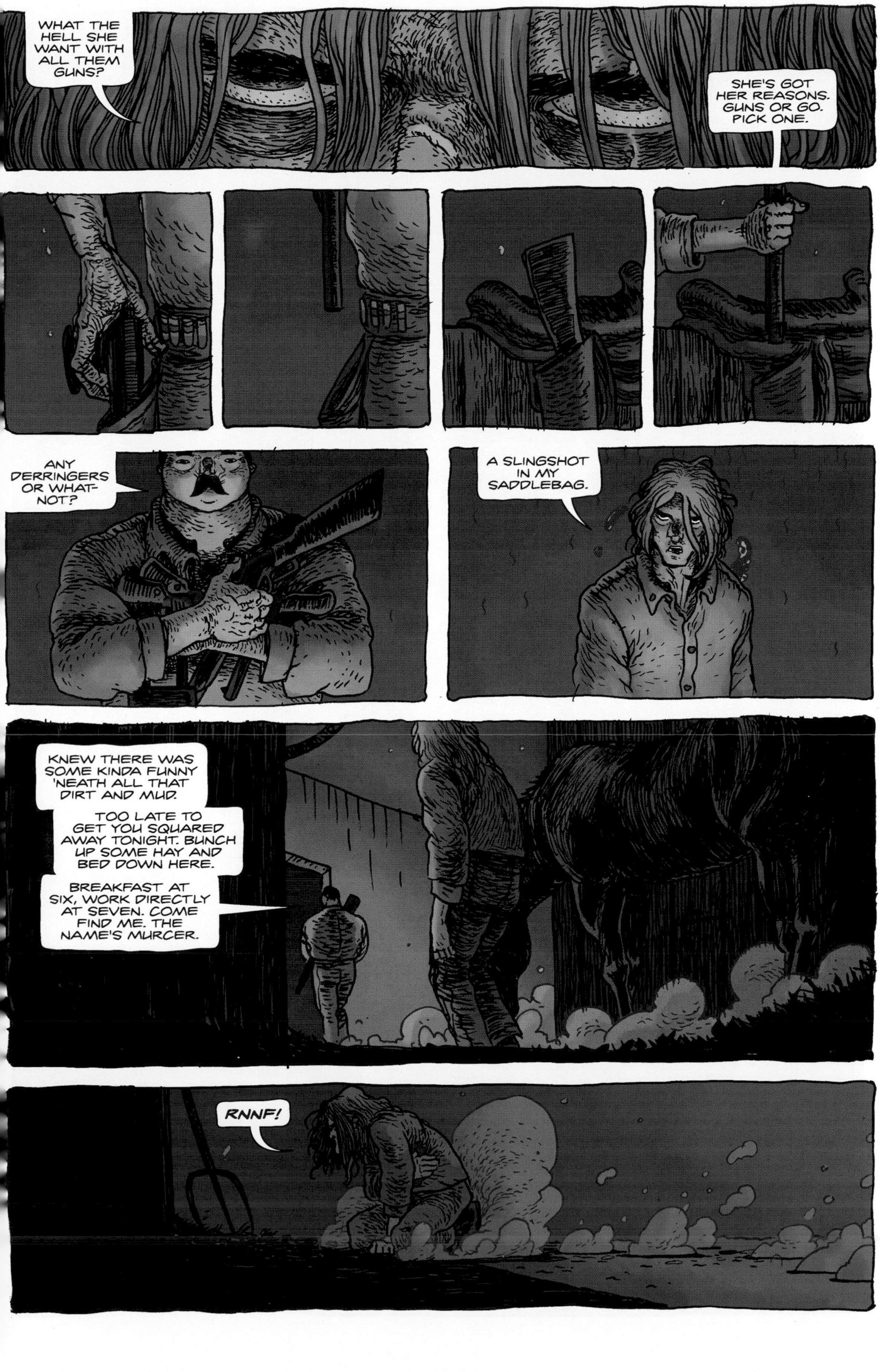
WHAT THE HELL SHE WANT WITH ALL THEM GUNS?
SHE'S GOT HER REASONS. GUNS OR GO. PICK ONE.
ANY DERRINGERS OR WHAT-NOT?
A SLINGSHOT IN MY SADDLEBAG.
KNEW THERE WAS SOME KINDA FUNNY 'NEATH ALL THAT DIRT AND MUD.
TOO LATE TO GET YOU SQUARED AWAY TONIGHT. BUNCH UP SOME HAY AND BED DOWN HERE.
BREAKFAST AT SIX, WORK DIRECTLY AT SEVEN. COME FIND ME. THE NAME'S MURCER.
RNNF!

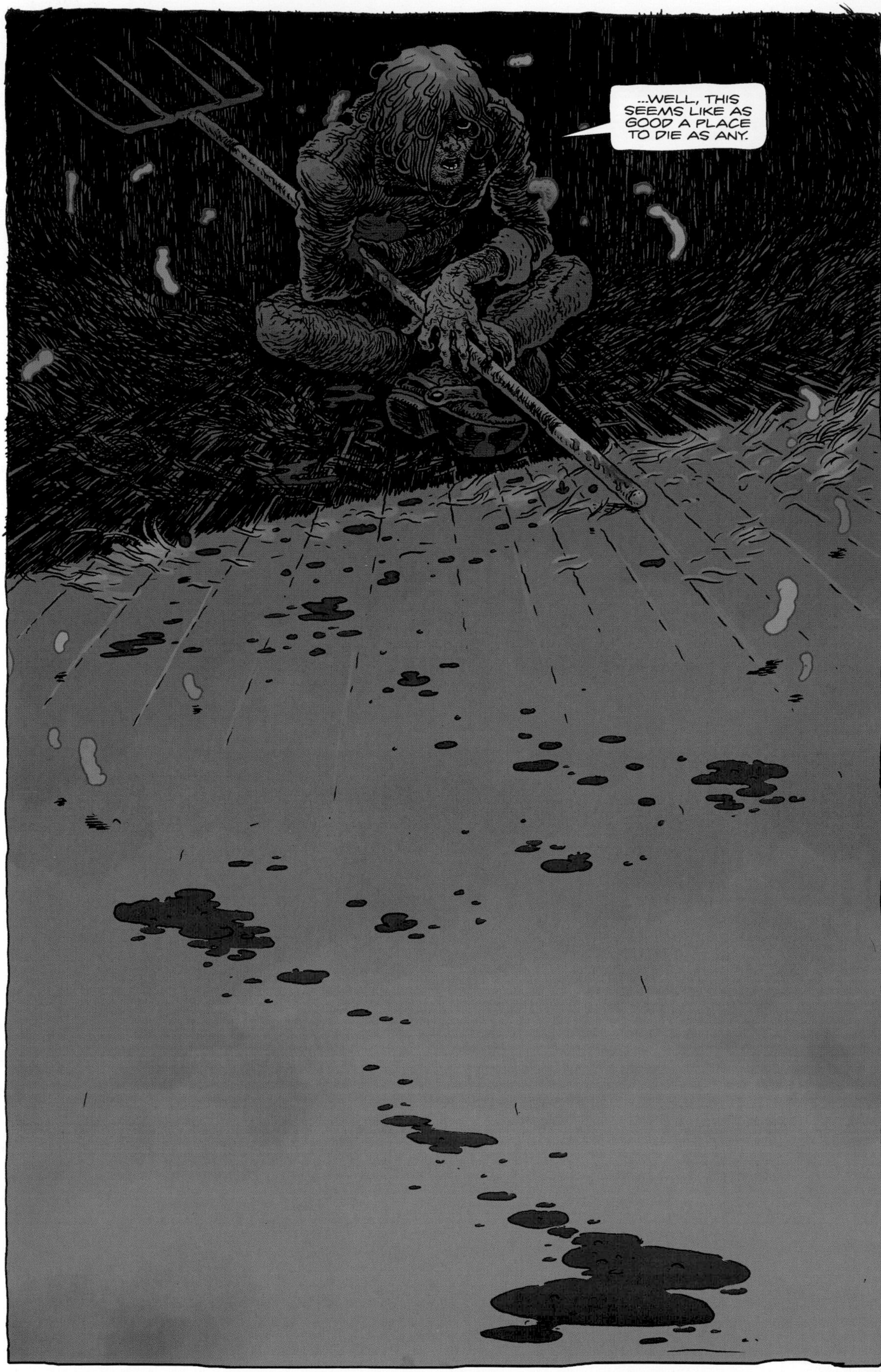
...WELL, THIS SEEMS LIKE AS GOOD A PLACE TO DIE AS ANY.

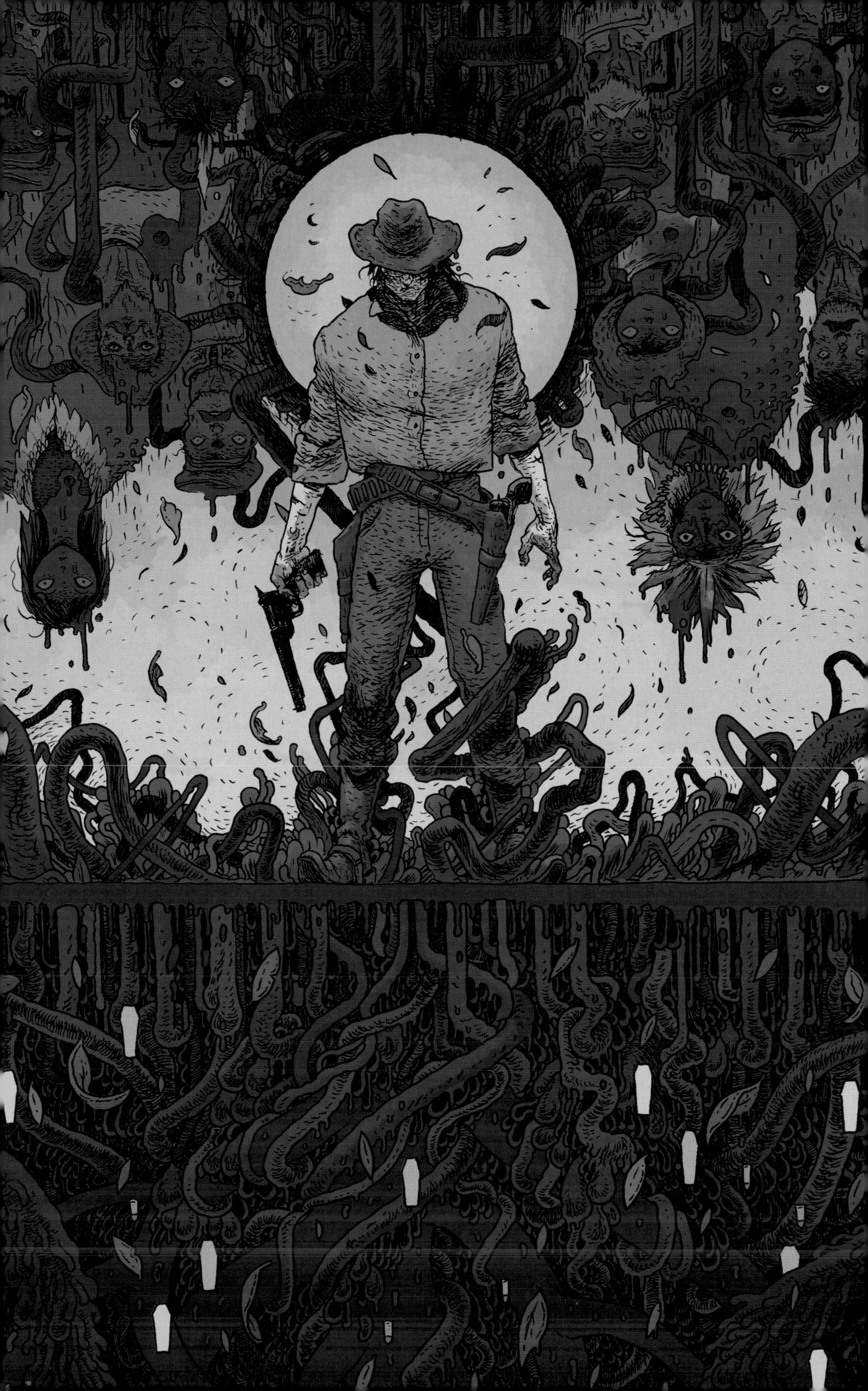

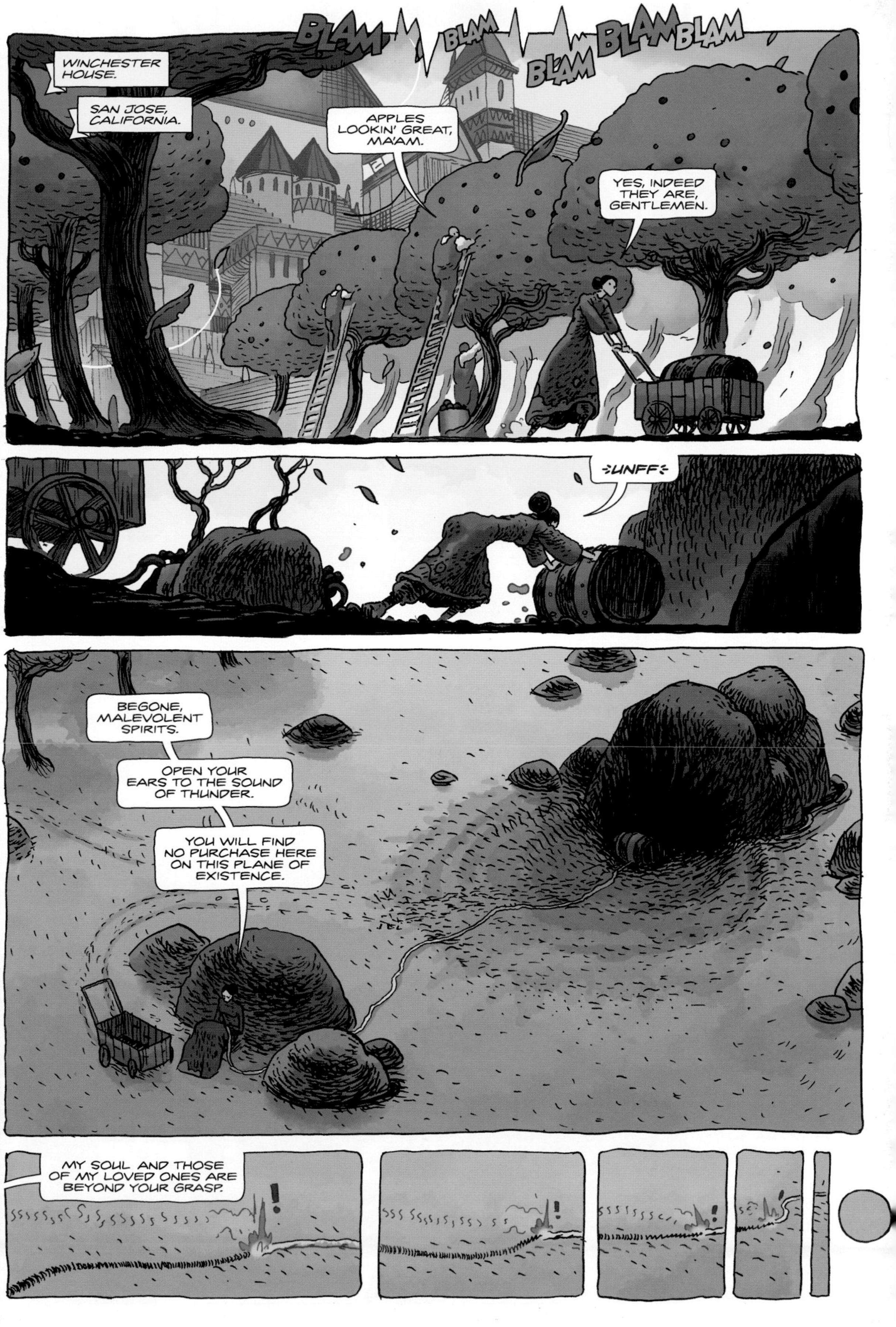
BLAM
BLAM
BLAM
BLAM
BLAM
WINCHESTER HOUSE.
SAN JOSE, CALIFORNIA.
APPLES LOOKIN' GREAT, MA'AM.
YES, INDEED THEY ARE, GENTLEMEN.
UNFF
BEGONE, MALEVOLENT SPIRITS.
OPEN YOUR EARS TO THE SOUND OF THUNDER.
YOU WILL FIND NO PURCHASE HERE ON THIS PLANE OF EXISTENCE.
MY SOUL AND THOSE OF MY LOVED ONES ARE BEYOND YOUR GRASP.
!
!
!

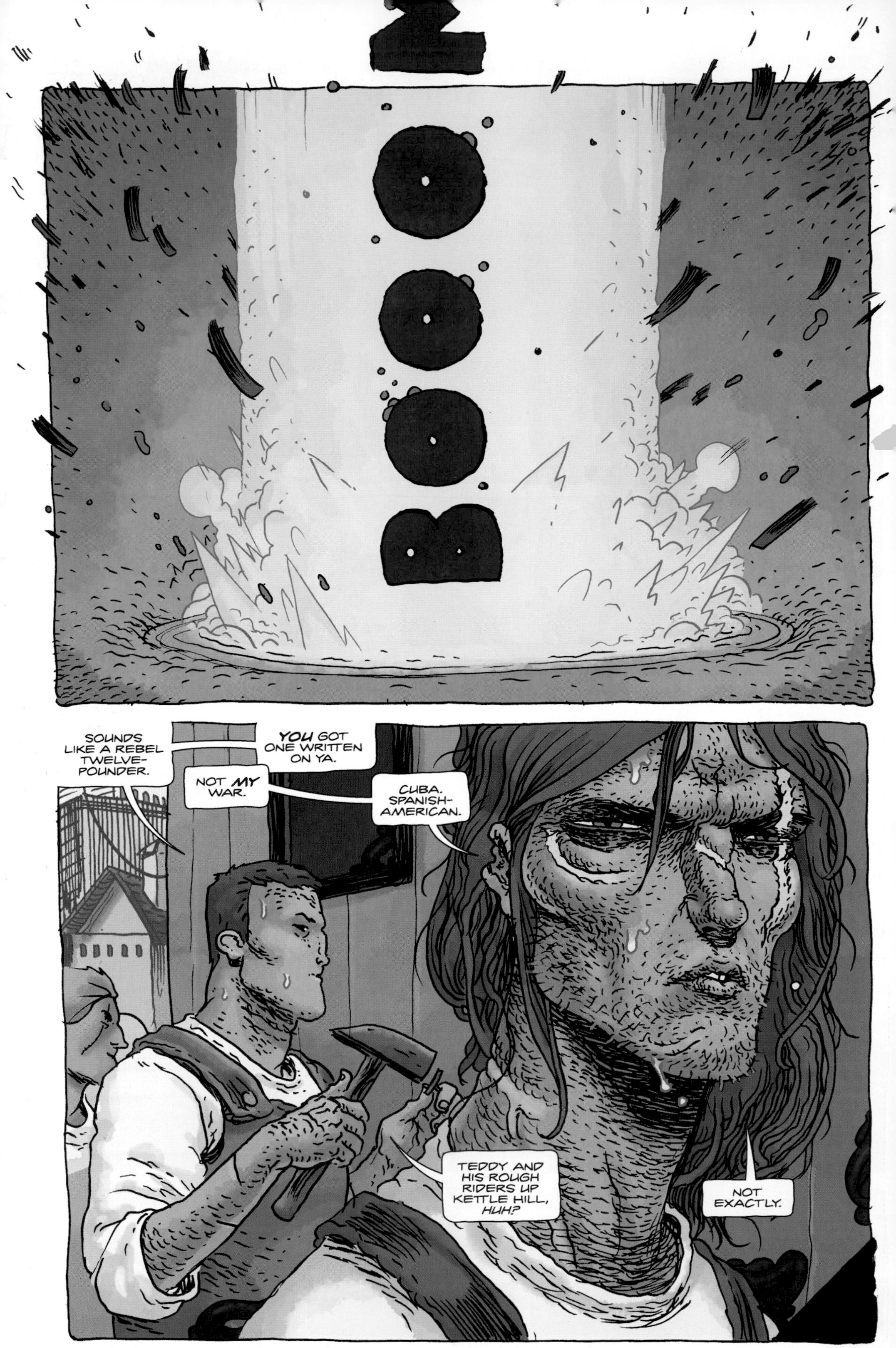
BOOO
SOUNDS LIKE A REBEL TWELVE-POUNDER.
NOT *MY* WAR.
YOU GOT ONE WRITTEN ON YA.
CUBA. SPANISH-AMERICAN.
TEDDY AND HIS ROUGH RIDERS UP KETTLE HILL, *HUH?*
NOT EXACTLY.

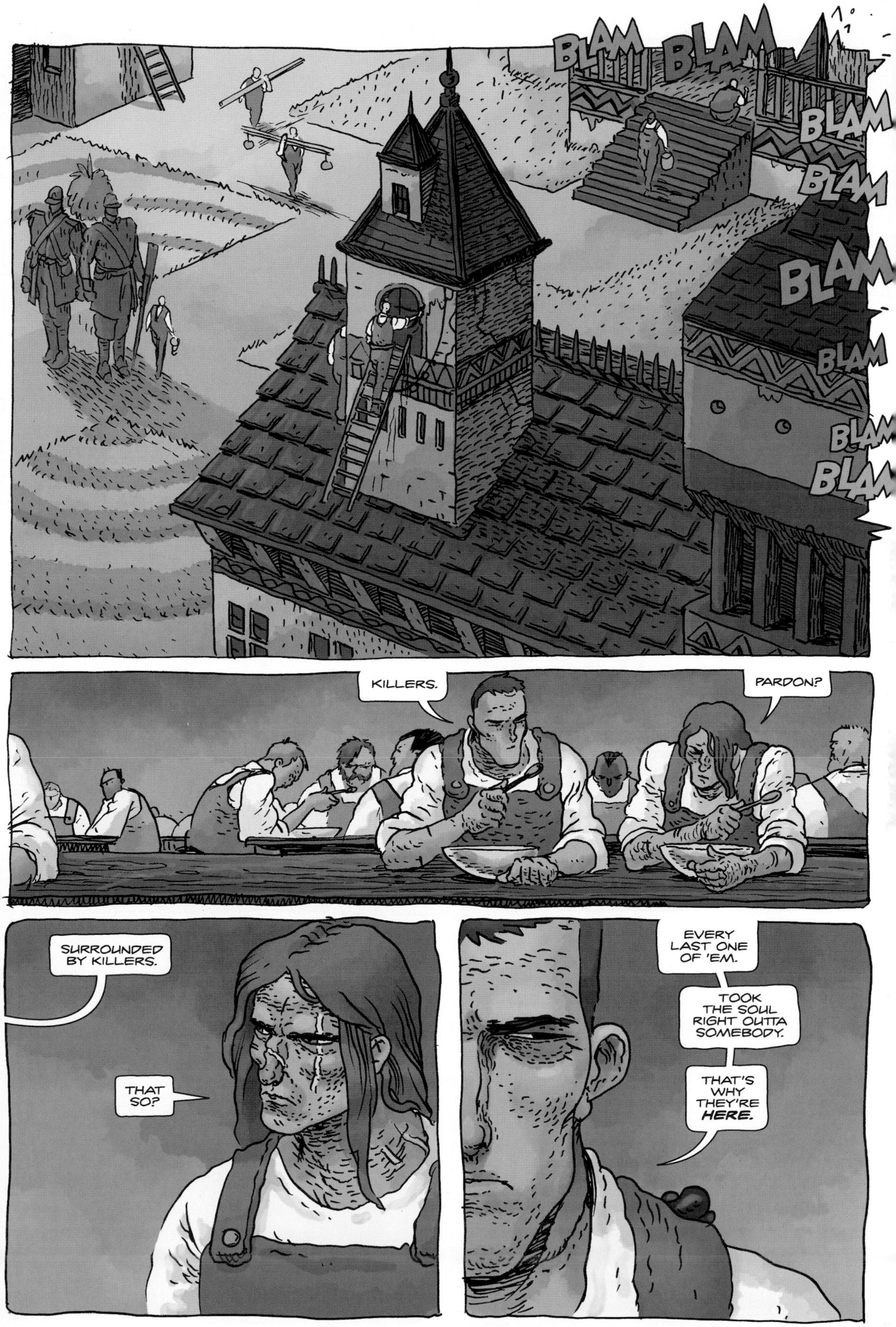
BLAM BLAM
BLAM
BLAM
BLAM
BLAM
BLAM
BLAM
KILLERS.
PARDON?
SURROUNDED BY KILLERS.
THAT SO?
EVERY LAST ONE OF 'EM.
TOOK THE SOUL RIGHT OUTTA SOMEBODY.
THAT'S WHY THEY'RE *HERE.*

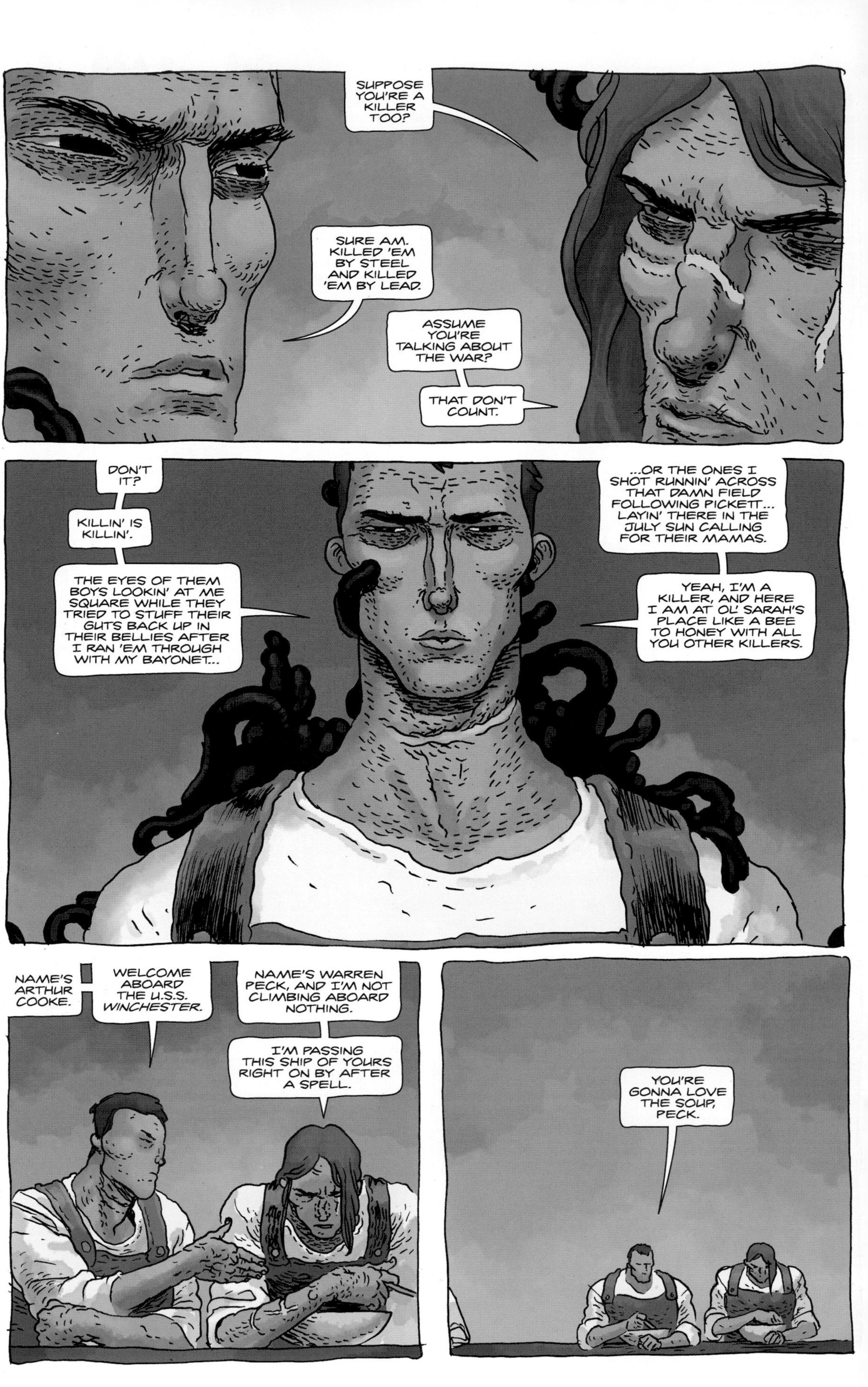
SUPPOSE YOU'RE A KILLER TOO?
SURE AM. KILLED 'EM BY STEEL AND KILLED 'EM BY LEAD.
ASSUME YOU'RE TALKING ABOUT THE WAR?
THAT DON'T COUNT.
DON'T IT?
KILLIN' IS KILLIN'.
THE EYES OF THEM BOYS LOOKIN' AT ME SQUARE WHILE THEY TRIED TO STUFF THEIR GUTS BACK UP IN THEIR BELLIES AFTER I RAN 'EM THROUGH WITH MY BAYONET...
...OR THE ONES I SHOT RUNNIN' ACROSS THAT DAMN FIELD FOLLOWING PICKETT... LAYIN' THERE IN THE JULY SUN CALLING FOR THEIR MAMAS.
YEAH, I'M A KILLER, AND HERE I AM AT OL' SARAH'S PLACE LIKE A BEE TO HONEY WITH ALL YOU OTHER KILLERS.
NAME'S ARTHUR COOKE.
WELCOME ABOARD THE U.S.S. WINCHESTER.
NAME'S WARREN PECK, AND I'M NOT CLIMBING ABOARD NOTHING.
I'M PASSING THIS SHIP OF YOURS RIGHT ON BY AFTER A SPELL.
YOU'RE GONNA LOVE THE SOUP, PECK.

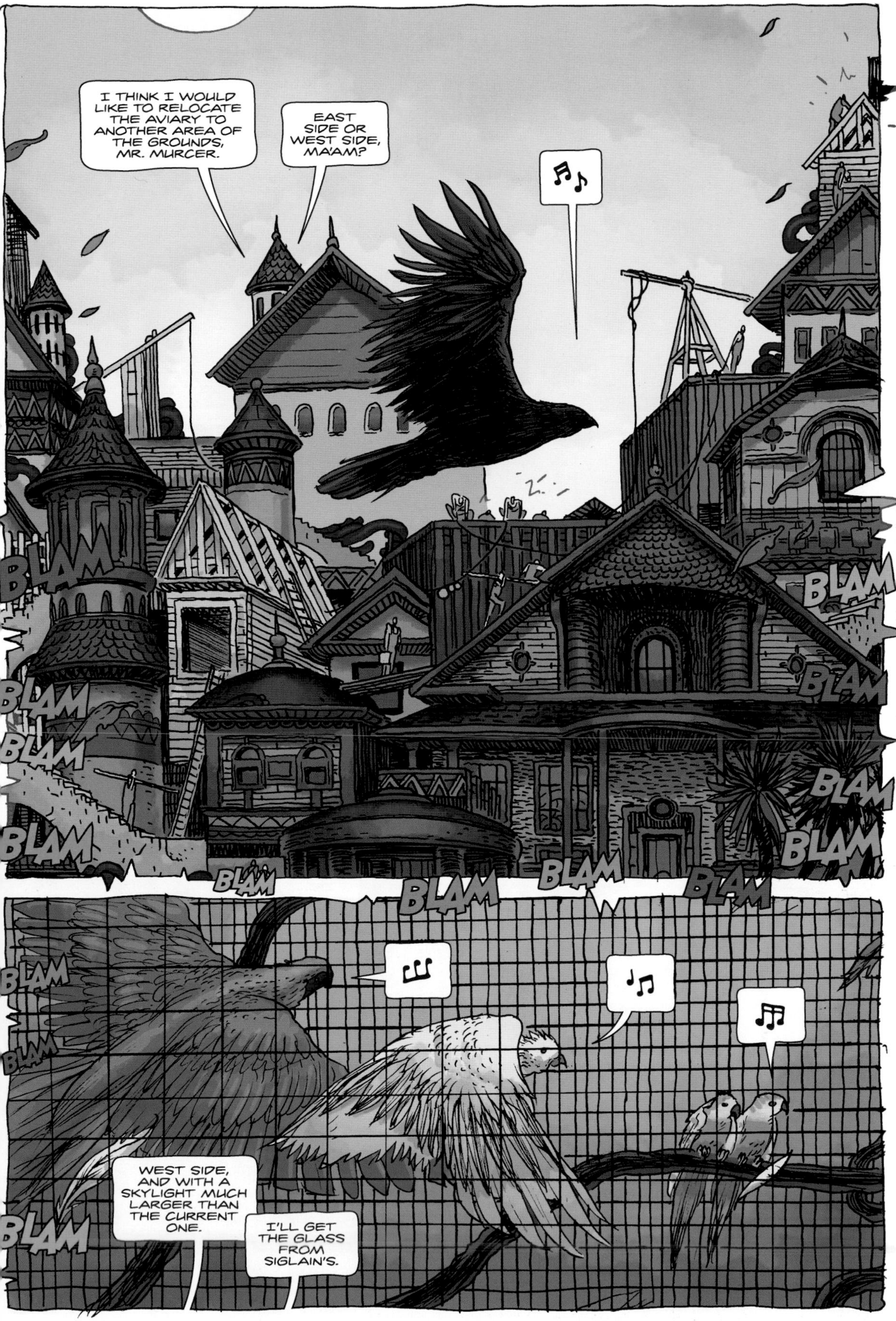

I THINK I WOULD LIKE TO RELOCATE THE AVIARY TO ANOTHER AREA OF THE GROUNDS, MR. MURCER.
EAST SIDE OR WEST SIDE, MA'AM?
BLAM
BLAM
BLAM
BLAM
BLAM
BLAM
BLAM
BLAM
BLAM
BLAM
BLAM
BLAM
BLAM
BLAM
BLAM
WEST SIDE, AND WITH A SKYLIGHT MUCH LARGER THAN THE CURRENT ONE.
I'LL GET THE GLASS FROM SIGLAIN'S.
BLAM

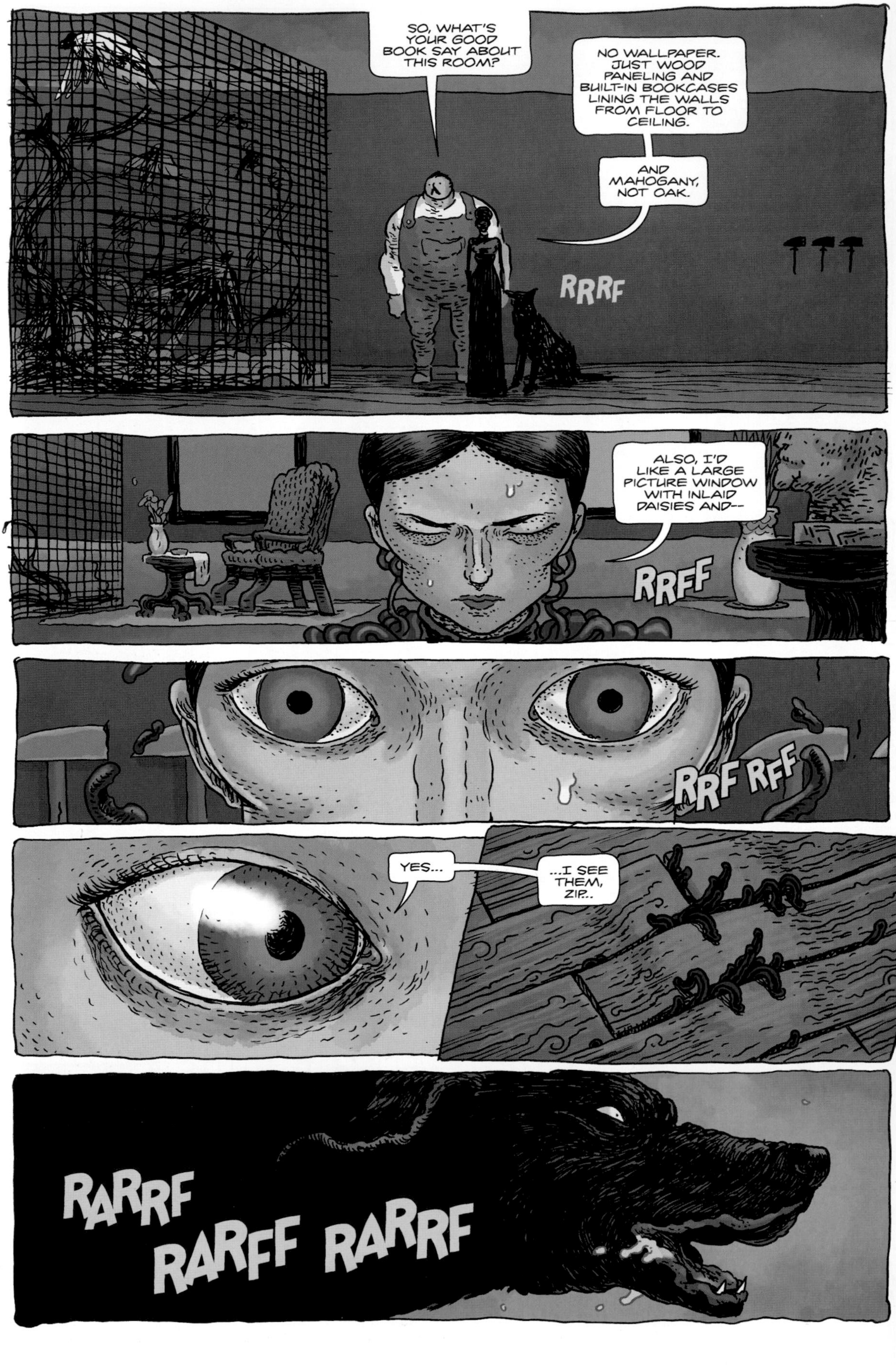

SO, WHAT'S YOUR GOOD BOOK SAY ABOUT THIS ROOM?
NO WALLPAPER. JUST WOOD PANELING AND BUILT-IN BOOKCASES LINING THE WALLS FROM FLOOR TO CEILING.
AND MAHOGANY, NOT OAK.
RRRF
ALSO, I'D LIKE A LARGE PICTURE WINDOW WITH INLAID DAISIES AND--
RRFF
RRF RFF
YES...
...I SEE THEM, ZIP...
RARRF
RARFF RARRF

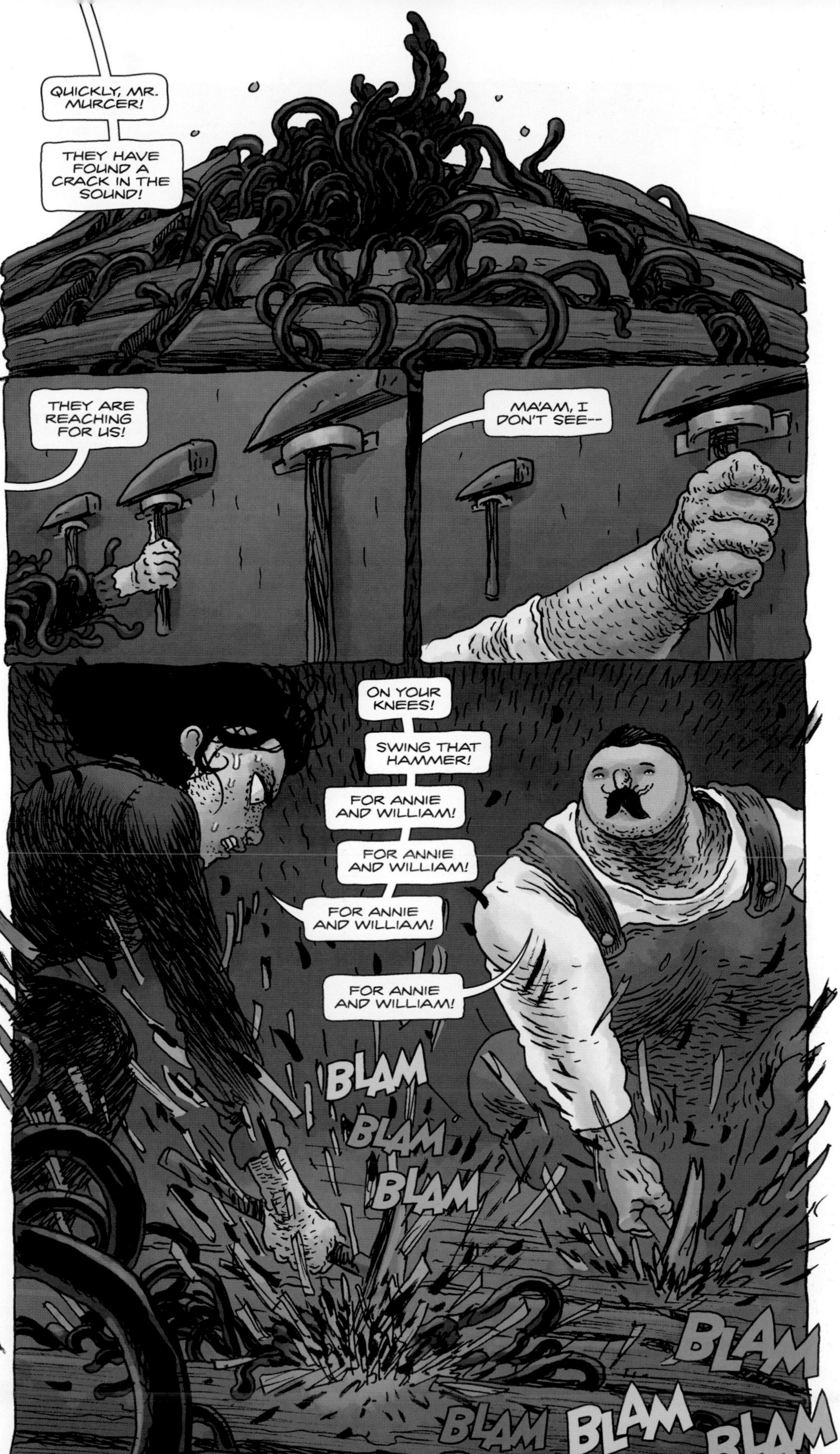
QUICKLY, MR. MURCER!
THEY HAVE FOUND A CRACK IN THE SOUND!
THEY ARE REACHING FOR US!
MA'AM, I DON'T SEE--
ON YOUR KNEES!
SWING THAT HAMMER!
FOR ANNIE AND WILLIAM!
FOR ANNIE AND WILLIAM!
FOR ANNIE AND WILLIAM!
FOR ANNIE AND WILLIAM!
BLAM
BLAM
BLAM
BLAM
BLAM BLAM BLAM

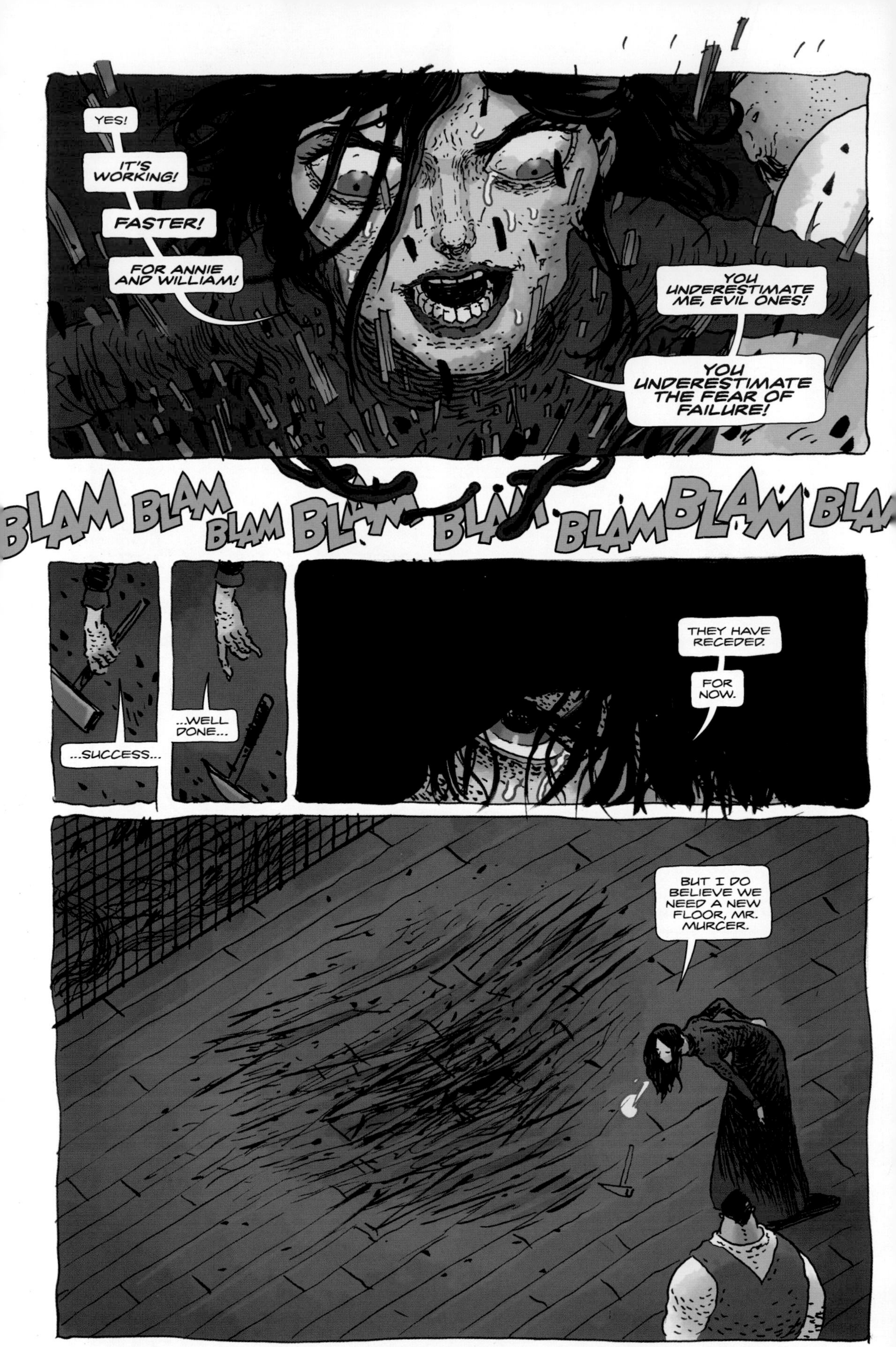
YES!
IT'S WORKING!
FASTER!
FOR ANNIE AND WILLIAM!
YOU UNDERESTIMATE ME, EVIL ONES!
YOU UNDERESTIMATE THE FEAR OF FAILURE!
BLAM BLAM BLAM BLAM BLAM BLAM BLAM BLAM
...SUCCESS...
...WELL DONE...
THEY HAVE RECEDED.
FOR NOW.
BUT I DO BELIEVE WE NEED A NEW FLOOR, MR. MURCER.

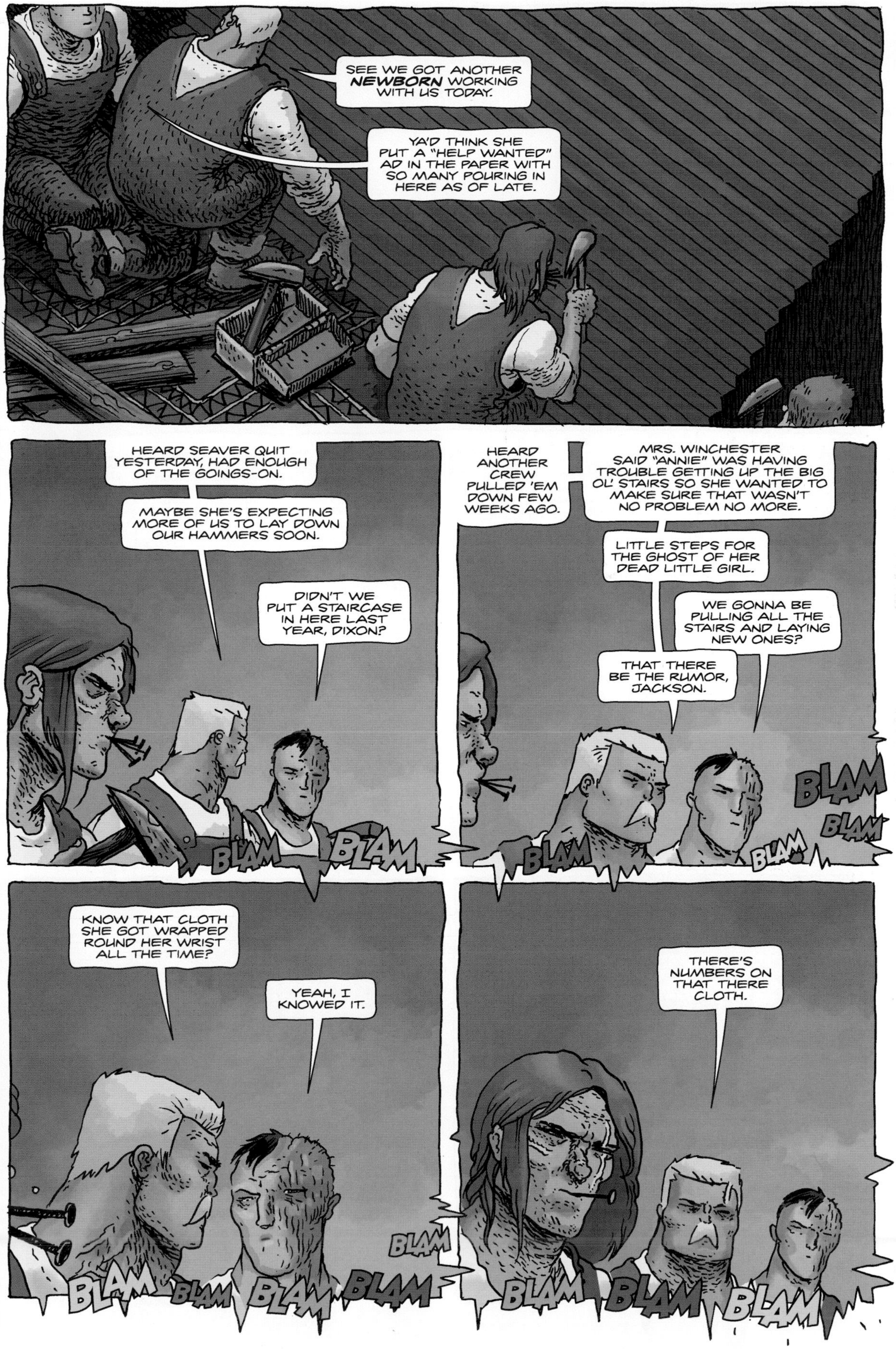
SEE WE GOT ANOTHER NEWBORN WORKING WITH US TODAY.
YA'D THINK SHE PUT A "HELP WANTED" AD IN THE PAPER WITH SO MANY POURING IN HERE AS OF LATE.
HEARD SEAVER QUIT YESTERDAY, HAD ENOUGH OF THE GOINGS-ON.
MAYBE SHE'S EXPECTING MORE OF US TO LAY DOWN OUR HAMMERS SOON.
DIDN'T WE PUT A STAIRCASE IN HERE LAST YEAR, DIXON?
BLAM BLAM
HEARD ANOTHER CREW PULLED 'EM DOWN FEW WEEKS AGO.
MRS. WINCHESTER SAID "ANNIE" WAS HAVING TROUBLE GETTING UP THE BIG OL' STAIRS SO SHE WANTED TO MAKE SURE THAT WASN'T NO PROBLEM NO MORE.
LITTLE STEPS FOR THE GHOST OF HER DEAD LITTLE GIRL.
WE GONNA BE PULLING ALL THE STAIRS AND LAYING NEW ONES?
THAT THERE BE THE RUMOR, JACKSON.
BLAM BLAM BLAM BLAM
KNOW THAT CLOTH SHE GOT WRAPPED ROUND HER WRIST ALL THE TIME?
YEAH, I KNOWED IT.
BLAM BLAM BLAM BLAM BLAM
THERE'S NUMBERS ON THAT THERE CLOTH.
BLAM BLAM BLAM

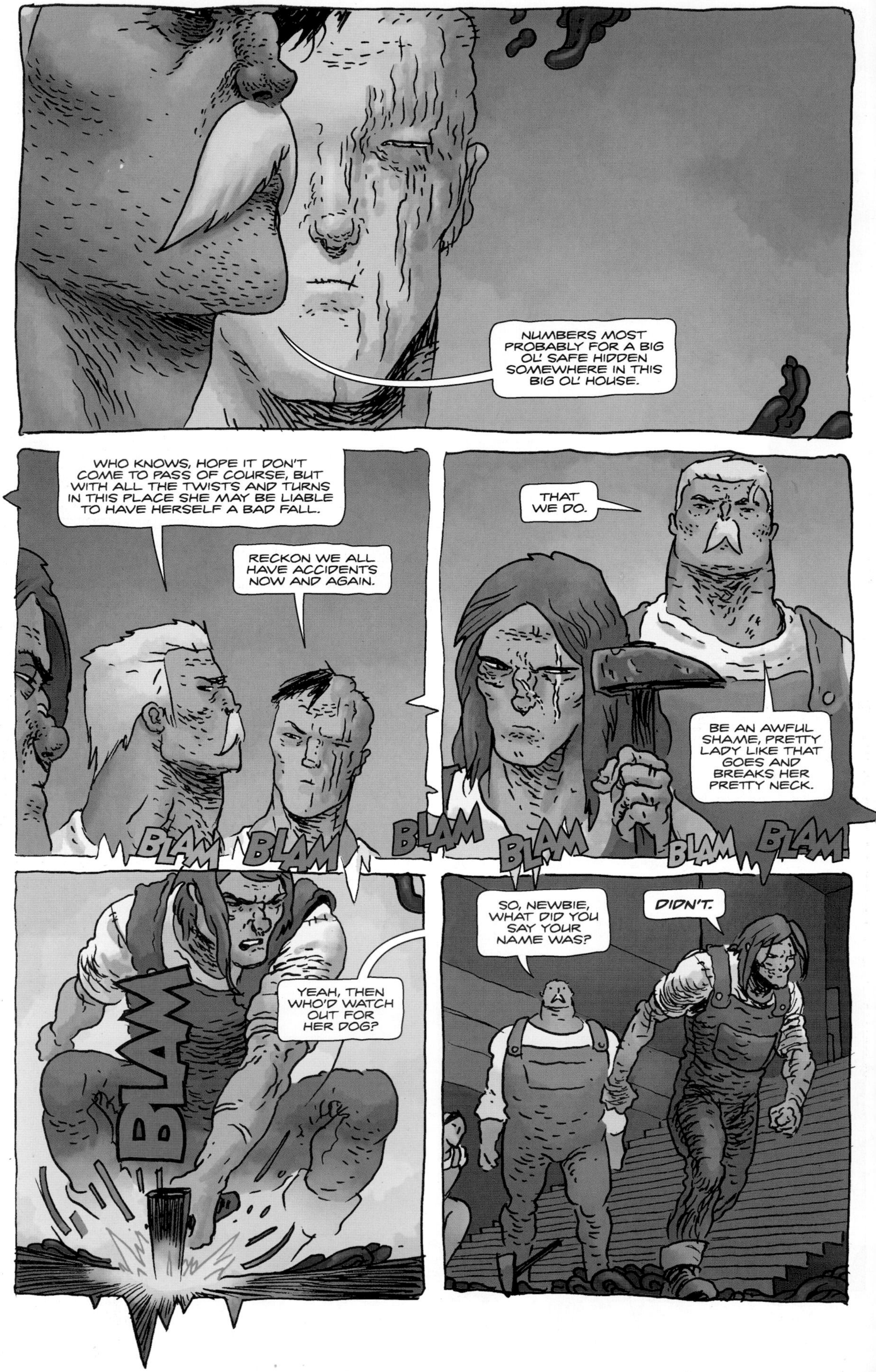
NUMBERS MOST PROBABLY FOR A BIG OL' SAFE HIDDEN SOMEWHERE IN THIS BIG OL' HOUSE.
WHO KNOWS, HOPE IT DON'T COME TO PASS OF COURSE, BUT WITH ALL THE TWISTS AND TURNS IN THIS PLACE SHE MAY BE LIABLE TO HAVE HERSELF A BAD FALL.
RECKON WE ALL HAVE ACCIDENTS NOW AND AGAIN.
THAT WE DO.
BE AN AWFUL SHAME, PRETTY LADY LIKE THAT GOES AND BREAKS HER PRETTY NECK.
BLAM BLAM BLAM BLAM BLAM BLAM
YEAH, THEN WHO'D WATCH OUT FOR HER DOG?
BLAM
SO, NEWBIE, WHAT DID YOU SAY YOUR NAME WAS?
DIDN'T.

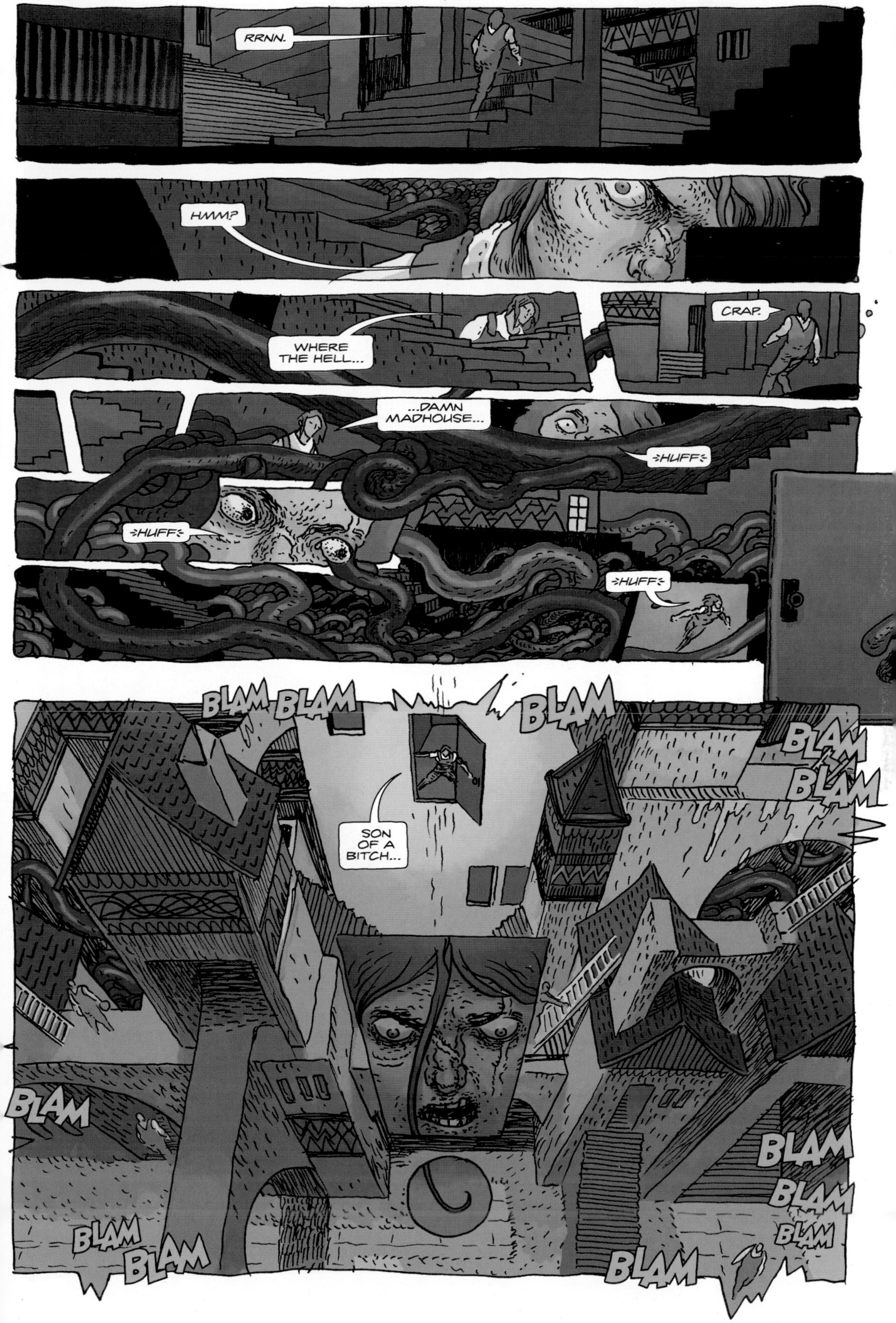
RRNN.
HMM?
WHERE THE HELL...
CRAP.
...DAMN MADHOUSE...
HUFF
HUFF
HUFF
BLAM BLAM
BLAM
BLAM BLAM
SON OF A BITCH...
BLAM
BLAM BLAM BLAM
BLAM BLAM
BLAM

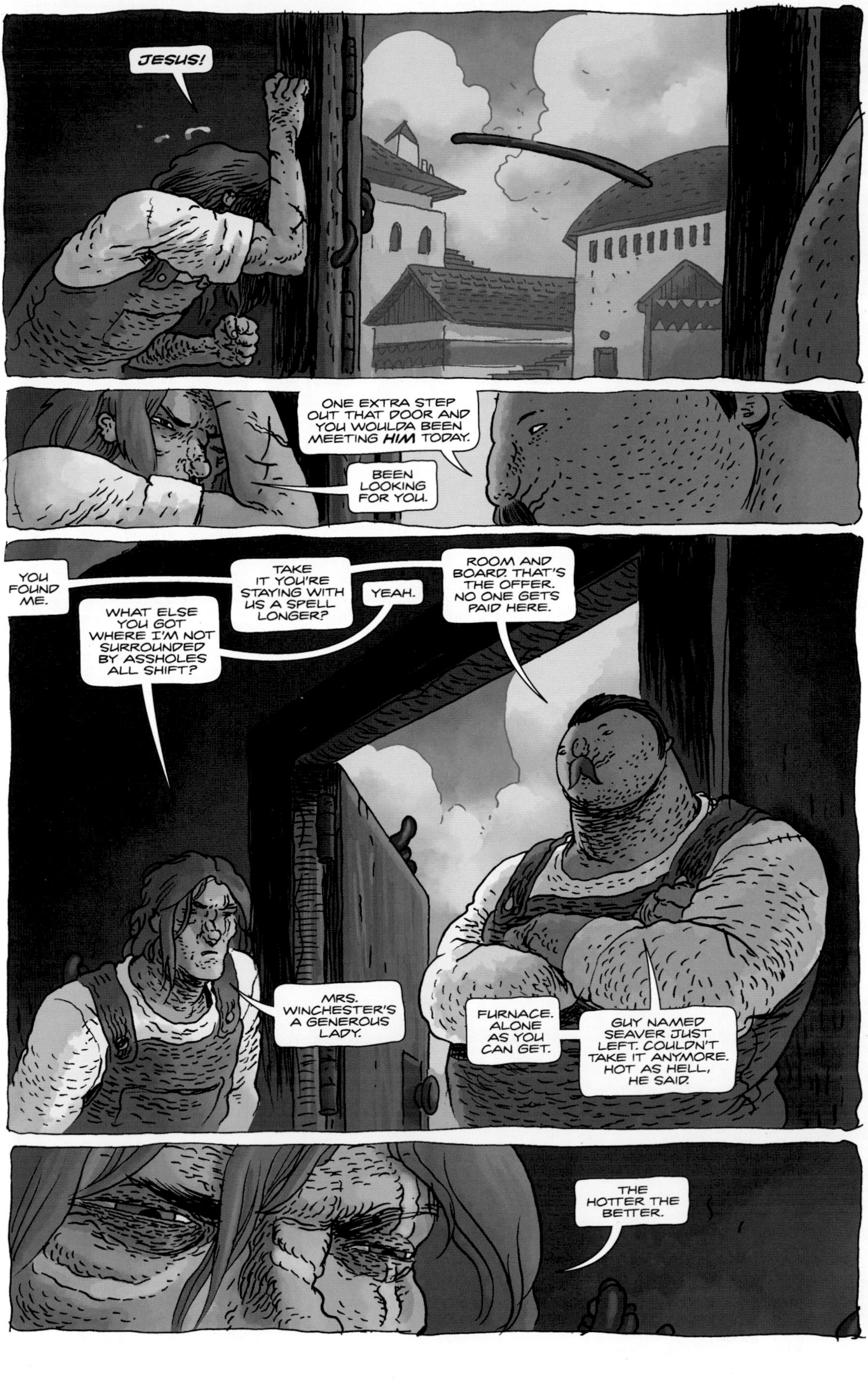
JESUS!
ONE EXTRA STEP OUT THAT DOOR AND YOU WOULDA BEEN MEETING HIM TODAY.
BEEN LOOKING FOR YOU.
YOU FOUND ME.
TAKE IT YOU'RE STAYING WITH US A SPELL LONGER?
YEAH.
ROOM AND BOARD. THAT'S THE OFFER. NO ONE GETS PAID HERE.
WHAT ELSE YOU GOT WHERE I'M NOT SURROUNDED BY ASSHOLES ALL SHIFT?
MRS. WINCHESTER'S A GENEROUS LADY.
FURNACE. ALONE AS YOU CAN GET.
GUY NAMED SEAVER JUST LEFT. COULDN'T TAKE IT ANYMORE. HOT AS HELL, HE SAID.
THE HOTTER THE BETTER.

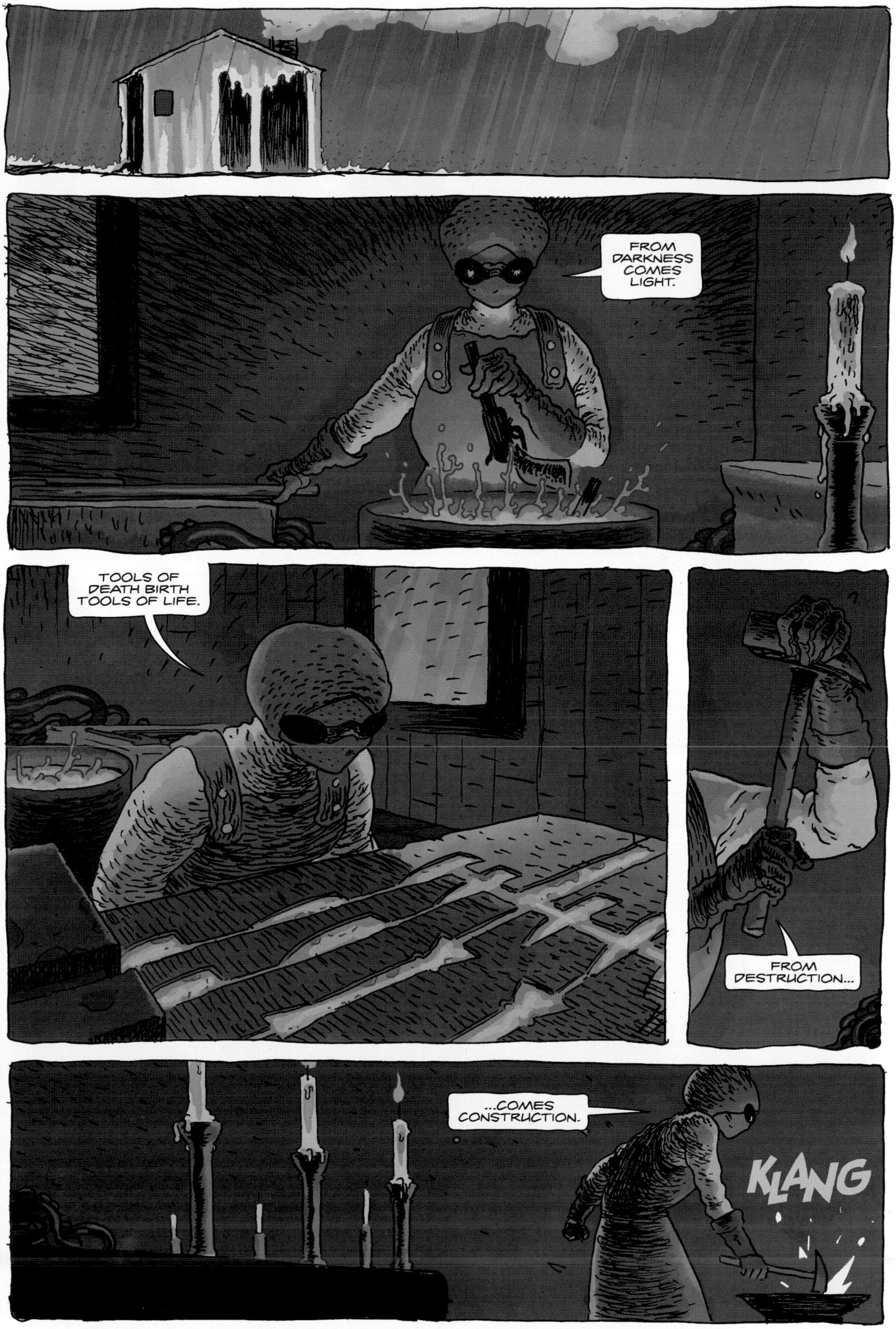
FROM DARKNESS COMES LIGHT.
TOOLS OF DEATH BIRTH TOOLS OF LIFE.
FROM DESTRUCTION...
...COMES CONSTRUCTION.
KLANG

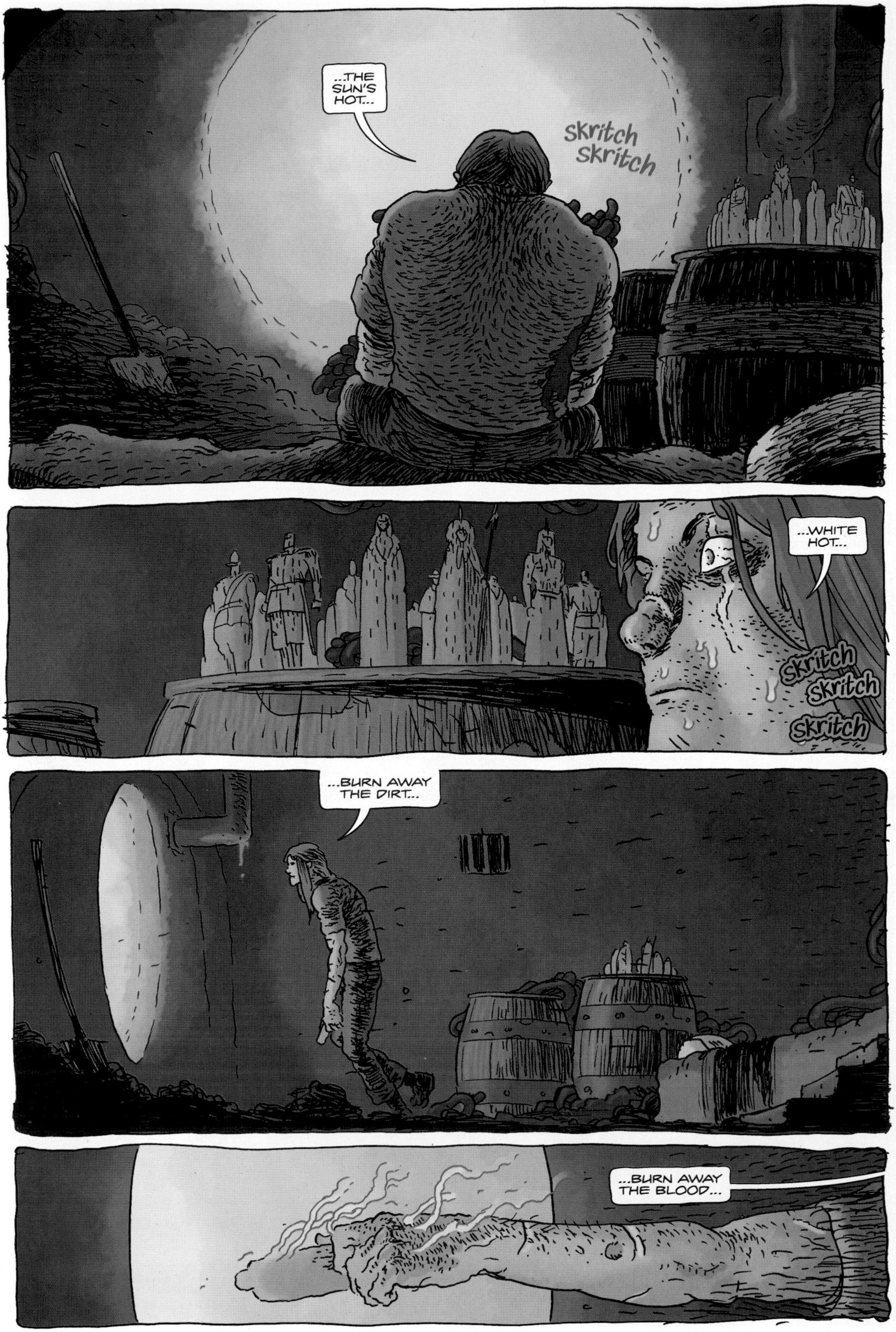
...THE SUN'S HOT...
skritch skritch
...WHITE HOT...
skritch skritch skritch
...BURN AWAY THE DIRT...
...BURN AWAY THE BLOOD...

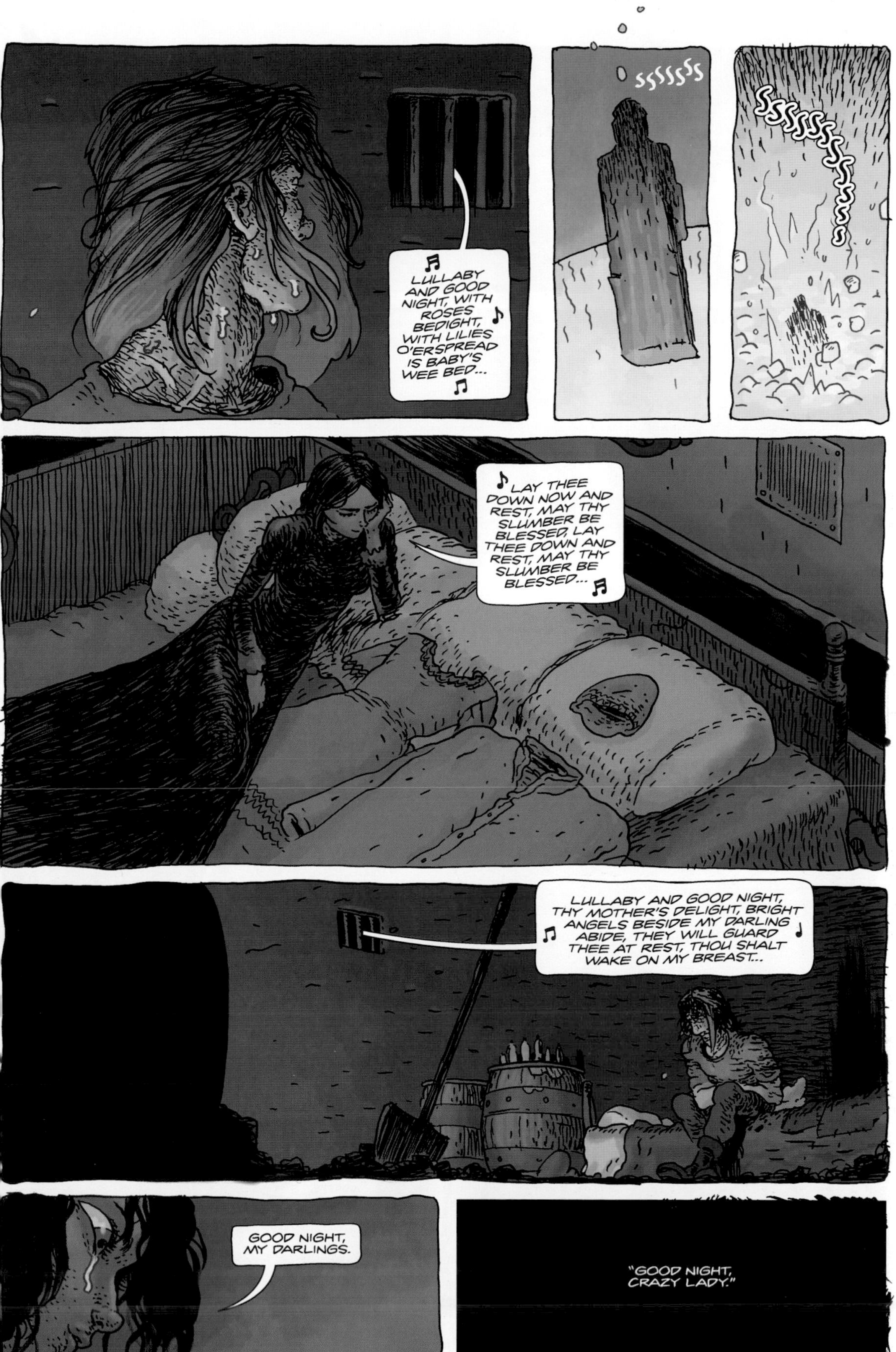
LULLABY AND GOOD NIGHT, WITH ROSES BEDIGHT, WITH LILIES O'ERSPREAD IS BABY'S WEE BED...
SSSSSSS
SSSSSSSSSSSSS
LAY THEE DOWN NOW AND REST, MAY THY SLUMBER BE BLESSED, LAY THEE DOWN AND REST, MAY THY SLUMBER BE BLESSED...
LULLABY AND GOOD NIGHT, THY MOTHER'S DELIGHT, BRIGHT ANGELS BESIDE MY DARLING ABIDE, THEY WILL GUARD THEE AT REST, THOU SHALT WAKE ON MY BREAST...
GOOD NIGHT, MY DARLINGS.
"GOOD NIGHT, CRAZY LADY."

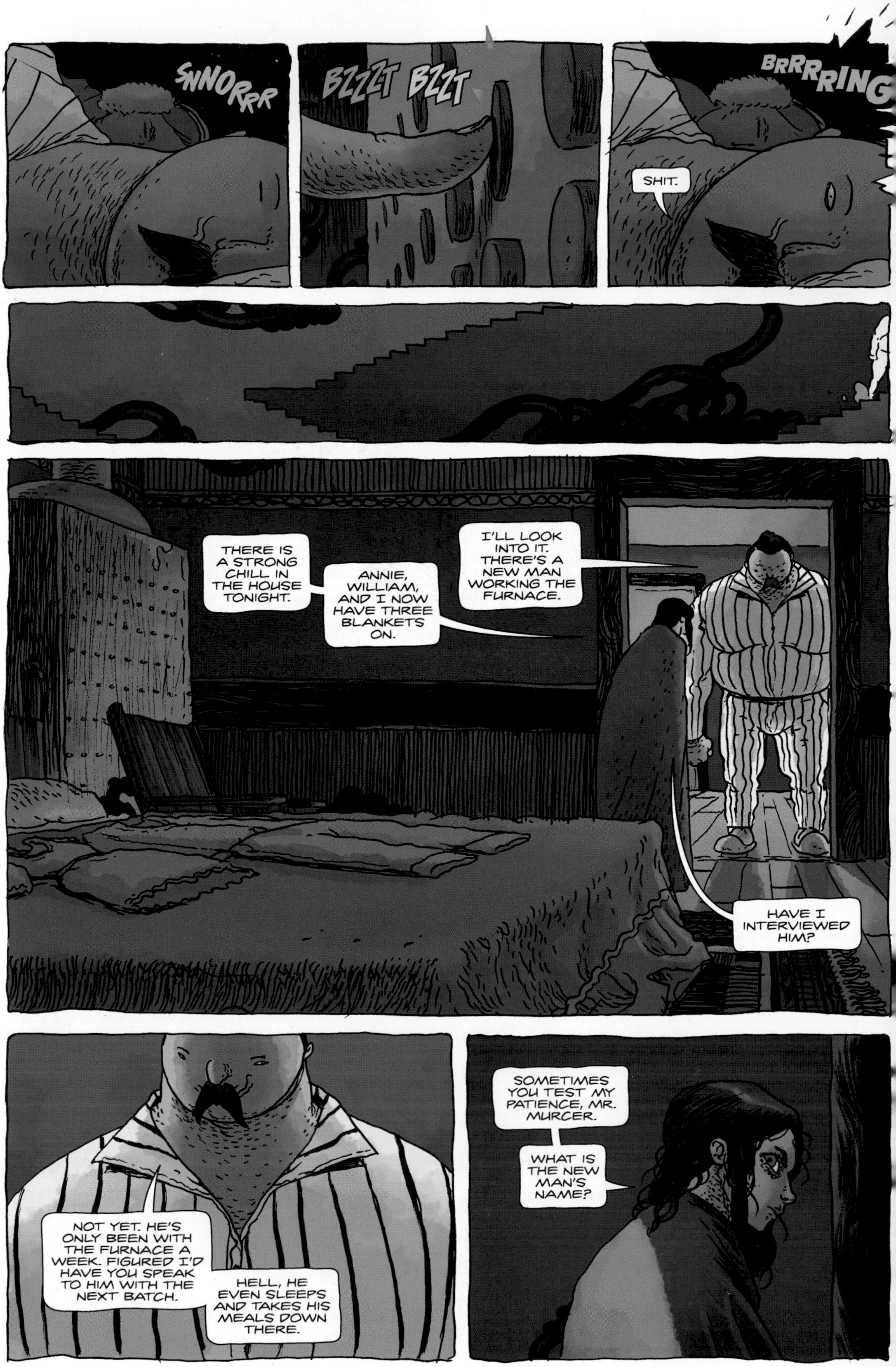
SNNORRRR
BZZZT BZZT
BRRRRING
SHIT.
THERE IS A STRONG CHILL IN THE HOUSE TONIGHT.
ANNIE, WILLIAM, AND I NOW HAVE THREE BLANKETS ON.
I'LL LOOK INTO IT. THERE'S A NEW MAN WORKING THE FURNACE.
HAVE I INTERVIEWED HIM?
NOT YET. HE'S ONLY BEEN WITH THE FURNACE A WEEK. FIGURED I'D HAVE YOU SPEAK TO HIM WITH THE NEXT BATCH.
HELL, HE EVEN SLEEPS AND TAKES HIS MEALS DOWN THERE.
SOMETIMES YOU TEST MY PATIENCE, MR. MURCER.
WHAT IS THE NEW MAN'S NAME?

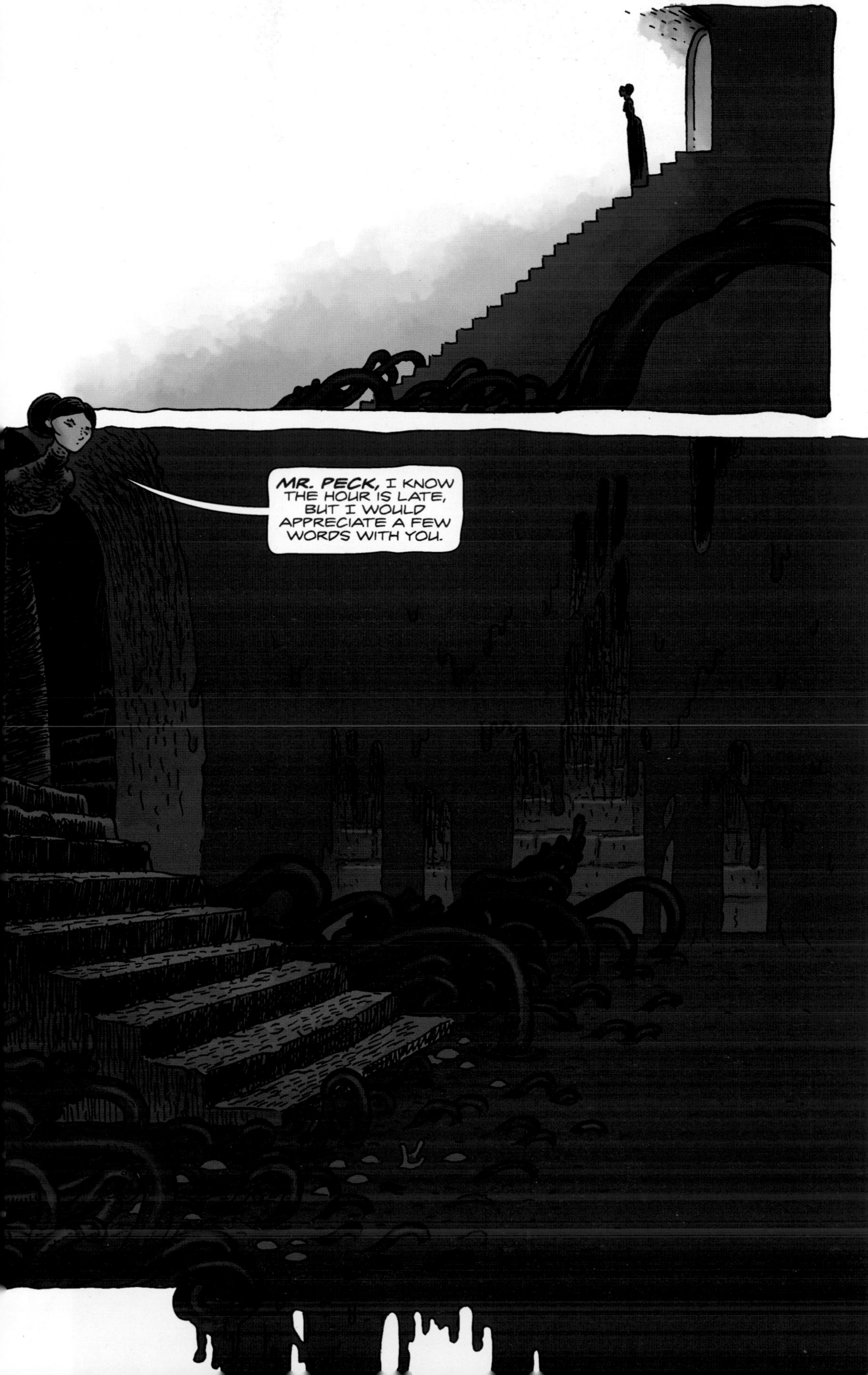
MR. PECK, I KNOW THE HOUR IS LATE, BUT I WOULD APPRECIATE A FEW WORDS WITH YOU.

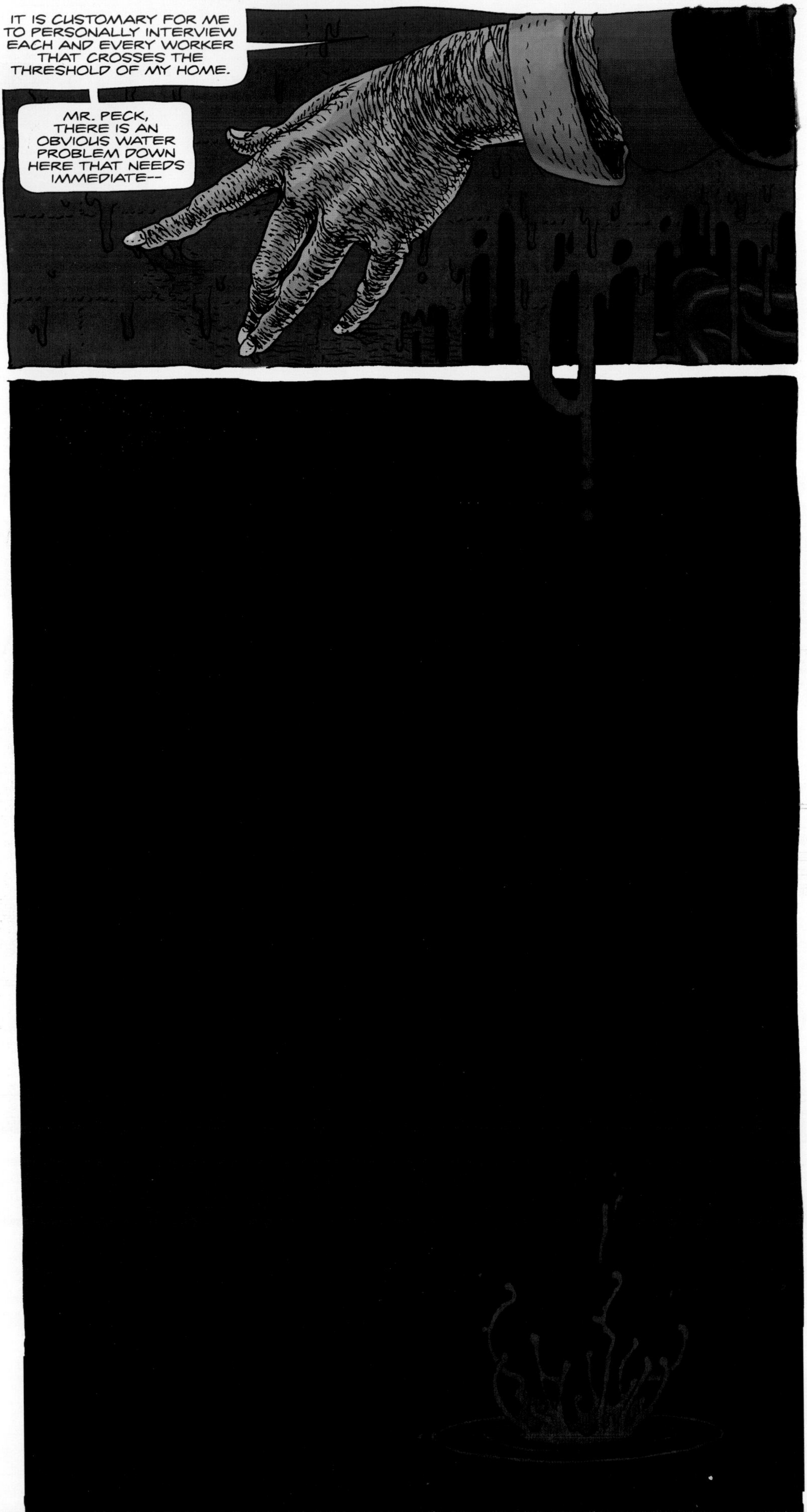
IT IS CUSTOMARY FOR ME TO PERSONALLY INTERVIEW EACH AND EVERY WORKER THAT CROSSES THE THRESHOLD OF MY HOME.
MR. PECK, THERE IS AN OBVIOUS WATER PROBLEM DOWN HERE THAT NEEDS IMMEDIATE--

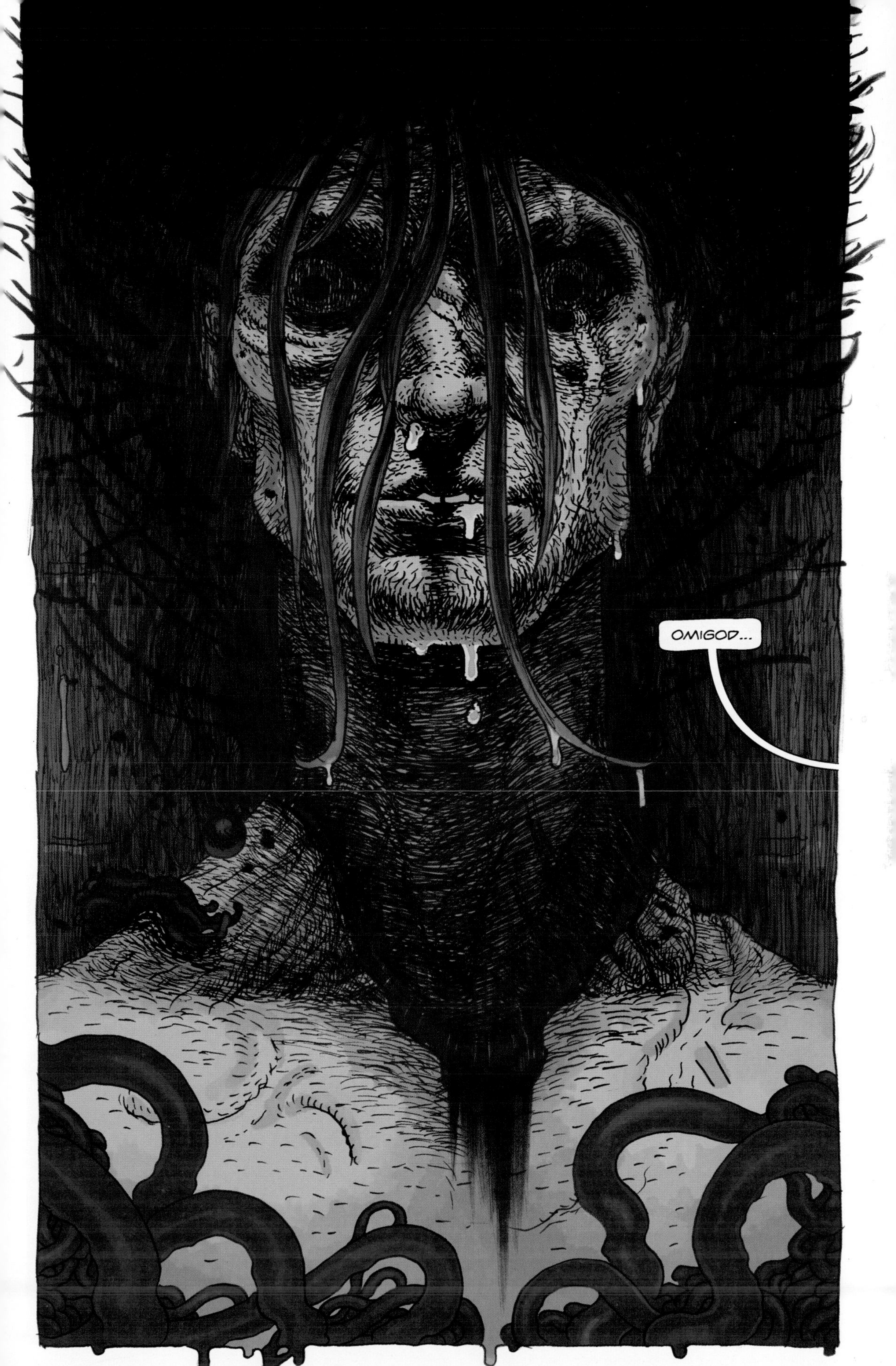
OMIGOD...

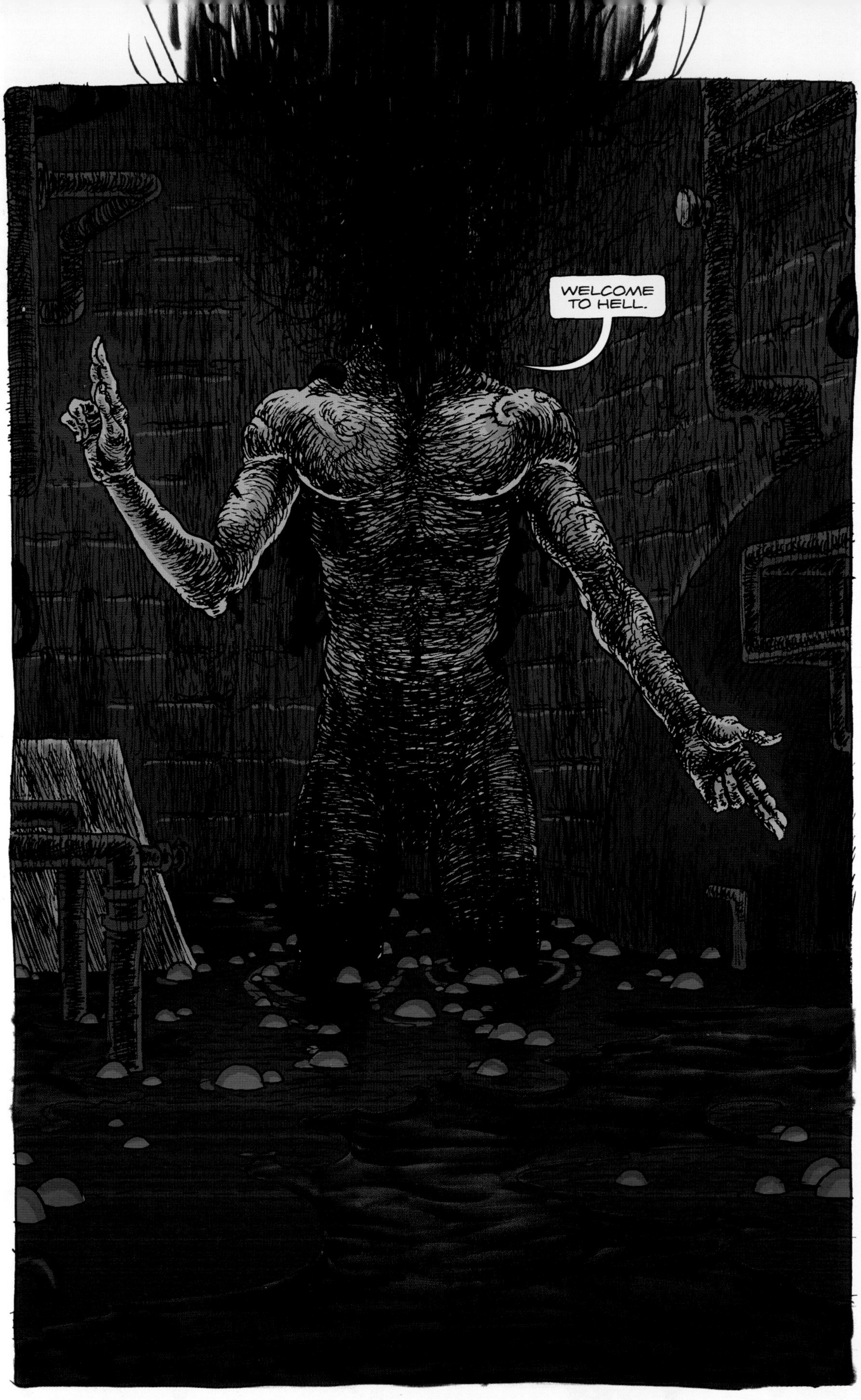
WELCOME TO HELL.

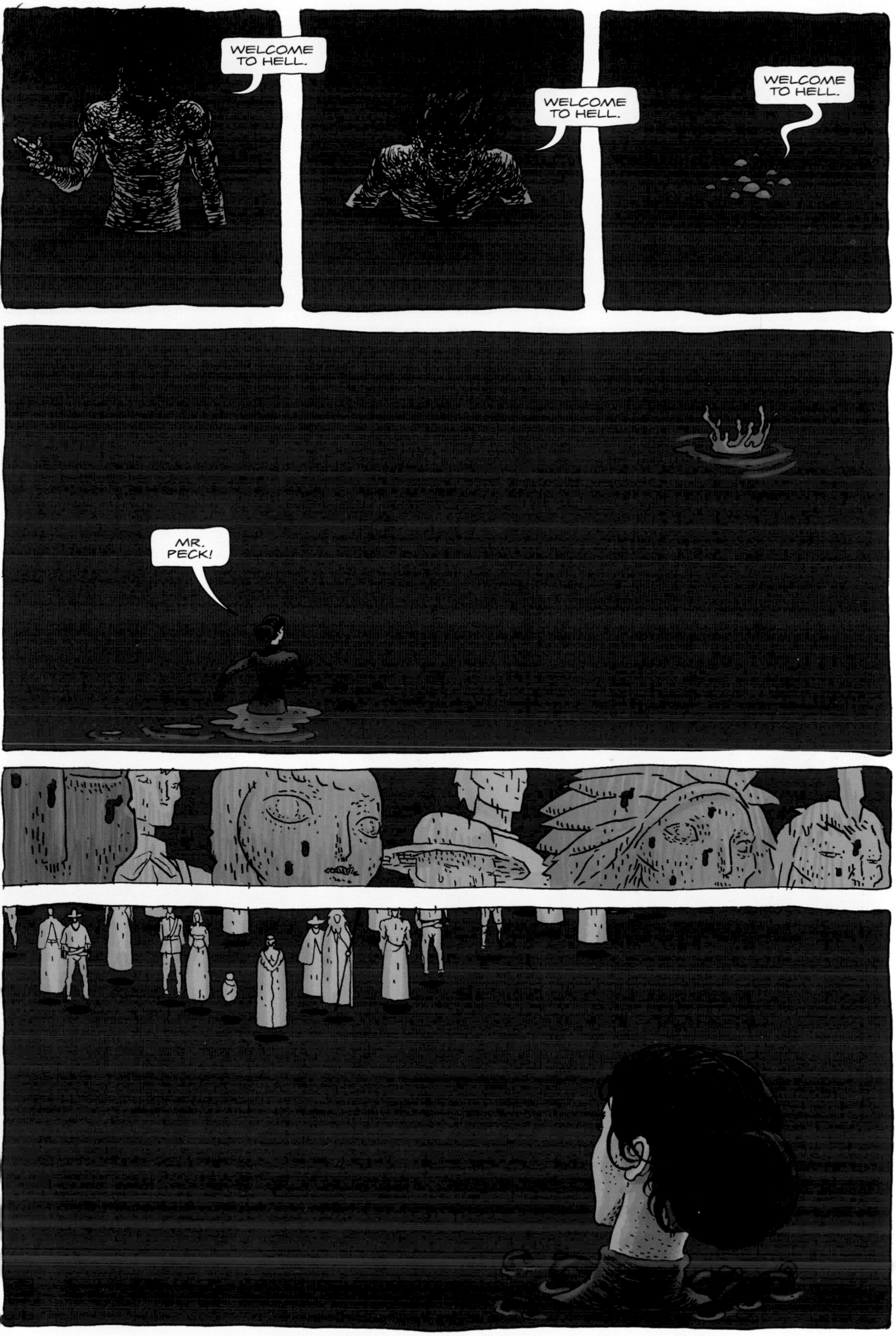
WELCOME TO HELL.
WELCOME TO HELL.
WELCOME TO HELL.
MR. PECK!

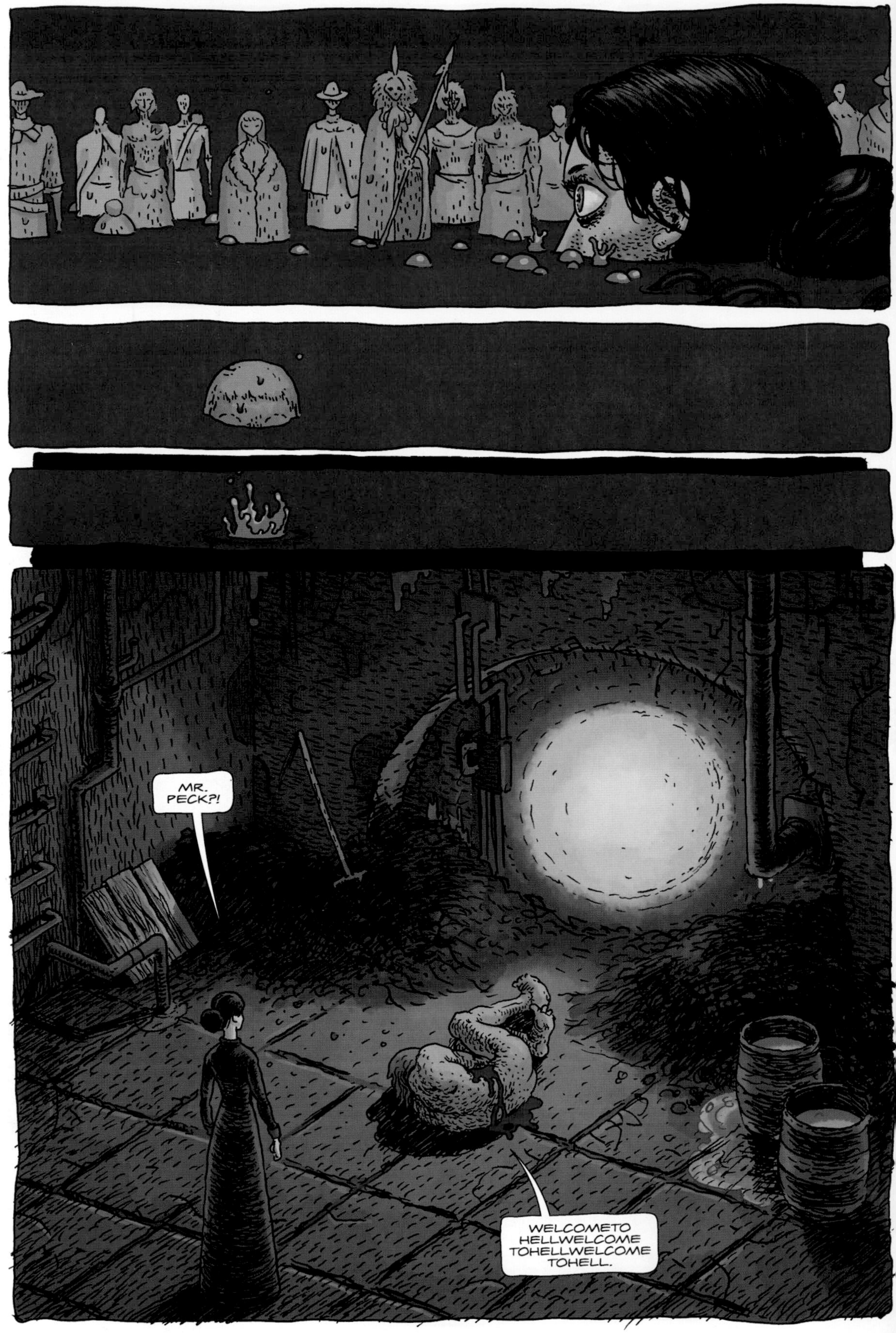
MR. PECK?!
WELCOMETO HELLWELCOME TOHELLWELCOME TOHELL.

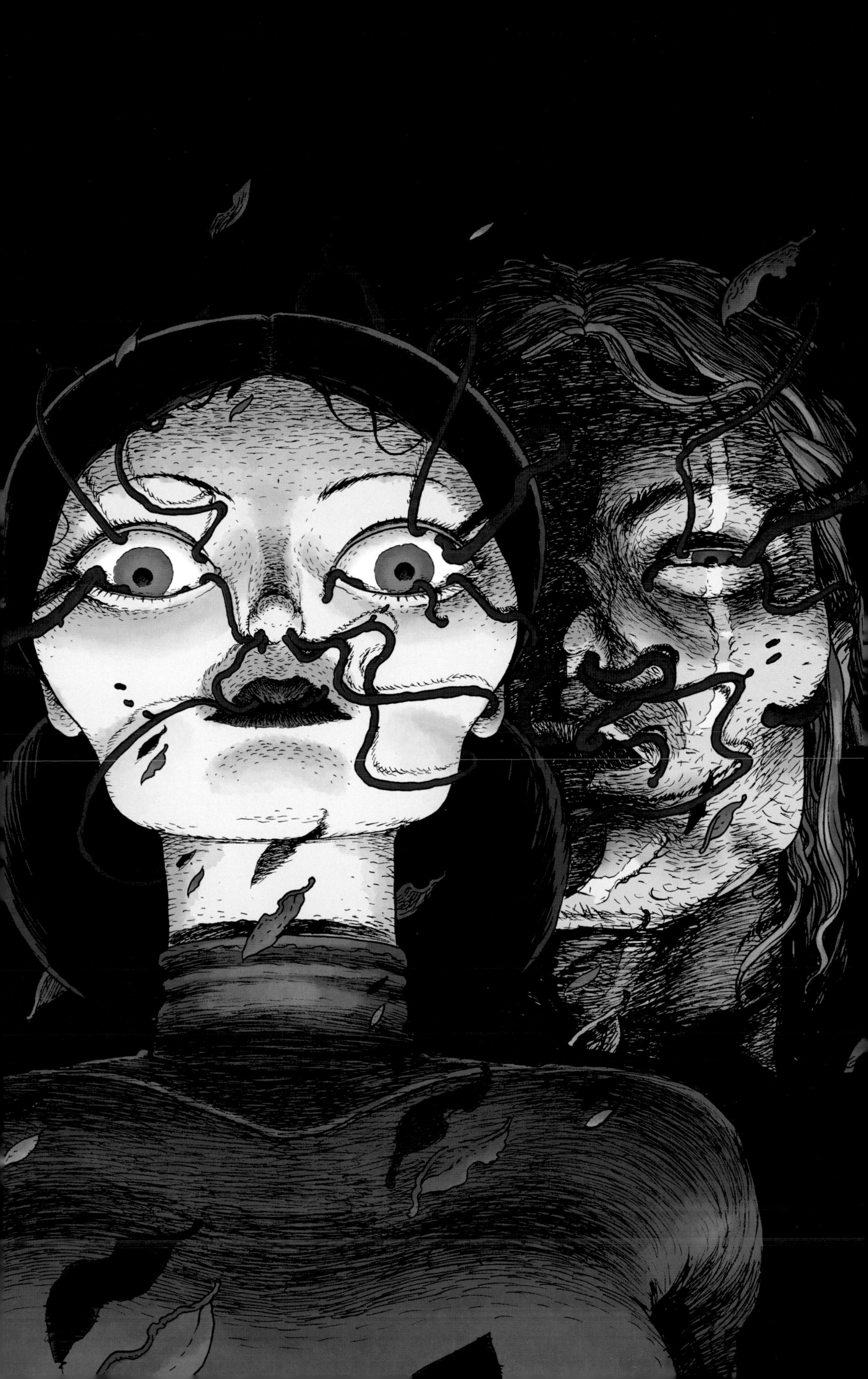

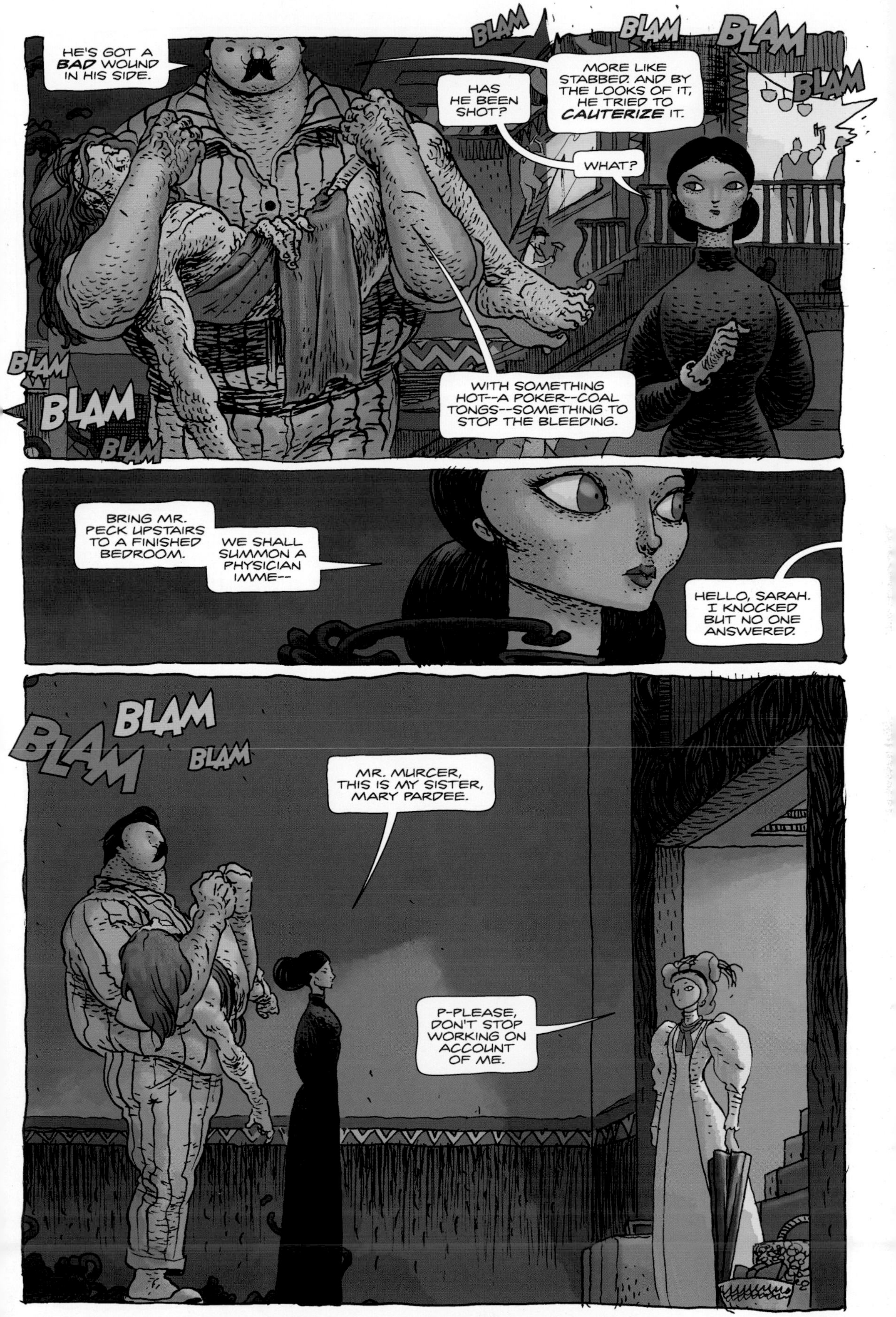
BLAM
BLAM
BLAM
BLAM
HE'S GOT A BAD WOUND IN HIS SIDE.
HAS HE BEEN SHOT?
MORE LIKE STABBED. AND BY THE LOOKS OF IT, HE TRIED TO CAUTERIZE IT.
WHAT?
WITH SOMETHING HOT--A POKER--COAL TONGS--SOMETHING TO STOP THE BLEEDING.
BLAM
BLAM
BLAM
BRING MR. PECK UPSTAIRS TO A FINISHED BEDROOM.
WE SHALL SUMMON A PHYSICIAN IMME--
HELLO, SARAH. I KNOCKED BUT NO ONE ANSWERED.
BLAM
BLAM
BLAM
MR. MURCER, THIS IS MY SISTER, MARY PARDEE.
P-PLEASE, DON'T STOP WORKING ON ACCOUNT OF ME.

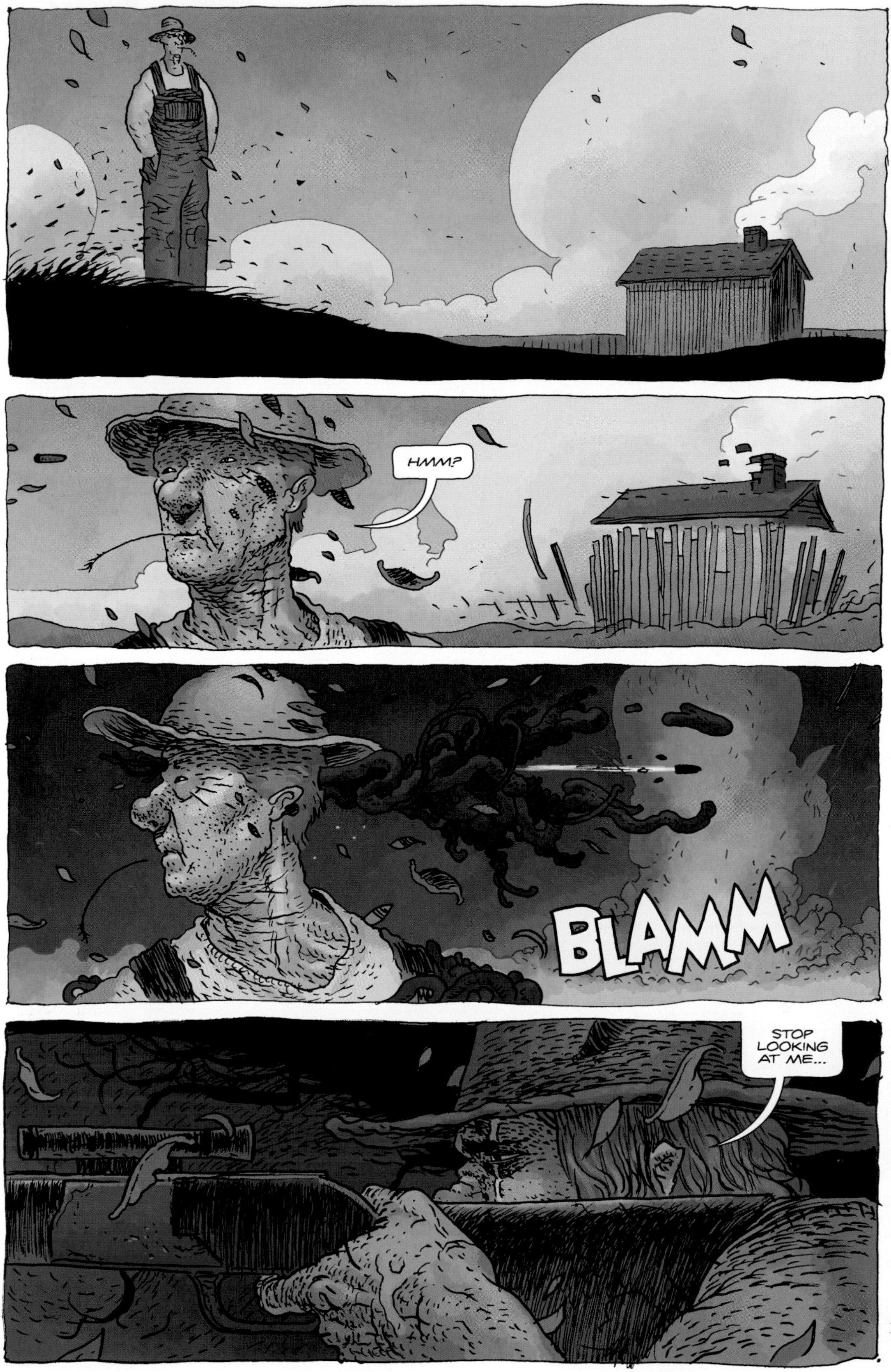
HMM?
BLAMM
STOP LOOKING AT ME...

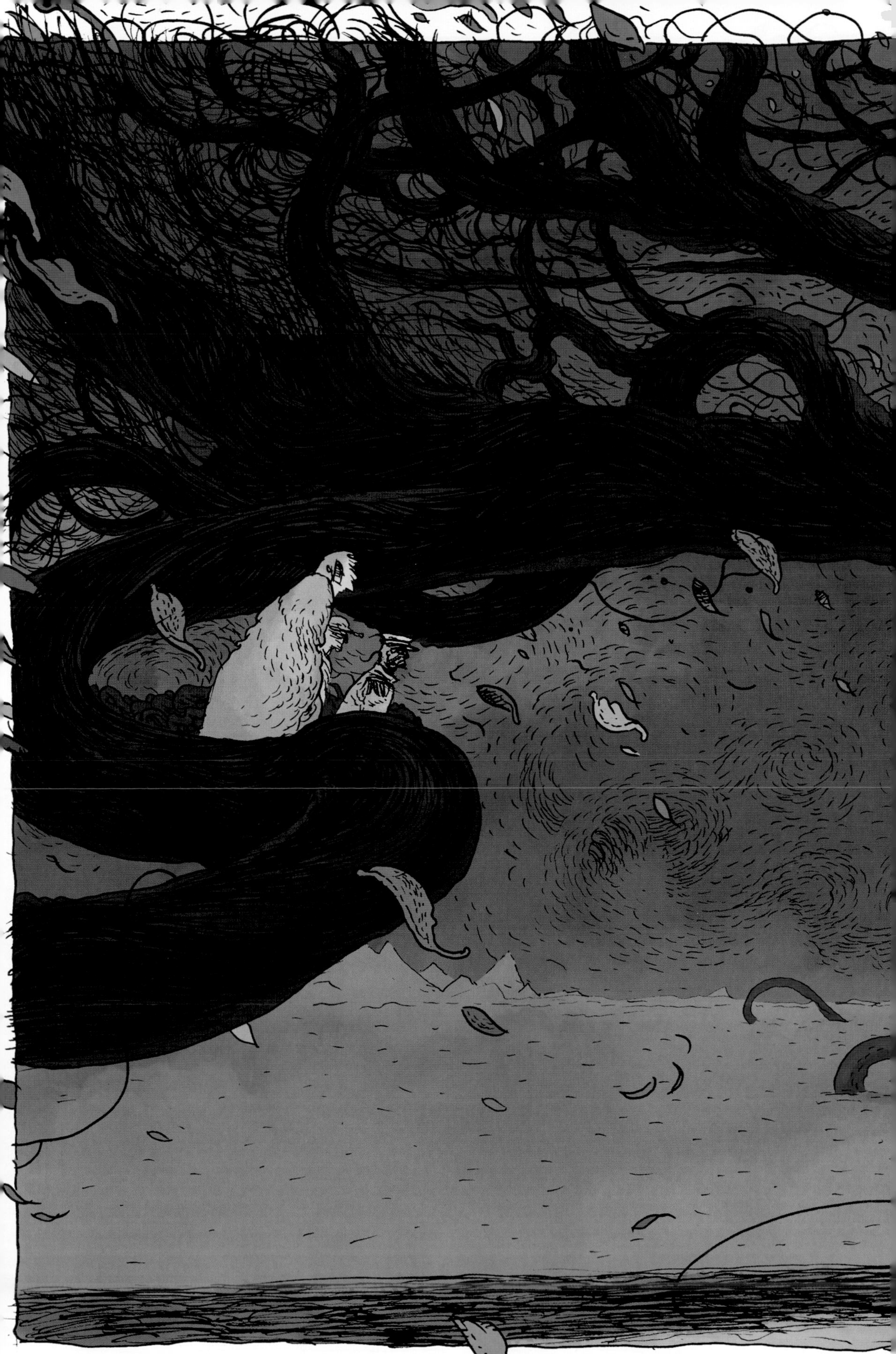

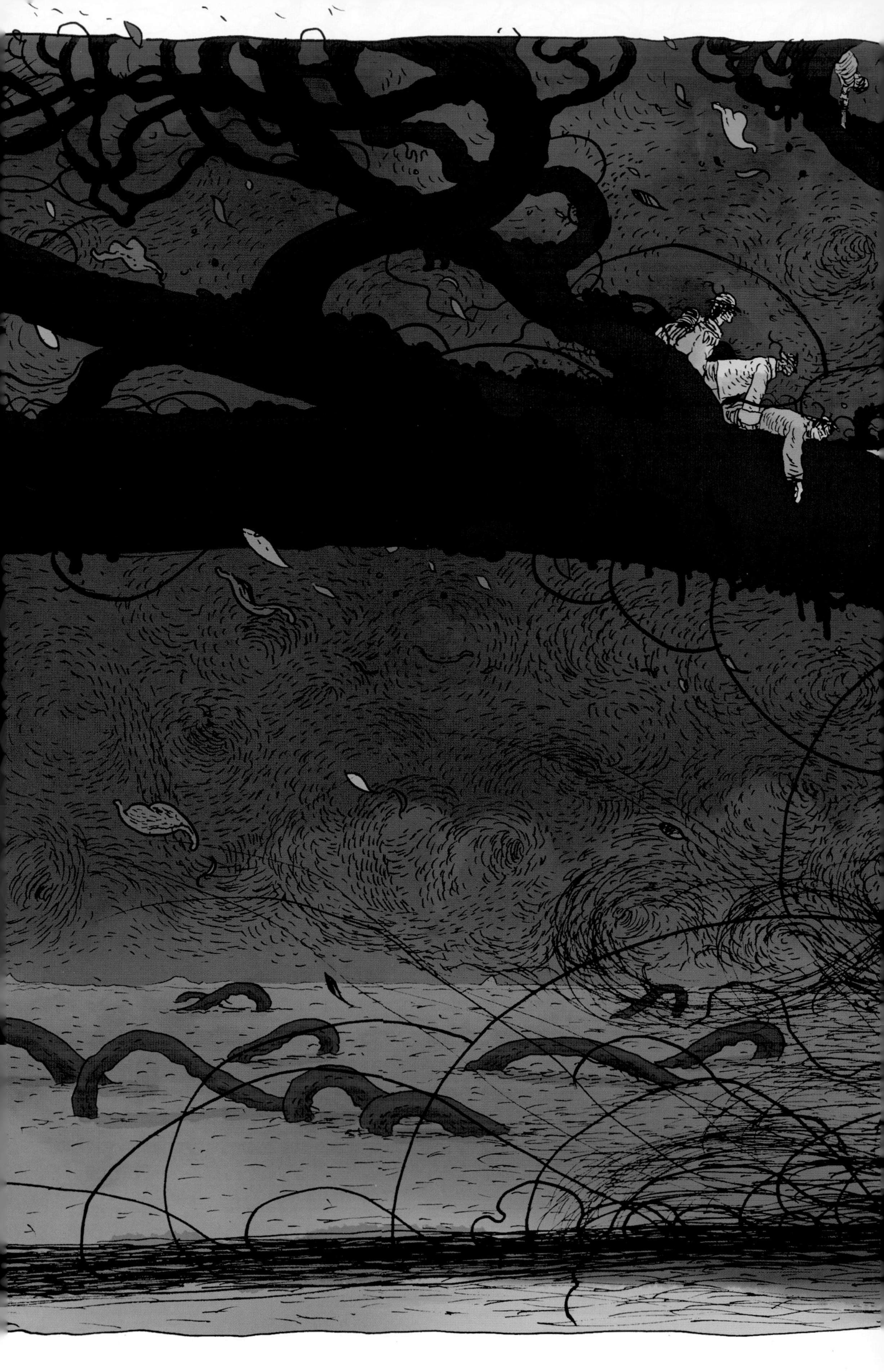

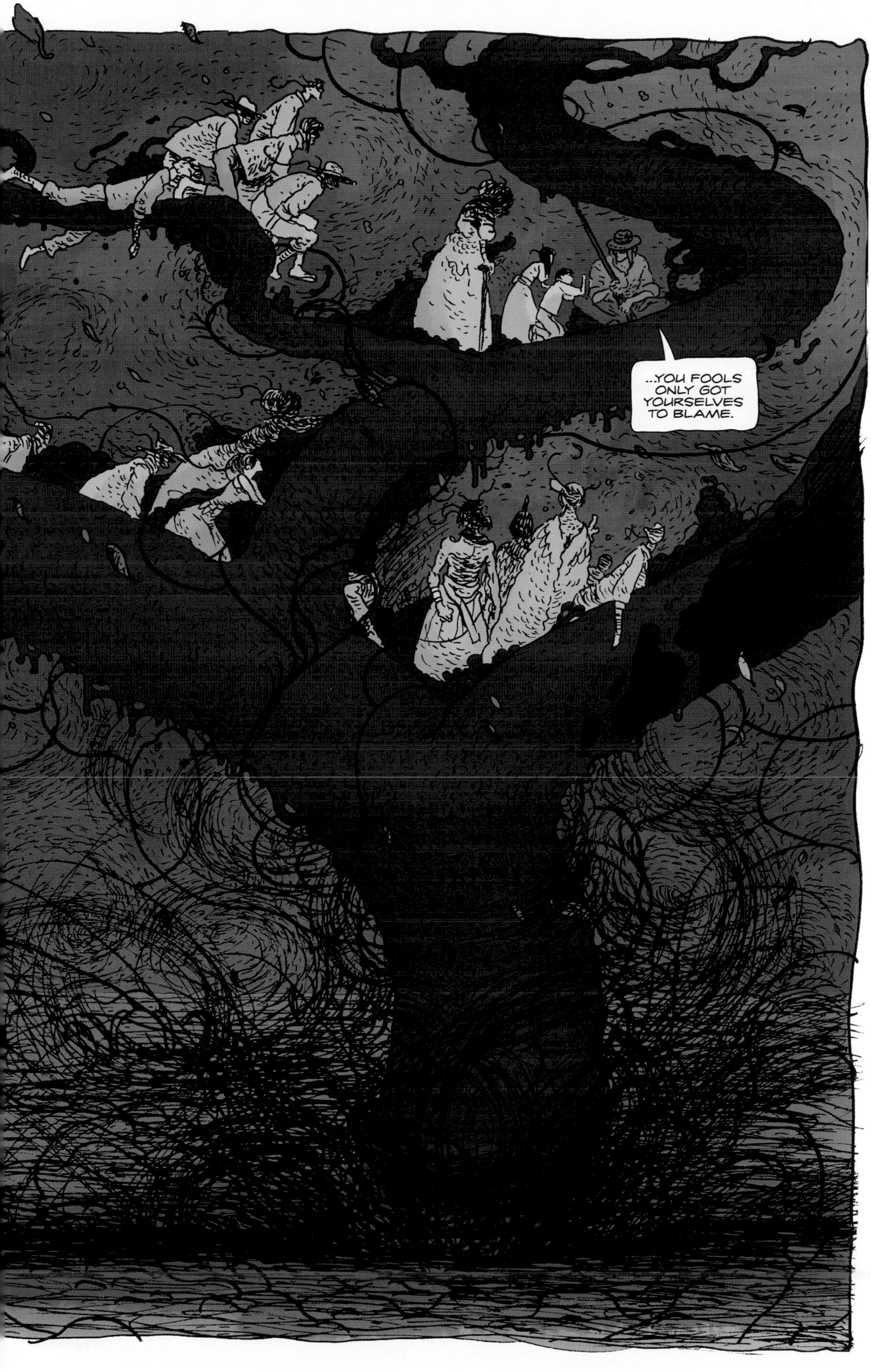
...YOU FOOLS ONLY GOT YOURSELVES TO BLAME.

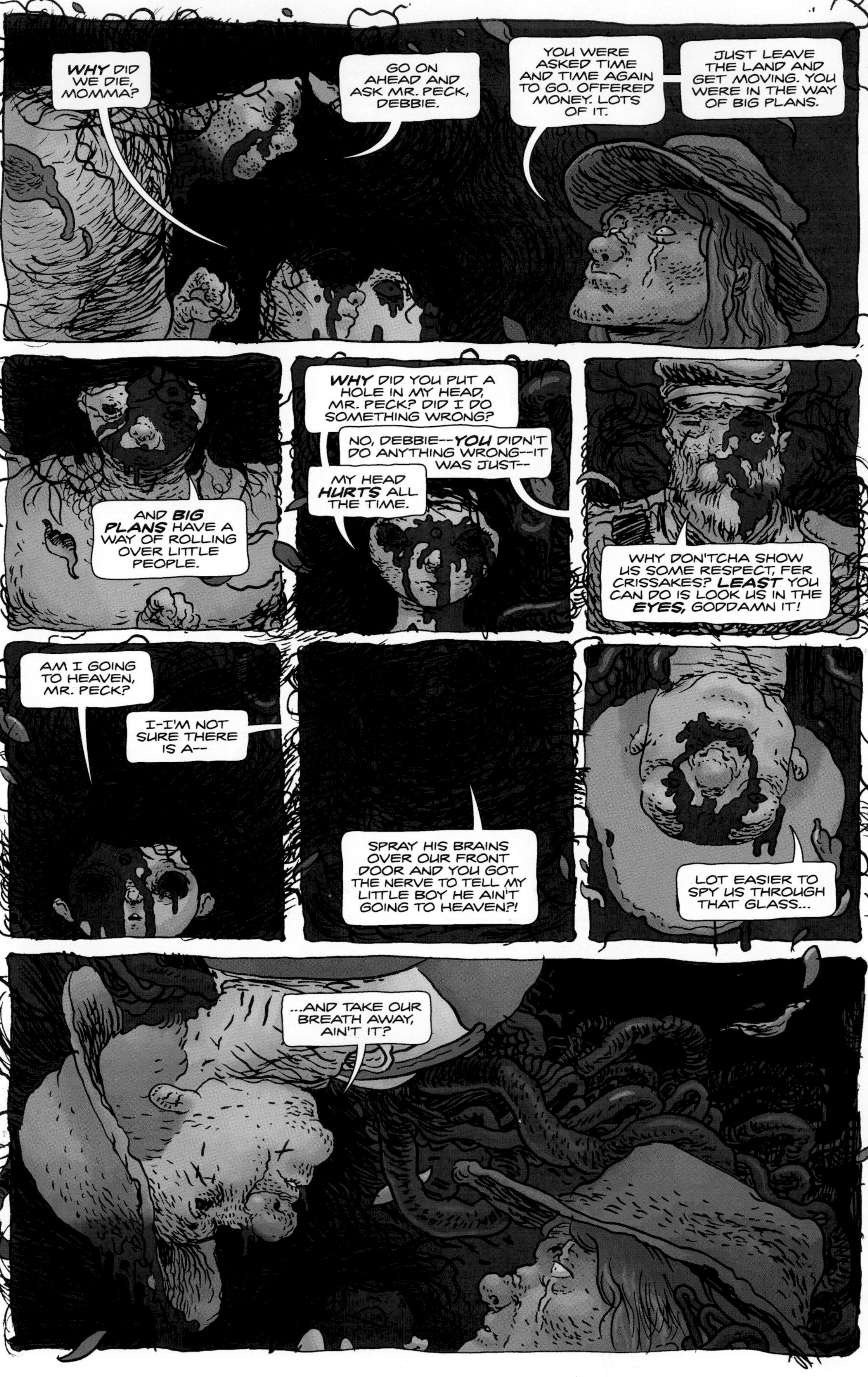
WHY DID WE DIE, MOMMA?
GO ON AHEAD AND ASK MR. PECK, DEBBIE.
YOU WERE ASKED TIME AND TIME AGAIN TO GO. OFFERED MONEY. LOTS OF IT.
JUST LEAVE THE LAND AND GET MOVING. YOU WERE IN THE WAY OF BIG PLANS.
AND BIG PLANS HAVE A WAY OF ROLLING OVER LITTLE PEOPLE.
WHY DID YOU PUT A HOLE IN MY HEAD, MR. PECK? DID I DO SOMETHING WRONG?
NO, DEBBIE--YOU DIDN'T DO ANYTHING WRONG--IT WAS JUST--
MY HEAD HURTS ALL THE TIME.
WHY DON'TCHA SHOW US SOME RESPECT, FER CRISSAKES? LEAST YOU CAN DO IS LOOK US IN THE EYES, GODDAMN IT!
AM I GOING TO HEAVEN, MR. PECK?
I-I'M NOT SURE THERE IS A--
SPRAY HIS BRAINS OVER OUR FRONT DOOR AND YOU GOT THE NERVE TO TELL MY LITTLE BOY HE AIN'T GOING TO HEAVEN?!
LOT EASIER TO SPY US THROUGH THAT GLASS...
...AND TAKE OUR BREATH AWAY, AIN'T IT?

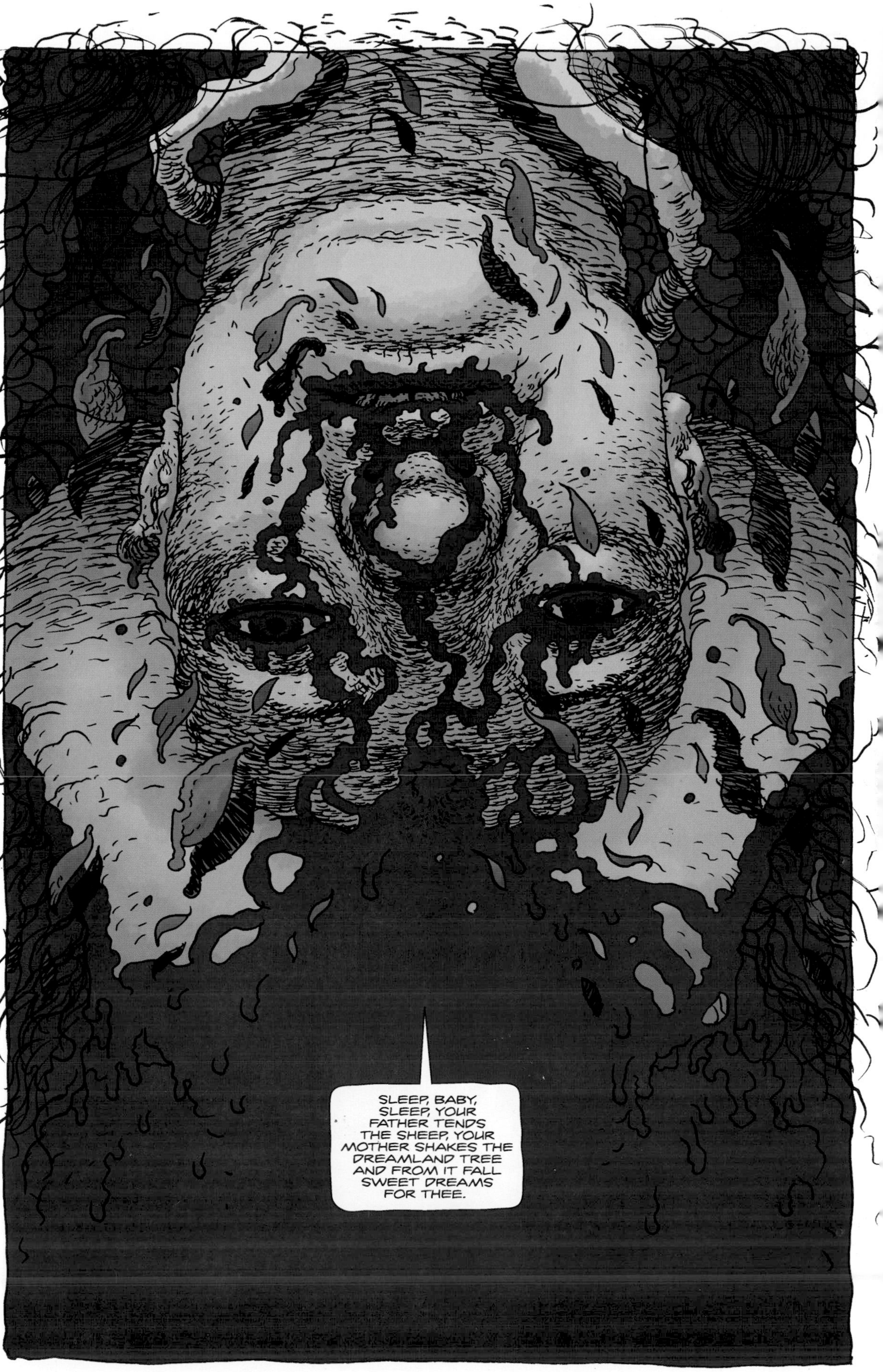
SLEEP, BABY, SLEEP, YOUR FATHER TENDS THE SHEEP, YOUR MOTHER SHAKES THE DREAMLAND TREE AND FROM IT FALL SWEET DREAMS FOR THEE.

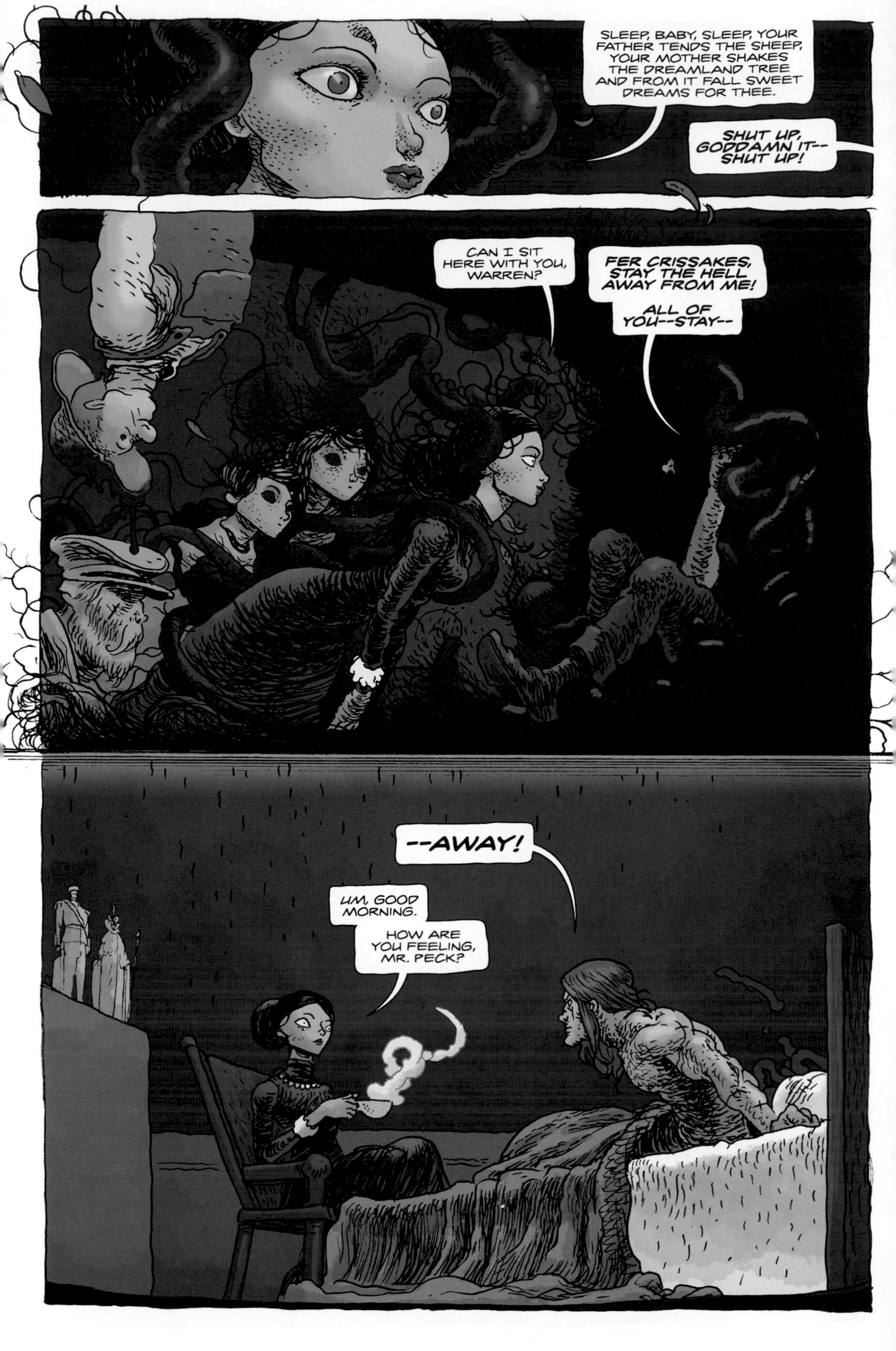
SLEEP, BABY, SLEEP, YOUR FATHER TENDS THE SHEEP, YOUR MOTHER SHAKES THE DREAMLAND TREE AND FROM IT FALL SWEET DREAMS FOR THEE.
SHUT UP, GODDAMN IT-- SHUT UP!
CAN I SIT HERE WITH YOU, WARREN?
FER CRISSAKES, STAY THE HELL AWAY FROM ME!
ALL OF YOU--STAY--
--AWAY!
UM, GOOD MORNING.
HOW ARE YOU FEELING, MR. PECK?

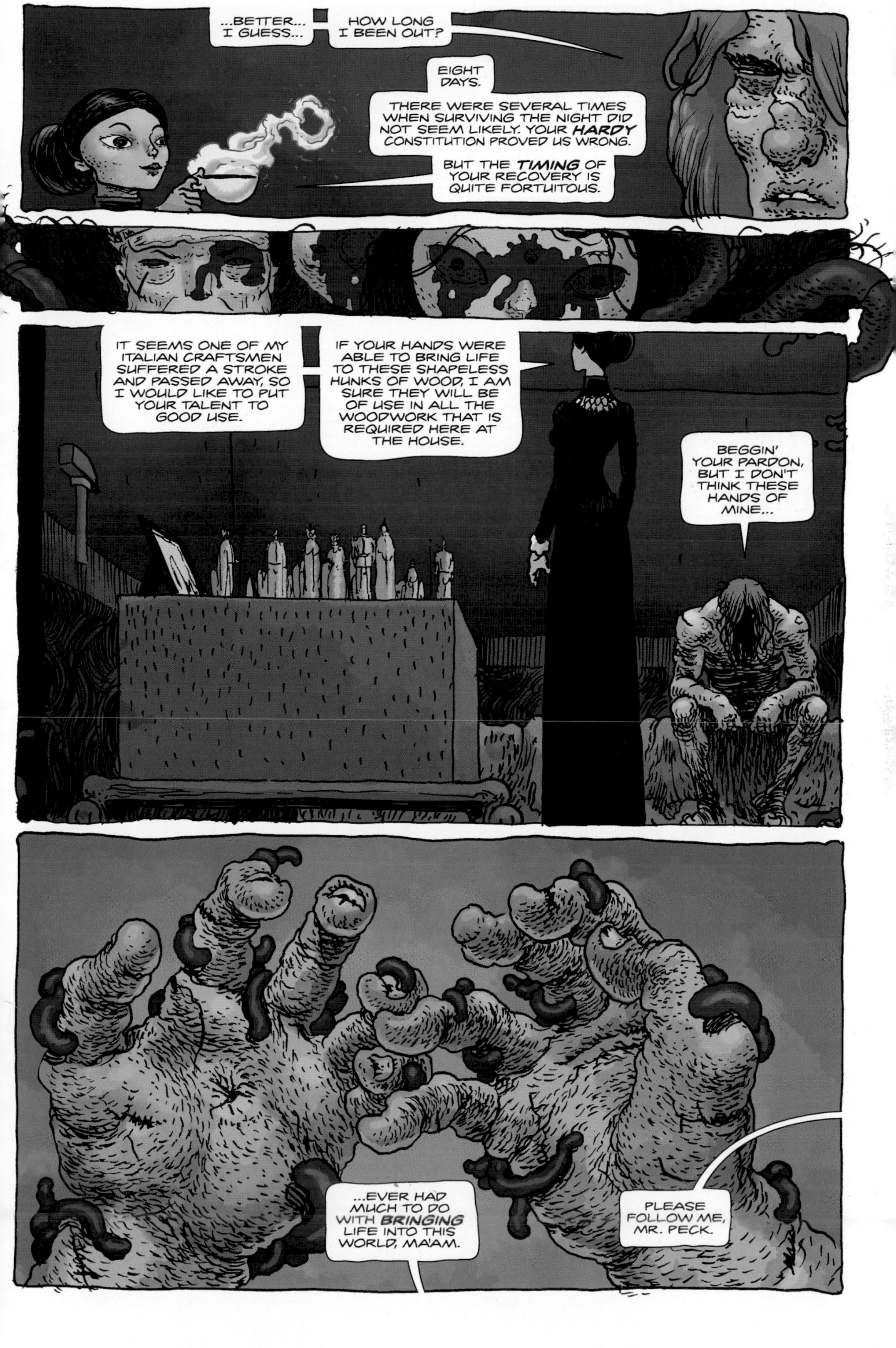
...BETTER... I GUESS...
HOW LONG I BEEN OUT?
EIGHT DAYS.
THERE WERE SEVERAL TIMES WHEN SURVIVING THE NIGHT DID NOT SEEM LIKELY. YOUR HARDY CONSTITUTION PROVED US WRONG.
BUT THE TIMING OF YOUR RECOVERY IS QUITE FORTUITOUS.
IT SEEMS ONE OF MY ITALIAN CRAFTSMEN SUFFERED A STROKE AND PASSED AWAY, SO I WOULD LIKE TO PUT YOUR TALENT TO GOOD USE.
IF YOUR HANDS WERE ABLE TO BRING LIFE TO THESE SHAPELESS HUNKS OF WOOD, I AM SURE THEY WILL BE OF USE IN ALL THE WOODWORK THAT IS REQUIRED HERE AT THE HOUSE.
BEGGIN' YOUR PARDON, BUT I DON'T THINK THESE HANDS OF MINE...
...EVER HAD MUCH TO DO WITH BRINGING LIFE INTO THIS WORLD, MA'AM.
PLEASE FOLLOW ME, MR. PECK.

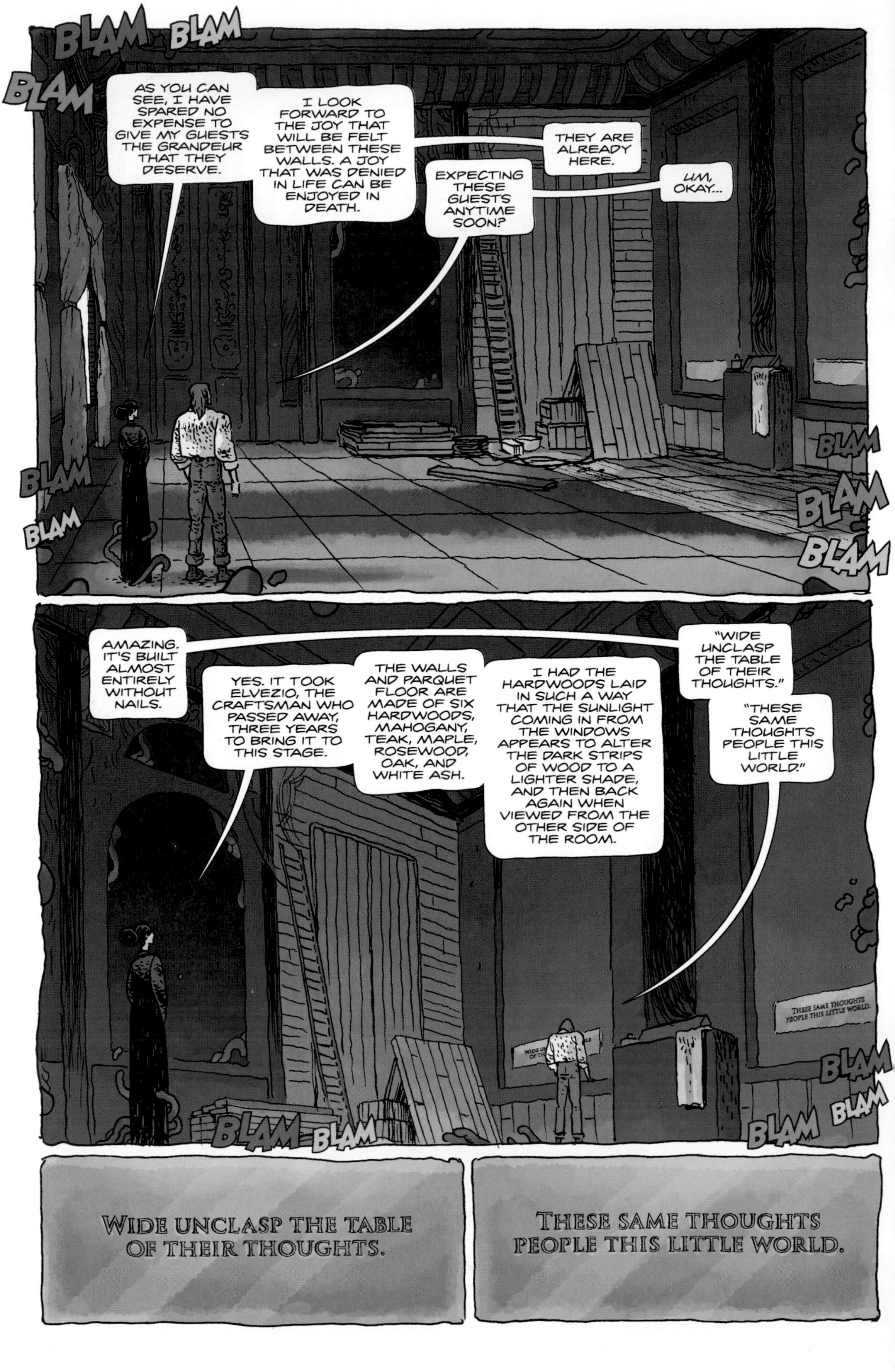
BLAM BLAM
BLAM
AS YOU CAN SEE, I HAVE SPARED NO EXPENSE TO GIVE MY GUESTS THE GRANDEUR THAT THEY DESERVE.
I LOOK FORWARD TO THE JOY THAT WILL BE FELT BETWEEN THESE WALLS. A JOY THAT WAS DENIED IN LIFE CAN BE ENJOYED IN DEATH.
EXPECTING THESE GUESTS ANYTIME SOON?
THEY ARE ALREADY HERE.
UM, OKAY...
BLAM
BLAM
BLAM
BLAM
BLAM
AMAZING. IT'S BUILT ALMOST ENTIRELY WITHOUT NAILS.
YES. IT TOOK ELVEZIO, THE CRAFTSMAN WHO PASSED AWAY, THREE YEARS TO BRING IT TO THIS STAGE.
THE WALLS AND PARQUET FLOOR ARE MADE OF SIX HARDWOODS, MAHOGANY, TEAK, MAPLE, ROSEWOOD, OAK, AND WHITE ASH.
I HAD THE HARDWOODS LAID IN SUCH A WAY THAT THE SUNLIGHT COMING IN FROM THE WINDOWS APPEARS TO ALTER THE DARK STRIPS OF WOOD TO A LIGHTER SHADE, AND THEN BACK AGAIN WHEN VIEWED FROM THE OTHER SIDE OF THE ROOM.
"WIDE UNCLASP THE TABLE OF THEIR THOUGHTS."
"THESE SAME THOUGHTS PEOPLE THIS LITTLE WORLD."
THESE SAME THOUGHTS PEOPLE THIS LITTLE WORLD.
BLAM BLAM
BLAM BLAM BLAM
WIDE UNCLASP THE TABLE OF THEIR THOUGHTS.
THESE SAME THOUGHTS PEOPLE THIS LITTLE WORLD.

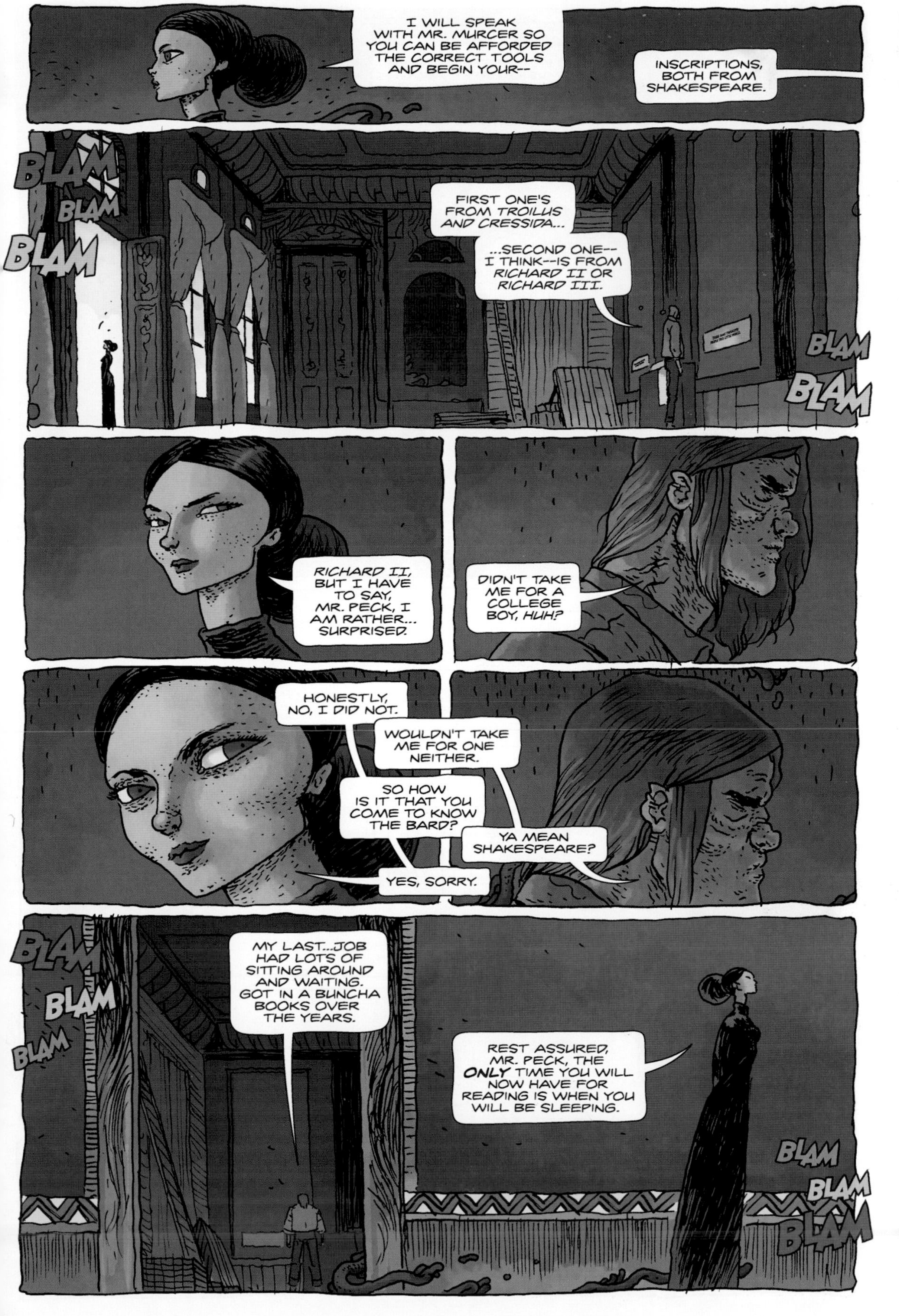
I WILL SPEAK WITH MR. MURCER SO YOU CAN BE AFFORDED THE CORRECT TOOLS AND BEGIN YOUR--
INSCRIPTIONS, BOTH FROM SHAKESPEARE.
BLAM
BLAM
BLAM
FIRST ONE'S FROM *TROILUS AND CRESSIDA*...
...SECOND ONE-- I THINK--IS FROM *RICHARD II* OR *RICHARD III*.
BLAM
BLAM
RICHARD II, BUT I HAVE TO SAY, MR. PECK, I AM RATHER... SURPRISED.
DIDN'T TAKE ME FOR A COLLEGE BOY, *HUH?*
HONESTLY, NO, I DID NOT.
WOULDN'T TAKE ME FOR ONE NEITHER.
SO HOW IS IT THAT YOU COME TO KNOW THE BARD?
YA MEAN SHAKESPEARE?
YES, SORRY.
BLAM
BLAM
BLAM
MY LAST...JOB HAD LOTS OF SITTING AROUND AND WAITING. GOT IN A BUNCHA BOOKS OVER THE YEARS.
REST ASSURED, MR. PECK, THE **ONLY** TIME YOU WILL NOW HAVE FOR READING IS WHEN YOU WILL BE SLEEPING.
BLAM
BLAM
BLAM

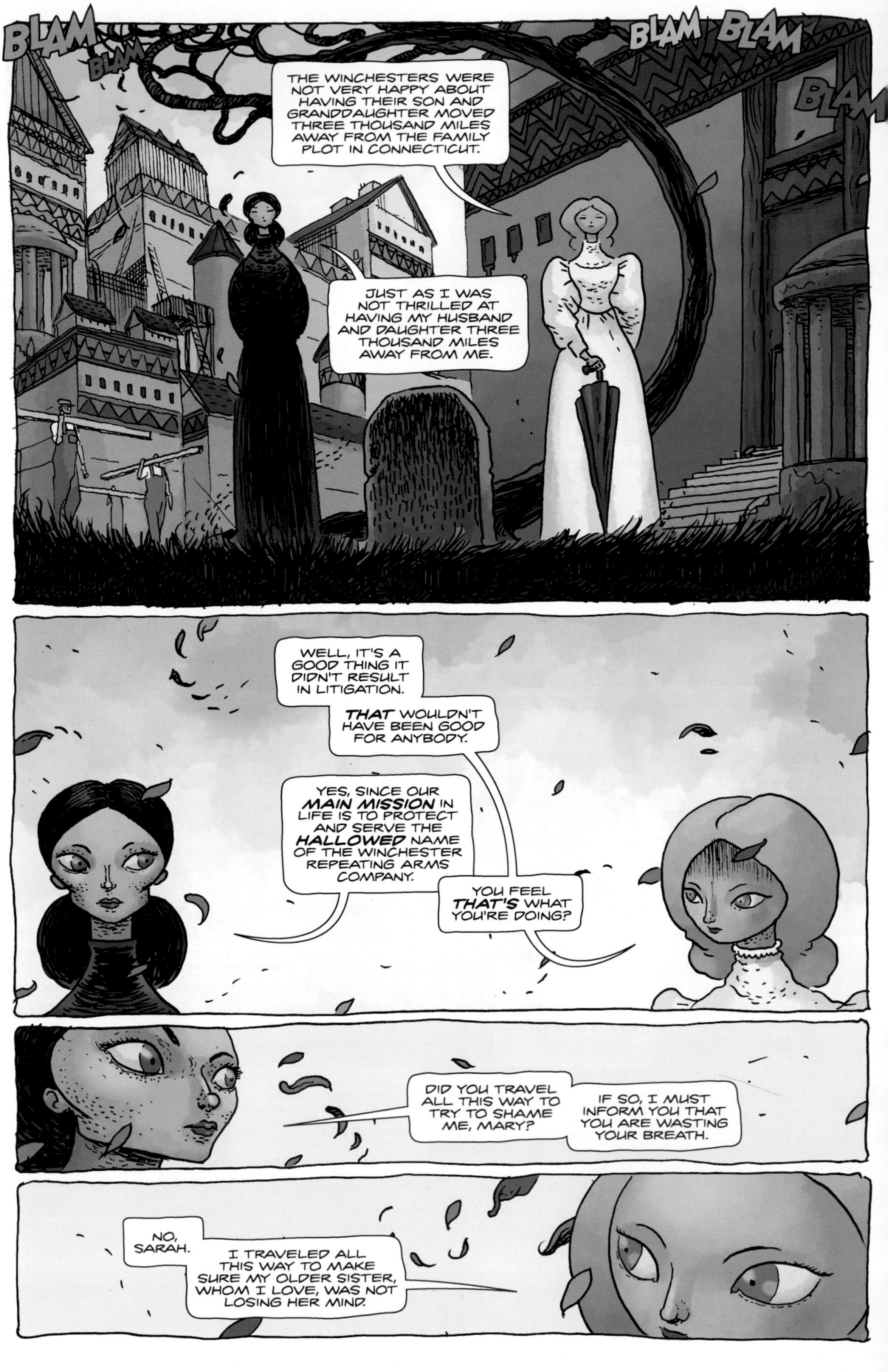
BLAM
BLAM
BLAM BLAM
BLAM
THE WINCHESTERS WERE NOT VERY HAPPY ABOUT HAVING THEIR SON AND GRANDDAUGHTER MOVED THREE THOUSAND MILES AWAY FROM THE FAMILY PLOT IN CONNECTICUT.
JUST AS I WAS NOT THRILLED AT HAVING MY HUSBAND AND DAUGHTER THREE THOUSAND MILES AWAY FROM ME.
WELL, IT'S A GOOD THING IT DIDN'T RESULT IN LITIGATION.
THAT WOULDN'T HAVE BEEN GOOD FOR ANYBODY.
YES, SINCE OUR MAIN MISSION IN LIFE IS TO PROTECT AND SERVE THE HALLOWED NAME OF THE WINCHESTER REPEATING ARMS COMPANY.
YOU FEEL THAT'S WHAT YOU'RE DOING?
DID YOU TRAVEL ALL THIS WAY TO TRY TO SHAME ME, MARY?
IF SO, I MUST INFORM YOU THAT YOU ARE WASTING YOUR BREATH.
NO, SARAH.
I TRAVELED ALL THIS WAY TO MAKE SURE MY OLDER SISTER, WHOM I LOVE, WAS NOT LOSING HER MIND.

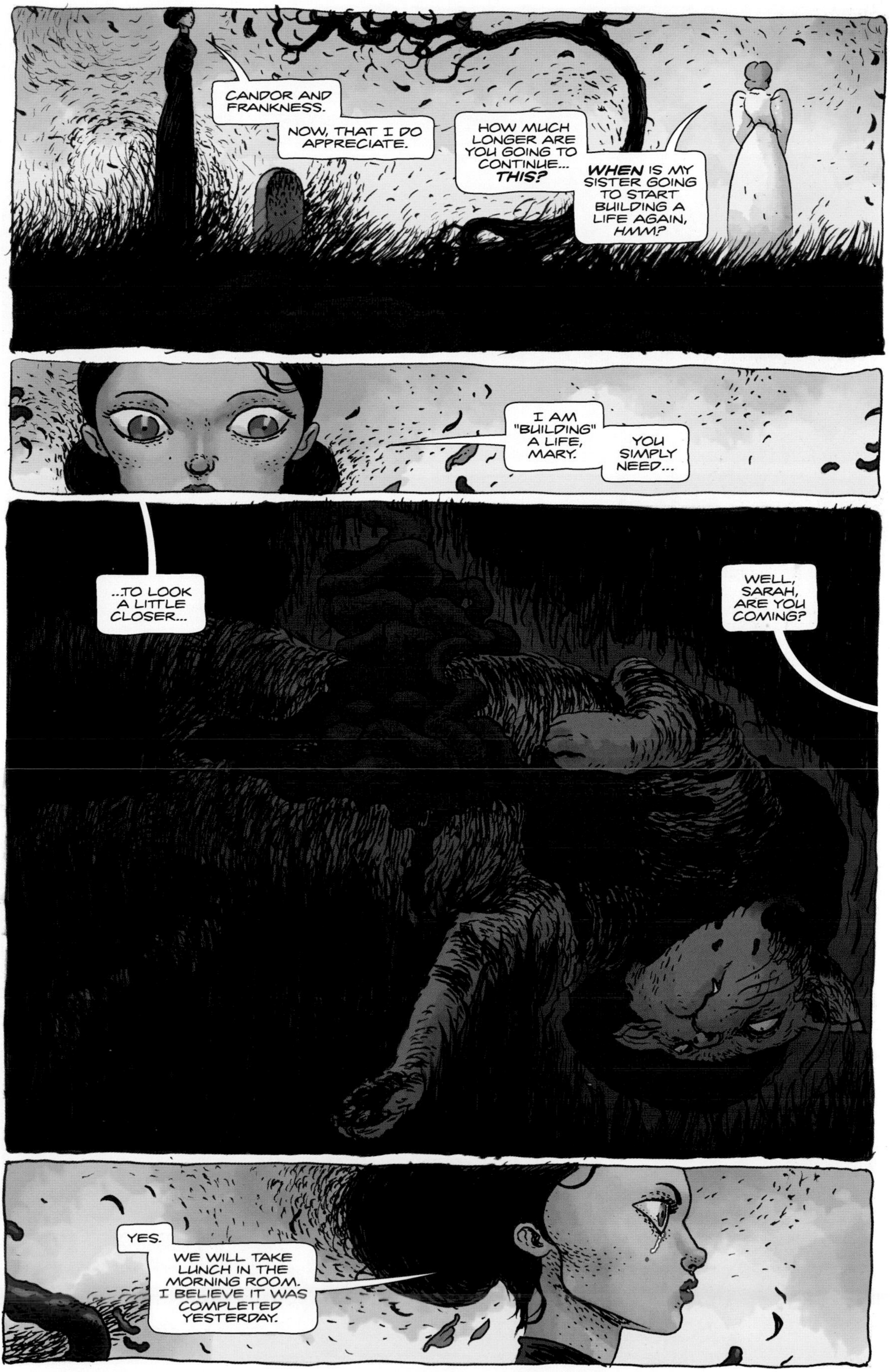
CANDOR AND FRANKNESS.
NOW, THAT I DO APPRECIATE.
HOW MUCH LONGER ARE YOU GOING TO CONTINUE... THIS?
WHEN IS MY SISTER GOING TO START BUILDING A LIFE AGAIN, HMM?
I AM "BUILDING" A LIFE, MARY.
YOU SIMPLY NEED...
...TO LOOK A LITTLE CLOSER...
WELL, SARAH, ARE YOU COMING?
YES.
WE WILL TAKE LUNCH IN THE MORNING ROOM. I BELIEVE IT WAS COMPLETED YESTERDAY.

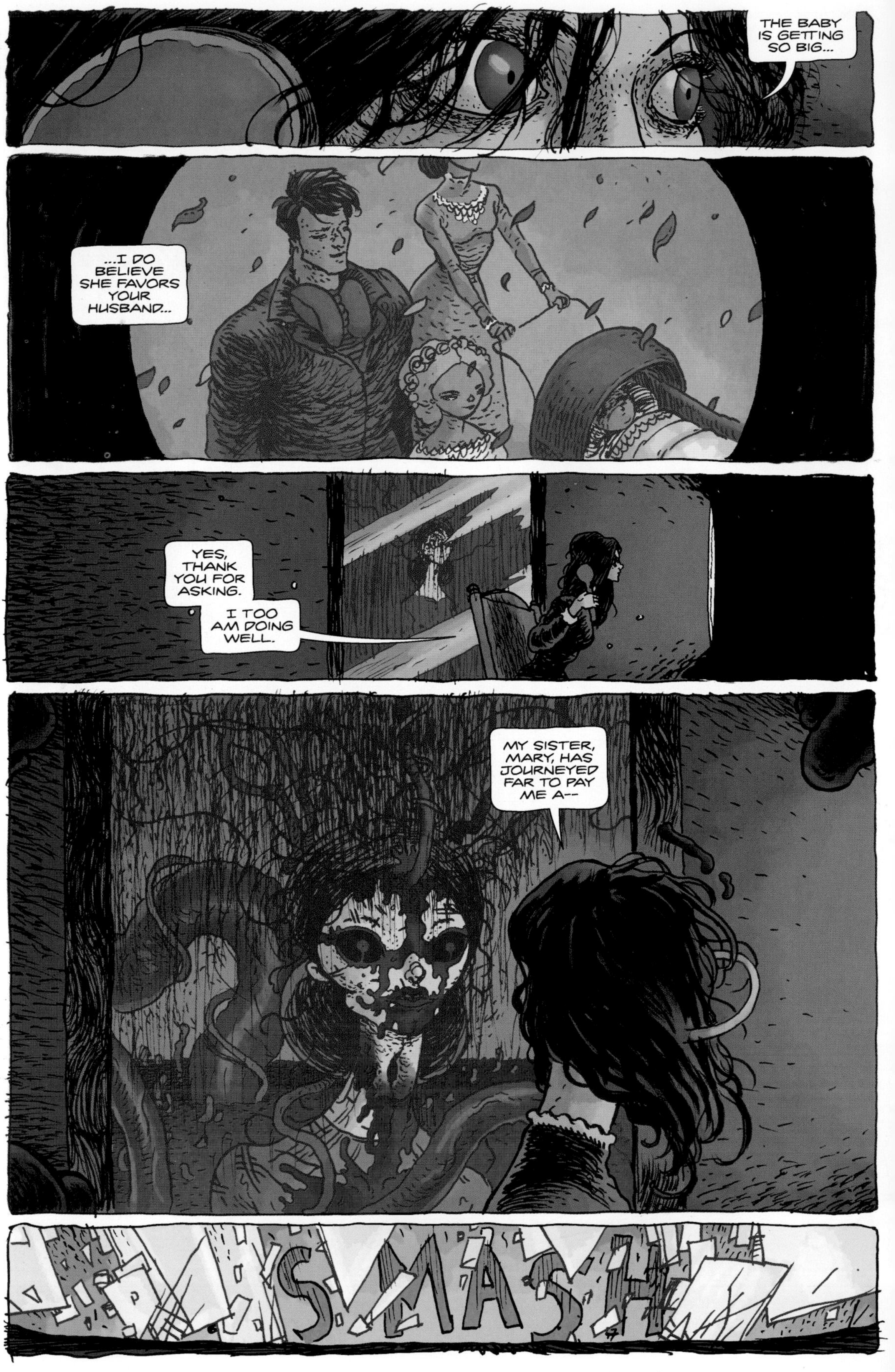
THE BABY IS GETTING SO BIG...
...I DO BELIEVE SHE FAVORS YOUR HUSBAND...
YES, THANK YOU FOR ASKING.
I TOO AM DOING WELL.
MY SISTER, MARY, HAS JOURNEYED FAR TO PAY ME A--
SMASH

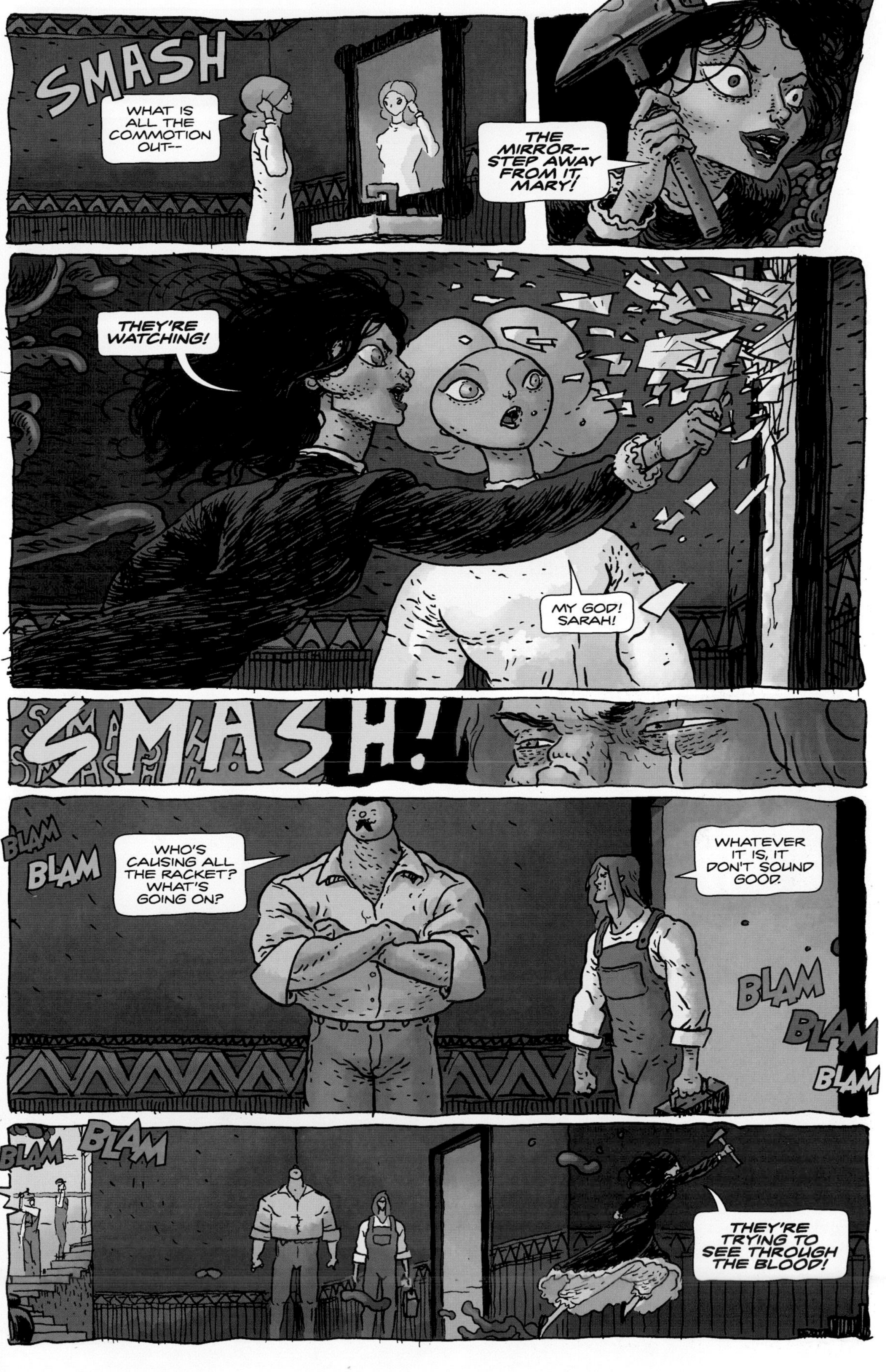
SMASH
WHAT IS ALL THE COMMOTION OUT--
THE MIRROR-- STEP AWAY FROM IT, MARY!
THEY'RE WATCHING!
MY GOD! SARAH!
SMASH!
BLAM
BLAM
WHO'S CAUSING ALL THE RACKET? WHAT'S GOING ON?
WHATEVER IT IS, IT DON'T SOUND GOOD.
BLAM
BLAM
BLAM
BLAM
BLAM
THEY'RE TRYING TO SEE THROUGH THE BLOOD!

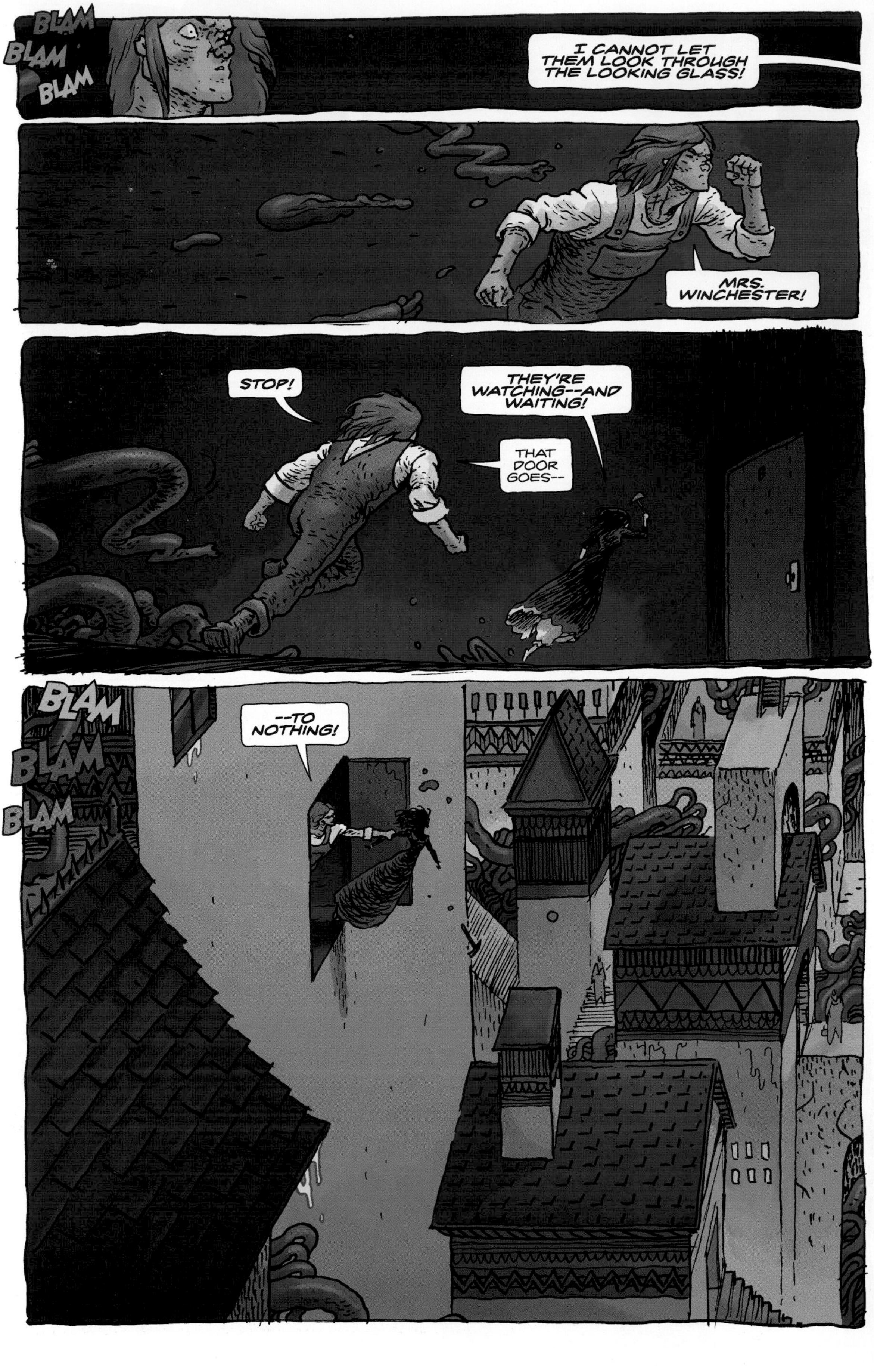
BLAM
BLAM
BLAM
I CANNOT LET THEM LOOK THROUGH THE LOOKING GLASS!
MRS. WINCHESTER!
STOP!
THEY'RE WATCHING--AND WAITING!
THAT DOOR GOES--
BLAM
BLAM
BLAM
--TO NOTHING!

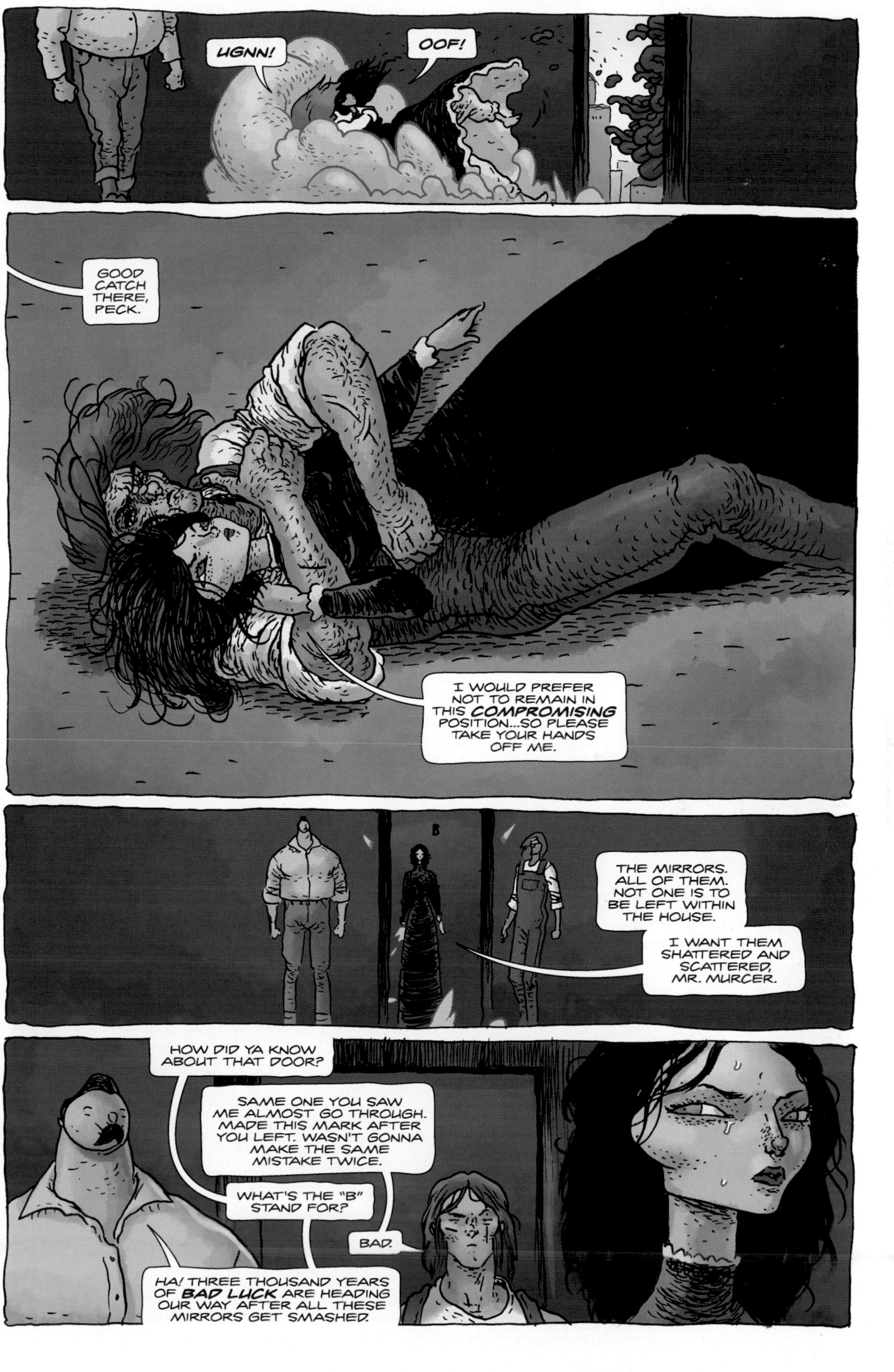
UGNN!
OOF!
GOOD CATCH THERE, PECK.
I WOULD PREFER NOT TO REMAIN IN THIS COMPROMISING POSITION...SO PLEASE TAKE YOUR HANDS OFF ME.
B
THE MIRRORS. ALL OF THEM. NOT ONE IS TO BE LEFT WITHIN THE HOUSE.
I WANT THEM SHATTERED AND SCATTERED, MR. MURCER.
HOW DID YA KNOW ABOUT THAT DOOR?
SAME ONE YOU SAW ME ALMOST GO THROUGH. MADE THIS MARK AFTER YOU LEFT. WASN'T GONNA MAKE THE SAME MISTAKE TWICE.
WHAT'S THE "B" STAND FOR?
BAD.
HA! THREE THOUSAND YEARS OF BAD LUCK ARE HEADING OUR WAY AFTER ALL THESE MIRRORS GET SMASHED.

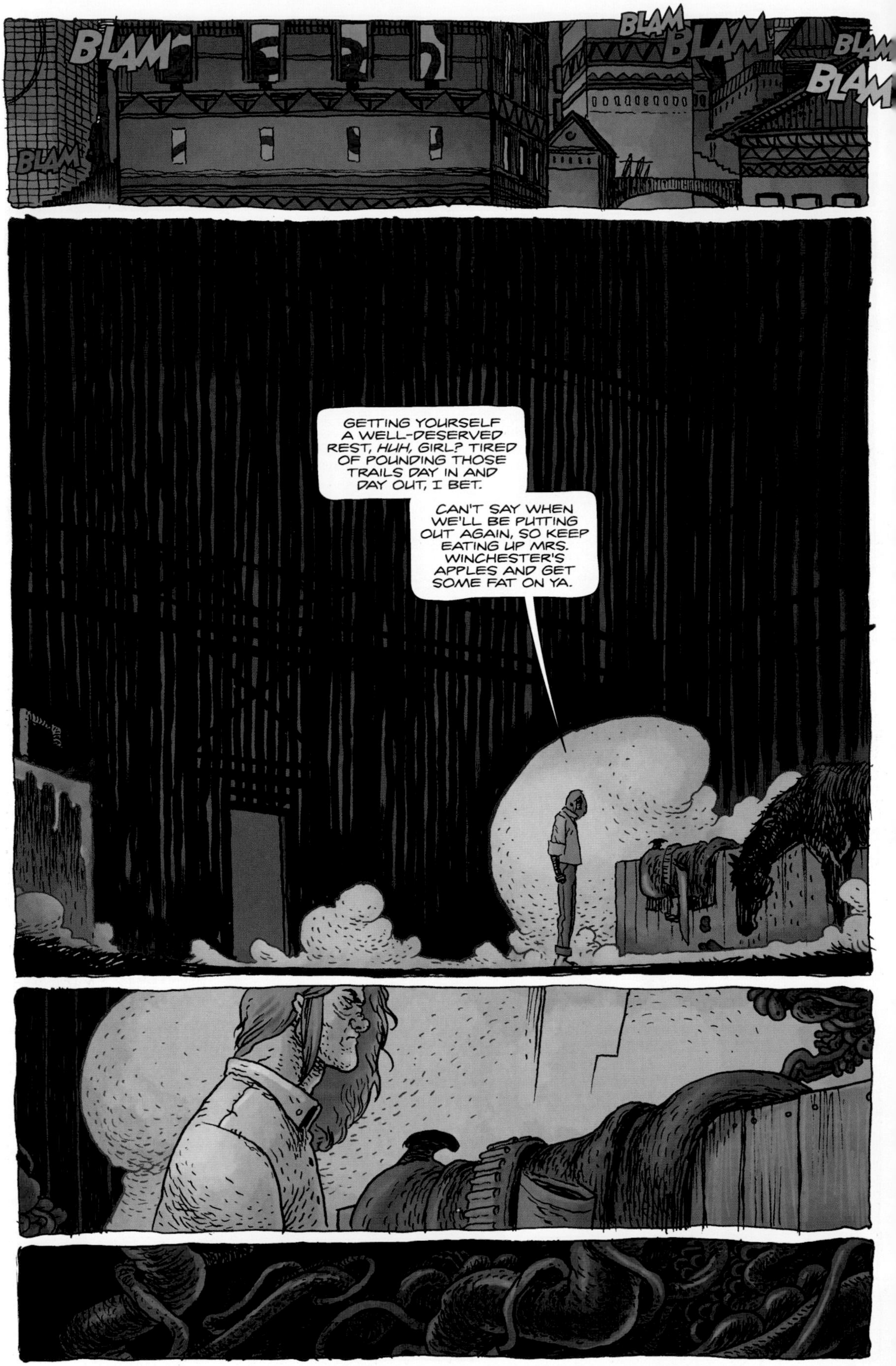
BLAM
BLAM
BLAM BLAM
BLAM BLAM
GETTING YOURSELF A WELL-DESERVED REST, *HUH,* GIRL? TIRED OF POUNDING THOSE TRAILS DAY IN AND DAY OUT, I BET.
CAN'T SAY WHEN WE'LL BE PUTTING OUT AGAIN, SO KEEP EATING UP MRS. WINCHESTER'S APPLES AND GET SOME FAT ON YA.

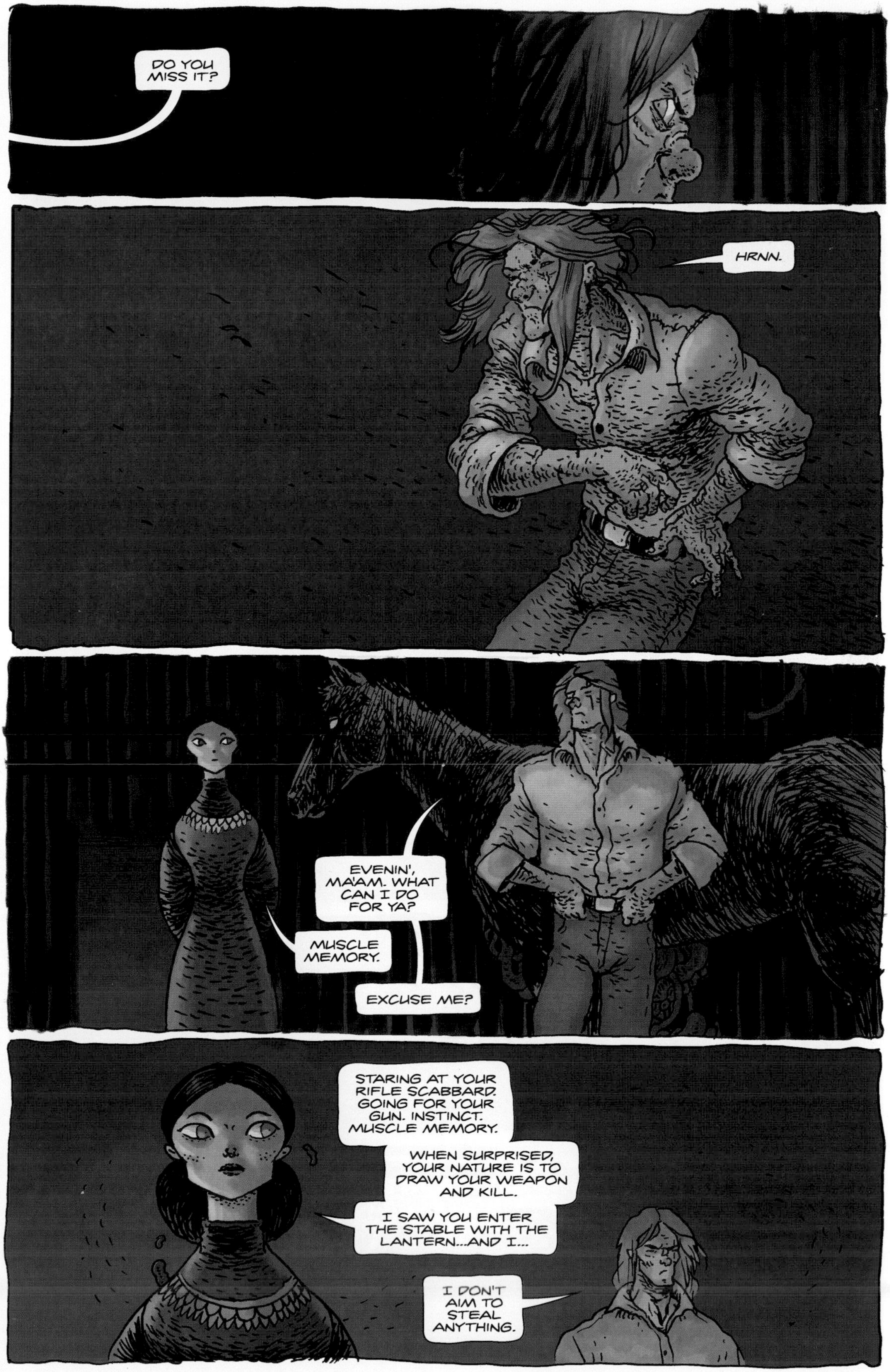
DO YOU MISS IT?
HRNN.
EVENIN', MA'AM. WHAT CAN I DO FOR YA?
MUSCLE MEMORY.
EXCUSE ME?
STARING AT YOUR RIFLE SCABBARD. GOING FOR YOUR GUN. INSTINCT. MUSCLE MEMORY.
WHEN SURPRISED, YOUR NATURE IS TO DRAW YOUR WEAPON AND KILL.
I SAW YOU ENTER THE STABLE WITH THE LANTERN...AND I...
I DON'T AIM TO STEAL ANYTHING.

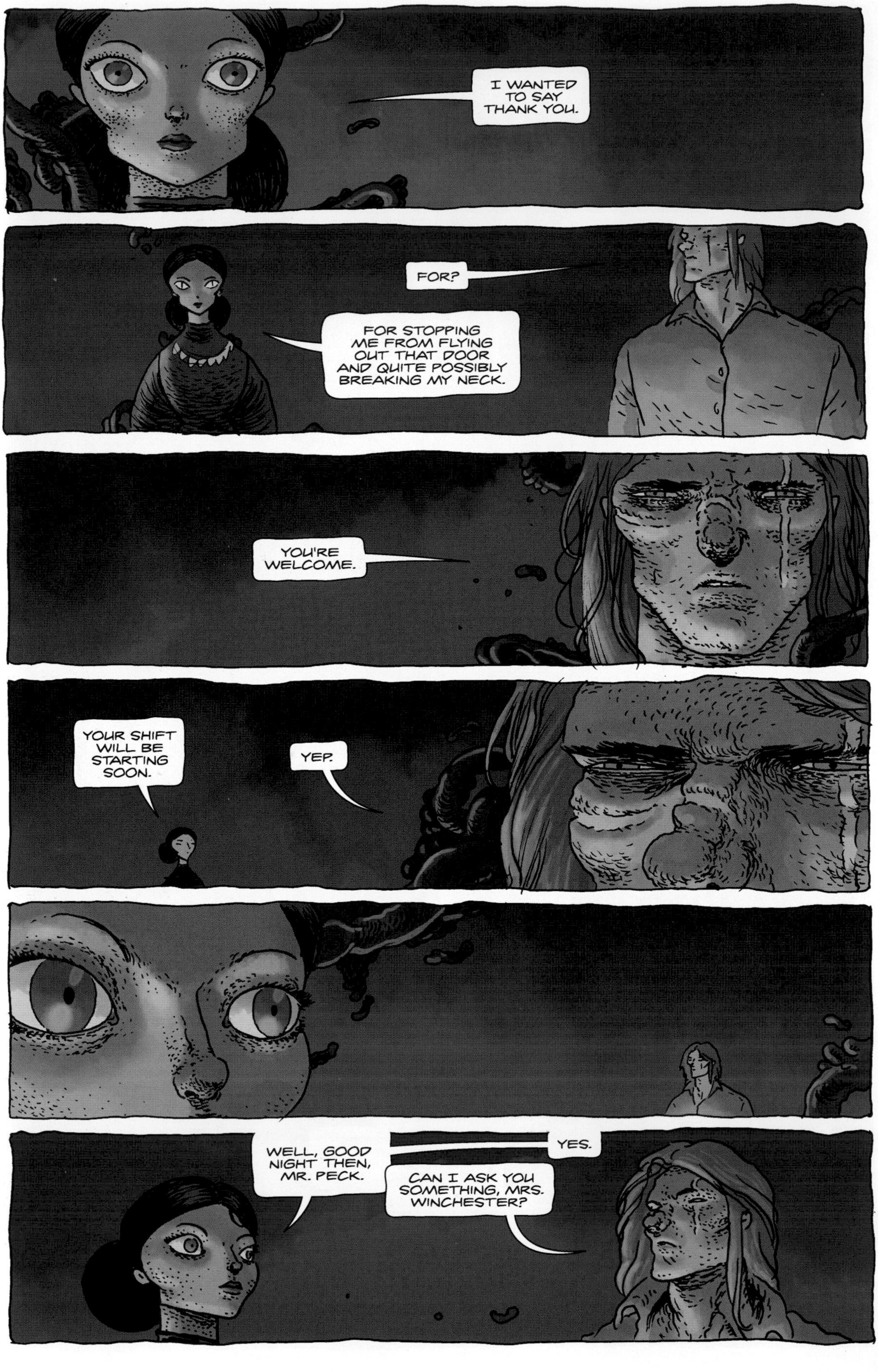
I WANTED TO SAY THANK YOU.
FOR?
FOR STOPPING ME FROM FLYING OUT THAT DOOR AND QUITE POSSIBLY BREAKING MY NECK.
YOU'RE WELCOME.
YOUR SHIFT WILL BE STARTING SOON.
YEP.
WELL, GOOD NIGHT THEN, MR. PECK.
CAN I ASK YOU SOMETHING, MRS. WINCHESTER?
YES.

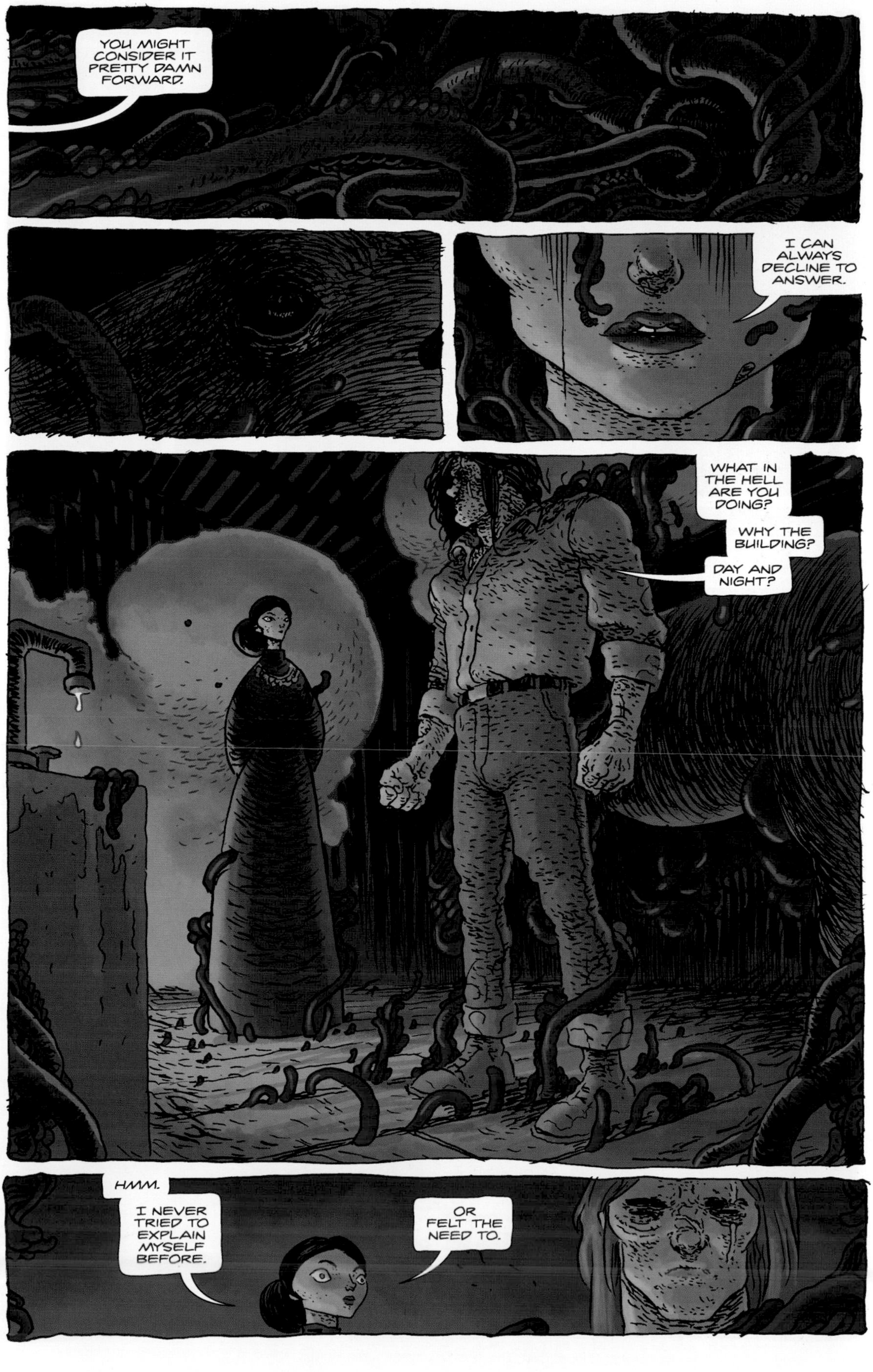
YOU MIGHT CONSIDER IT PRETTY DAMN FORWARD.
I CAN ALWAYS DECLINE TO ANSWER.
WHAT IN THE HELL ARE YOU DOING?
WHY THE BUILDING?
DAY AND NIGHT?
HMM.
I NEVER TRIED TO EXPLAIN MYSELF BEFORE.
OR FELT THE NEED TO.

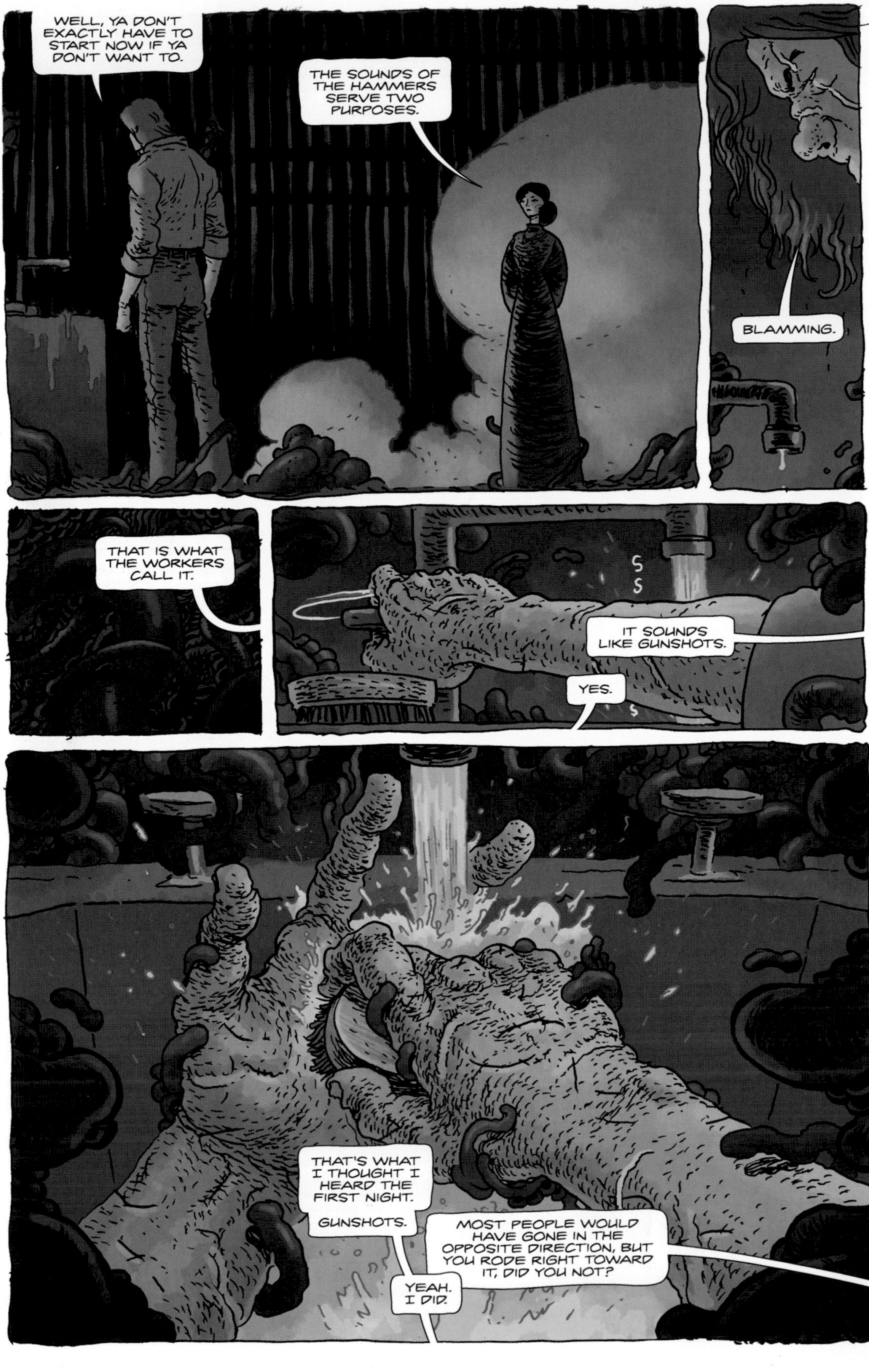
WELL, YA DON'T EXACTLY HAVE TO START NOW IF YA DON'T WANT TO.
THE SOUNDS OF THE HAMMERS SERVE TWO PURPOSES.
BLAMMING.
THAT IS WHAT THE WORKERS CALL IT.
IT SOUNDS LIKE GUNSHOTS.
YES.
THAT'S WHAT I THOUGHT I HEARD THE FIRST NIGHT.
GUNSHOTS.
MOST PEOPLE WOULD HAVE GONE IN THE OPPOSITE DIRECTION, BUT YOU RODE RIGHT TOWARD IT, DID YOU NOT?
YEAH. I DID.

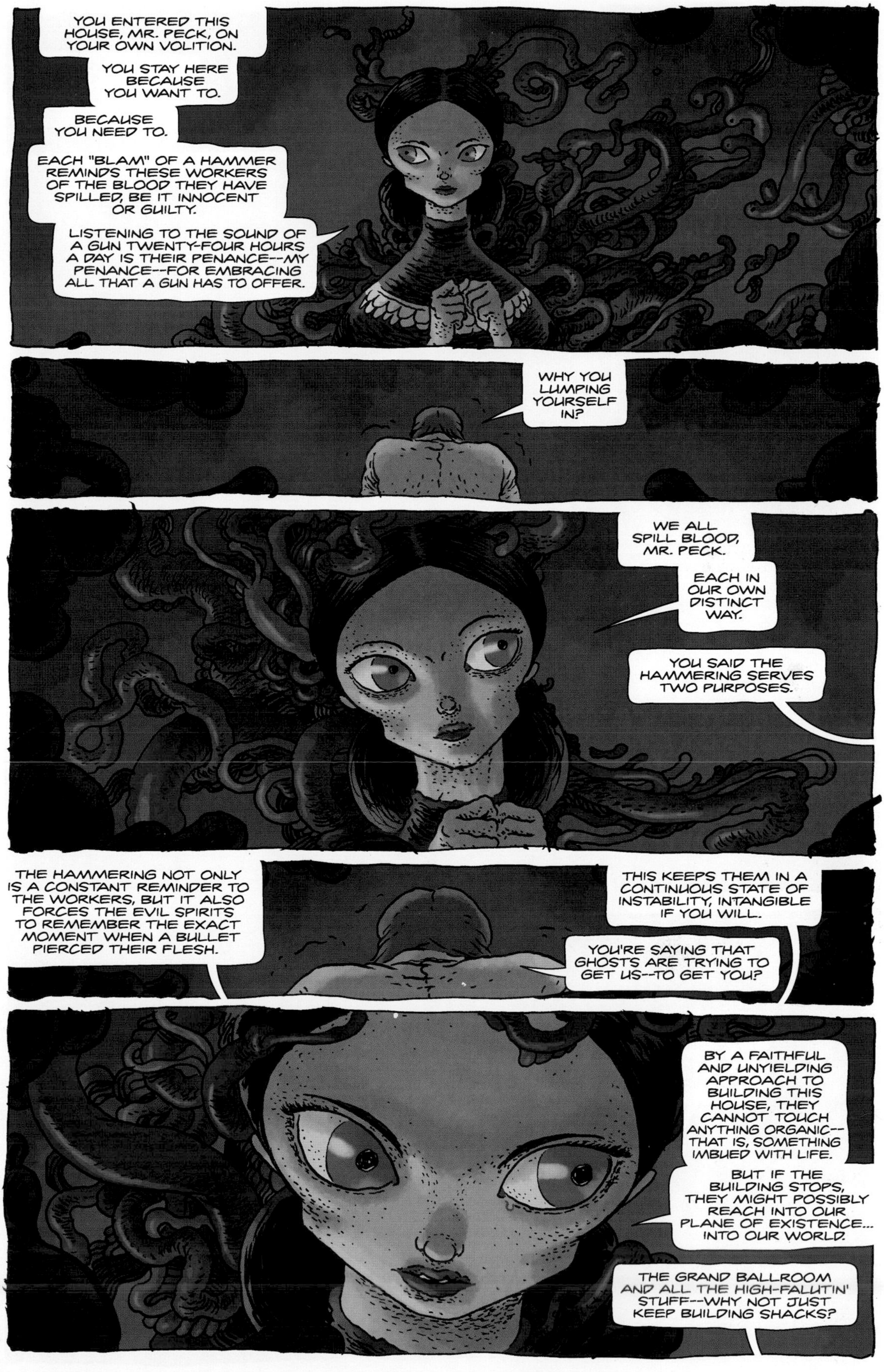
YOU ENTERED THIS HOUSE, MR. PECK, ON YOUR OWN VOLITION.
YOU STAY HERE BECAUSE YOU WANT TO.
BECAUSE YOU NEED TO.
EACH "BLAM" OF A HAMMER REMINDS THESE WORKERS OF THE BLOOD THEY HAVE SPILLED, BE IT INNOCENT OR GUILTY.
LISTENING TO THE SOUND OF A GUN TWENTY-FOUR HOURS A DAY IS THEIR PENANCE--MY PENANCE--FOR EMBRACING ALL THAT A GUN HAS TO OFFER.
WHY YOU LUMPING YOURSELF IN?
WE ALL SPILL BLOOD, MR. PECK.
EACH IN OUR OWN DISTINCT WAY.
YOU SAID THE HAMMERING SERVES TWO PURPOSES.
THE HAMMERING NOT ONLY IS A CONSTANT REMINDER TO THE WORKERS, BUT IT ALSO FORCES THE EVIL SPIRITS TO REMEMBER THE EXACT MOMENT WHEN A BULLET PIERCED THEIR FLESH.
THIS KEEPS THEM IN A CONTINUOUS STATE OF INSTABILITY, INTANGIBLE IF YOU WILL.
YOU'RE SAYING THAT GHOSTS ARE TRYING TO GET US--TO GET YOU?
BY A FAITHFUL AND UNYIELDING APPROACH TO BUILDING THIS HOUSE, THEY CANNOT TOUCH ANYTHING ORGANIC--THAT IS, SOMETHING IMBUED WITH LIFE.
BUT IF THE BUILDING STOPS, THEY MIGHT POSSIBLY REACH INTO OUR PLANE OF EXISTENCE... INTO OUR WORLD.
THE GRAND BALLROOM AND ALL THE HIGH-FALUTIN' STUFF--WHY NOT JUST KEEP BUILDING SHACKS?

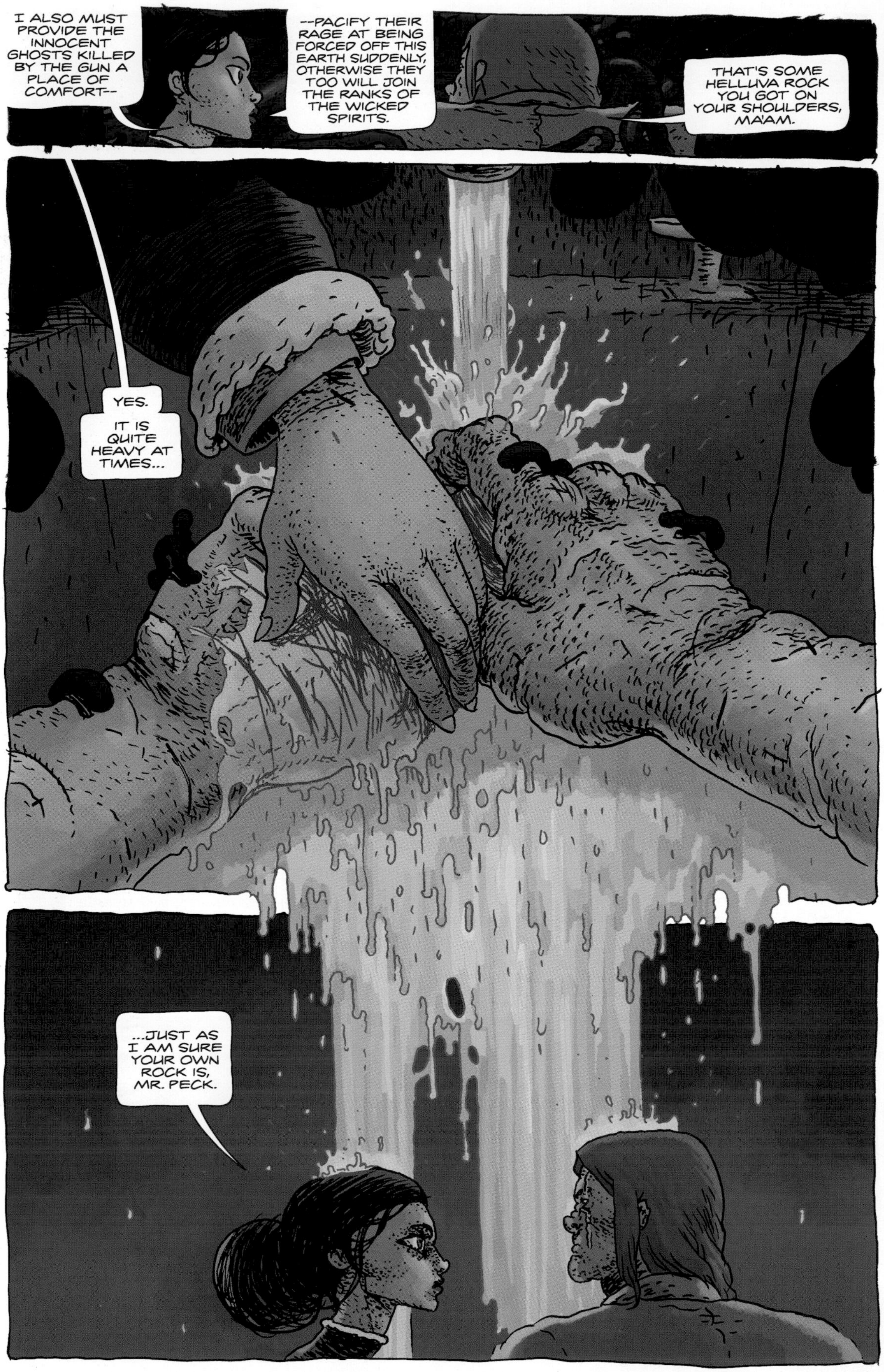
I ALSO MUST PROVIDE THE INNOCENT GHOSTS KILLED BY THE GUN A PLACE OF COMFORT--
--PACIFY THEIR RAGE AT BEING FORCED OFF THIS EARTH SUDDENLY, OTHERWISE THEY TOO WILL JOIN THE RANKS OF THE WICKED SPIRITS.
THAT'S SOME HELLUVA ROCK YOU GOT ON YOUR SHOULDERS, MA'AM.
YES.
IT IS QUITE HEAVY AT TIMES...
...JUST AS I AM SURE YOUR OWN ROCK IS, MR. PECK.

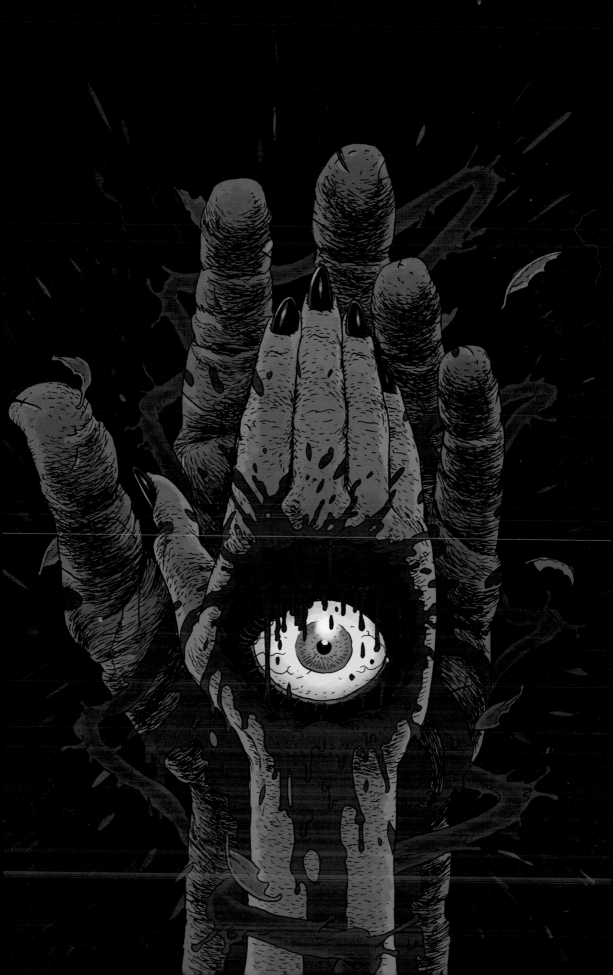

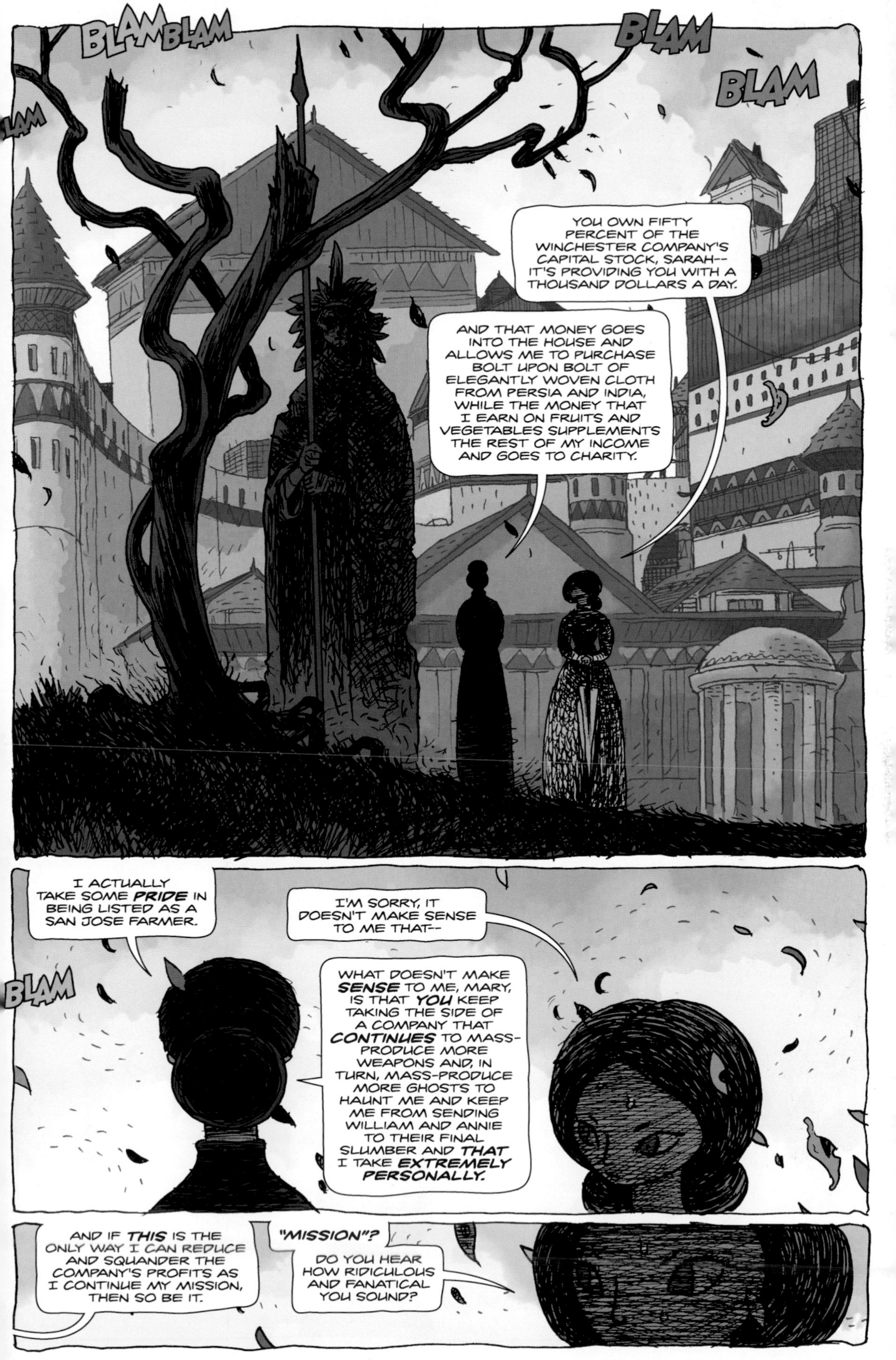
BLAM BLAM
BLAM
BLAM
YOU OWN FIFTY PERCENT OF THE WINCHESTER COMPANY'S CAPITAL STOCK, SARAH-- IT'S PROVIDING YOU WITH A THOUSAND DOLLARS A DAY.
AND THAT MONEY GOES INTO THE HOUSE AND ALLOWS ME TO PURCHASE BOLT UPON BOLT OF ELEGANTLY WOVEN CLOTH FROM PERSIA AND INDIA, WHILE THE MONEY THAT I EARN ON FRUITS AND VEGETABLES SUPPLEMENTS THE REST OF MY INCOME AND GOES TO CHARITY.
I ACTUALLY TAKE SOME PRIDE IN BEING LISTED AS A SAN JOSE FARMER.
I'M SORRY, IT DOESN'T MAKE SENSE TO ME THAT--
BLAM
WHAT DOESN'T MAKE SENSE TO ME, MARY, IS THAT YOU KEEP TAKING THE SIDE OF A COMPANY THAT CONTINUES TO MASS-PRODUCE MORE WEAPONS AND, IN TURN, MASS-PRODUCE MORE GHOSTS TO HAUNT ME AND KEEP ME FROM SENDING WILLIAM AND ANNIE TO THEIR FINAL SLUMBER AND THAT I TAKE EXTREMELY PERSONALLY.
AND IF THIS IS THE ONLY WAY I CAN REDUCE AND SQUANDER THE COMPANY'S PROFITS AS I CONTINUE MY MISSION, THEN SO BE IT.
"MISSION"?
DO YOU HEAR HOW RIDICULOUS AND FANATICAL YOU SOUND?

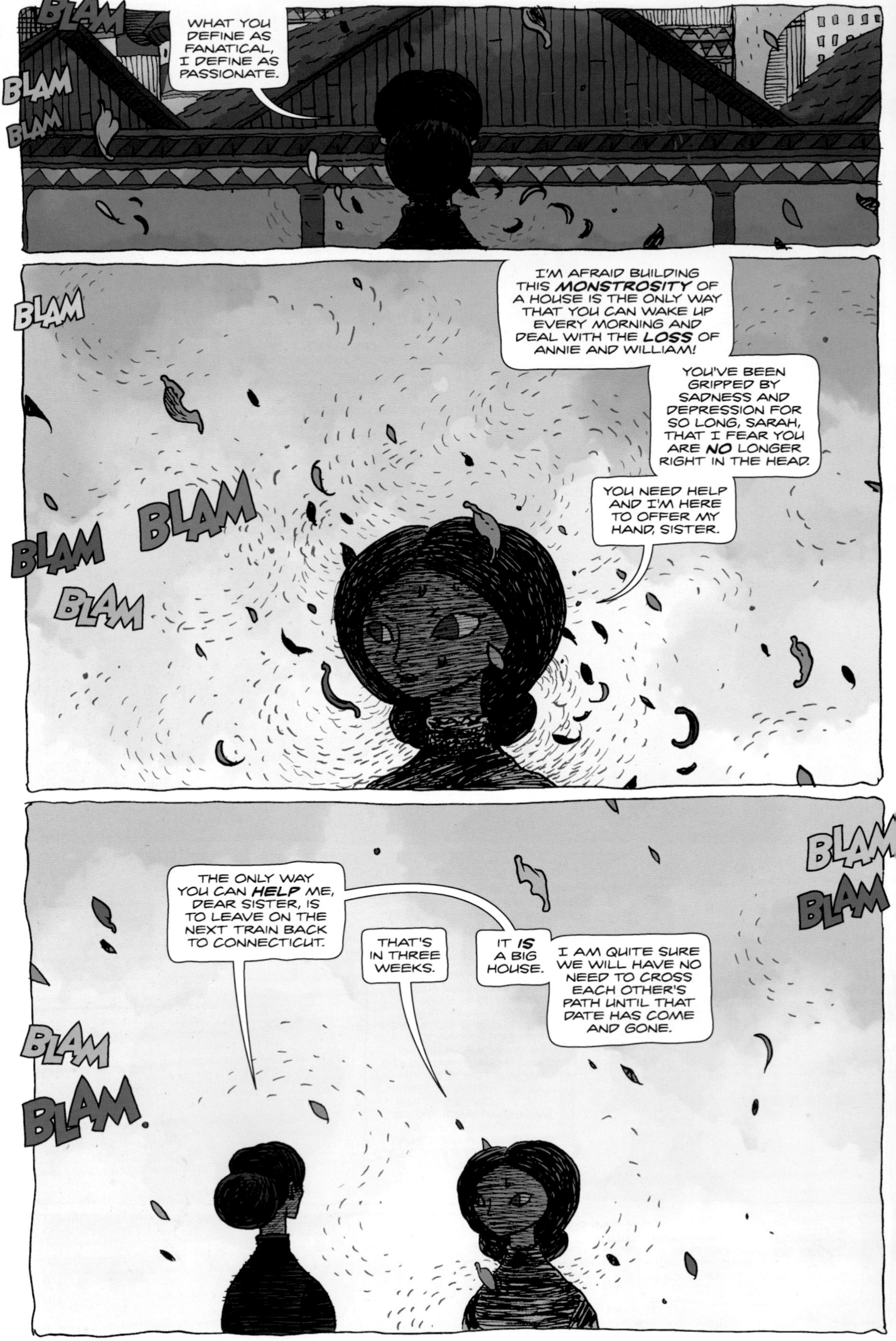
BLAM
BLAM
BLAM
WHAT YOU DEFINE AS FANATICAL, I DEFINE AS PASSIONATE.
BLAM
I'M AFRAID BUILDING THIS MONSTROSITY OF A HOUSE IS THE ONLY WAY THAT YOU CAN WAKE UP EVERY MORNING AND DEAL WITH THE LOSS OF ANNIE AND WILLIAM!
YOU'VE BEEN GRIPPED BY SADNESS AND DEPRESSION FOR SO LONG, SARAH, THAT I FEAR YOU ARE NO LONGER RIGHT IN THE HEAD.
YOU NEED HELP AND I'M HERE TO OFFER MY HAND, SISTER.
BLAM
BLAM
BLAM
THE ONLY WAY YOU CAN HELP ME, DEAR SISTER, IS TO LEAVE ON THE NEXT TRAIN BACK TO CONNECTICUT.
THAT'S IN THREE WEEKS.
IT IS A BIG HOUSE.
I AM QUITE SURE WE WILL HAVE NO NEED TO CROSS EACH OTHER'S PATH UNTIL THAT DATE HAS COME AND GONE.
BLAM
BLAM
BLAM
BLAM.

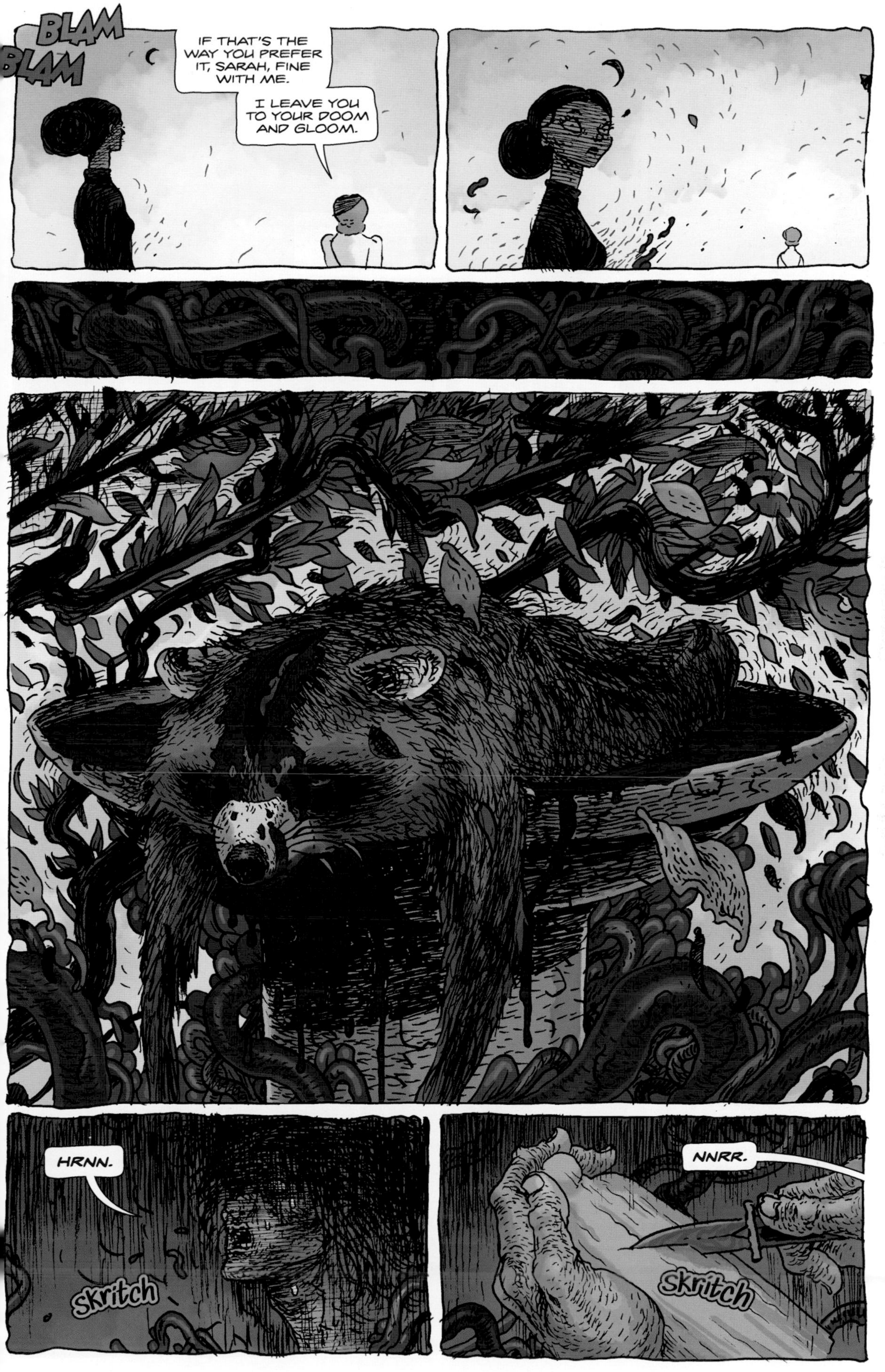
BLAM
BLAM
IF THAT'S THE WAY YOU PREFER IT, SARAH, FINE WITH ME.
I LEAVE YOU TO YOUR DOOM AND GLOOM.
HRNN.
SKRITCH
NNRR.
SKRITCH

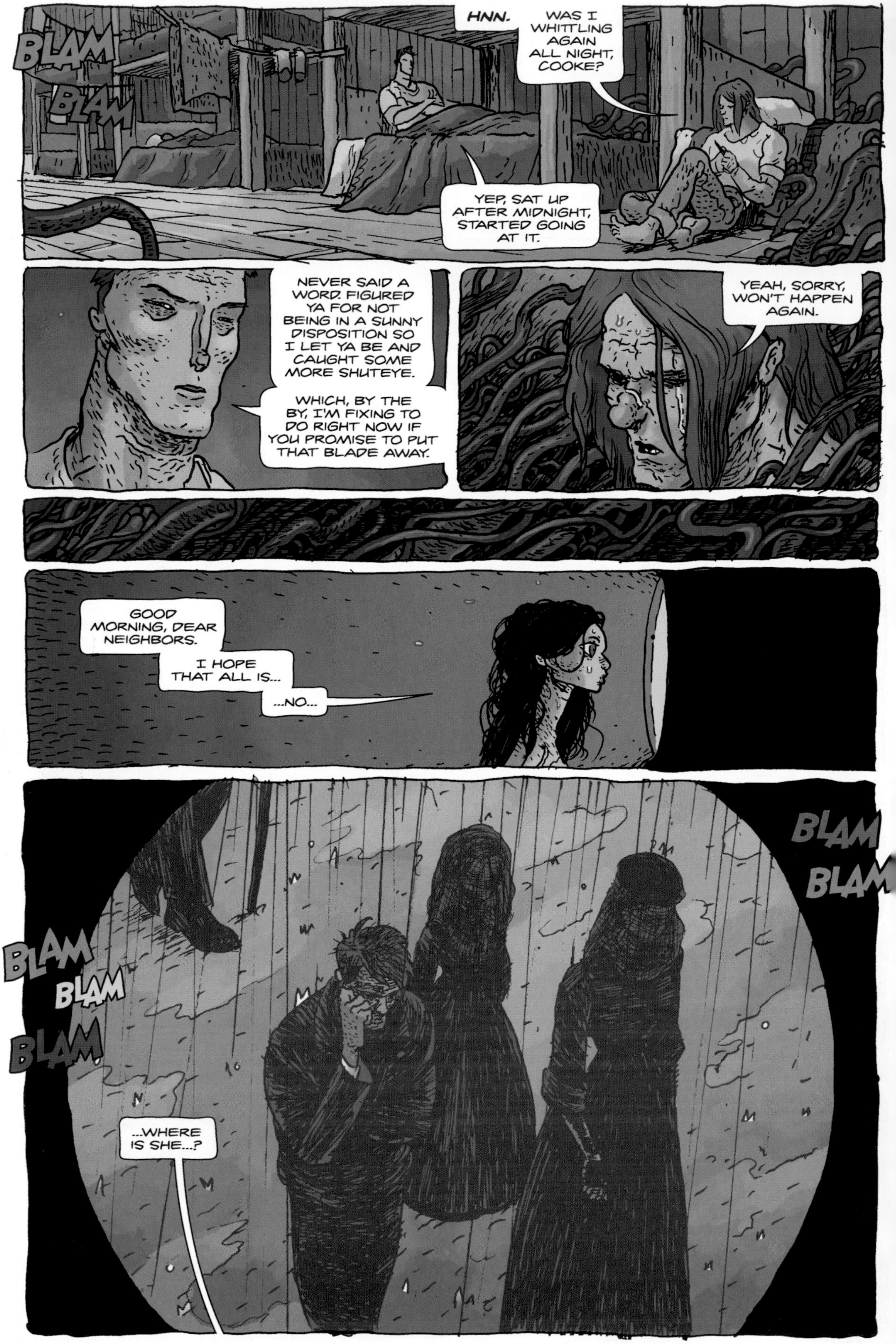
BLAM
BLAM
HNN.
WAS I WHITTLING AGAIN ALL NIGHT, COOKE?
YEP, SAT UP AFTER MIDNIGHT, STARTED GOING AT IT.
NEVER SAID A WORD. FIGURED YA FOR NOT BEING IN A SUNNY DISPOSITION SO I LET YA BE AND CAUGHT SOME MORE SHUTEYE.
WHICH, BY THE BY, I'M FIXING TO DO RIGHT NOW IF YOU PROMISE TO PUT THAT BLADE AWAY.
YEAH, SORRY, WON'T HAPPEN AGAIN.
GOOD MORNING, DEAR NEIGHBORS.
I HOPE THAT ALL IS...
...NO...
BLAM
BLAM
BLAM
BLAM
BLAM
...WHERE IS SHE...?

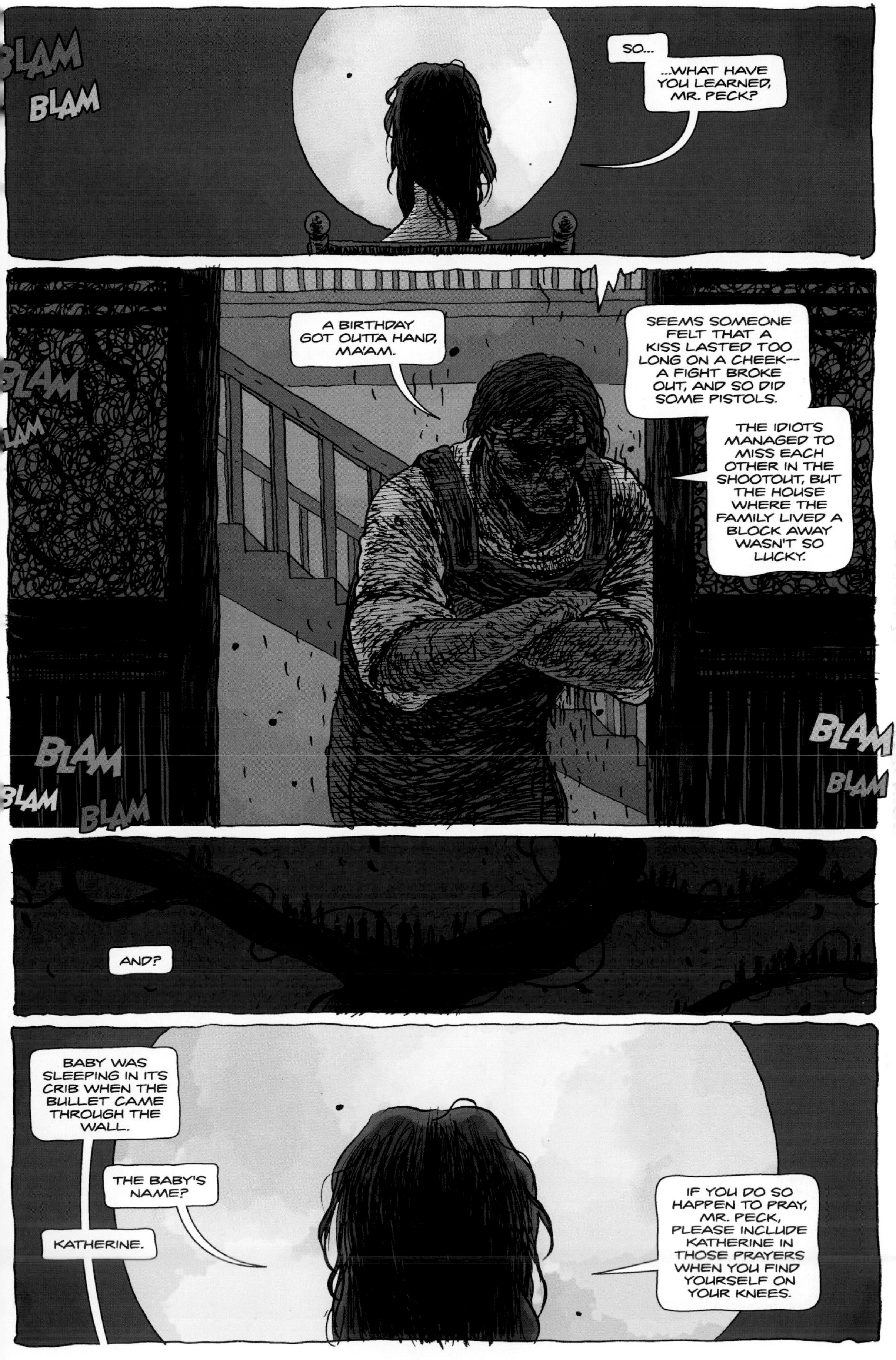
BLAM
BLAM
SO...
...WHAT HAVE YOU LEARNED, MR. PECK?
A BIRTHDAY GOT OUTTA HAND, MA'AM.
SEEMS SOMEONE FELT THAT A KISS LASTED TOO LONG ON A CHEEK-- A FIGHT BROKE OUT, AND SO DID SOME PISTOLS.
THE IDIOTS MANAGED TO MISS EACH OTHER IN THE SHOOTOUT, BUT THE HOUSE WHERE THE FAMILY LIVED A BLOCK AWAY WASN'T SO LUCKY.
BLAM
BLAM
BLAM
BLAM
BLAM
BLAM
AND?
BABY WAS SLEEPING IN ITS CRIB WHEN THE BULLET CAME THROUGH THE WALL.
THE BABY'S NAME?
KATHERINE.
IF YOU DO SO HAPPEN TO PRAY, MR. PECK, PLEASE INCLUDE KATHERINE IN THOSE PRAYERS WHEN YOU FIND YOURSELF ON YOUR KNEES.

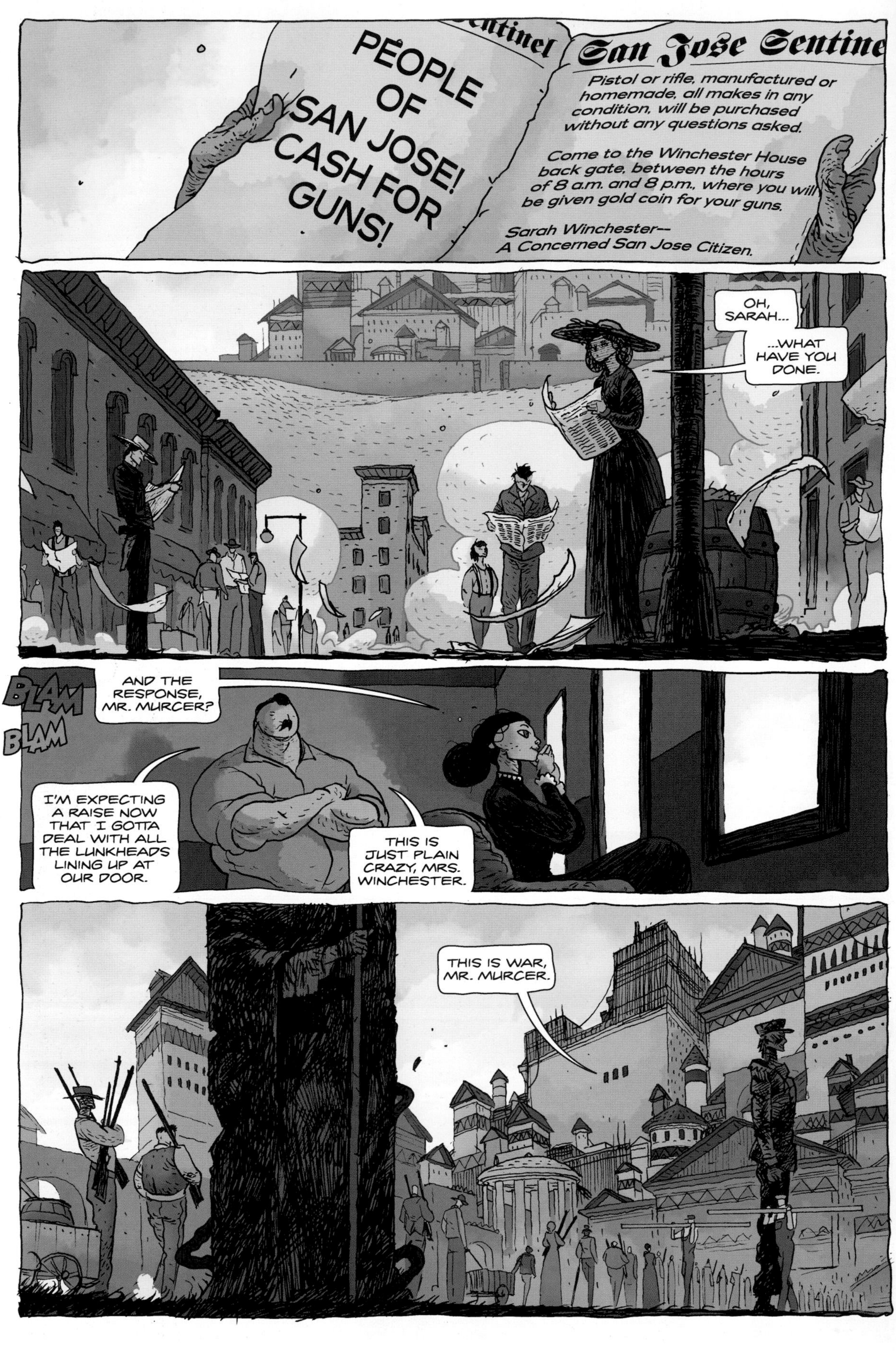
Sentinel
PEOPLE OF SAN JOSE! CASH FOR GUNS!
San Jose Sentine
Pistol or rifle, manufactured or homemade, all makes in any condition, will be purchased without any questions asked.
Come to the Winchester House back gate, between the hours of 8 a.m. and 8 p.m., where you will be given gold coin for your guns.
Sarah Winchester— A Concerned San Jose Citizen.
OH, SARAH...
...WHAT HAVE YOU DONE.
BLAM
BLAM
AND THE RESPONSE, MR. MURCER?
I'M EXPECTING A RAISE NOW THAT I GOTTA DEAL WITH ALL THE LUNKHEADS LINING UP AT OUR DOOR.
THIS IS JUST PLAIN CRAZY, MRS. WINCHESTER.
THIS IS WAR, MR. MURCER.

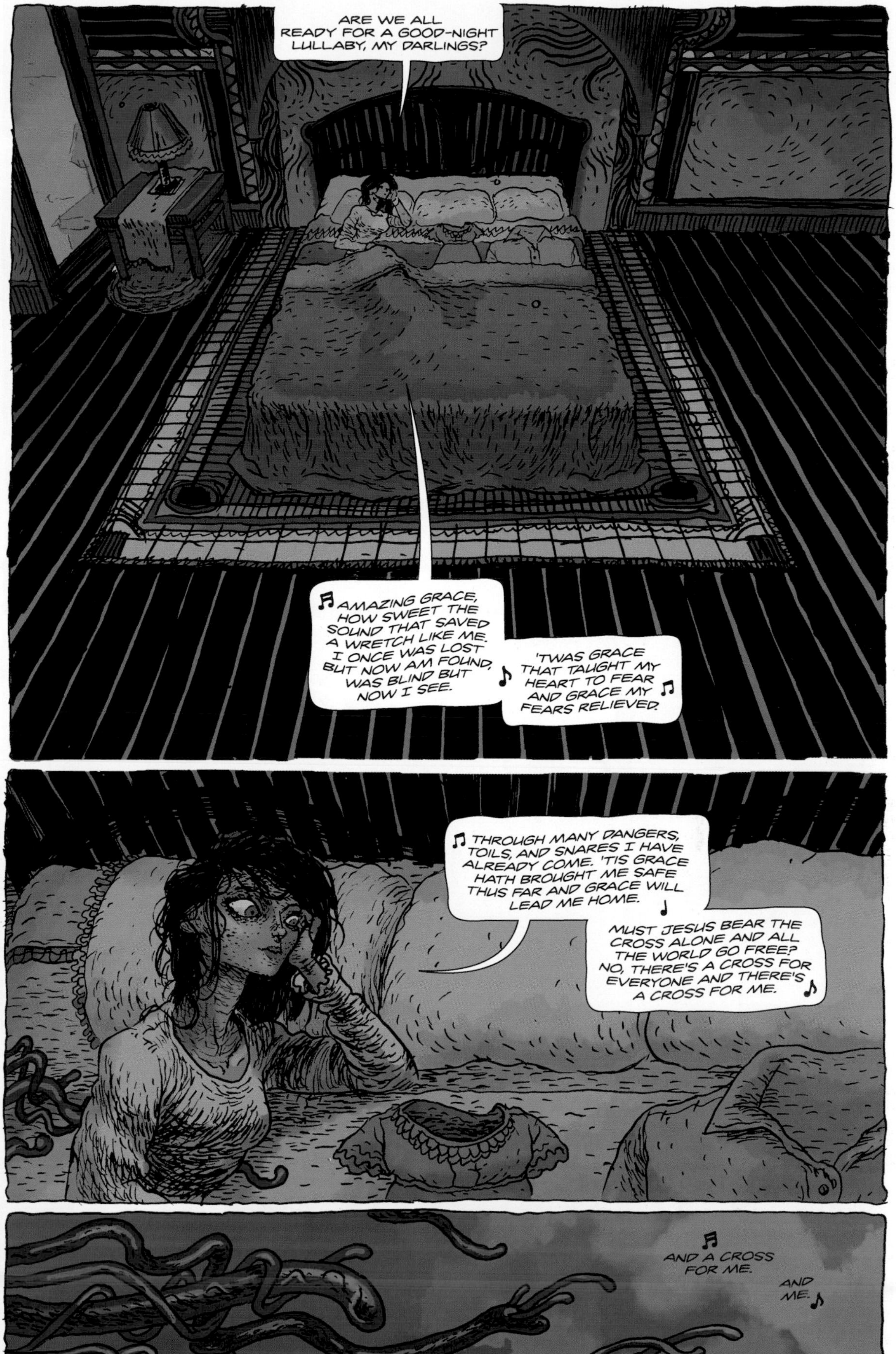
ARE WE ALL READY FOR A GOOD-NIGHT LULLABY, MY DARLINGS?
♫ AMAZING GRACE, HOW SWEET THE SOUND THAT SAVED A WRETCH LIKE ME. I ONCE WAS LOST BUT NOW AM FOUND, WAS BLIND BUT NOW I SEE. ♪
'TWAS GRACE THAT TAUGHT MY HEART TO FEAR AND GRACE MY FEARS RELIEVED. ♫
♫ THROUGH MANY DANGERS, TOILS, AND SNARES I HAVE ALREADY COME. 'TIS GRACE HATH BROUGHT ME SAFE THUS FAR AND GRACE WILL LEAD ME HOME. ♩
MUST JESUS BEAR THE CROSS ALONE AND ALL THE WORLD GO FREE? NO, THERE'S A CROSS FOR EVERYONE AND THERE'S A CROSS FOR ME. ♪
♫ AND A CROSS FOR ME.
AND ME. ♪

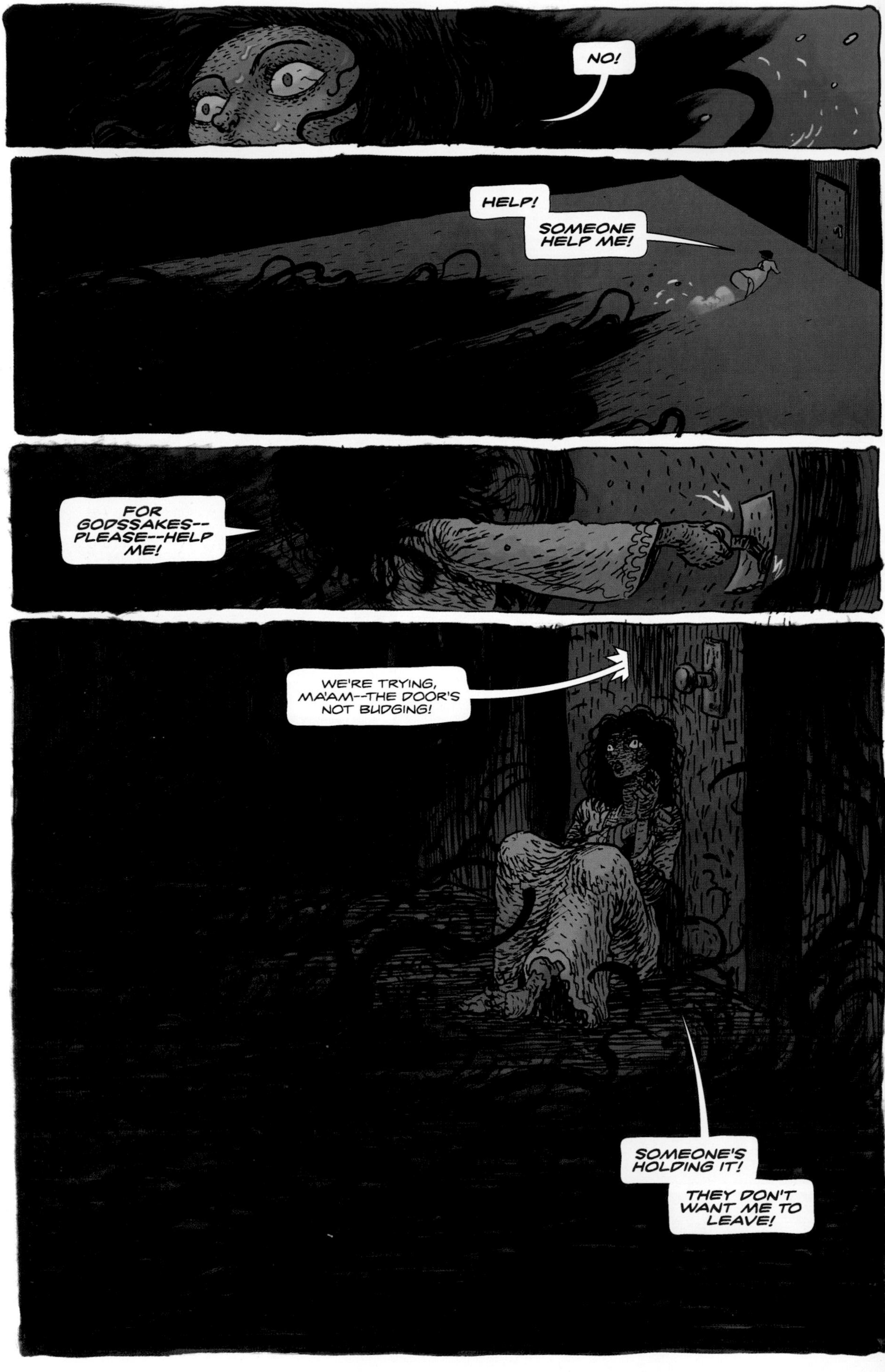
NO!
HELP!
SOMEONE HELP ME!
FOR GODSSAKES-- PLEASE--HELP ME!
WE'RE TRYING, MA'AM--THE DOOR'S NOT BUDGING!
SOMEONE'S HOLDING IT!
THEY DON'T WANT ME TO LEAVE!

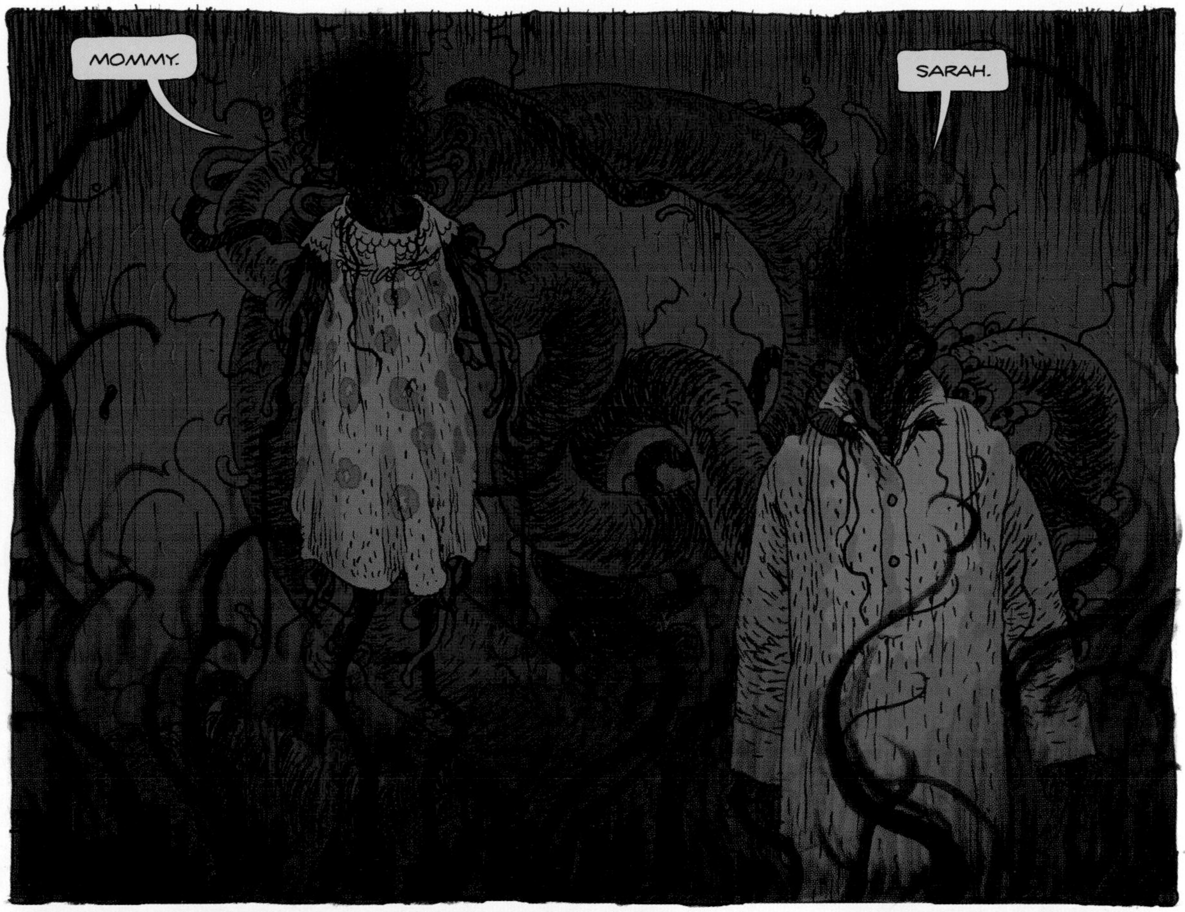
MOMMY.
SARAH.

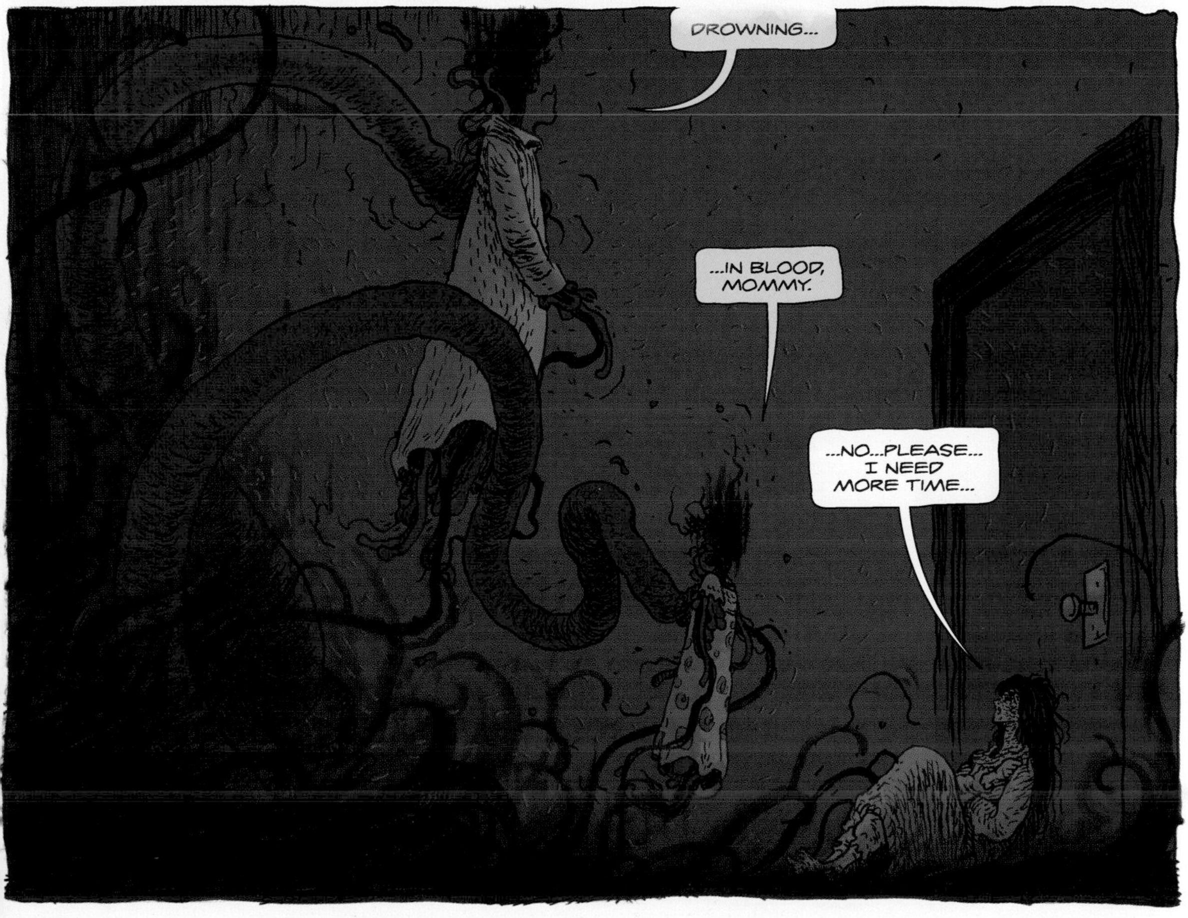
DROWNING...
...IN BLOOD, MOMMY.
...NO...PLEASE... I NEED MORE TIME...

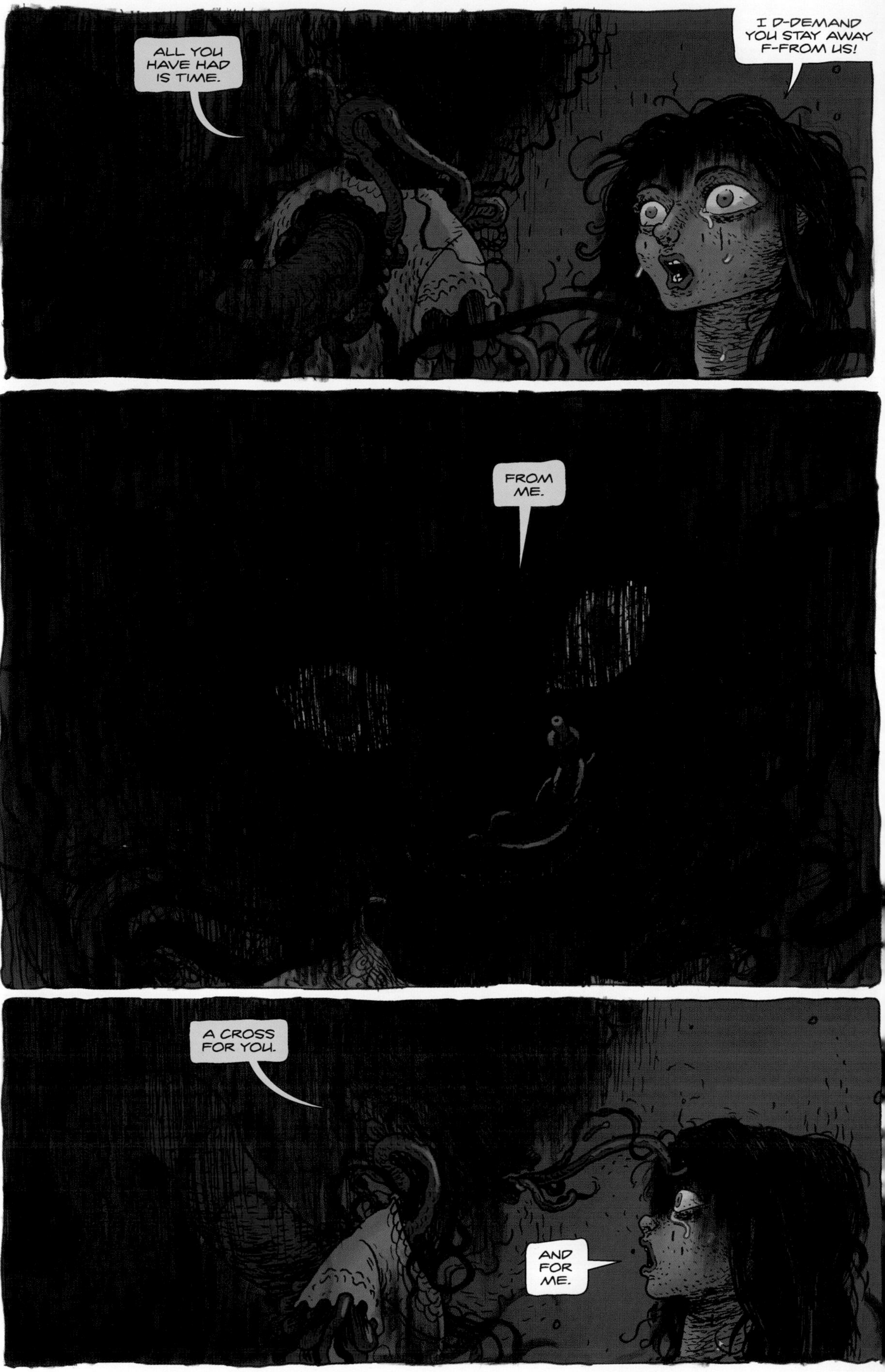

ALL YOU HAVE HAD IS TIME.
I D-DEMAND YOU STAY AWAY F-FROM US!
FROM ME.
A CROSS FOR YOU.
AND FOR ME.

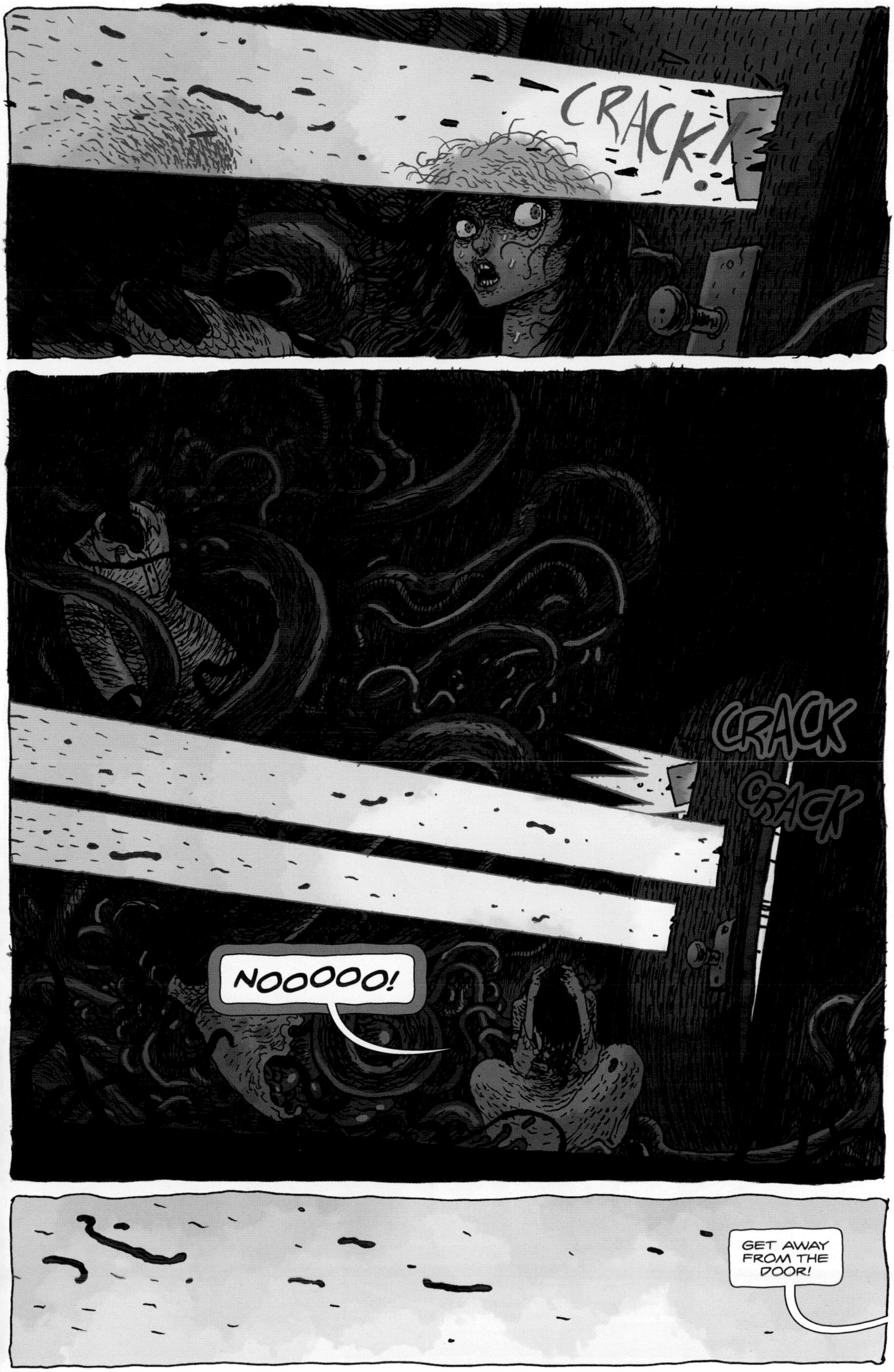
CRACK!
CRACK
CRACK
NOOOOO!
GET AWAY FROM THE DOOR!

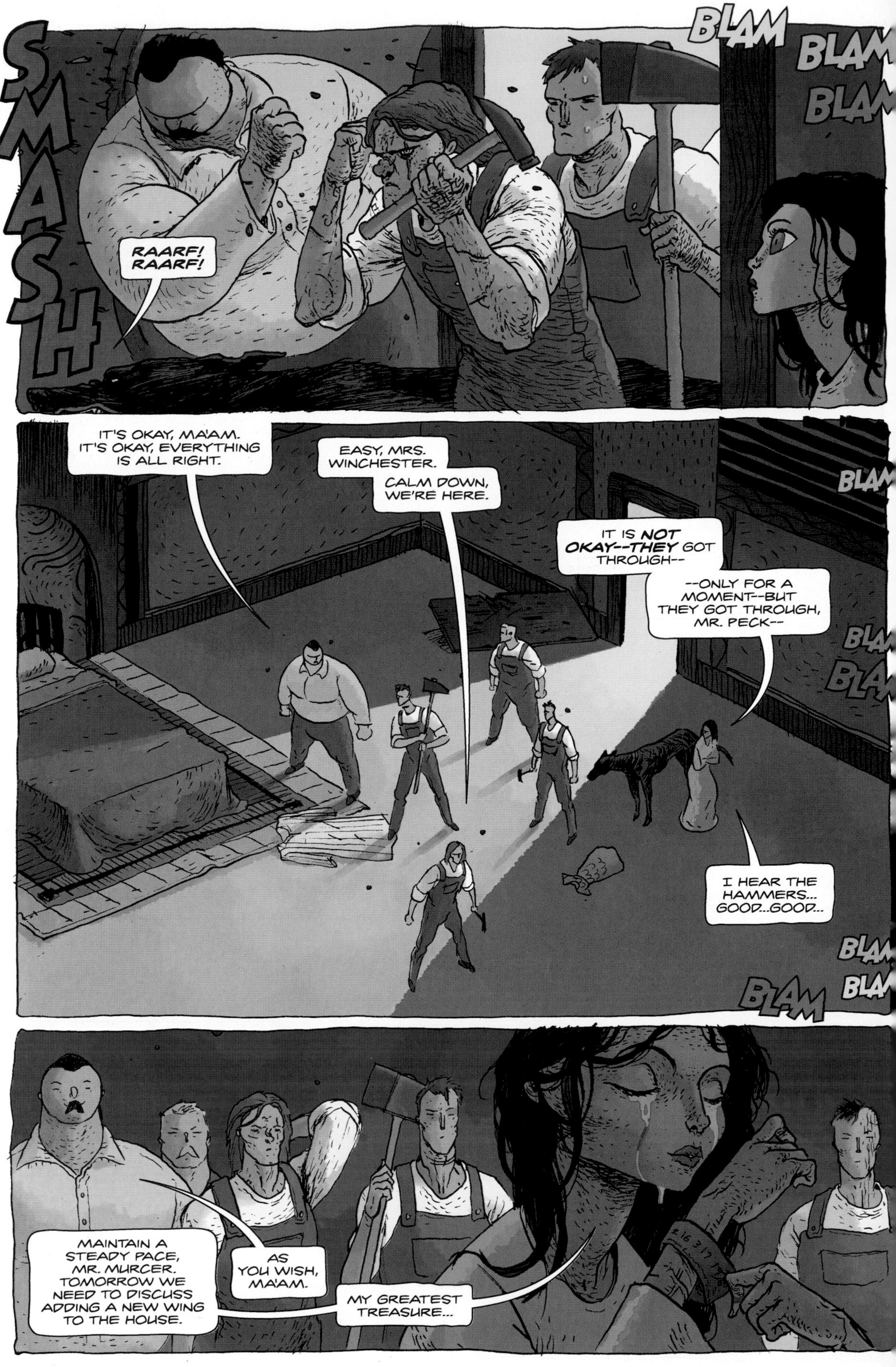
SMASH
BLAM
BLAM
BLAM
RAARF! RAARF!
IT'S OKAY, MA'AM. IT'S OKAY, EVERYTHING IS ALL RIGHT.
EASY, MRS. WINCHESTER.
CALM DOWN, WE'RE HERE.
BLAM
IT IS **NOT OKAY--THEY** GOT THROUGH--
--ONLY FOR A MOMENT--BUT THEY GOT THROUGH, MR. PECK--
BLAM
BLAM
I HEAR THE HAMMERS... GOOD...GOOD...
BLAM
BLAM
BLAM
MAINTAIN A STEADY PACE, MR. MURCER. TOMORROW WE NEED TO DISCUSS ADDING A NEW WING TO THE HOUSE.
AS YOU WISH, MA'AM.
MY GREATEST TREASURE...

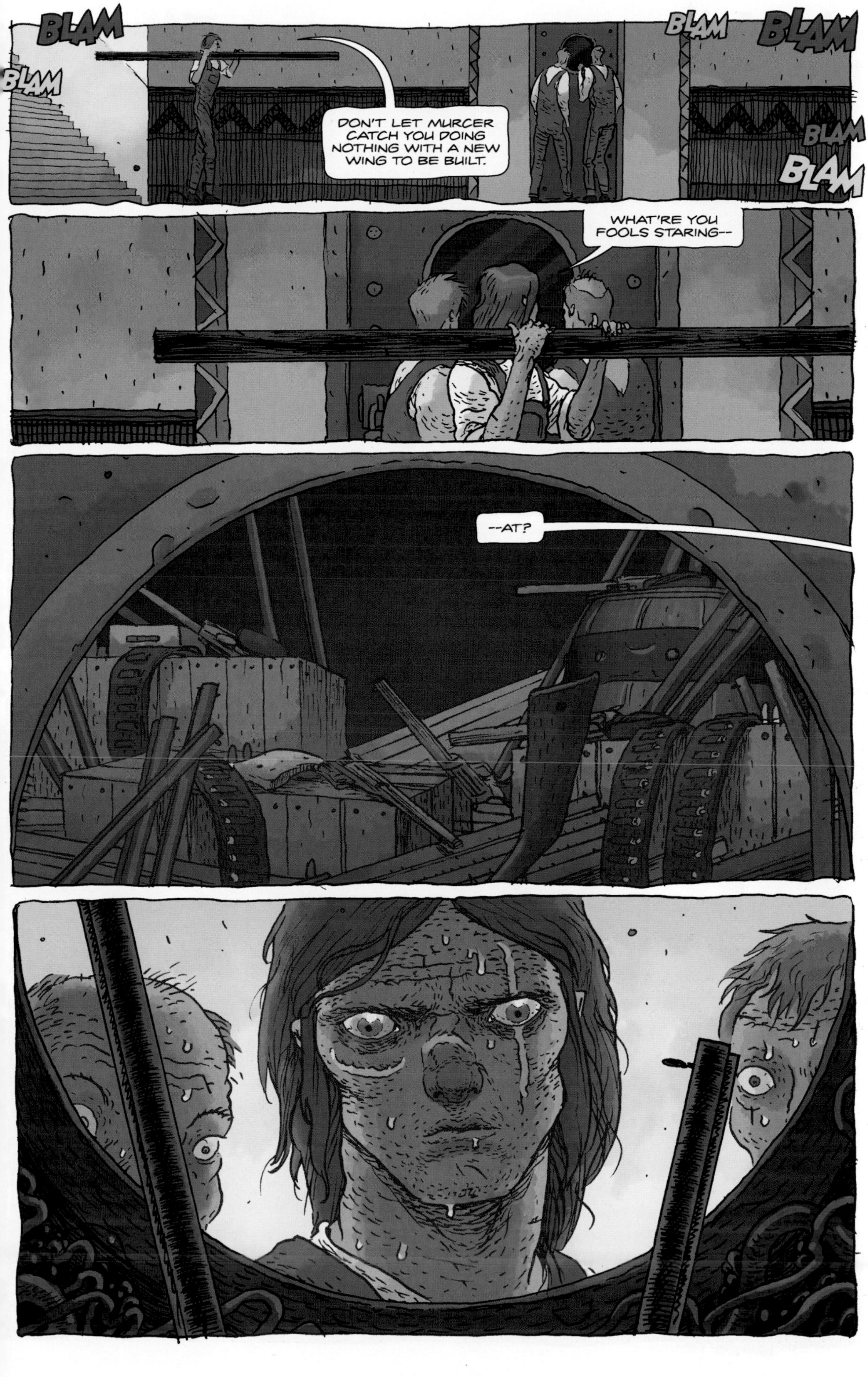
BLAM
BLAM
DON'T LET MURCER CATCH YOU DOING NOTHING WITH A NEW WING TO BE BUILT.
BLAM
BLAM
BLAM
BLAM
WHAT'RE YOU FOOLS STARING--
--AT?

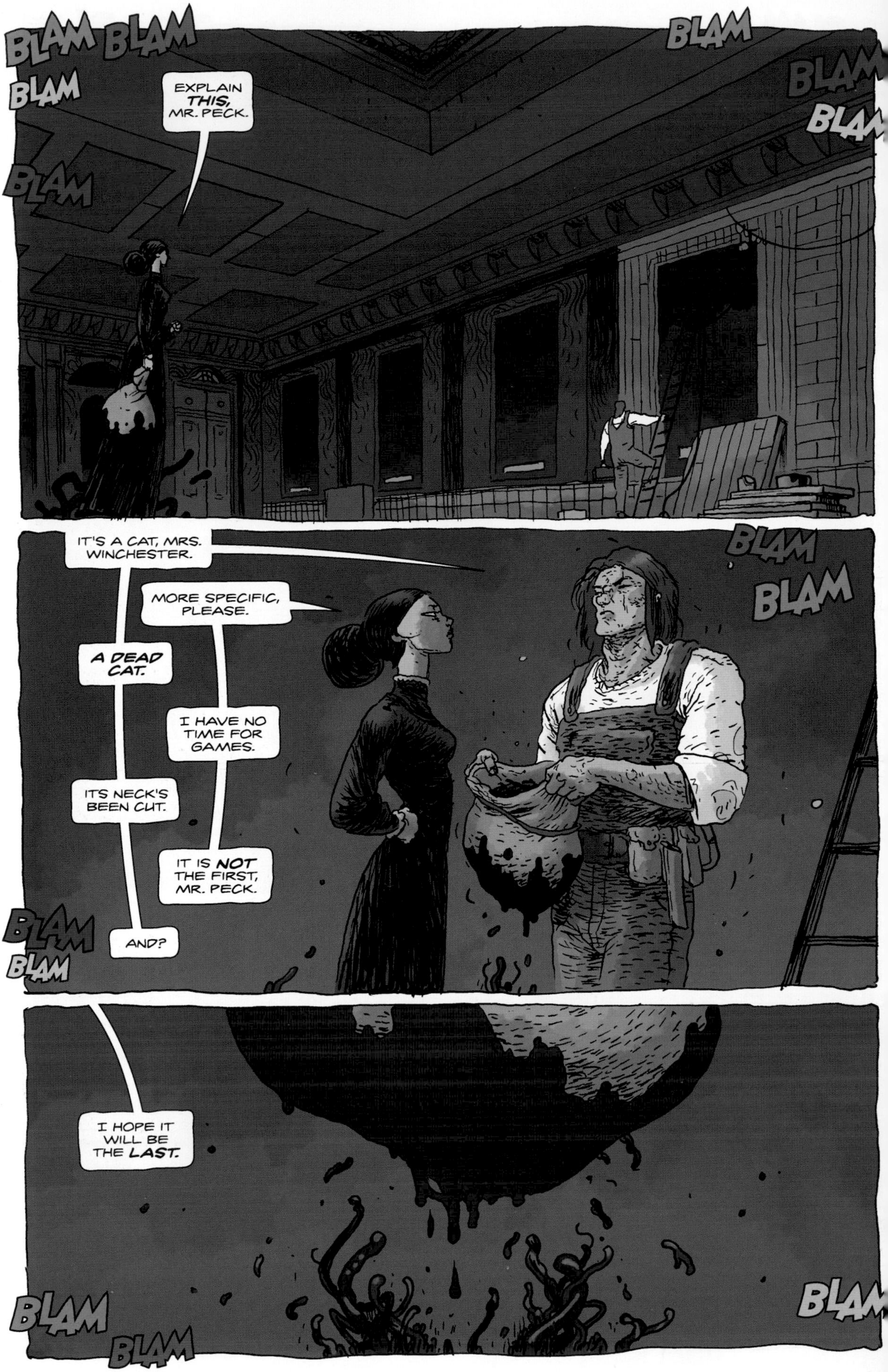
BLAM BLAM
BLAM
BLAM
BLAM
BLAM
BLAM
EXPLAIN THIS, MR. PECK.
IT'S A CAT, MRS. WINCHESTER.
BLAM
BLAM
MORE SPECIFIC, PLEASE.
A DEAD CAT.
I HAVE NO TIME FOR GAMES.
ITS NECK'S BEEN CUT.
IT IS NOT THE FIRST, MR. PECK.
BLAM
BLAM
AND?
I HOPE IT WILL BE THE LAST.
BLAM
BLAM
BLAM

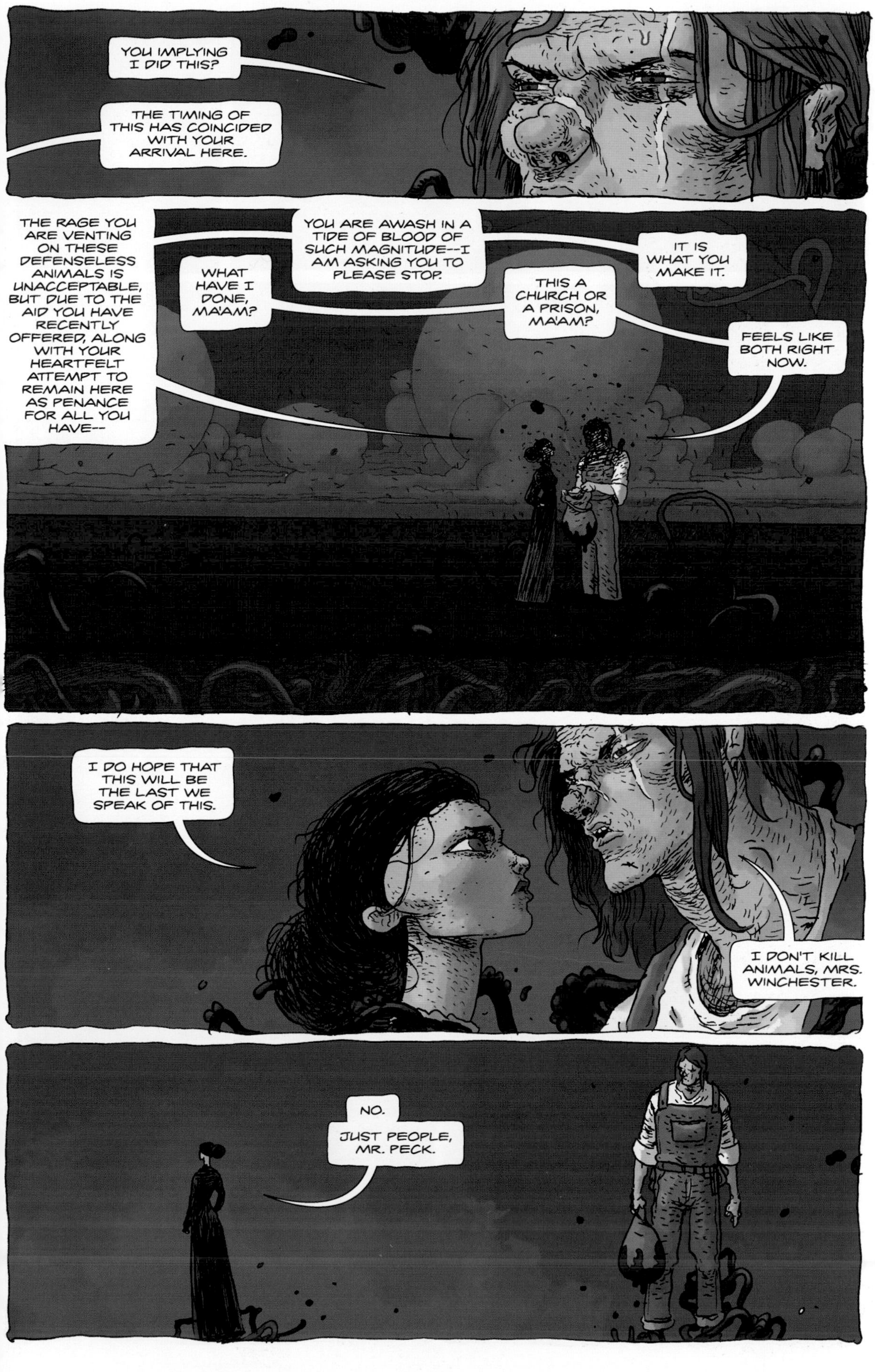
YOU IMPLYING I DID THIS?
THE TIMING OF THIS HAS COINCIDED WITH YOUR ARRIVAL HERE.
THE RAGE YOU ARE VENTING ON THESE DEFENSELESS ANIMALS IS UNACCEPTABLE, BUT DUE TO THE AID YOU HAVE RECENTLY OFFERED, ALONG WITH YOUR HEARTFELT ATTEMPT TO REMAIN HERE AS PENANCE FOR ALL YOU HAVE--
YOU ARE AWASH IN A TIDE OF BLOOD OF SUCH MAGNITUDE--I AM ASKING YOU TO PLEASE STOP.
IT IS WHAT YOU MAKE IT.
WHAT HAVE I DONE, MA'AM?
THIS A CHURCH OR A PRISON, MA'AM?
FEELS LIKE BOTH RIGHT NOW.
I DO HOPE THAT THIS WILL BE THE LAST WE SPEAK OF THIS.
I DON'T KILL ANIMALS, MRS. WINCHESTER.
NO.
JUST PEOPLE, MR. PECK.

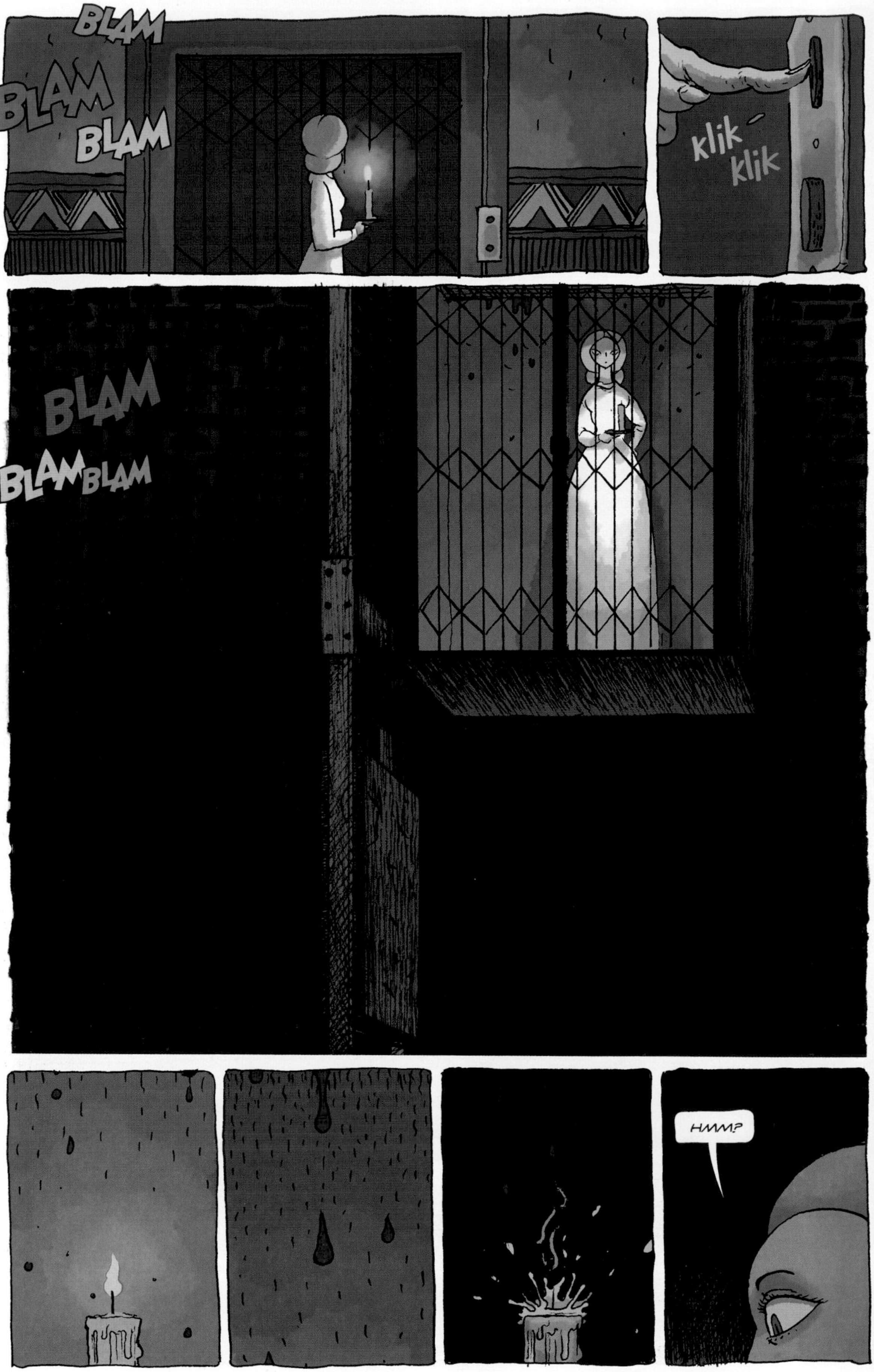
BLAM
BLAM
BLAM
klik
klik
BLAM
BLAMBLAM
HMM?

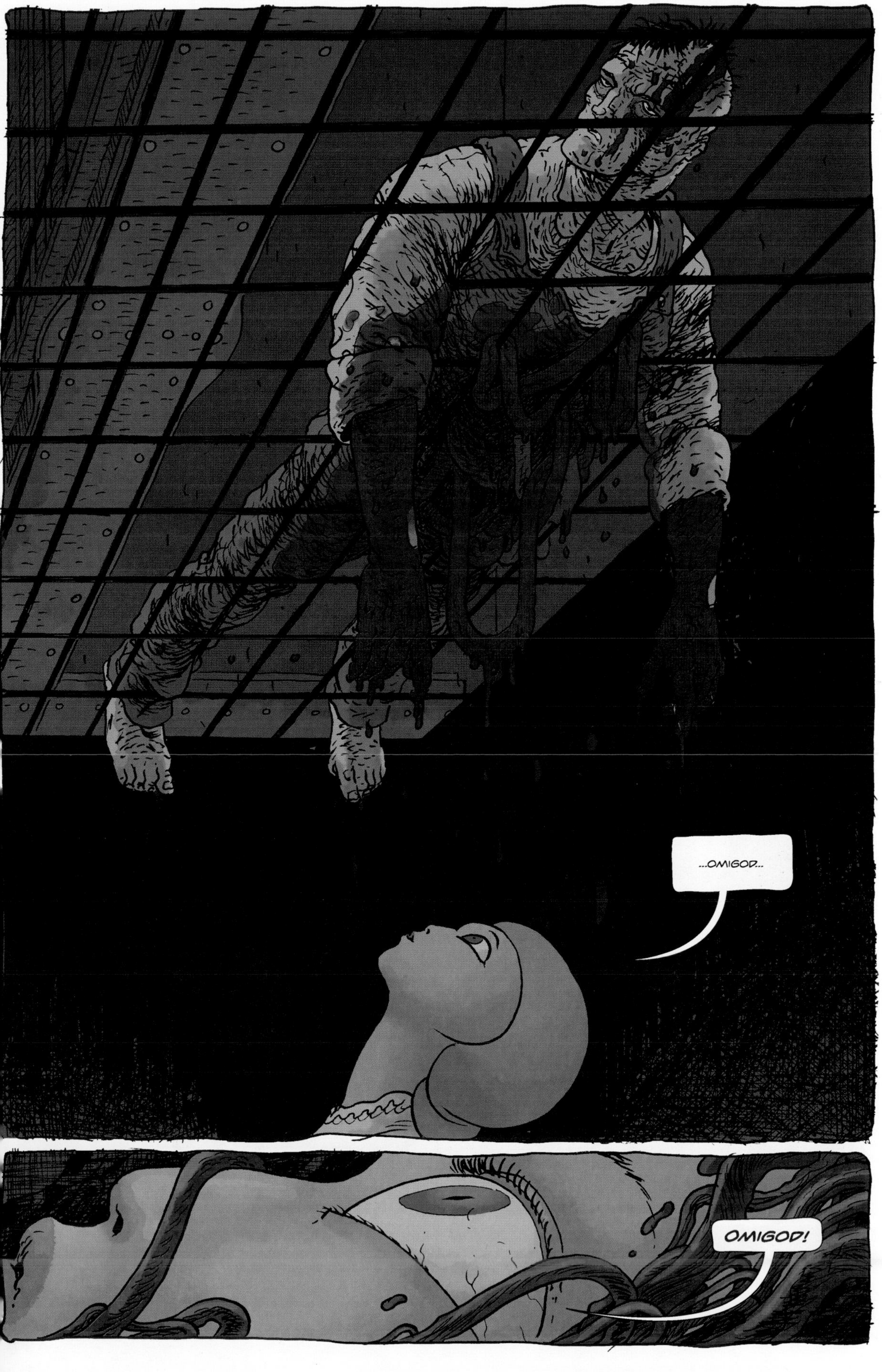
...OMIGOD...
OMIGOD!

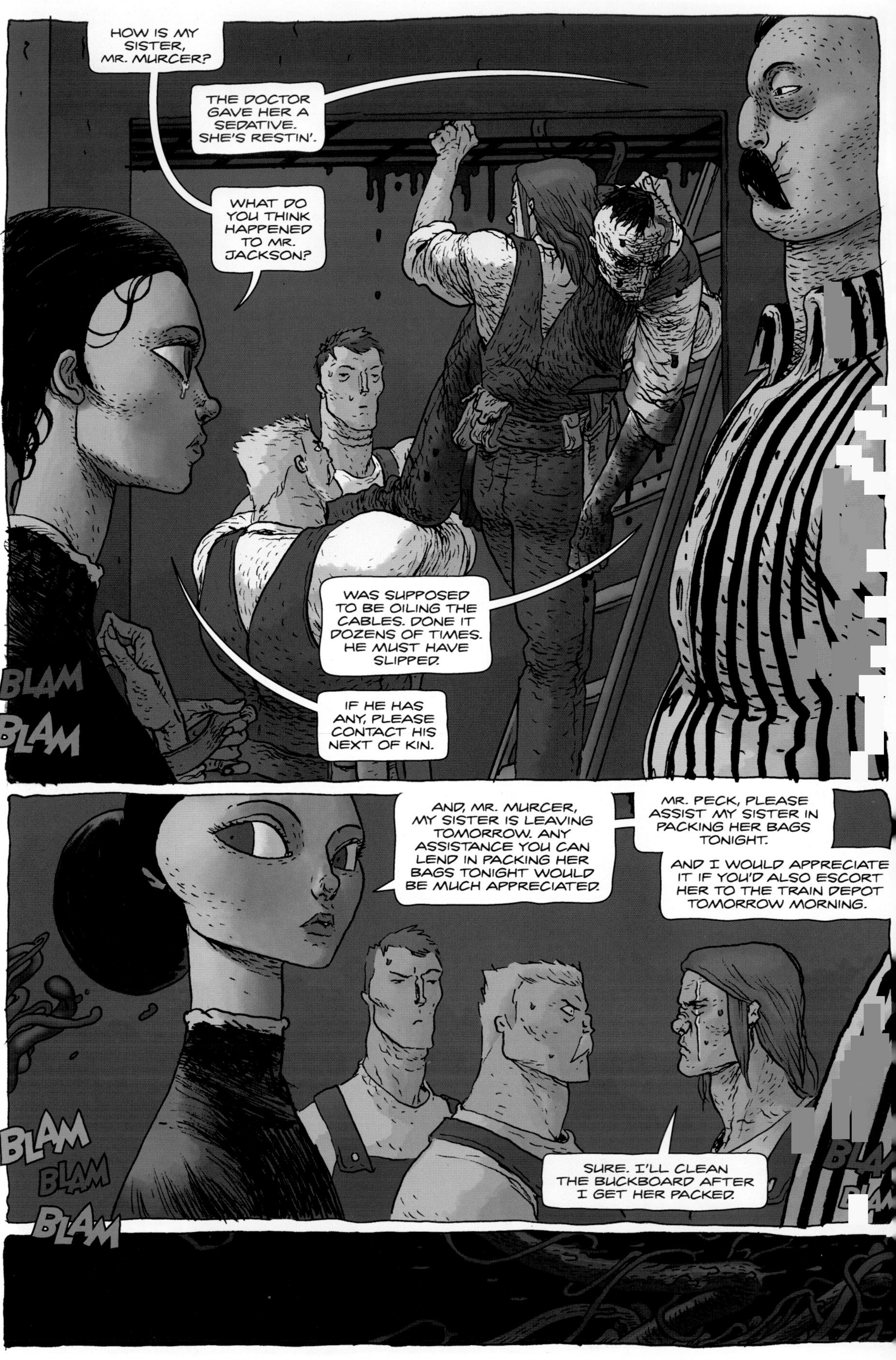
HOW IS MY SISTER, MR. MURCER?
THE DOCTOR GAVE HER A SEDATIVE. SHE'S RESTIN'.
WHAT DO YOU THINK HAPPENED TO MR. JACKSON?
WAS SUPPOSED TO BE OILING THE CABLES. DONE IT DOZENS OF TIMES. HE MUST HAVE SLIPPED.
IF HE HAS ANY, PLEASE CONTACT HIS NEXT OF KIN.
BLAM
BLAM
AND, MR. MURCER, MY SISTER IS LEAVING TOMORROW. ANY ASSISTANCE YOU CAN LEND IN PACKING HER BAGS TONIGHT WOULD BE MUCH APPRECIATED.
MR. PECK, PLEASE ASSIST MY SISTER IN PACKING HER BAGS TONIGHT.
AND I WOULD APPRECIATE IT IF YOU'D ALSO ESCORT HER TO THE TRAIN DEPOT TOMORROW MORNING.
SURE. I'LL CLEAN THE BUCKBOARD AFTER I GET HER PACKED.
BLAM
BLAM
BLAM

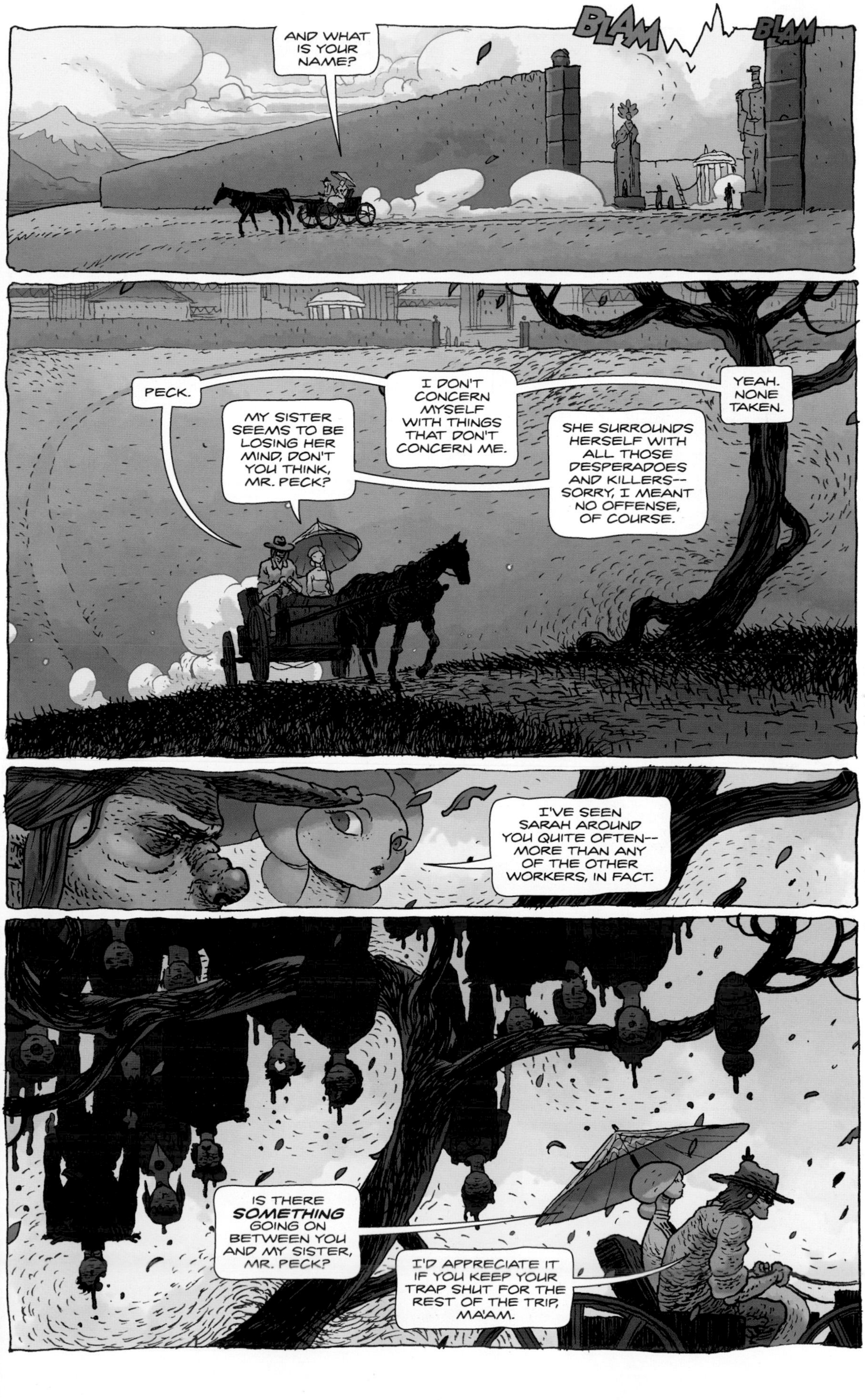
AND WHAT IS YOUR NAME?
BLAM
BLAM
PECK.
MY SISTER SEEMS TO BE LOSING HER MIND, DON'T YOU THINK, MR. PECK?
I DON'T CONCERN MYSELF WITH THINGS THAT DON'T CONCERN ME.
SHE SURROUNDS HERSELF WITH ALL THOSE DESPERADOES AND KILLERS-- SORRY, I MEANT NO OFFENSE, OF COURSE.
YEAH. NONE TAKEN.
I'VE SEEN SARAH AROUND YOU QUITE OFTEN-- MORE THAN ANY OF THE OTHER WORKERS, IN FACT.
IS THERE *SOMETHING* GOING ON BETWEEN YOU AND MY SISTER, MR. PECK?
I'D APPRECIATE IT IF YOU KEEP YOUR TRAP SHUT FOR THE REST OF THE TRIP, MA'AM.

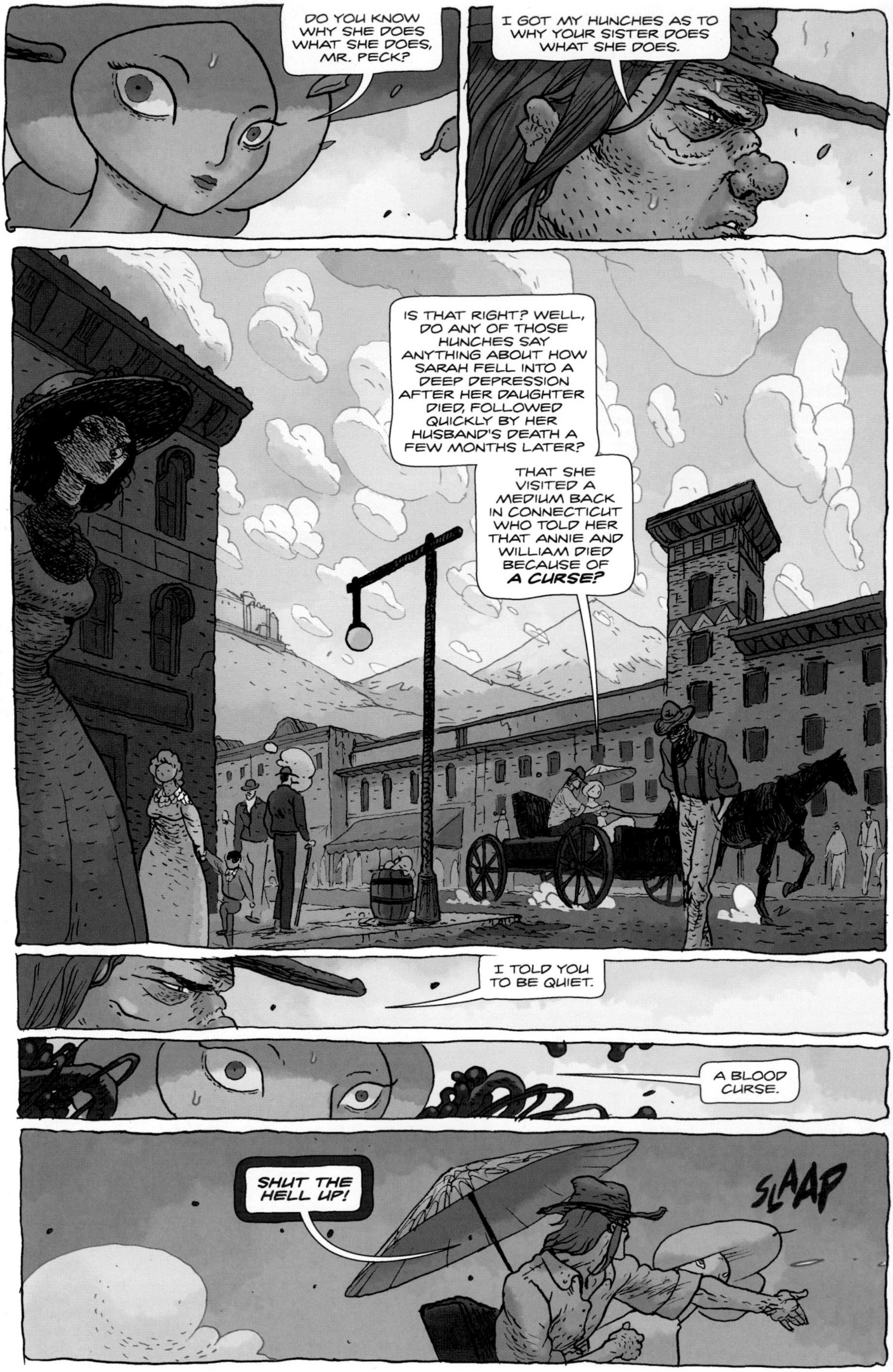
DO YOU KNOW WHY SHE DOES WHAT SHE DOES, MR. PECK?
I GOT MY HUNCHES AS TO WHY YOUR SISTER DOES WHAT SHE DOES.
IS THAT RIGHT? WELL, DO ANY OF THOSE HUNCHES SAY ANYTHING ABOUT HOW SARAH FELL INTO A DEEP DEPRESSION AFTER HER DAUGHTER DIED, FOLLOWED QUICKLY BY HER HUSBAND'S DEATH A FEW MONTHS LATER?
THAT SHE VISITED A MEDIUM BACK IN CONNECTICUT WHO TOLD HER THAT ANNIE AND WILLIAM DIED BECAUSE OF ***A CURSE?***
I TOLD YOU TO BE QUIET.
A BLOOD CURSE.
SHUT THE HELL UP!
SLAAP

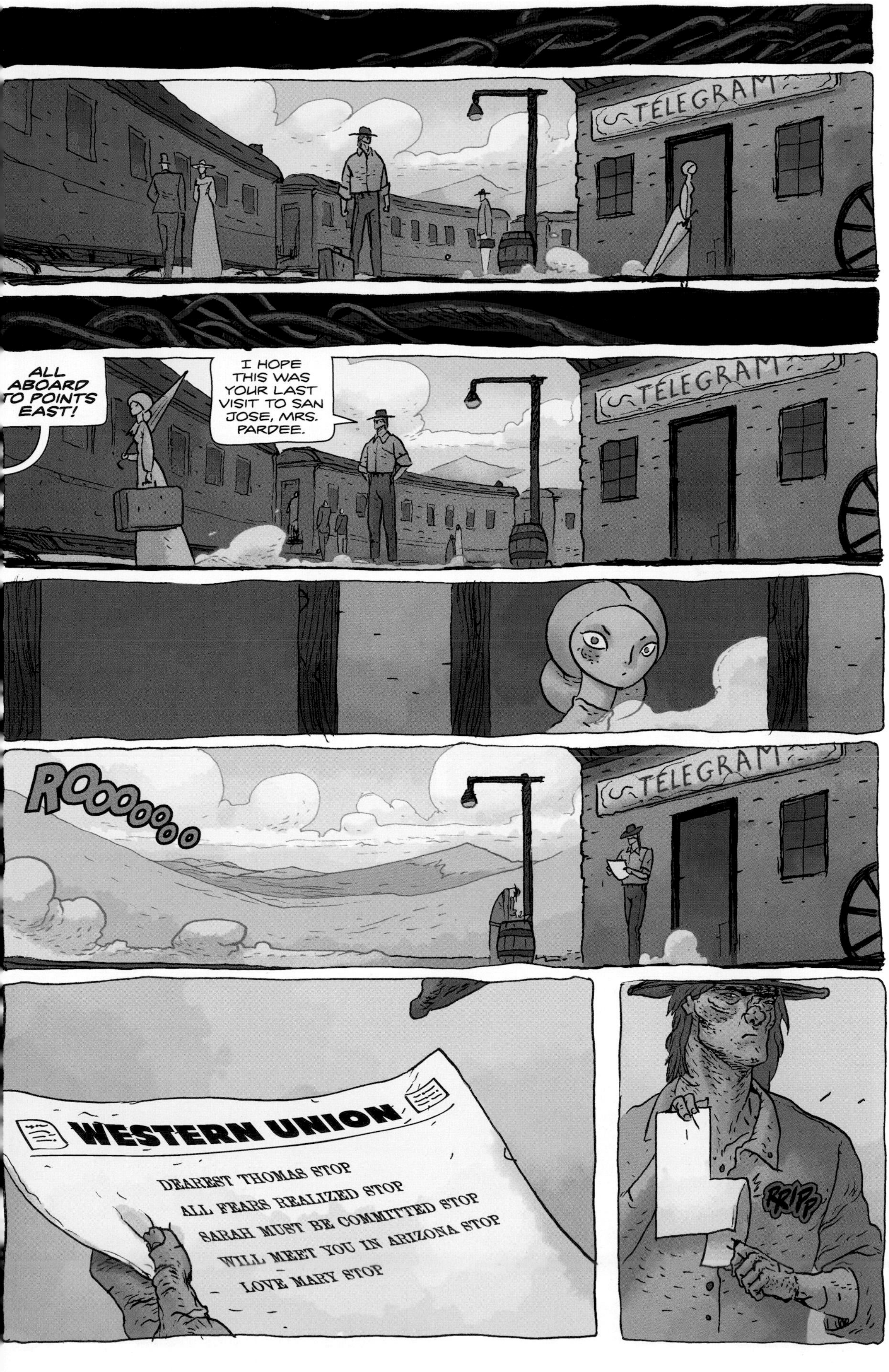
TELEGRAM
ALL ABOARD TO POINTS EAST!
I HOPE THIS WAS YOUR LAST VISIT TO SAN JOSE, MRS. PARDEE.
ROOOOOOOO
WESTERN UNION
DEAREST THOMAS STOP
ALL FEARS REALIZED STOP
SARAH MUST BE COMMITTED STOP
WILL MEET YOU IN ARIZONA STOP
LOVE MARY STOP
RRIPP

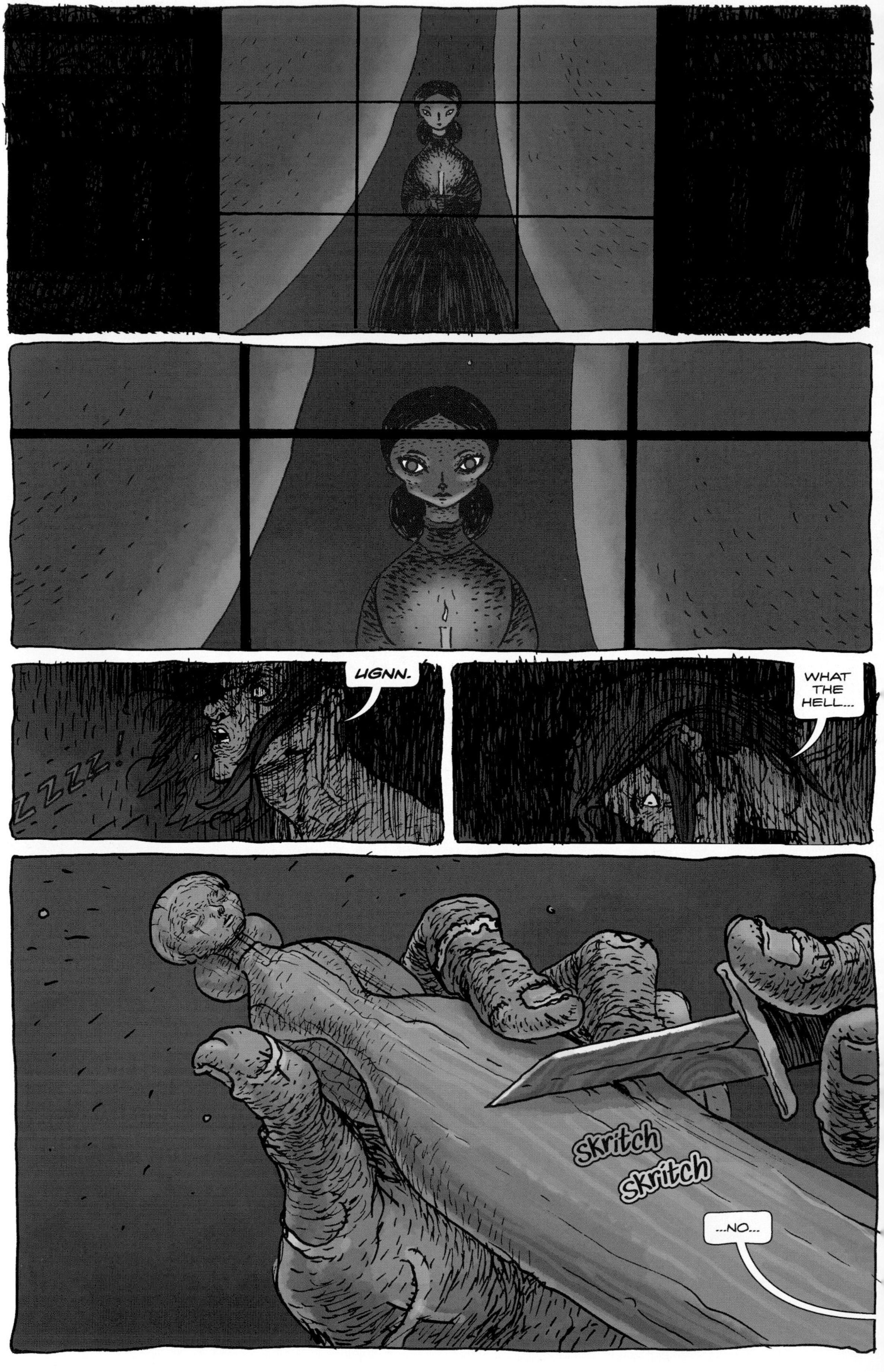
UGNN.
ZZZZ!
WHAT THE HELL...
SKRITCH
SKRITCH
...NO...

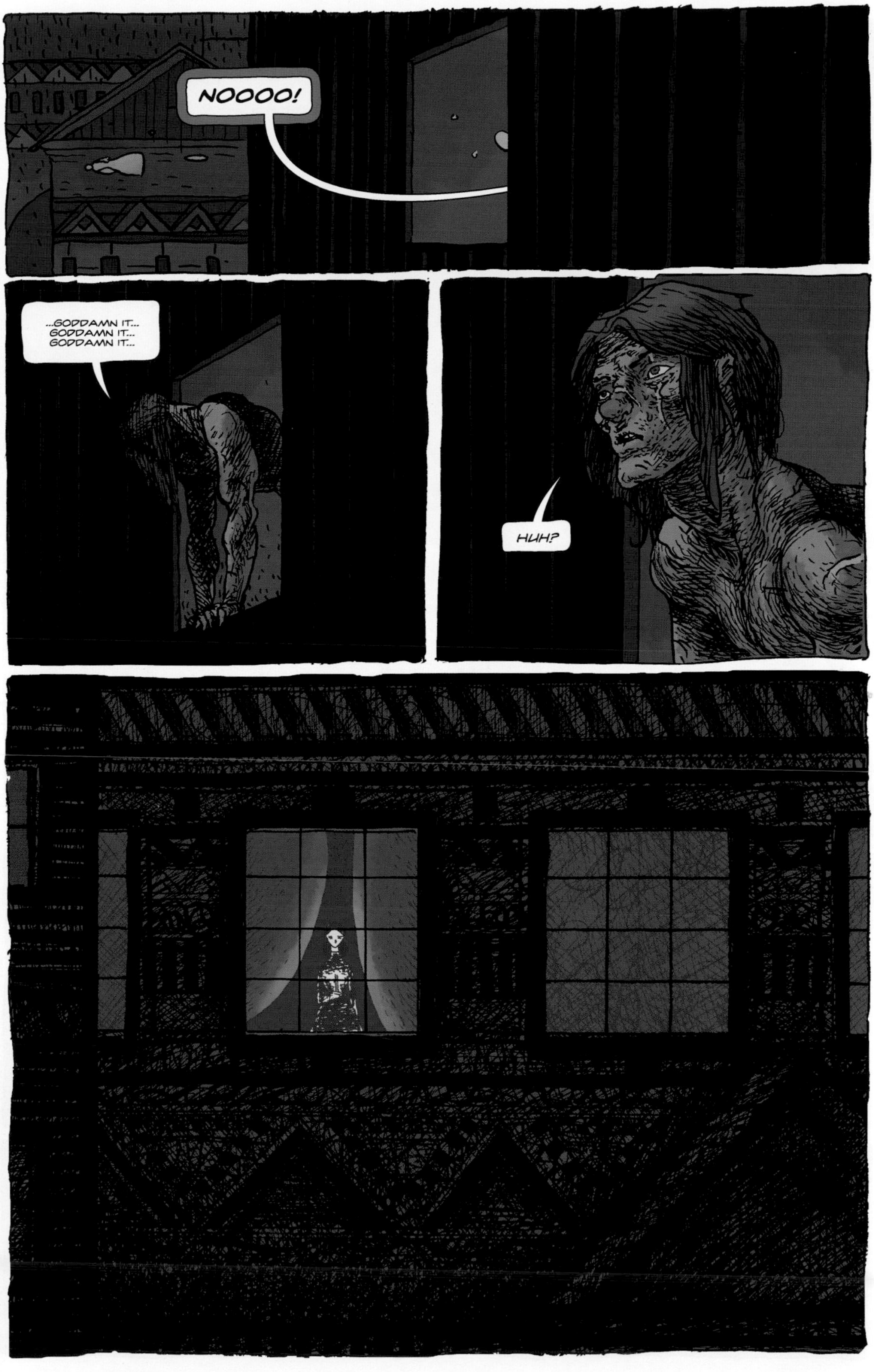
NOOOO!
...GODDAMN IT...
GODDAMN IT...
GODDAMN IT...
HUH?

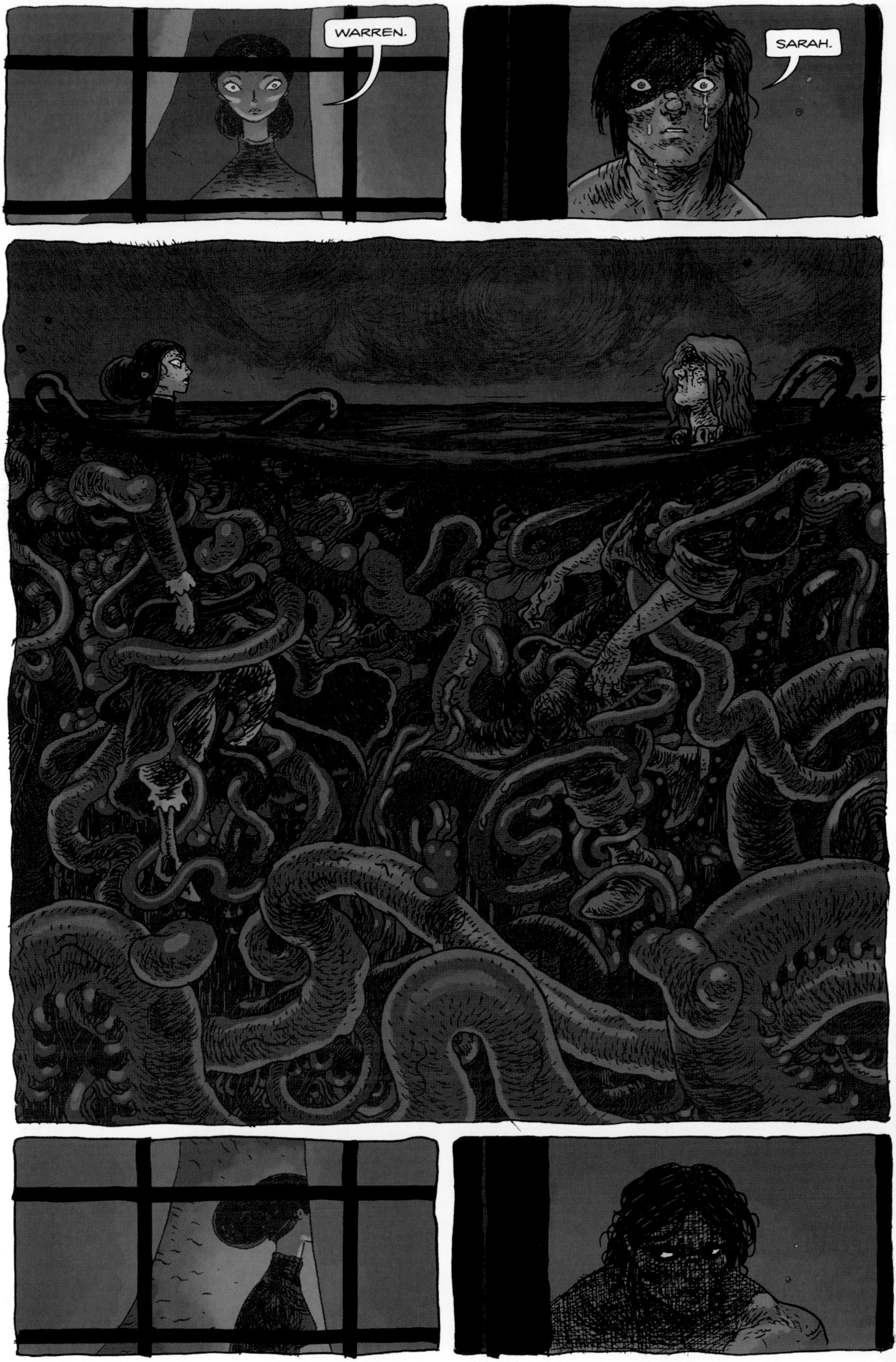
WARREN.
SARAH.

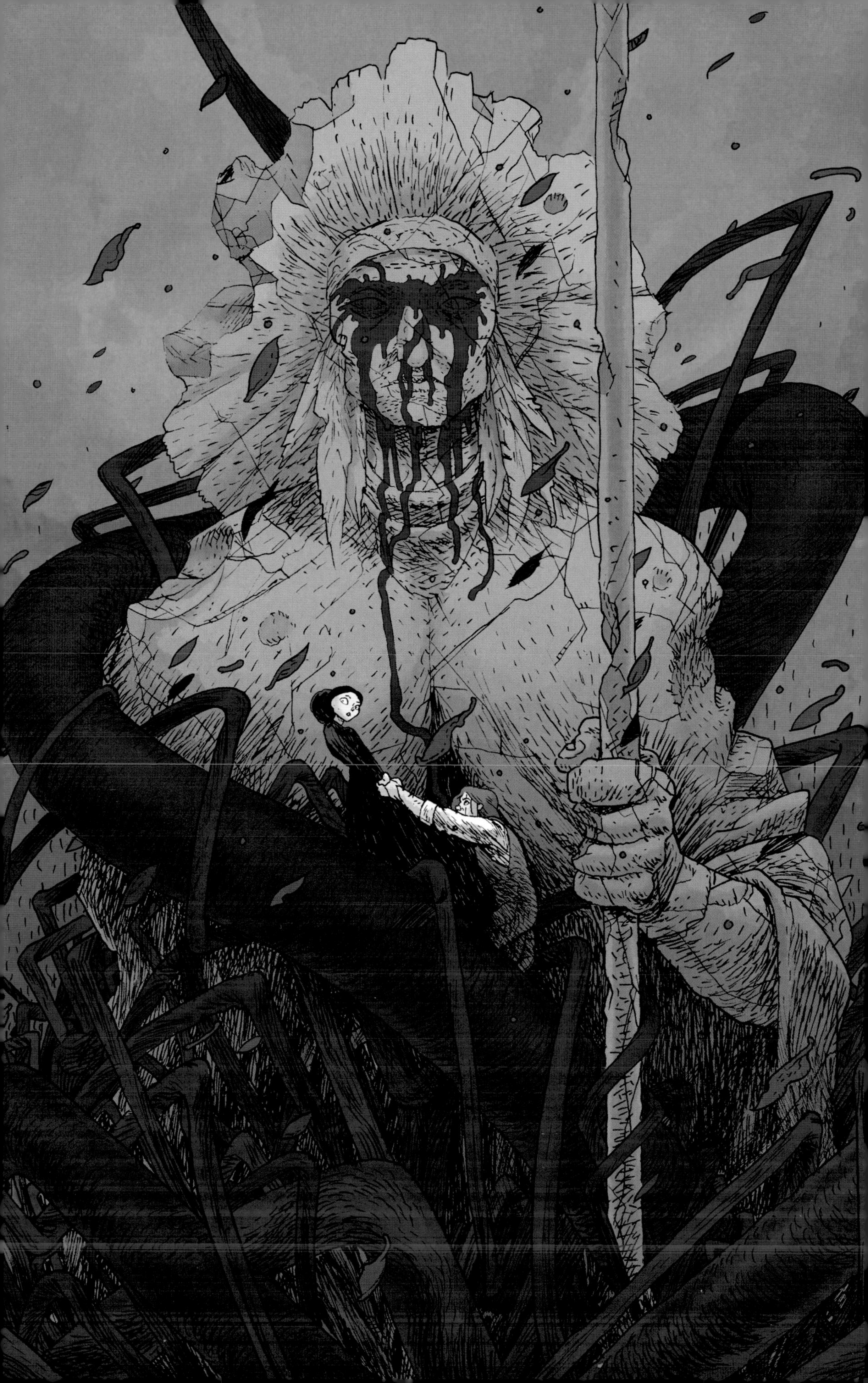

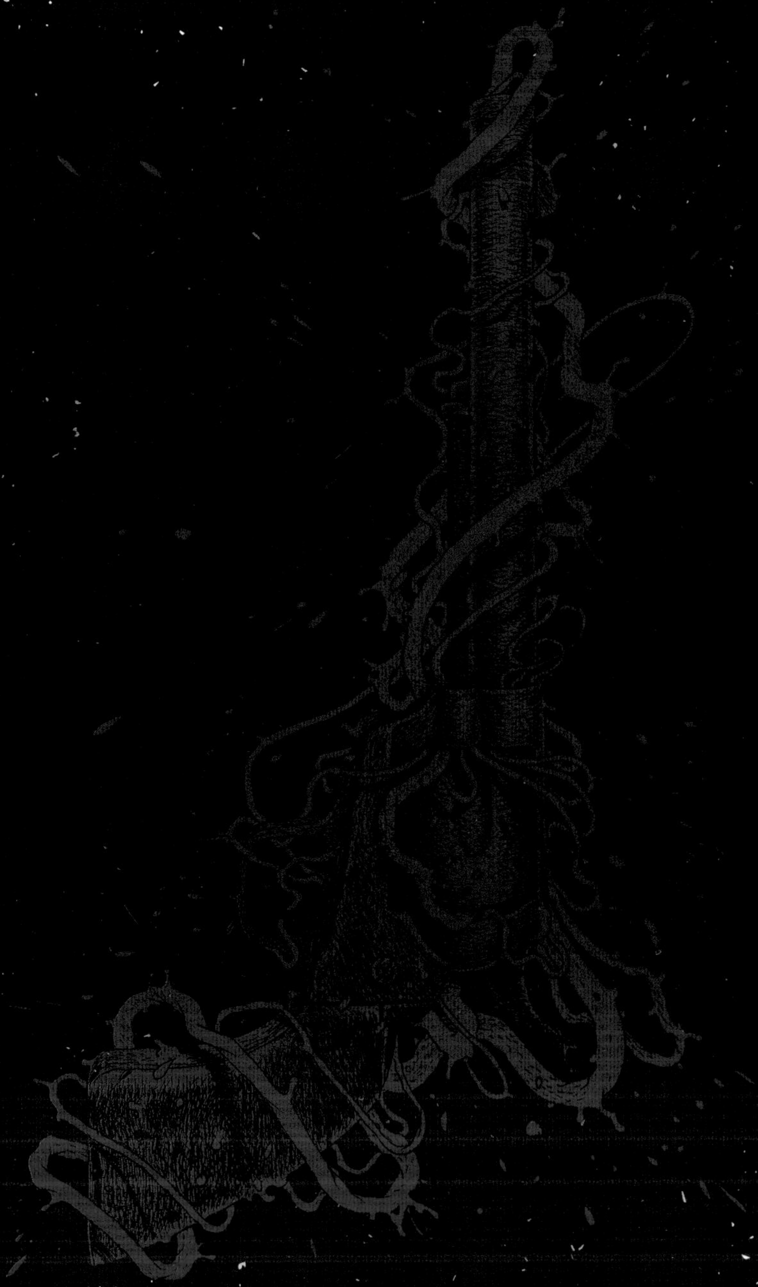

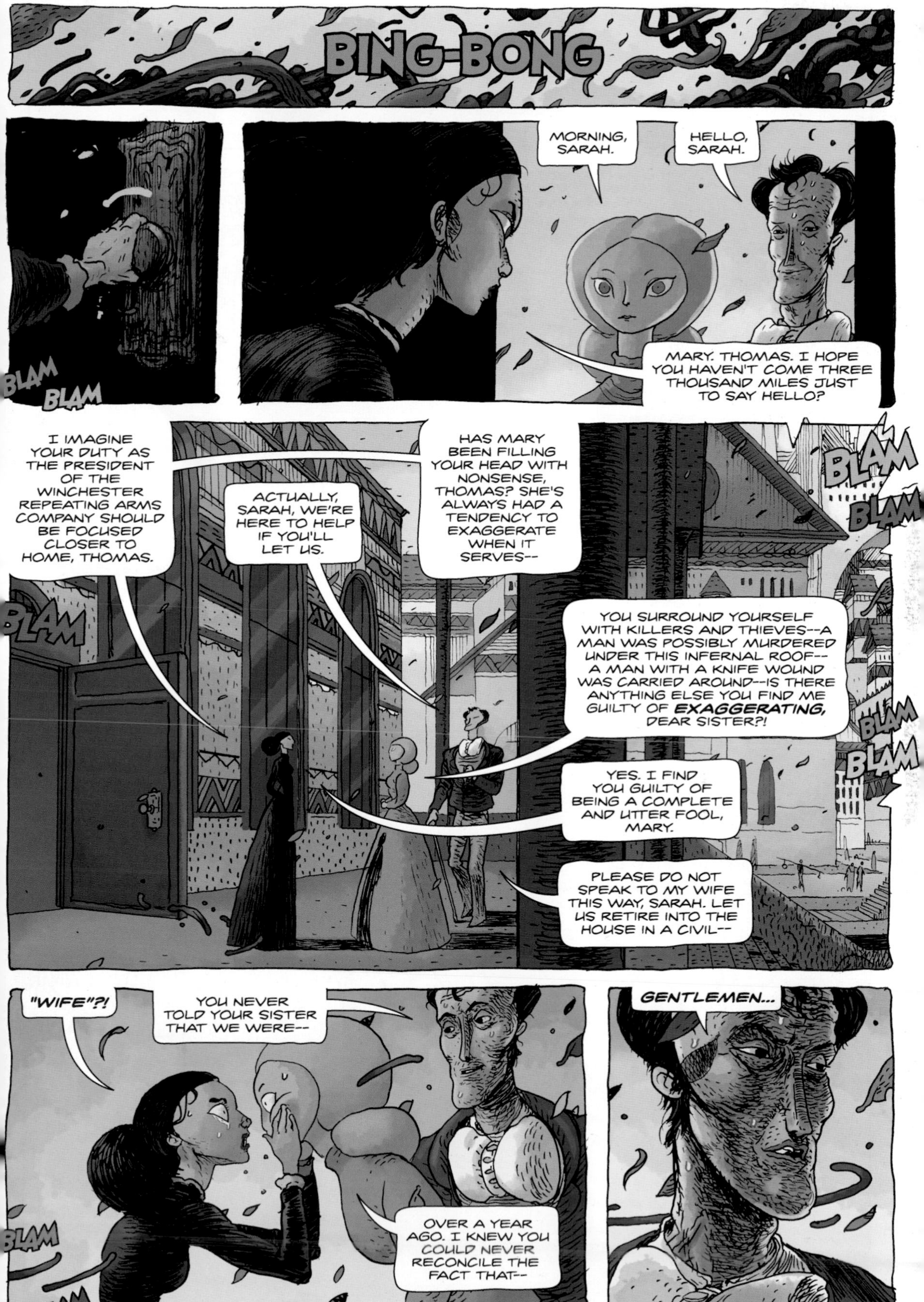
BING-BONG
BLAM
BLAM
MORNING, SARAH.
HELLO, SARAH.
MARY. THOMAS. I HOPE YOU HAVEN'T COME THREE THOUSAND MILES JUST TO SAY HELLO?
BLAM
BLAM
I IMAGINE YOUR DUTY AS THE PRESIDENT OF THE WINCHESTER REPEATING ARMS COMPANY SHOULD BE FOCUSED CLOSER TO HOME, THOMAS.
ACTUALLY, SARAH, WE'RE HERE TO HELP IF YOU'LL LET US.
HAS MARY BEEN FILLING YOUR HEAD WITH NONSENSE, THOMAS? SHE'S ALWAYS HAD A TENDENCY TO EXAGGERATE WHEN IT SERVES--
BLAM
YOU SURROUND YOURSELF WITH KILLERS AND THIEVES--A MAN WAS POSSIBLY MURDERED UNDER THIS INFERNAL ROOF--A MAN WITH A KNIFE WOUND WAS CARRIED AROUND--IS THERE ANYTHING ELSE YOU FIND ME GUILTY OF *EXAGGERATING,* DEAR SISTER?!
BLAM
BLAM
YES. I FIND YOU GUILTY OF BEING A COMPLETE AND UTTER FOOL, MARY.
PLEASE DO NOT SPEAK TO MY WIFE THIS WAY, SARAH. LET US RETIRE INTO THE HOUSE IN A CIVIL--
"WIFE"?!
YOU NEVER TOLD YOUR SISTER THAT WE WERE--
OVER A YEAR AGO. I KNEW YOU COULD NEVER RECONCILE THE FACT THAT--
BLAM
BLAM
GENTLEMEN...

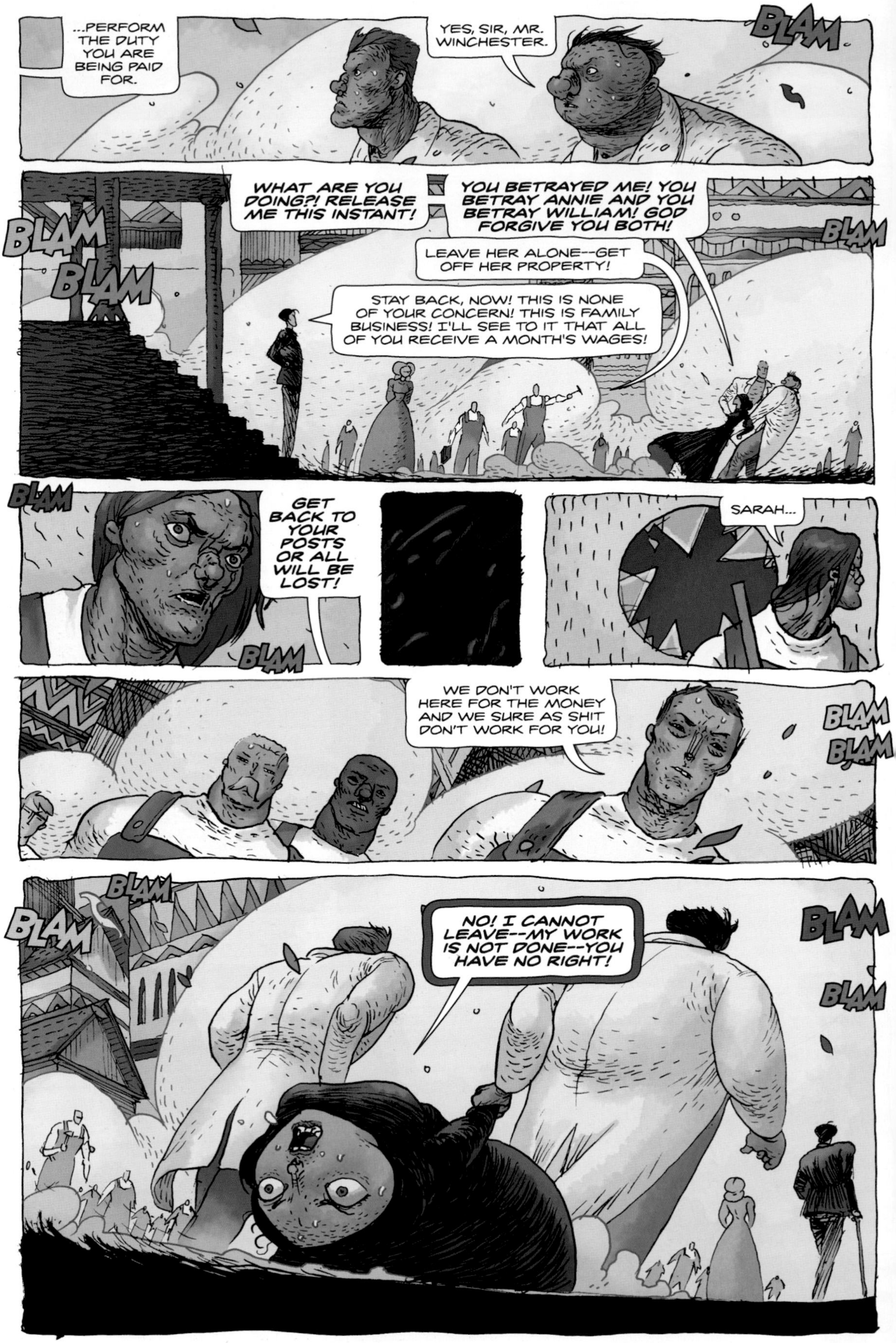
...PERFORM THE DUTY YOU ARE BEING PAID FOR.
YES, SIR, MR. WINCHESTER.
BLAM
BLAM
BLAM
WHAT ARE YOU DOING?! RELEASE ME THIS INSTANT!
YOU BETRAYED ME! YOU BETRAY ANNIE AND YOU BETRAY WILLIAM! GOD FORGIVE YOU BOTH!
BLAM
LEAVE HER ALONE--GET OFF HER PROPERTY!
STAY BACK, NOW! THIS IS NONE OF YOUR CONCERN! THIS IS FAMILY BUSINESS! I'LL SEE TO IT THAT ALL OF YOU RECEIVE A MONTH'S WAGES!
BLAM
GET BACK TO YOUR POSTS OR ALL WILL BE LOST!
BLAM
SARAH...
WE DON'T WORK HERE FOR THE MONEY AND WE SURE AS SHIT DON'T WORK FOR YOU!
BLAM
BLAM
BLAM
BLAM
NO! I CANNOT LEAVE--MY WORK IS NOT DONE--YOU HAVE NO RIGHT!
BLAM
BLAM

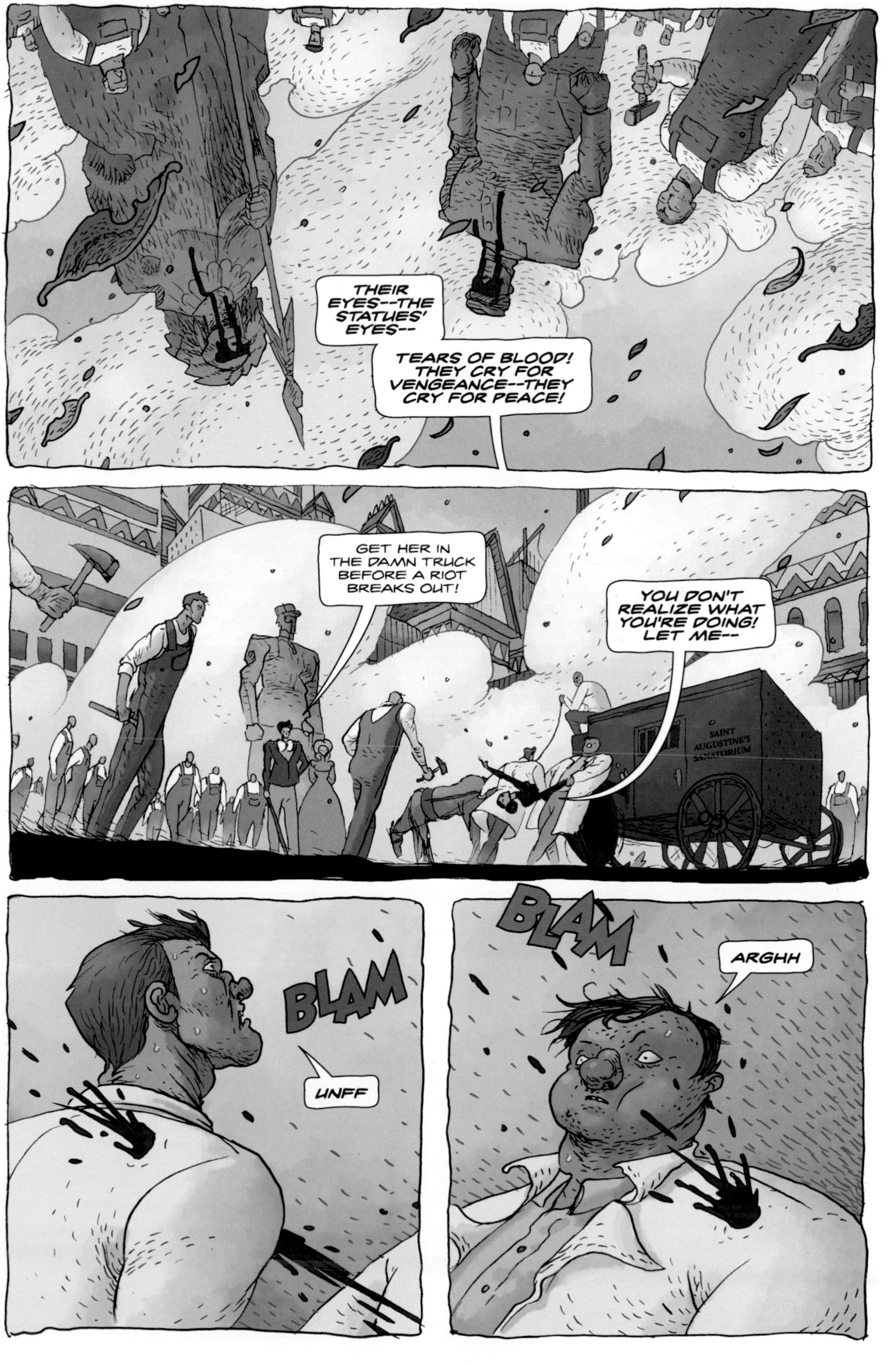
THEIR EYES--THE STATUES' EYES--
TEARS OF BLOOD! THEY CRY FOR VENGEANCE--THEY CRY FOR PEACE!
GET HER IN THE DAMN TRUCK BEFORE A RIOT BREAKS OUT!
YOU DON'T REALIZE WHAT YOU'RE DOING! LET ME--
SAINT AUGUSTINE'S SANATORIUM
BLAM
UNFF
BLAM
ARGHH

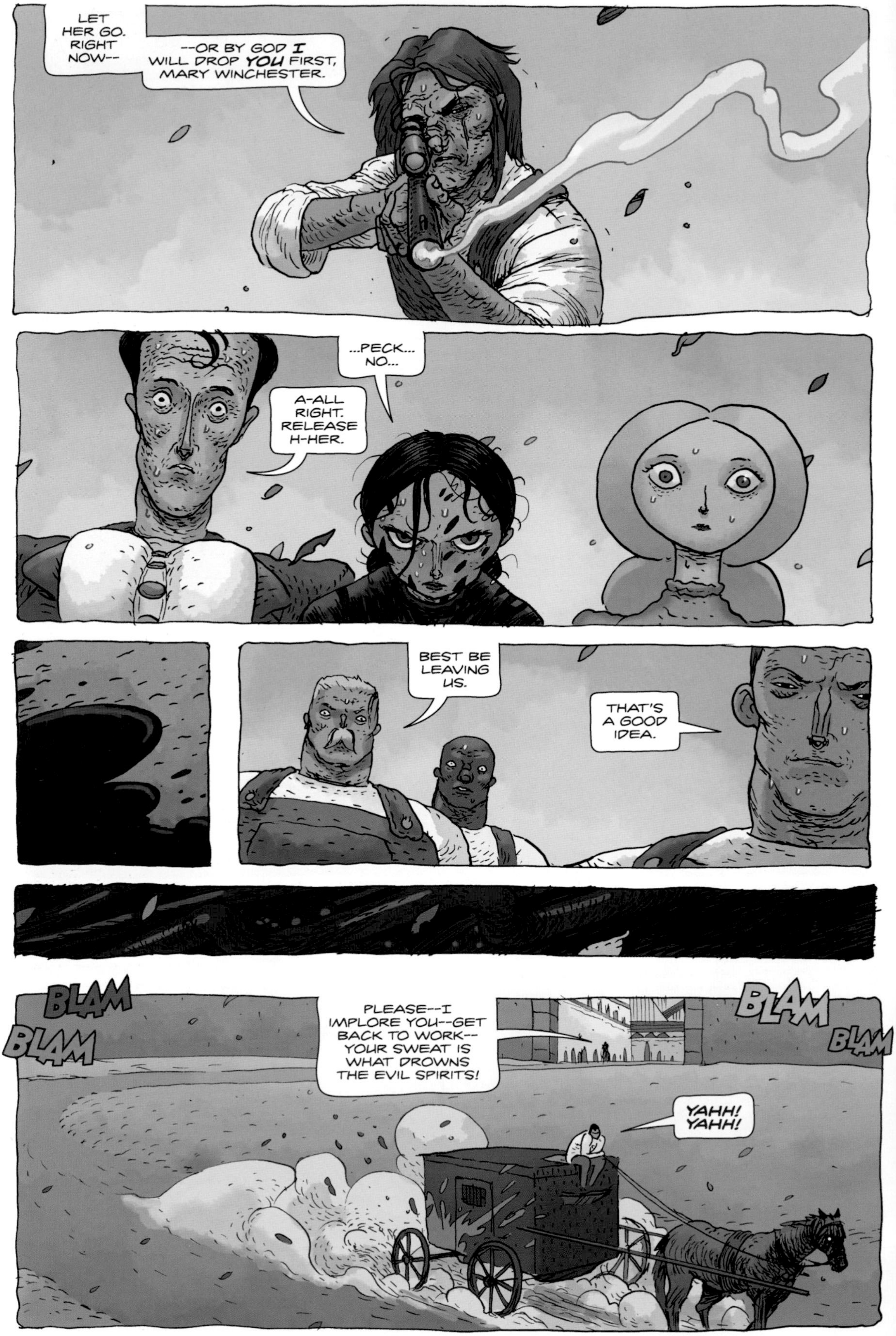
LET HER GO. RIGHT NOW--
--OR BY GOD I WILL DROP YOU FIRST, MARY WINCHESTER.
...PECK... NO...
A-ALL RIGHT. RELEASE H-HER.
BEST BE LEAVING US.
THAT'S A GOOD IDEA.
BLAM
BLAM
PLEASE--I IMPLORE YOU--GET BACK TO WORK-- YOUR SWEAT IS WHAT DROWNS THE EVIL SPIRITS!
BLAM
BLAM
YAHH! YAHH!

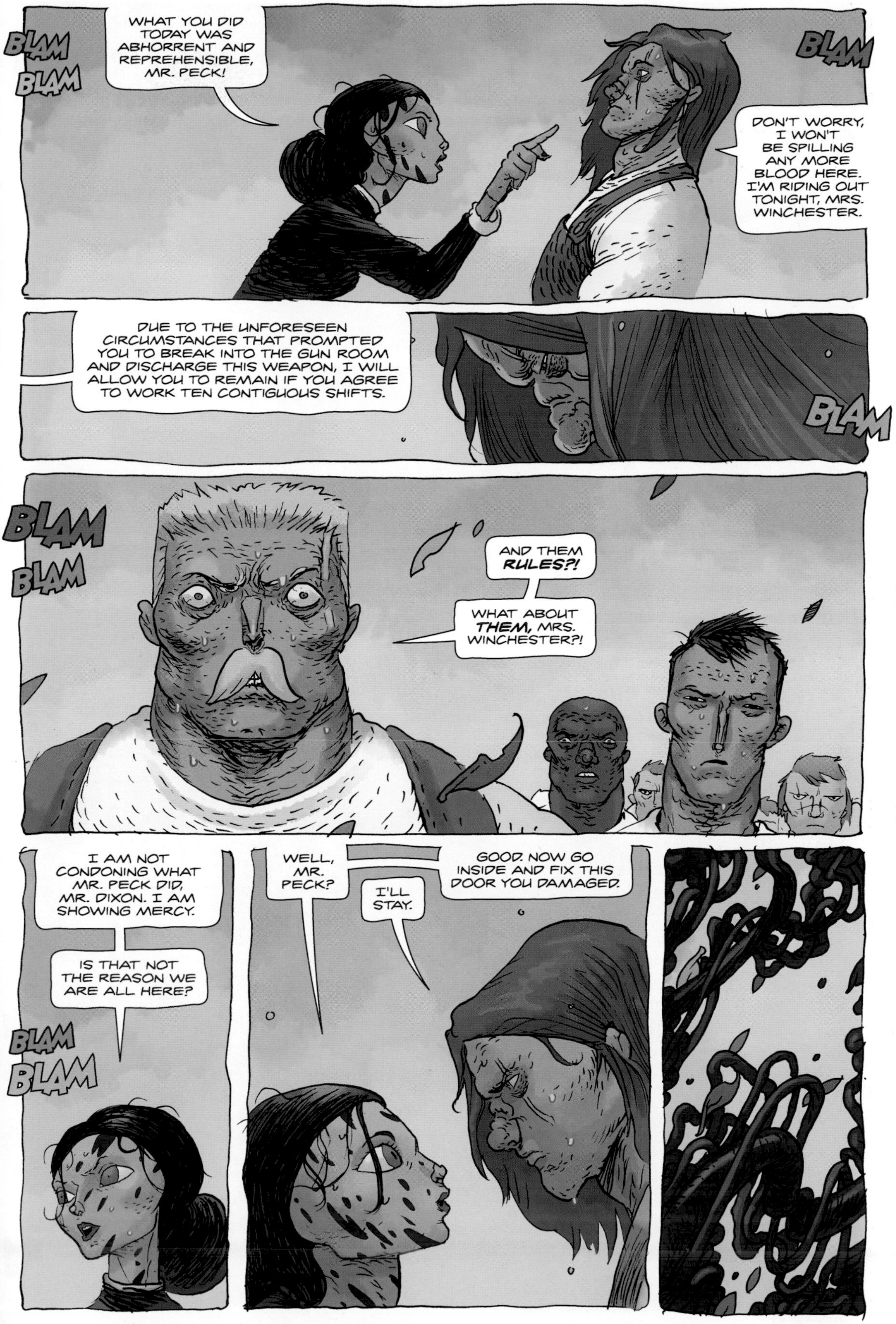
BLAM
BLAM
WHAT YOU DID TODAY WAS ABHORRENT AND REPREHENSIBLE, MR. PECK!
BLAM
DON'T WORRY, I WON'T BE SPILLING ANY MORE BLOOD HERE. I'M RIDING OUT TONIGHT, MRS. WINCHESTER.
DUE TO THE UNFORESEEN CIRCUMSTANCES THAT PROMPTED YOU TO BREAK INTO THE GUN ROOM AND DISCHARGE THIS WEAPON, I WILL ALLOW YOU TO REMAIN IF YOU AGREE TO WORK TEN CONTIGUOUS SHIFTS.
BLAM
BLAM
BLAM
AND THEM RULES?!
WHAT ABOUT THEM, MRS. WINCHESTER?!
I AM NOT CONDONING WHAT MR. PECK DID, MR. DIXON. I AM SHOWING MERCY.
IS THAT NOT THE REASON WE ARE ALL HERE?
BLAM
BLAM
WELL, MR. PECK?
I'LL STAY.
GOOD. NOW GO INSIDE AND FIX THIS DOOR YOU DAMAGED.

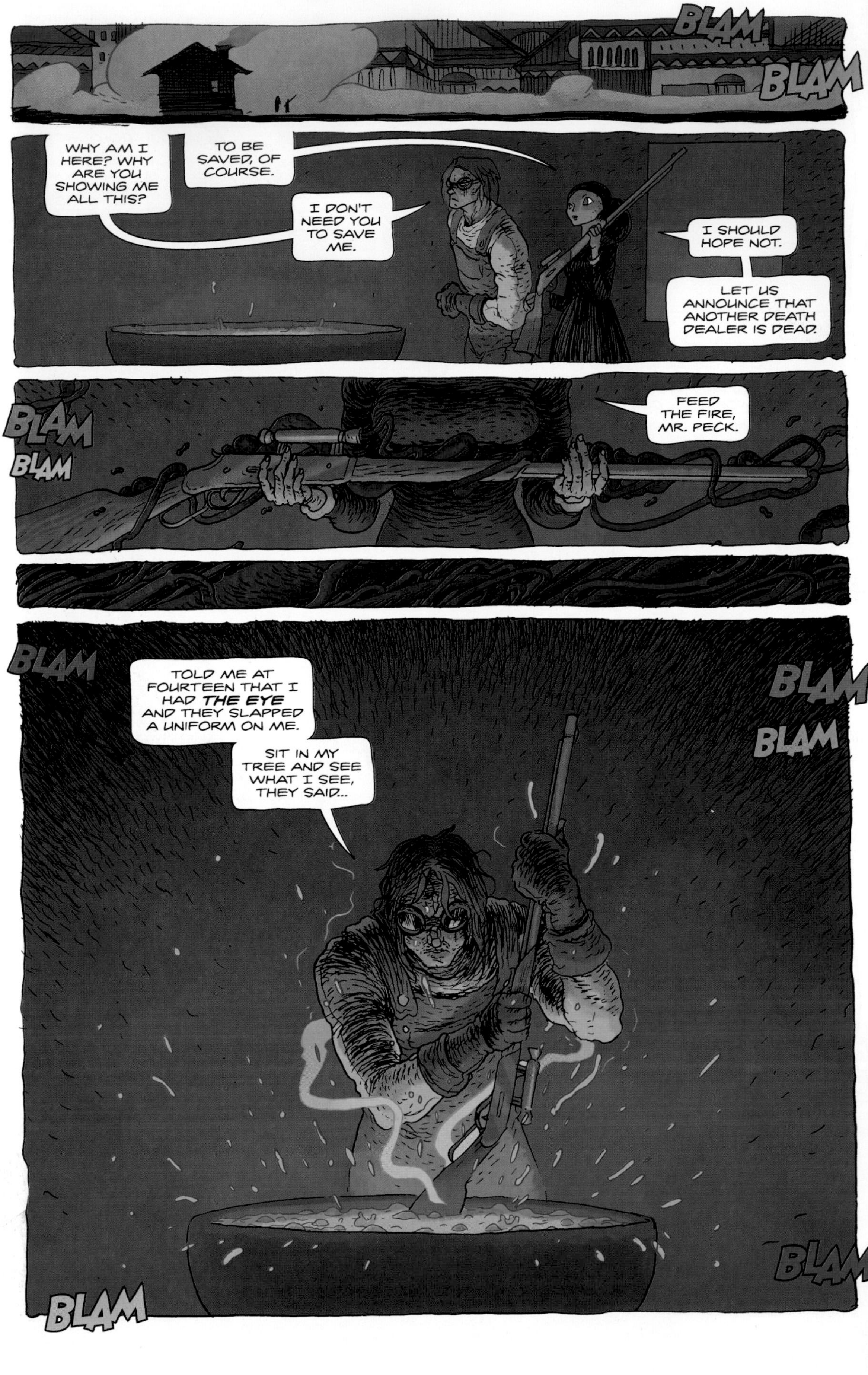
BLAM
BLAM
WHY AM I HERE? WHY ARE YOU SHOWING ME ALL THIS?
TO BE SAVED, OF COURSE.
I DON'T NEED YOU TO SAVE ME.
I SHOULD HOPE NOT.
LET US ANNOUNCE THAT ANOTHER DEATH DEALER IS DEAD.
BLAM
BLAM
FEED THE FIRE, MR. PECK.
BLAM
TOLD ME AT FOURTEEN THAT I HAD THE EYE AND THEY SLAPPED A UNIFORM ON ME.
SIT IN MY TREE AND SEE WHAT I SEE, THEY SAID...
BLAM
BLAM
BLAM
BLAM

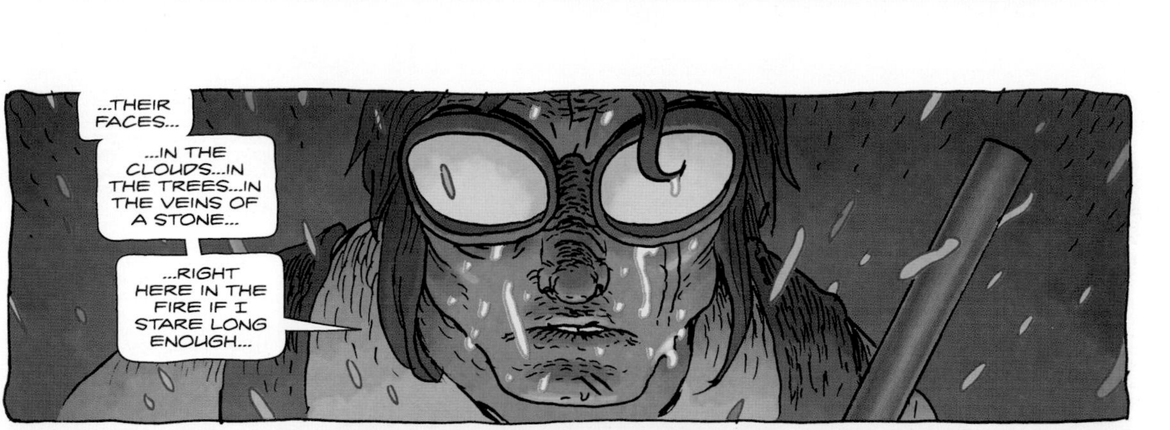
...THEIR FACES...
...IN THE CLOUDS...IN THE TREES...IN THE VEINS OF A STONE...
...RIGHT HERE IN THE FIRE IF I STARE LONG ENOUGH...

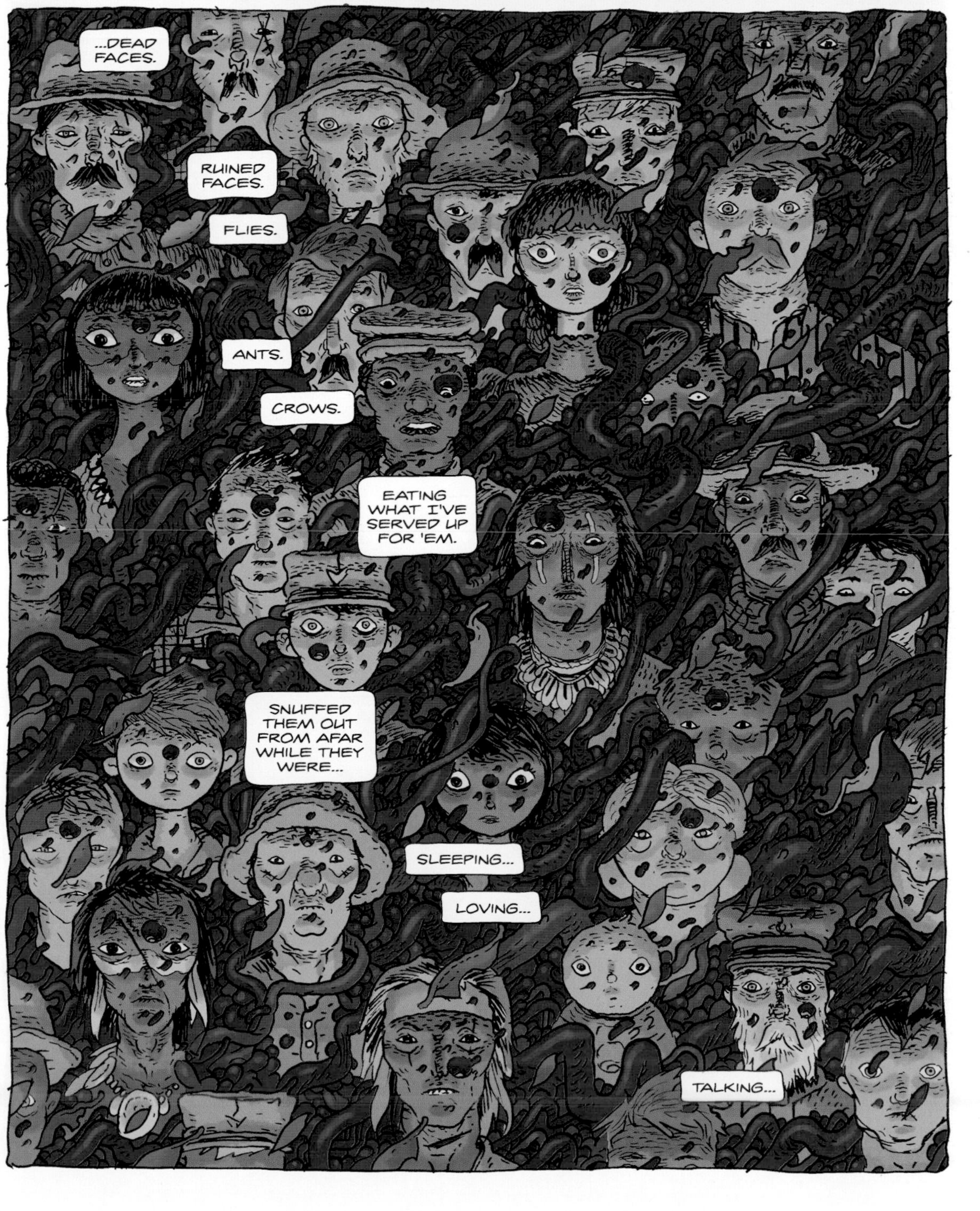
...DEAD FACES.
RUINED FACES.
FLIES.
ANTS.
CROWS.
EATING WHAT I'VE SERVED UP FOR 'EM.
SNUFFED THEM OUT FROM AFAR WHILE THEY WERE...
SLEEPING...
LOVING...
TALKING...

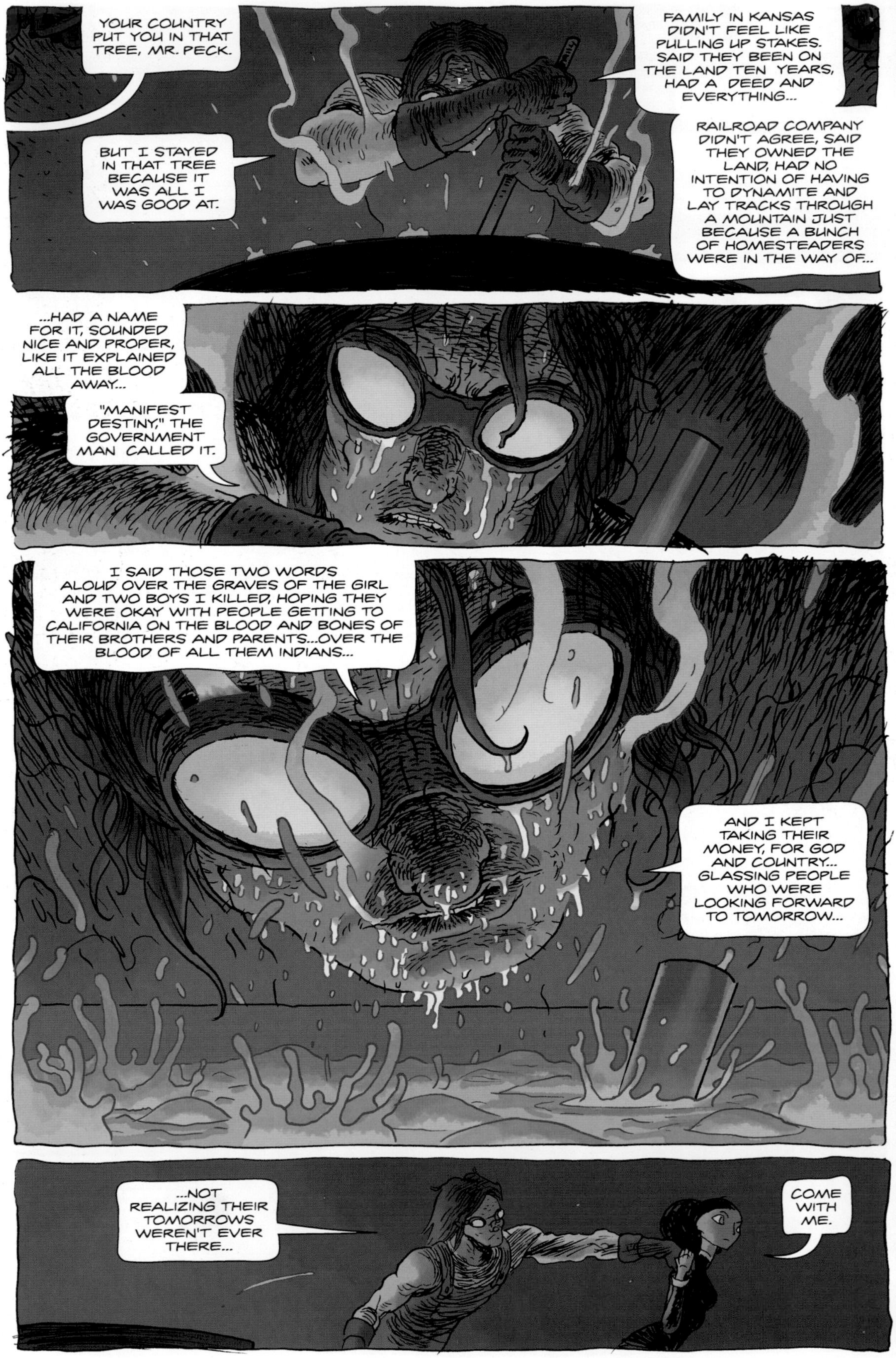
YOUR COUNTRY PUT YOU IN THAT TREE, MR. PECK.
BUT I STAYED IN THAT TREE BECAUSE IT WAS ALL I WAS GOOD AT.
FAMILY IN KANSAS DIDN'T FEEL LIKE PULLING UP STAKES. SAID THEY BEEN ON THE LAND TEN YEARS, HAD A DEED AND EVERYTHING...
RAILROAD COMPANY DIDN'T AGREE, SAID THEY OWNED THE LAND, HAD NO INTENTION OF HAVING TO DYNAMITE AND LAY TRACKS THROUGH A MOUNTAIN JUST BECAUSE A BUNCH OF HOMESTEADERS WERE IN THE WAY OF...
...HAD A NAME FOR IT, SOUNDED NICE AND PROPER, LIKE IT EXPLAINED ALL THE BLOOD AWAY...
"MANIFEST DESTINY," THE GOVERNMENT MAN CALLED IT.
I SAID THOSE TWO WORDS ALOUD OVER THE GRAVES OF THE GIRL AND TWO BOYS I KILLED, HOPING THEY WERE OKAY WITH PEOPLE GETTING TO CALIFORNIA ON THE BLOOD AND BONES OF THEIR BROTHERS AND PARENTS...OVER THE BLOOD OF ALL THEM INDIANS...
AND I KEPT TAKING THEIR MONEY, FOR GOD AND COUNTRY... GLASSING PEOPLE WHO WERE LOOKING FORWARD TO TOMORROW...
...NOT REALIZING THEIR TOMORROWS WEREN'T EVER THERE...
COME WITH ME.

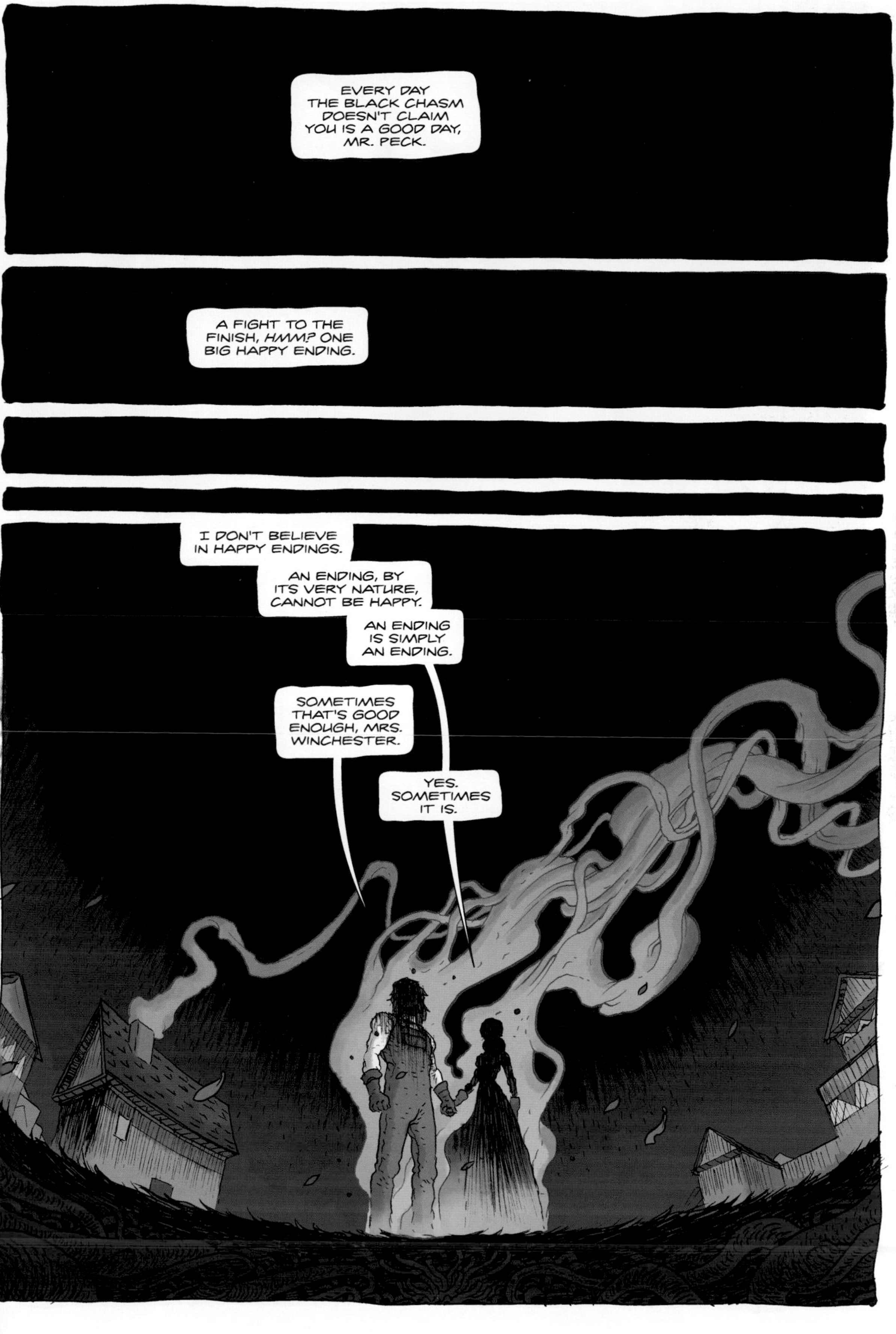
EVERY DAY THE BLACK CHASM DOESN'T CLAIM YOU IS A GOOD DAY, MR. PECK.
A FIGHT TO THE FINISH, *HMM?* ONE BIG HAPPY ENDING.
I DON'T BELIEVE IN HAPPY ENDINGS.
AN ENDING, BY ITS VERY NATURE, CANNOT BE HAPPY.
AN ENDING IS SIMPLY AN ENDING.
SOMETIMES THAT'S GOOD ENOUGH, MRS. WINCHESTER.
YES. SOMETIMES IT IS.

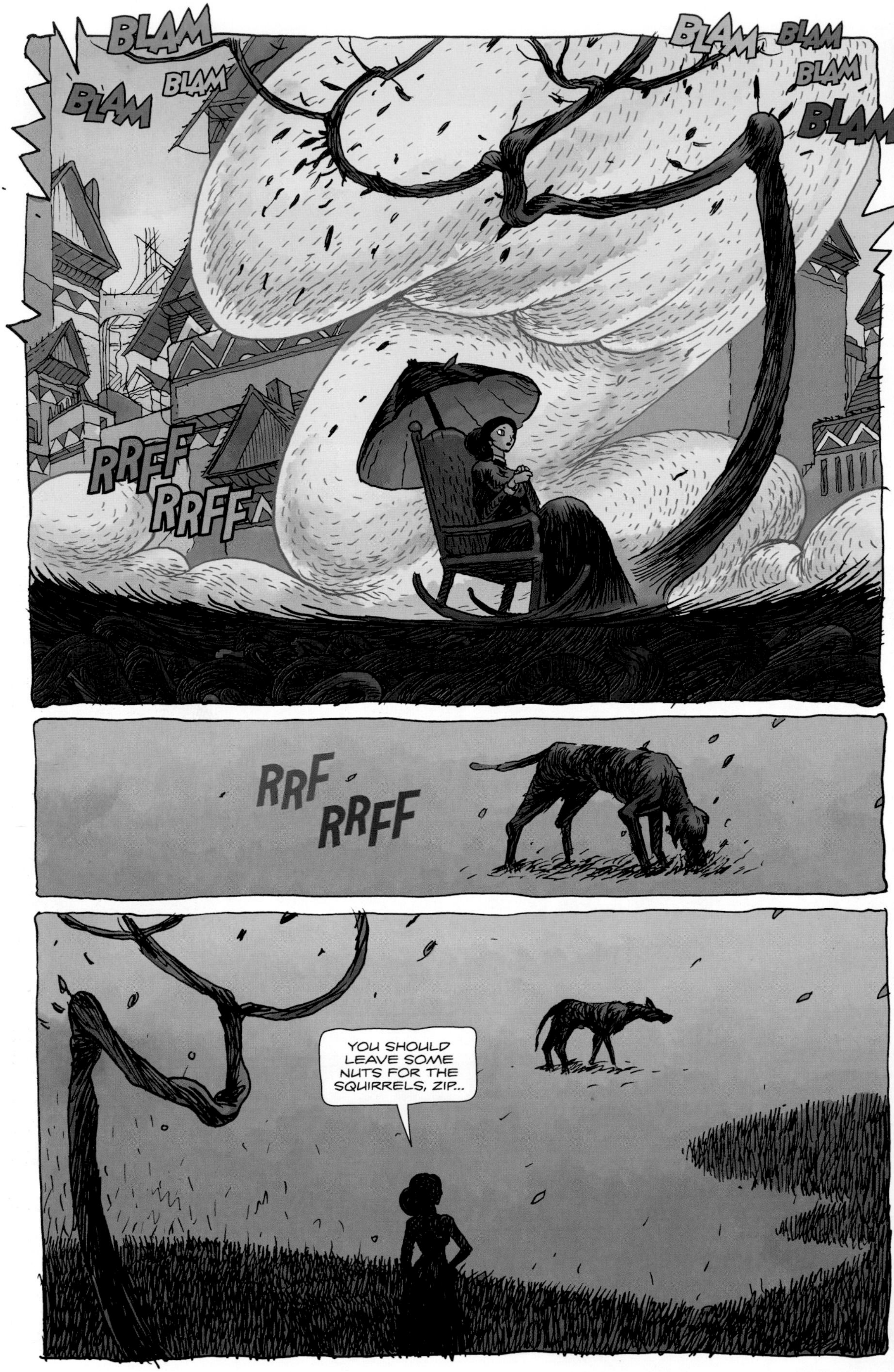
BLAM
BLAM
BLAM
BLAM
BLAM
BLAM
BLAM
RRFF
RRFF
RRF
RRFF
YOU SHOULD LEAVE SOME NUTS FOR THE SQUIRRELS, ZIP...

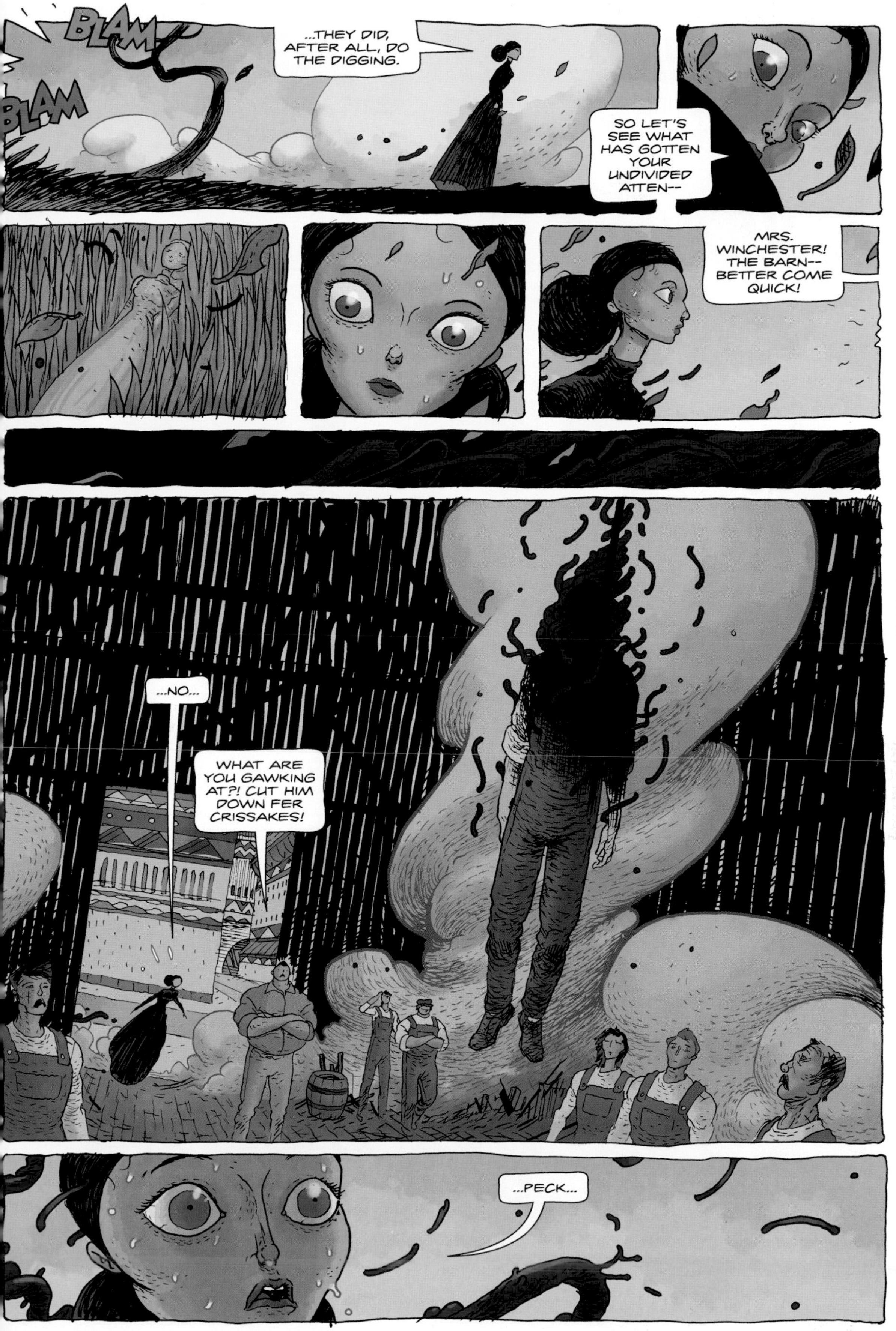
BLAM
BLAM
...THEY DID, AFTER ALL, DO THE DIGGING.
SO LET'S SEE WHAT HAS GOTTEN YOUR UNDIVIDED ATTEN--
MRS. WINCHESTER! THE BARN-- BETTER COME QUICK!
...NO...
WHAT ARE YOU GAWKING AT?! CUT HIM DOWN FER CRISSAKES!
...PECK...

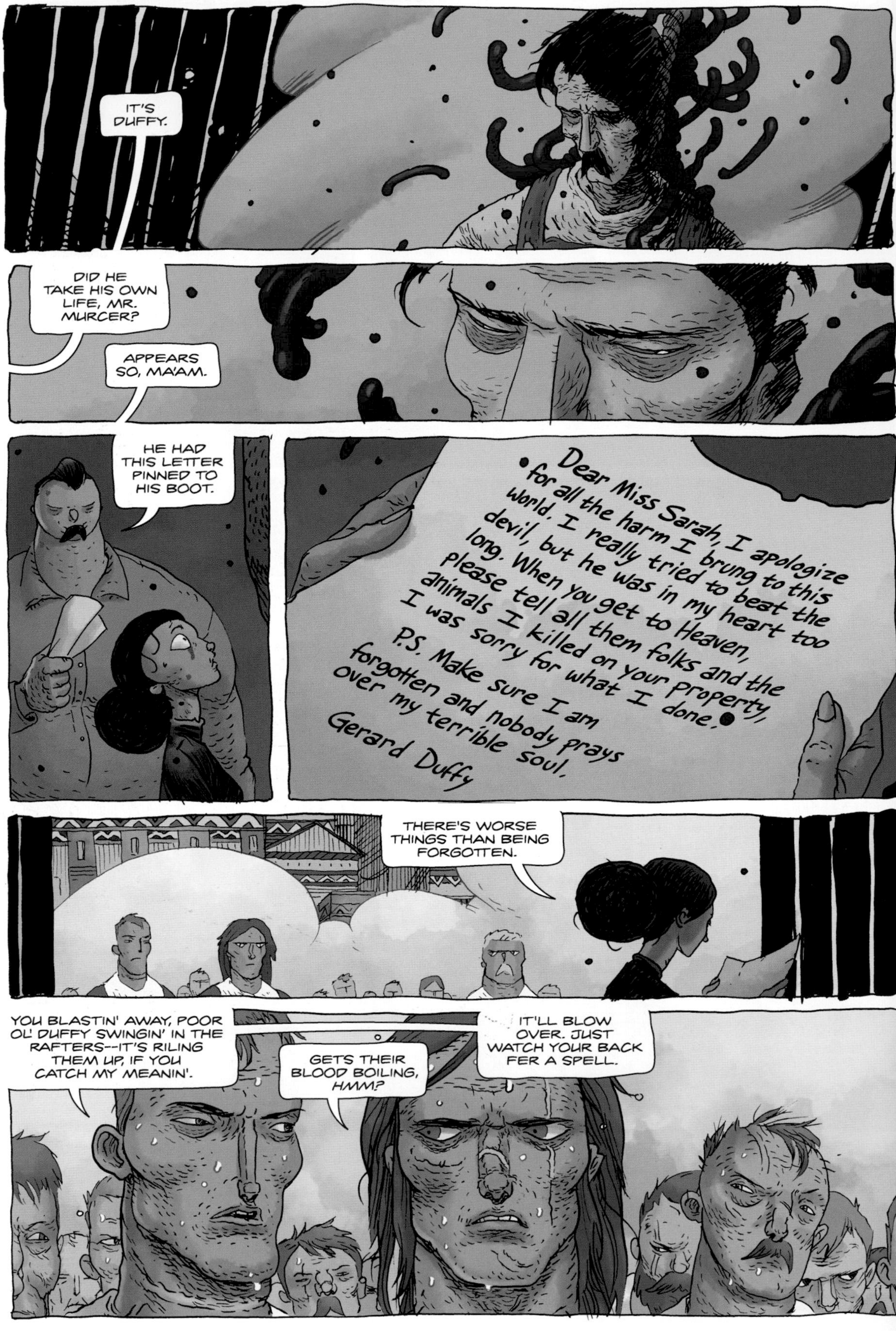
IT'S DUFFY.
DID HE TAKE HIS OWN LIFE, MR. MURCER?
APPEARS SO, MA'AM.
HE HAD THIS LETTER PINNED TO HIS BOOT.
Dear Miss Sarah, I apologize for all the harm I brung to this world. I really tried to beat the devil, but he was in my heart too long. When you get to Heaven, please tell all them folks and the animals I killed on your property, I was sorry for what I done.
P.S. Make sure I am forgotten and nobody prays over my terrible soul.
Gerard Duffy
THERE'S WORSE THINGS THAN BEING FORGOTTEN.
YOU BLASTIN' AWAY, POOR OL' DUFFY SWINGIN' IN THE RAFTERS--IT'S RILING THEM UP, IF YOU CATCH MY MEANIN'.
GETS THEIR BLOOD BOILING, HMM?
IT'LL BLOW OVER. JUST WATCH YOUR BACK FER A SPELL.

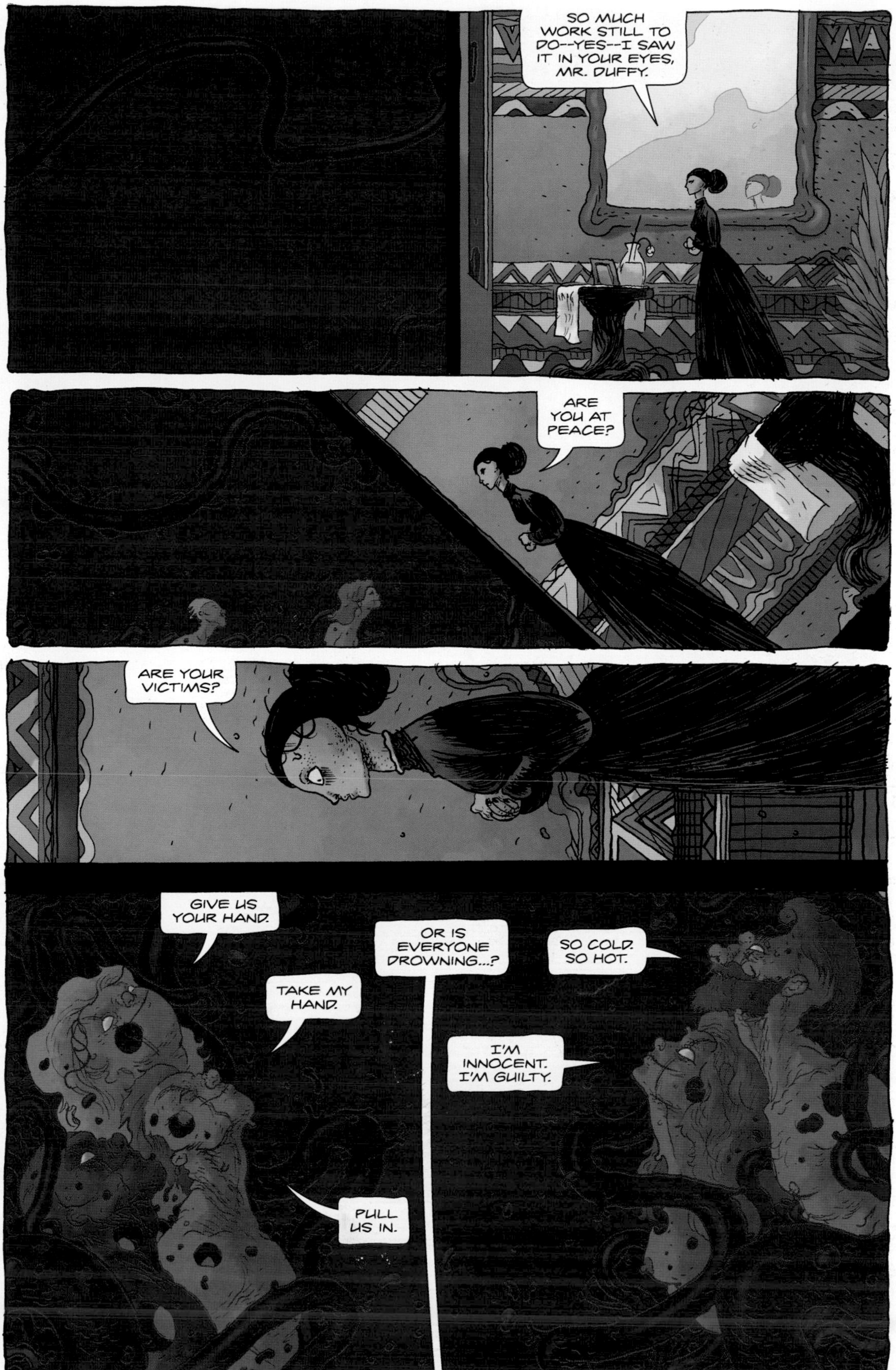

SO MUCH WORK STILL TO DO--YES--I SAW IT IN YOUR EYES, MR. DUFFY.
ARE YOU AT PEACE?
ARE YOUR VICTIMS?
GIVE US YOUR HAND.
TAKE MY HAND.
PULL US IN.
OR IS EVERYONE DROWNING...?
SO COLD. SO HOT.
I'M INNOCENT. I'M GUILTY.

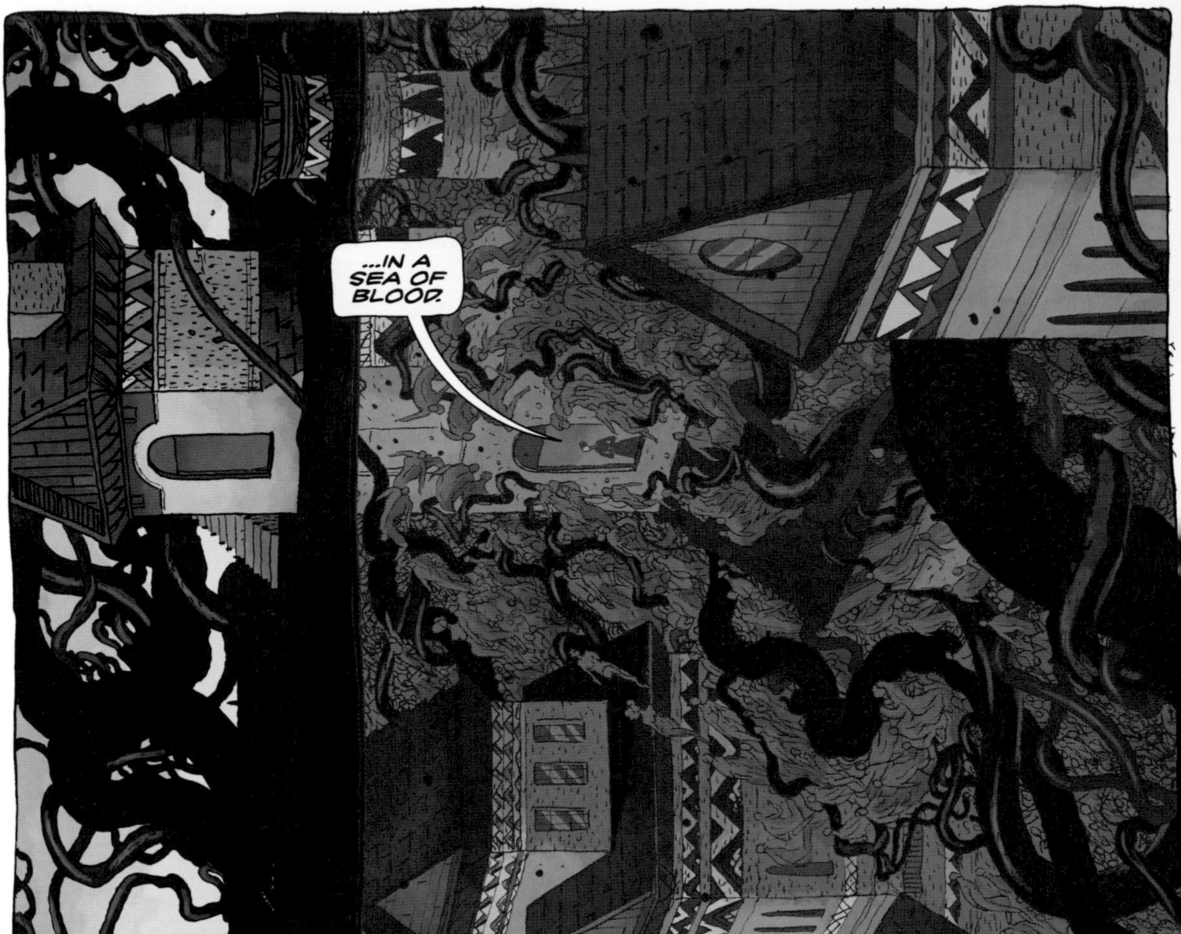
...IN A SEA OF BLOOD.

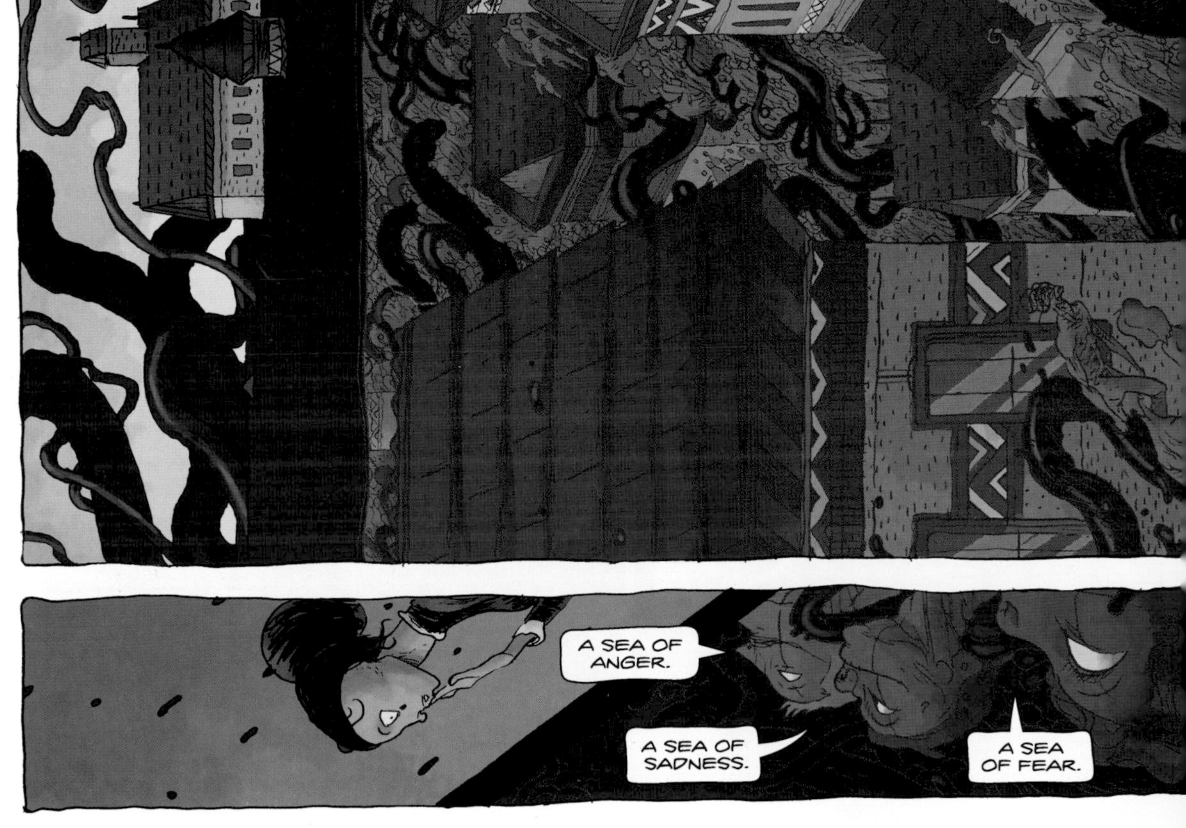
A SEA OF ANGER.
A SEA OF SADNESS.
A SEA OF FEAR.

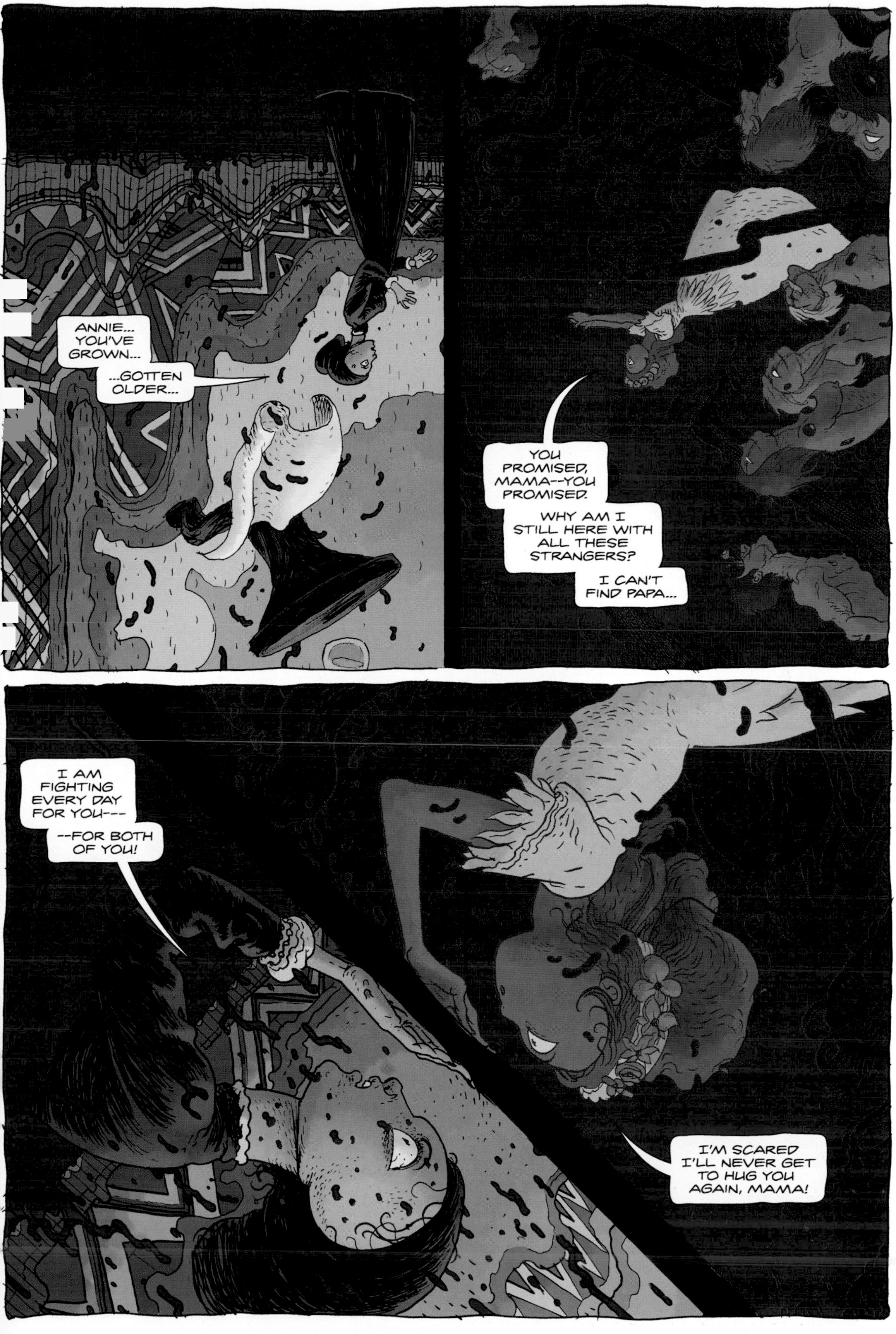

ANNIE... YOU'VE GROWN...
...GOTTEN OLDER...
YOU PROMISED, MAMA--YOU PROMISED.
WHY AM I STILL HERE WITH ALL THESE STRANGERS?
I CAN'T FIND PAPA...
I AM FIGHTING EVERY DAY FOR YOU---
--FOR BOTH OF YOU!
I'M SCARED I'LL NEVER GET TO HUG YOU AGAIN, MAMA!

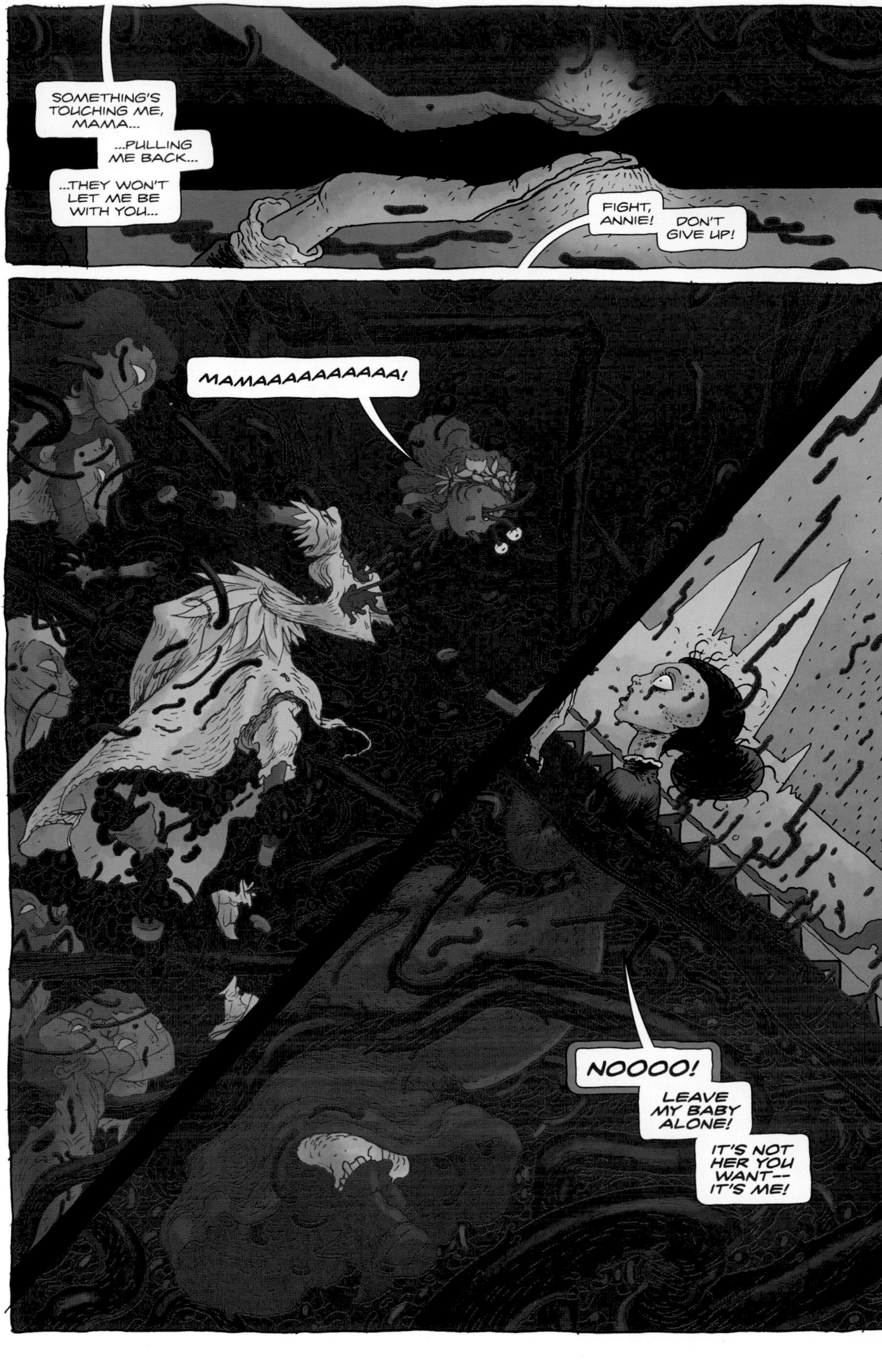
SOMETHING'S TOUCHING ME, MAMA...
...PULLING ME BACK...
...THEY WON'T LET ME BE WITH YOU...
FIGHT, ANNIE!
DON'T GIVE UP!
MAMAAAAAAAAAAA!
NOOOO!
LEAVE MY BABY ALONE!
IT'S NOT HER YOU WANT-- IT'S ME!

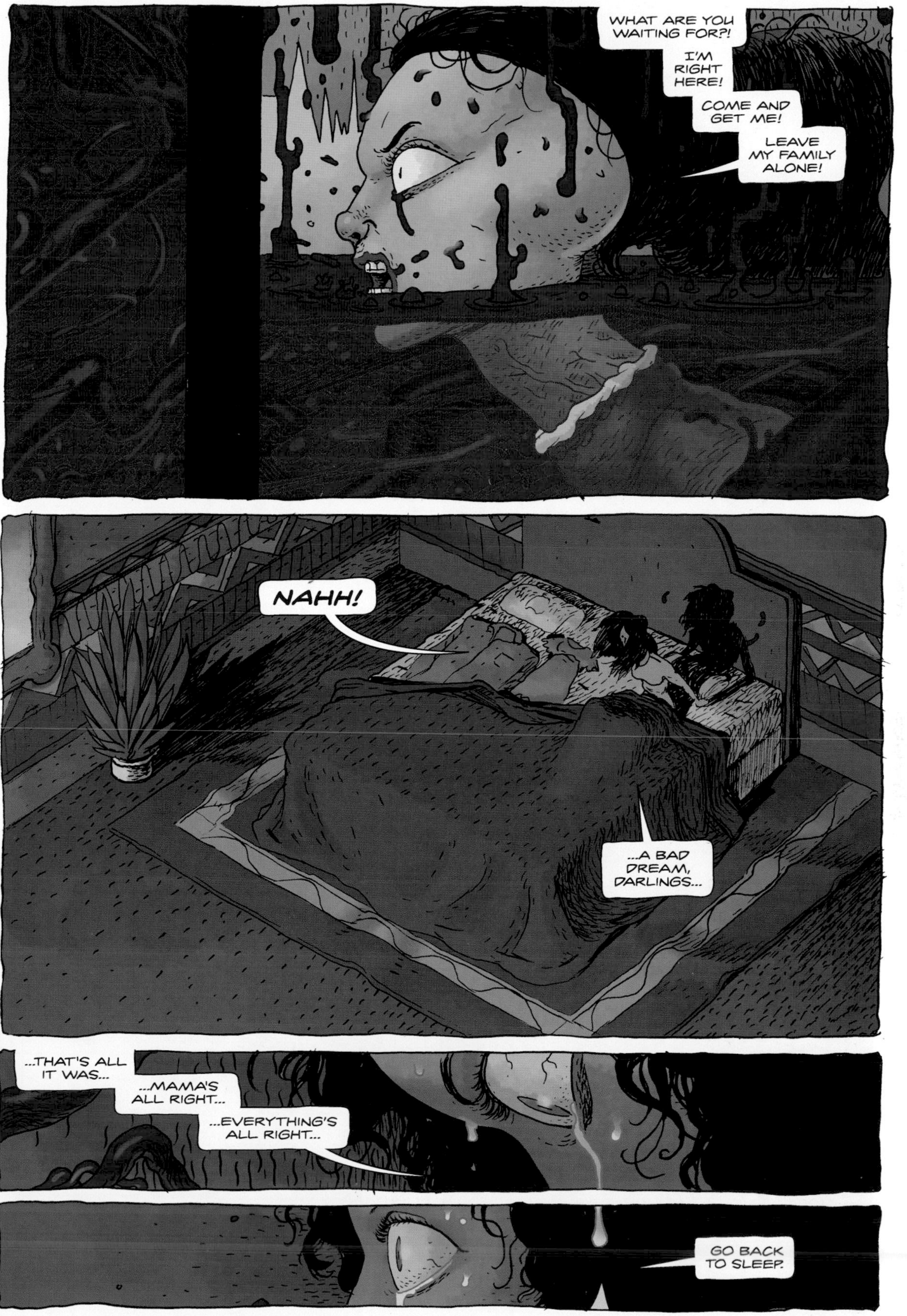
WHAT ARE YOU WAITING FOR?!
I'M RIGHT HERE!
COME AND GET ME!
LEAVE MY FAMILY ALONE!
NAHH!
...A BAD DREAM, DARLINGS...
...THAT'S ALL IT WAS...
...MAMA'S ALL RIGHT...
...EVERYTHING'S ALL RIGHT...
GO BACK TO SLEEP.

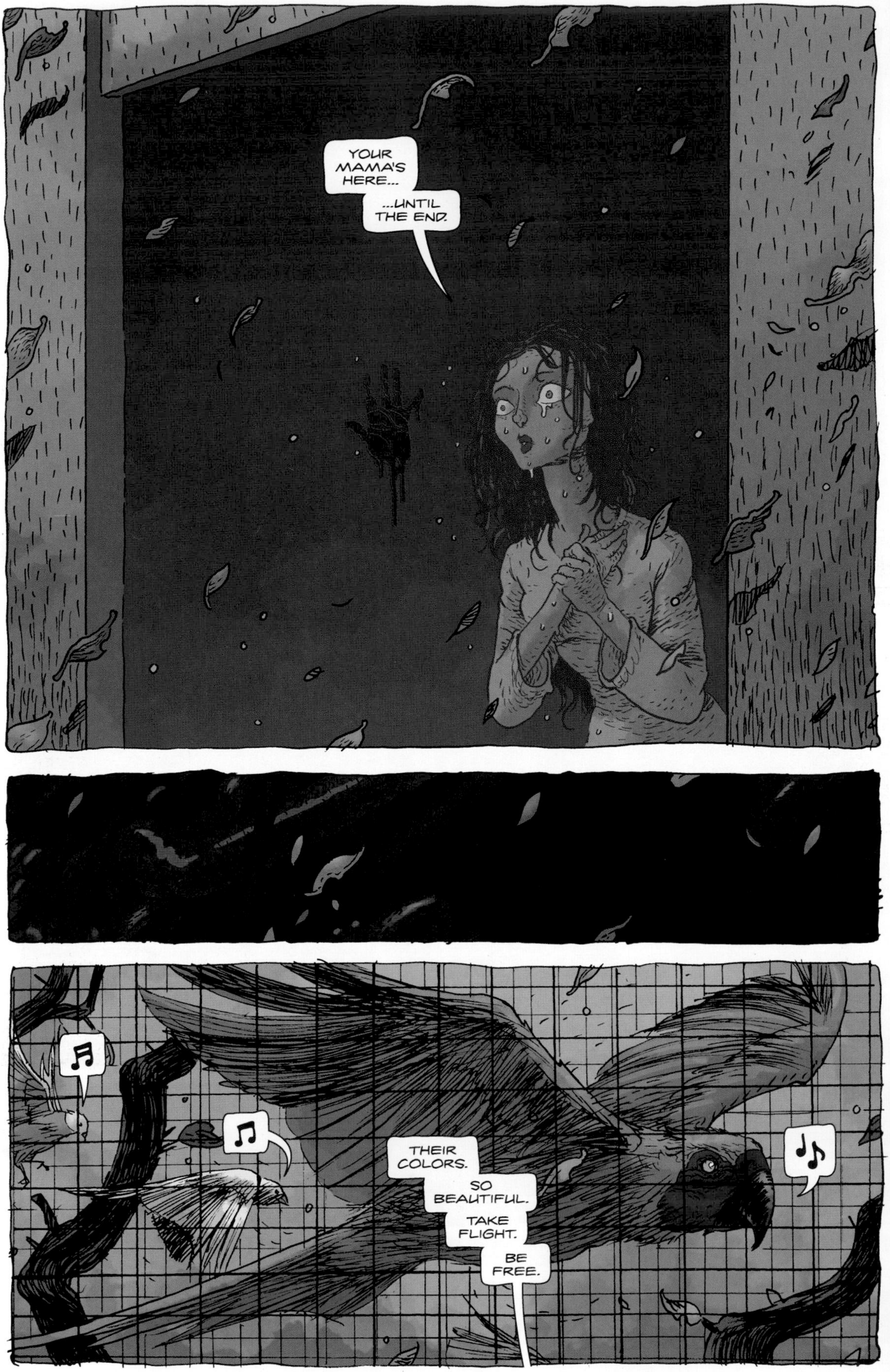
YOUR MAMA'S HERE...
...UNTIL THE END.
♬
♫
THEIR COLORS.
SO BEAUTIFUL.
TAKE FLIGHT.
BE FREE.
♪♪

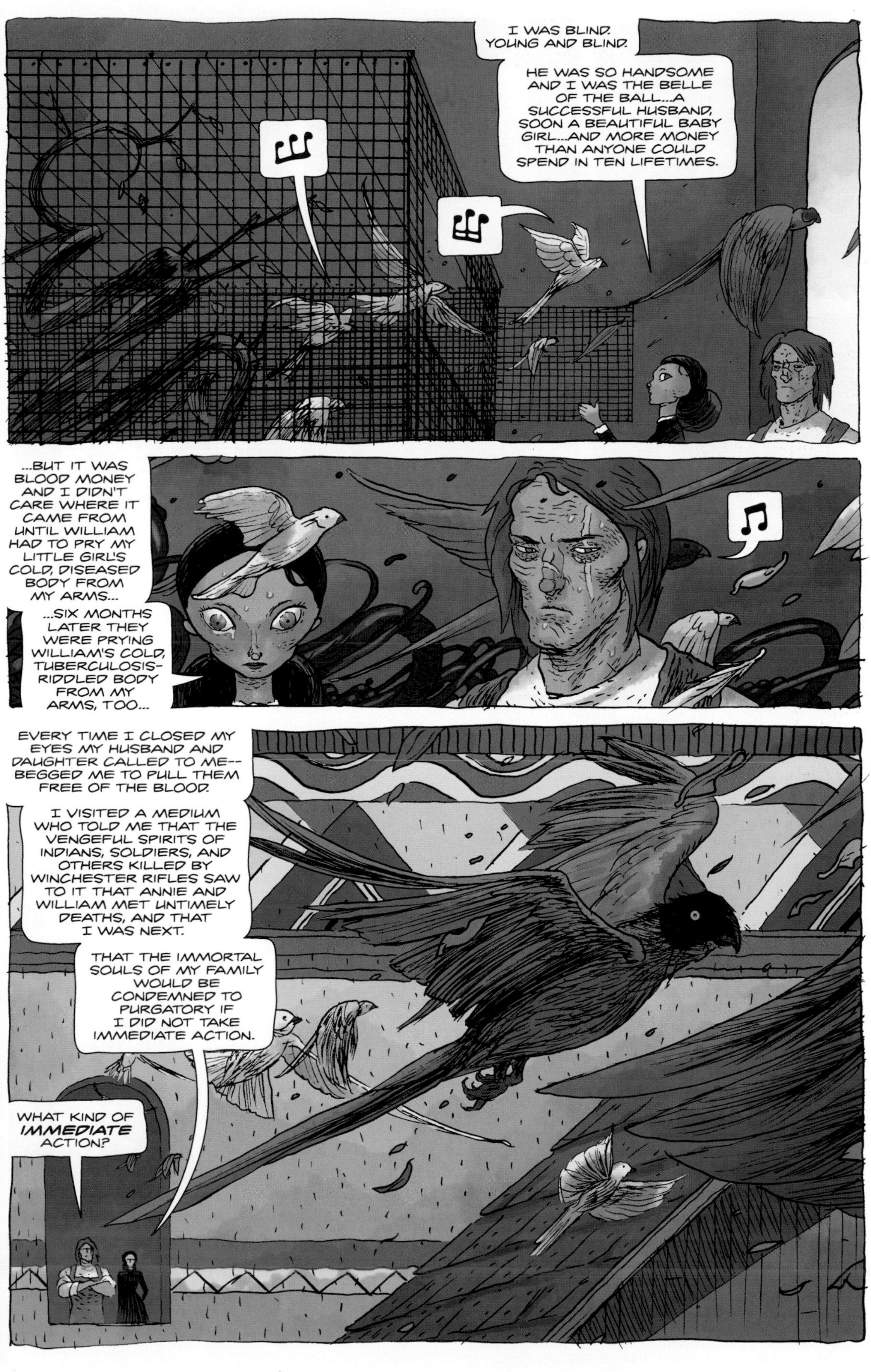
I WAS BLIND. YOUNG AND BLIND.
HE WAS SO HANDSOME AND I WAS THE BELLE OF THE BALL...A SUCCESSFUL HUSBAND, SOON A BEAUTIFUL BABY GIRL...AND MORE MONEY THAN ANYONE COULD SPEND IN TEN LIFETIMES.
...BUT IT WAS BLOOD MONEY AND I DIDN'T CARE WHERE IT CAME FROM UNTIL WILLIAM HAD TO PRY MY LITTLE GIRL'S COLD, DISEASED BODY FROM MY ARMS...
...SIX MONTHS LATER THEY WERE PRYING WILLIAM'S COLD, TUBERCULOSIS-RIDDLED BODY FROM MY ARMS, TOO...
EVERY TIME I CLOSED MY EYES MY HUSBAND AND DAUGHTER CALLED TO ME--BEGGED ME TO PULL THEM FREE OF THE BLOOD.
I VISITED A MEDIUM WHO TOLD ME THAT THE VENGEFUL SPIRITS OF INDIANS, SOLDIERS, AND OTHERS KILLED BY WINCHESTER RIFLES SAW TO IT THAT ANNIE AND WILLIAM MET UNTIMELY DEATHS, AND THAT I WAS NEXT.
THAT THE IMMORTAL SOULS OF MY FAMILY WOULD BE CONDEMNED TO PURGATORY IF I DID NOT TAKE IMMEDIATE ACTION.
WHAT KIND OF ***IMMEDIATE*** ACTION?

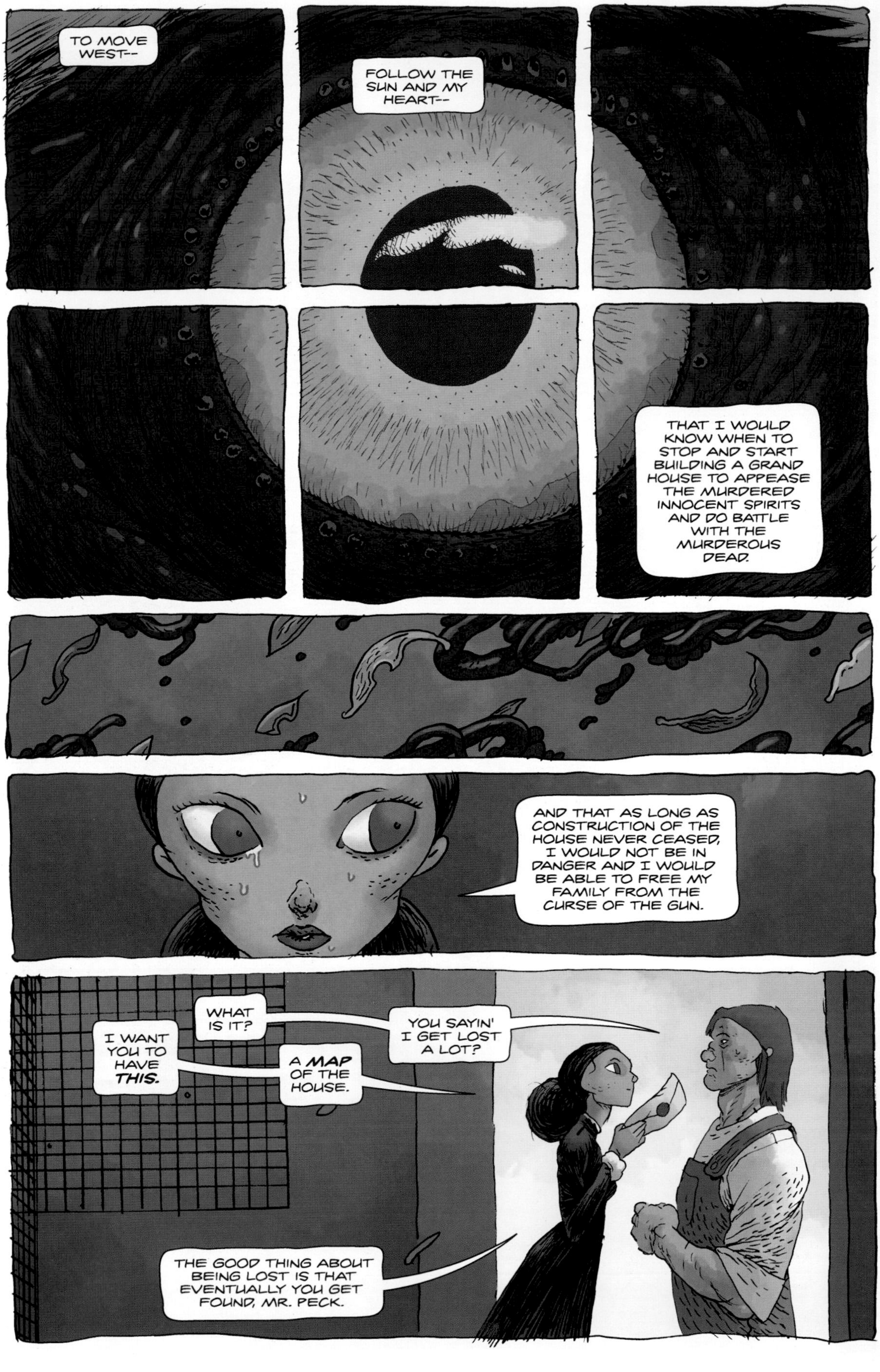
TO MOVE WEST--
FOLLOW THE SUN AND MY HEART--
THAT I WOULD KNOW WHEN TO STOP AND START BUILDING A GRAND HOUSE TO APPEASE THE MURDERED INNOCENT SPIRITS AND DO BATTLE WITH THE MURDEROUS DEAD.
AND THAT AS LONG AS CONSTRUCTION OF THE HOUSE NEVER CEASED, I WOULD NOT BE IN DANGER AND I WOULD BE ABLE TO FREE MY FAMILY FROM THE CURSE OF THE GUN.
I WANT YOU TO HAVE **THIS.**
WHAT IS IT?
A ***MAP*** OF THE HOUSE.
YOU SAYIN' I GET LOST A LOT?
THE GOOD THING ABOUT BEING LOST IS THAT EVENTUALLY YOU GET FOUND, MR. PECK.

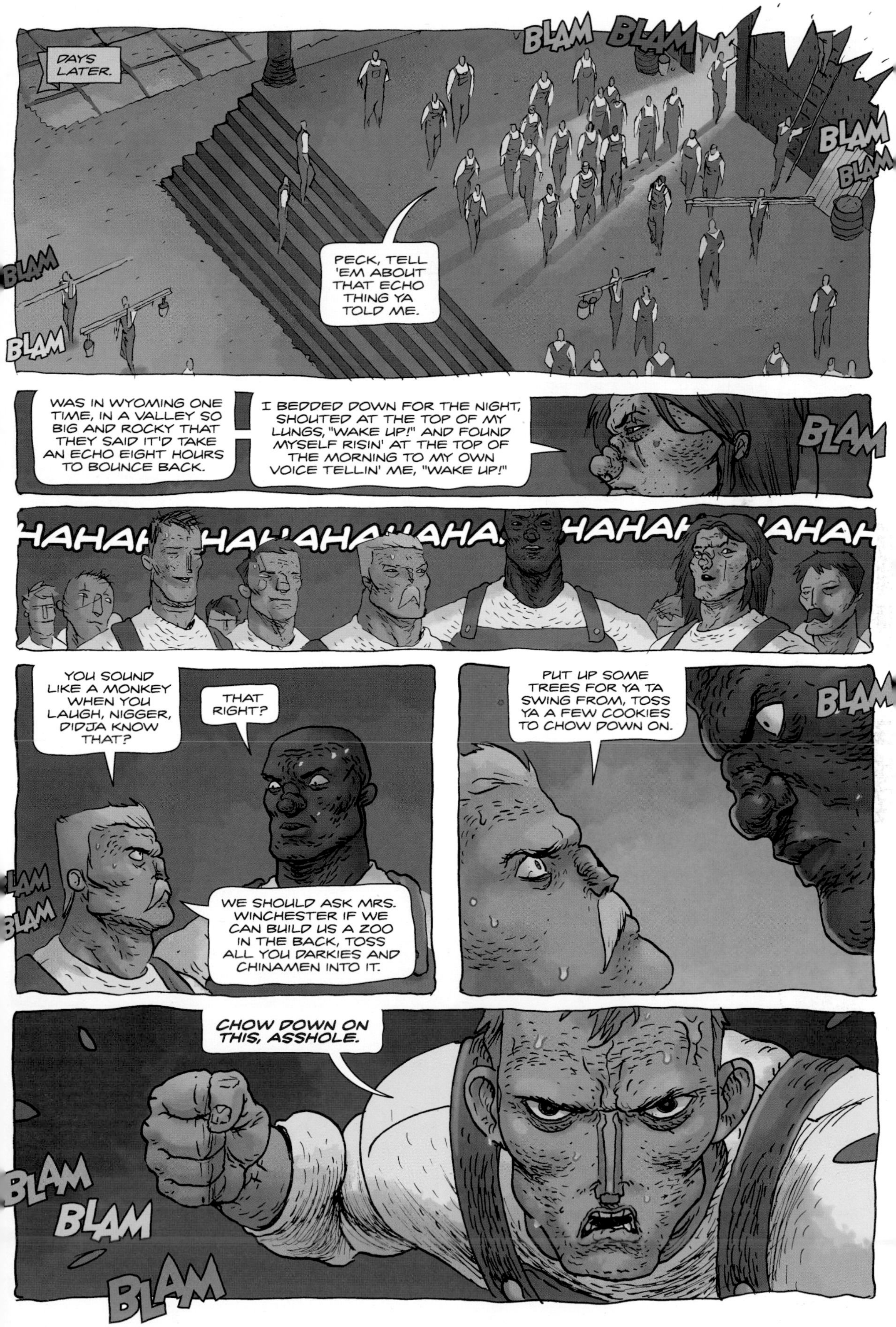
DAYS LATER.
BLAM BLAM
BLAM BLAM
BLAM
BLAM
PECK, TELL 'EM ABOUT THAT ECHO THING YA TOLD ME.
WAS IN WYOMING ONE TIME, IN A VALLEY SO BIG AND ROCKY THAT THEY SAID IT'D TAKE AN ECHO EIGHT HOURS TO BOUNCE BACK.
I BEDDED DOWN FOR THE NIGHT, SHOUTED AT THE TOP OF MY LUNGS, "WAKE UP!" AND FOUND MYSELF RISIN' AT THE TOP OF THE MORNING TO MY OWN VOICE TELLIN' ME, "WAKE UP!"
BLAM
HAHAHAHAHAHAHAHAHAHAHAHAHAH
YOU SOUND LIKE A MONKEY WHEN YOU LAUGH, NIGGER, DIDJA KNOW THAT?
THAT RIGHT?
WE SHOULD ASK MRS. WINCHESTER IF WE CAN BUILD US A ZOO IN THE BACK, TOSS ALL YOU DARKIES AND CHINAMEN INTO IT.
BLAM
PUT UP SOME TREES FOR YA TA SWING FROM, TOSS YA A FEW COOKIES TO CHOW DOWN ON.
BLAM
CHOW DOWN ON THIS, ASSHOLE.
BLAM
BLAM
BLAM

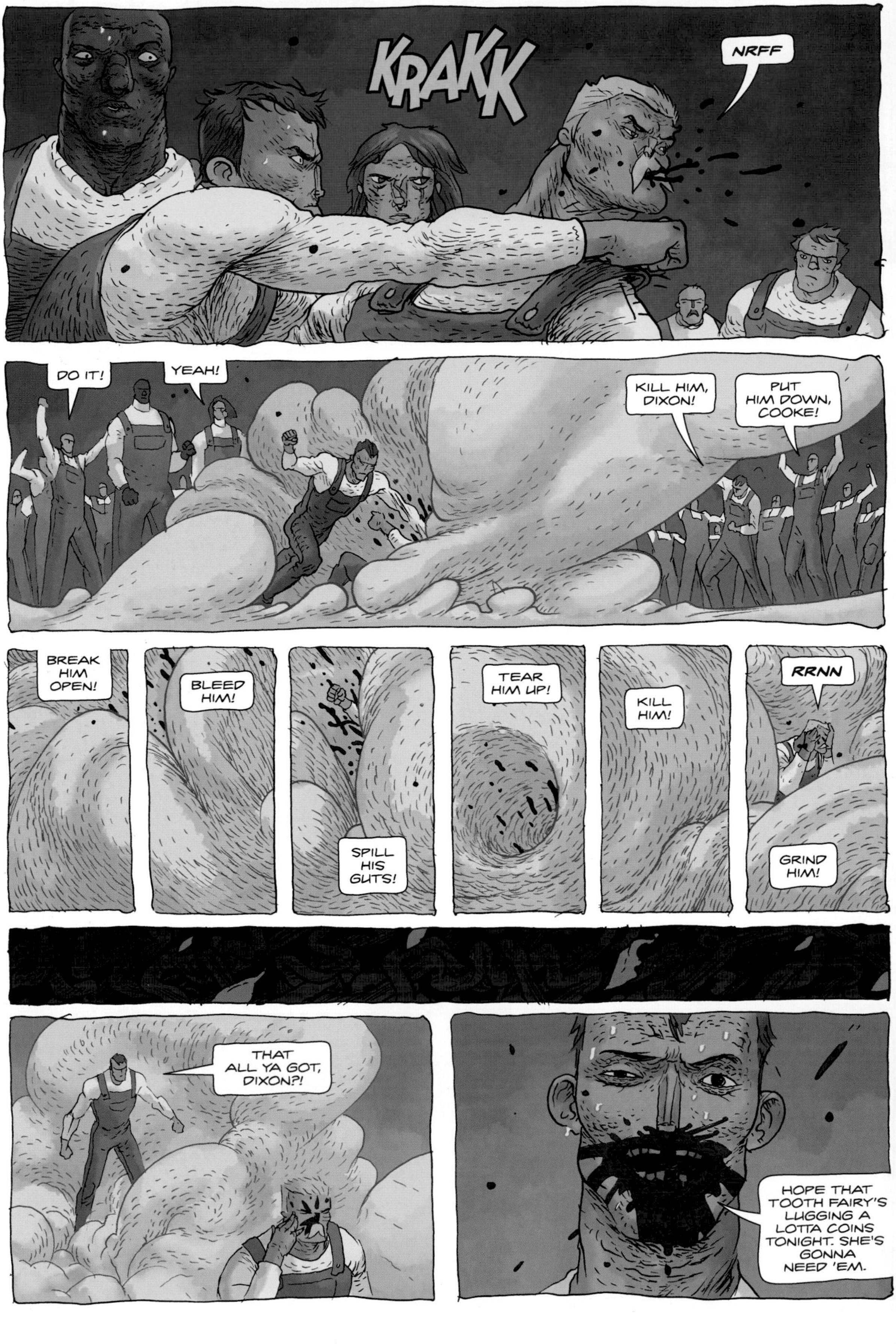
KRAKK
NRFF
DO IT!
YEAH!
KILL HIM, DIXON!
PUT HIM DOWN, COOKE!
BREAK HIM OPEN!
BLEED HIM!
SPILL HIS GUTS!
TEAR HIM UP!
KILL HIM!
RRNN
GRIND HIM!
THAT ALL YA GOT, DIXON?!
HOPE THAT TOOTH FAIRY'S LUGGING A LOTTA COINS TONIGHT. SHE'S GONNA NEED 'EM.

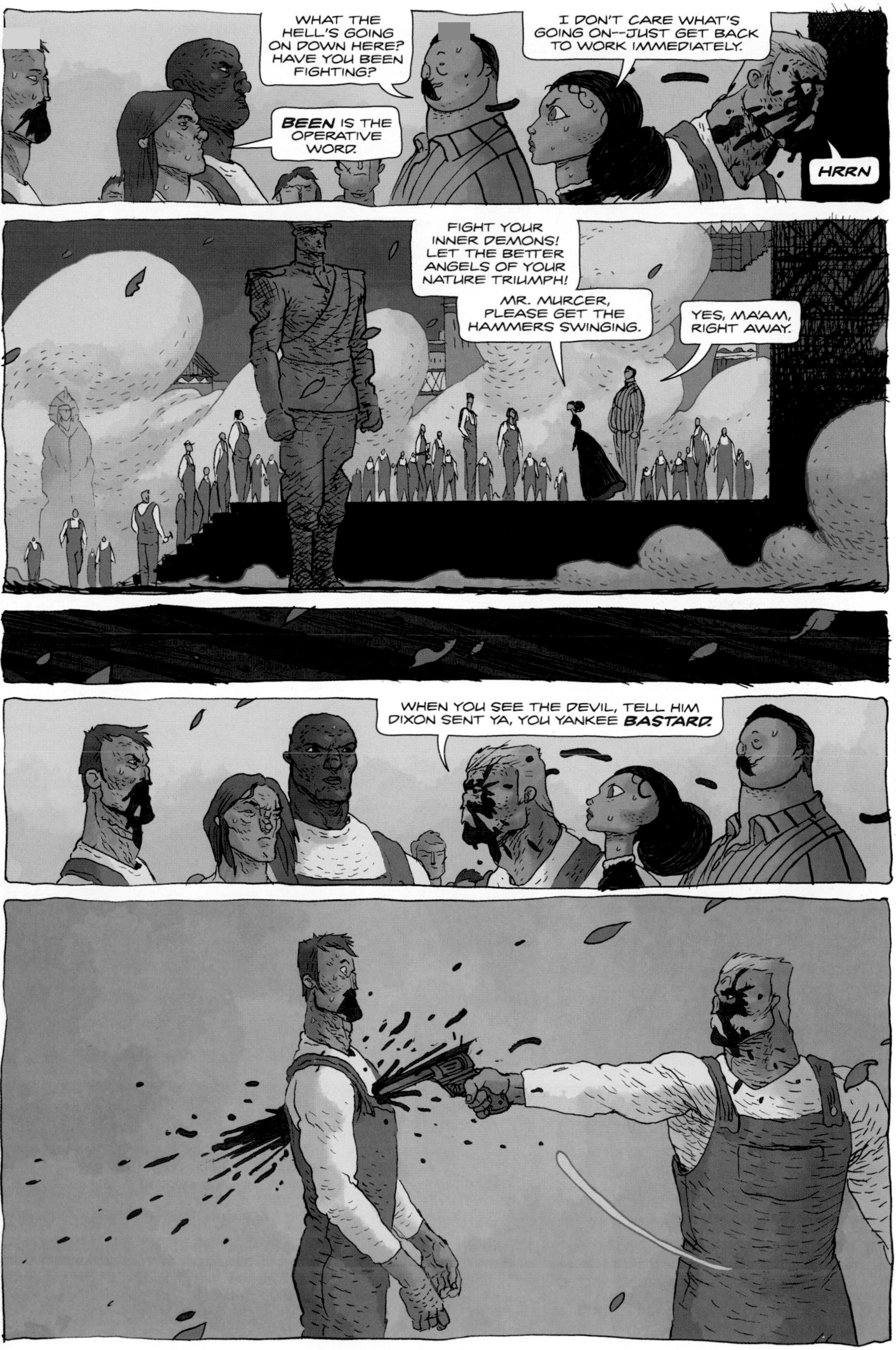
WHAT THE HELL'S GOING ON DOWN HERE? HAVE YOU BEEN FIGHTING?
BEEN IS THE OPERATIVE WORD.
I DON'T CARE WHAT'S GOING ON--JUST GET BACK TO WORK IMMEDIATELY.
HRRN
FIGHT YOUR INNER DEMONS! LET THE BETTER ANGELS OF YOUR NATURE TRIUMPH!
MR. MURCER, PLEASE GET THE HAMMERS SWINGING.
YES, MA'AM, RIGHT AWAY.
WHEN YOU SEE THE DEVIL, TELL HIM DIXON SENT YA, YOU YANKEE **BASTARD**.

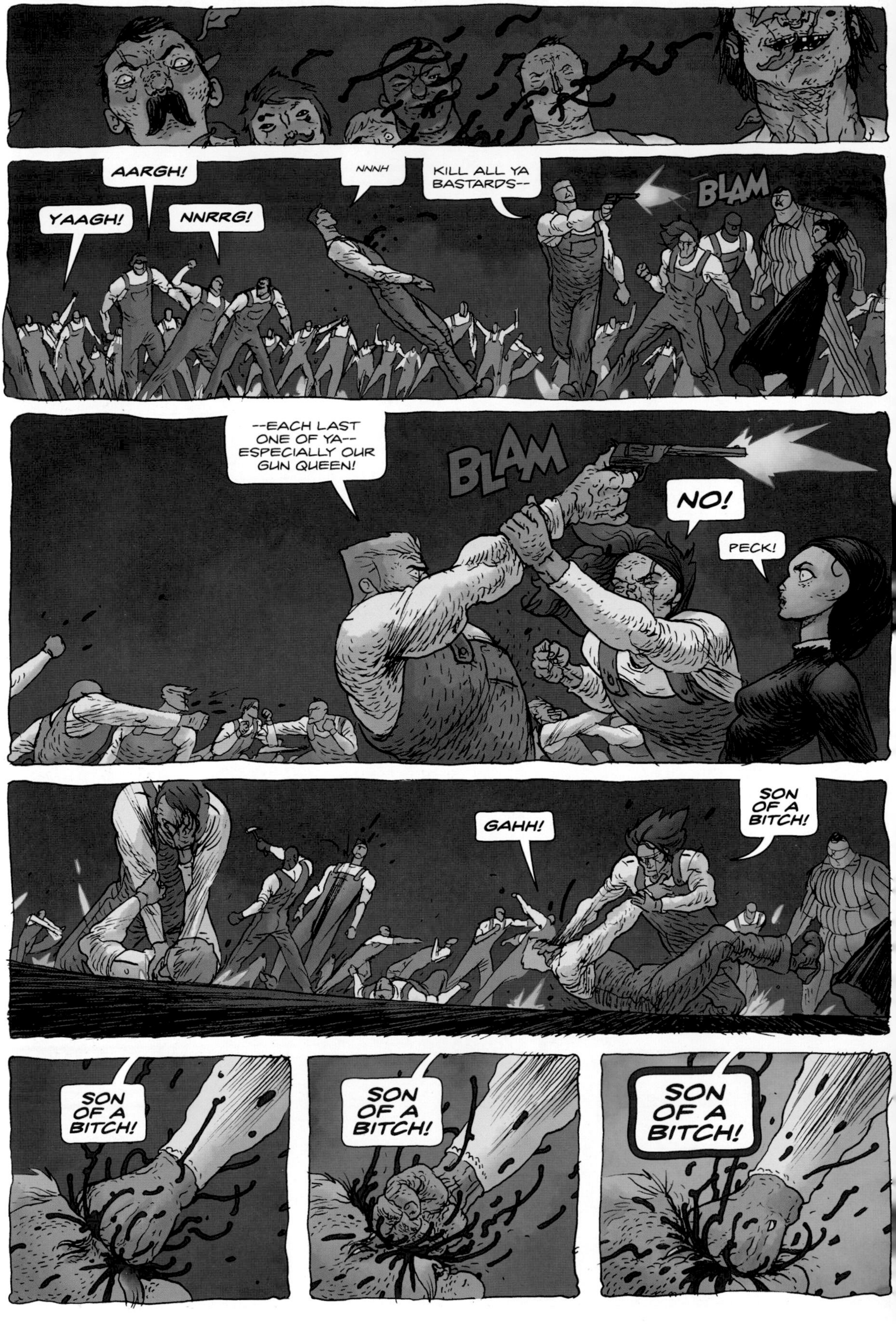
YAAGH!
AARGH!
NNRRG!
NNNH
KILL ALL YA BASTARDS--
BLAM
--EACH LAST ONE OF YA-- ESPECIALLY OUR GUN QUEEN!
BLAM
NO!
PECK!
GAHH!
SON OF A BITCH!
SON OF A BITCH!
SON OF A BITCH!
SON OF A BITCH!

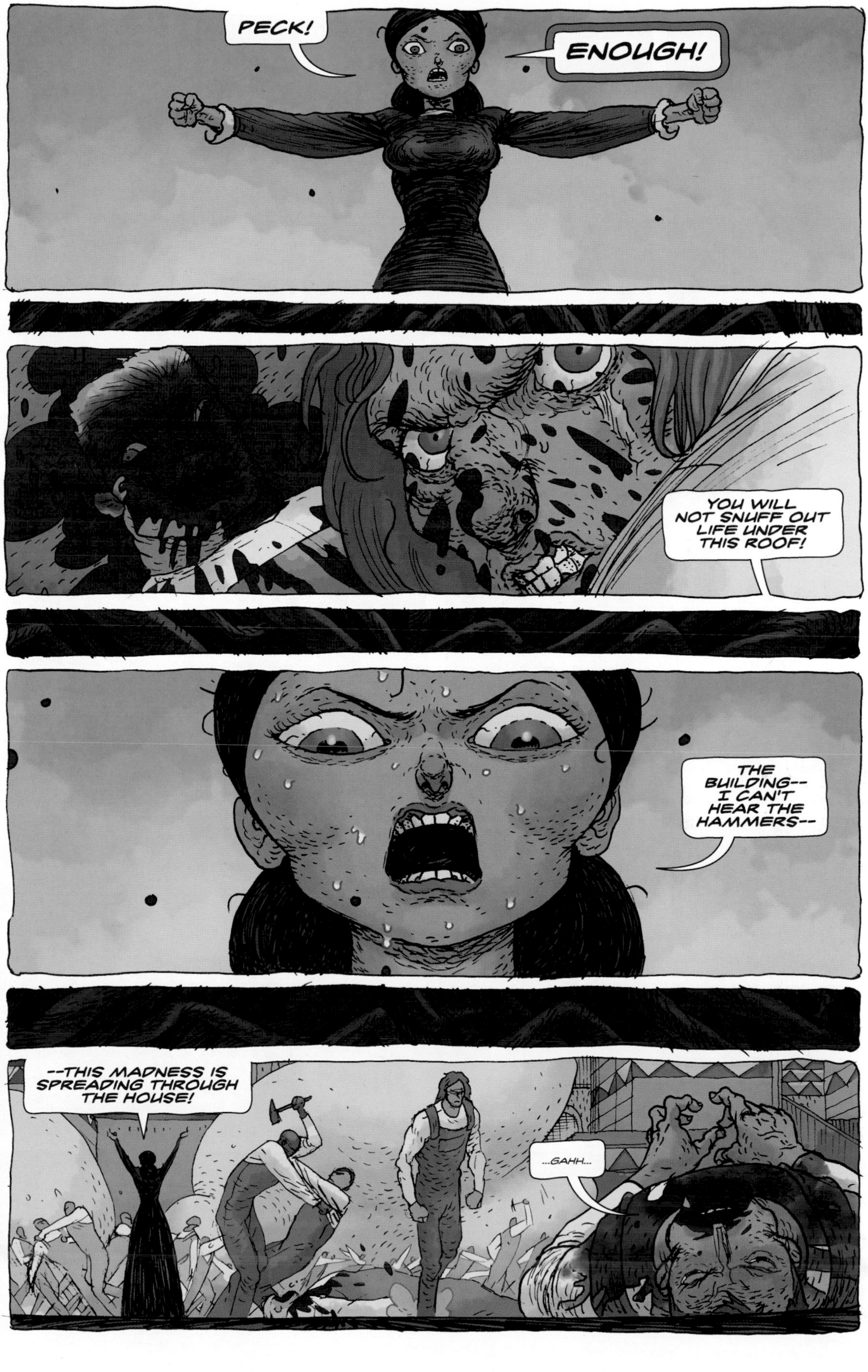
PECK!
ENOUGH!
YOU WILL NOT SNUFF OUT LIFE UNDER THIS ROOF!
THE BUILDING-- I CAN'T HEAR THE HAMMERS--
--THIS MADNESS IS SPREADING THROUGH THE HOUSE!
...GAHH...

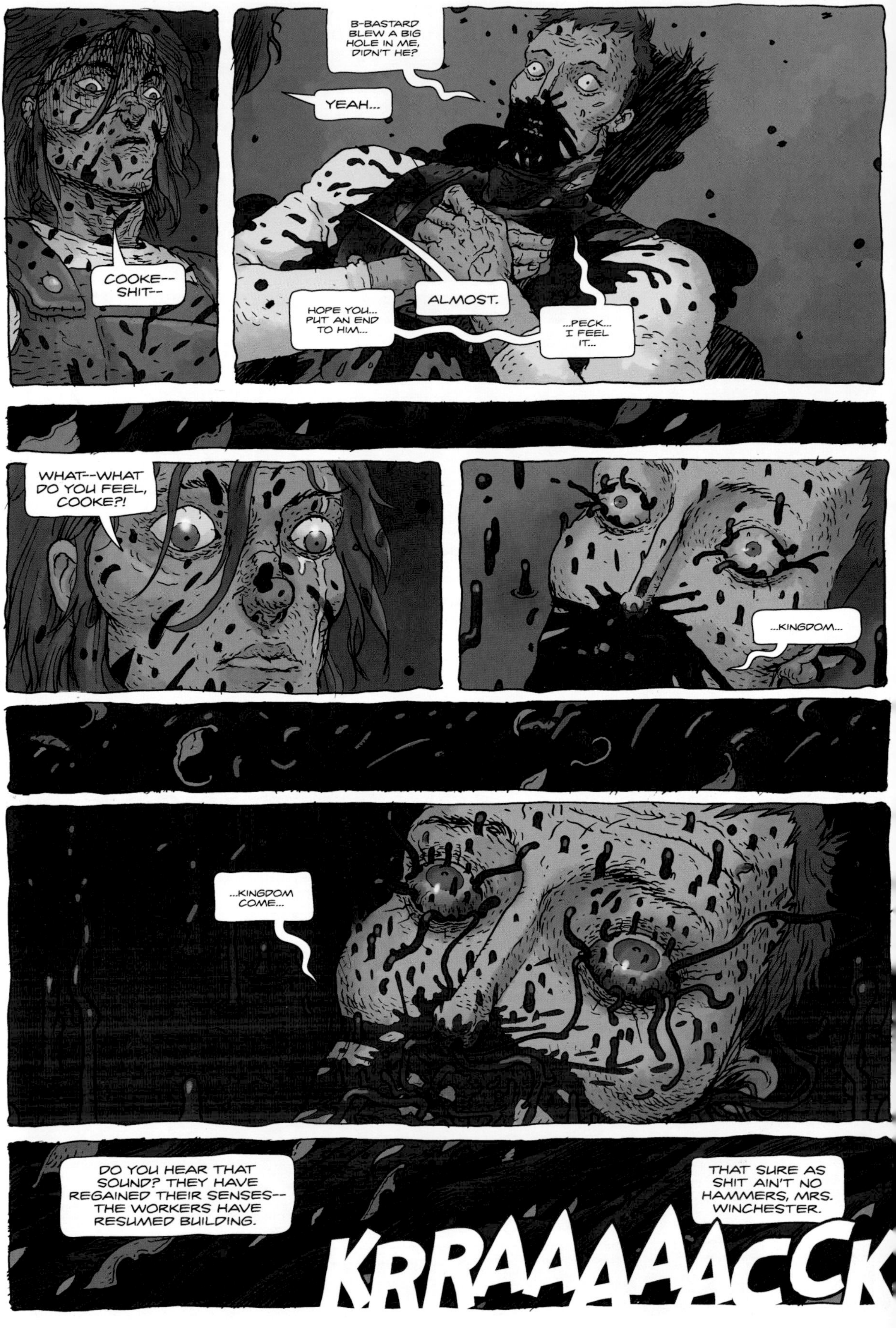
COOKE--
SHIT--
B-BASTARD BLEW A BIG HOLE IN ME, DIDN'T HE?
YEAH...
ALMOST.
HOPE YOU... PUT AN END TO HIM...
...PECK... I FEEL IT...
WHAT--WHAT DO YOU FEEL, COOKE?!
...KINGDOM...
...KINGDOM COME...
DO YOU HEAR THAT SOUND? THEY HAVE REGAINED THEIR SENSES-- THE WORKERS HAVE RESUMED BUILDING.
THAT SURE AS SHIT AIN'T NO HAMMERS, MRS. WINCHESTER.
KRRAAAAACCK

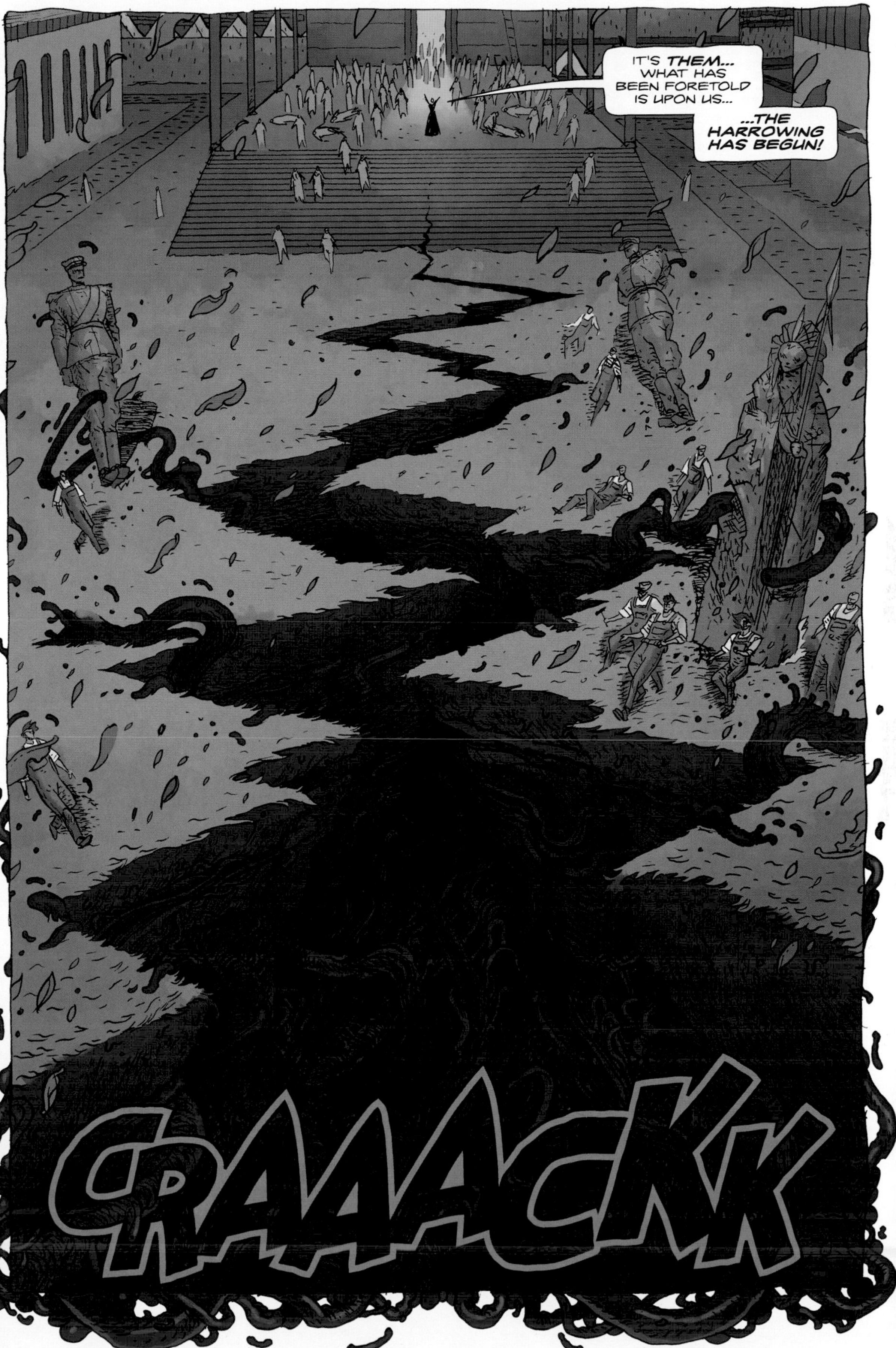
IT'S THEM... WHAT HAS BEEN FORETOLD IS UPON US...
...THE HARROWING HAS BEGUN!
CRAAACKK

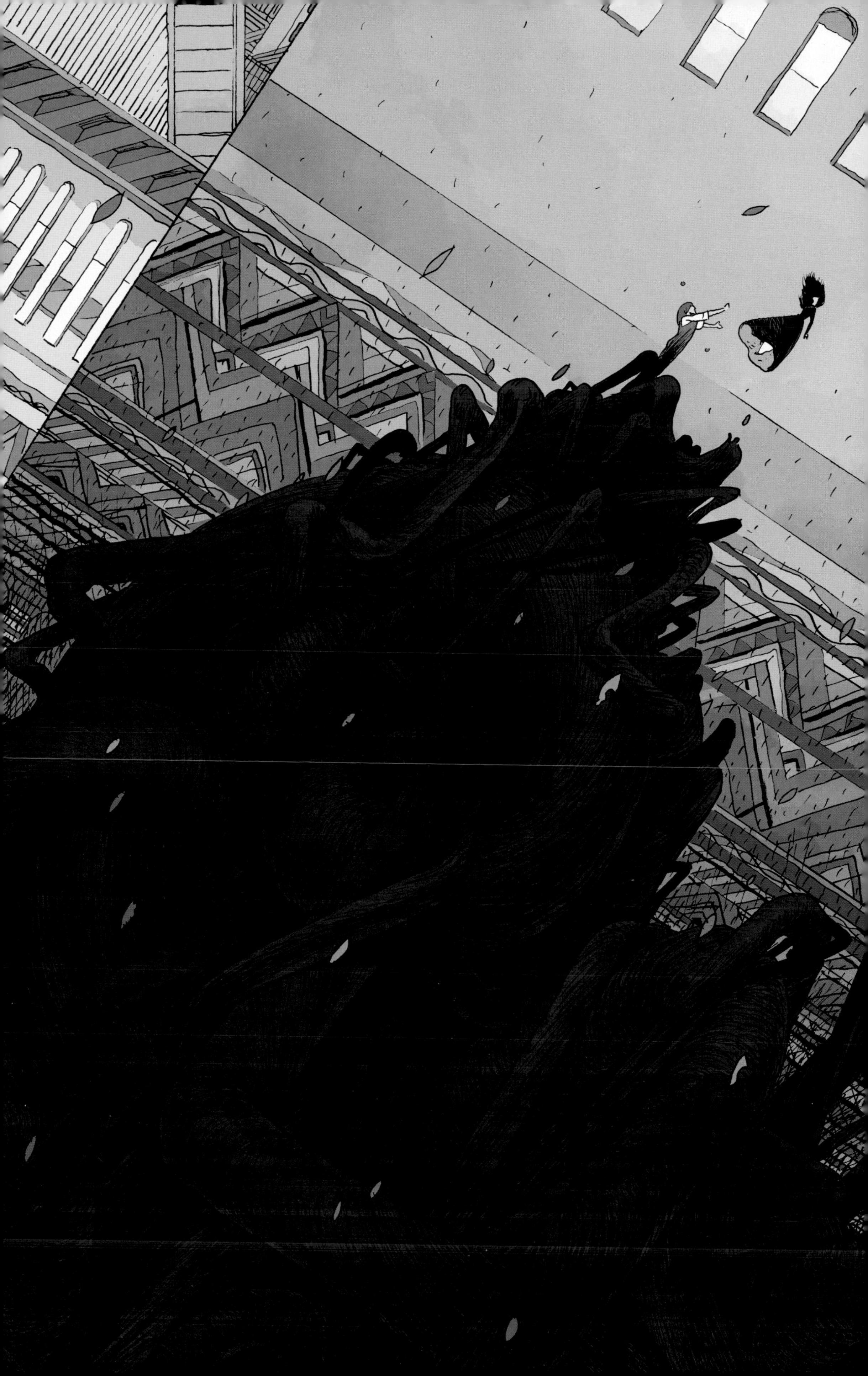

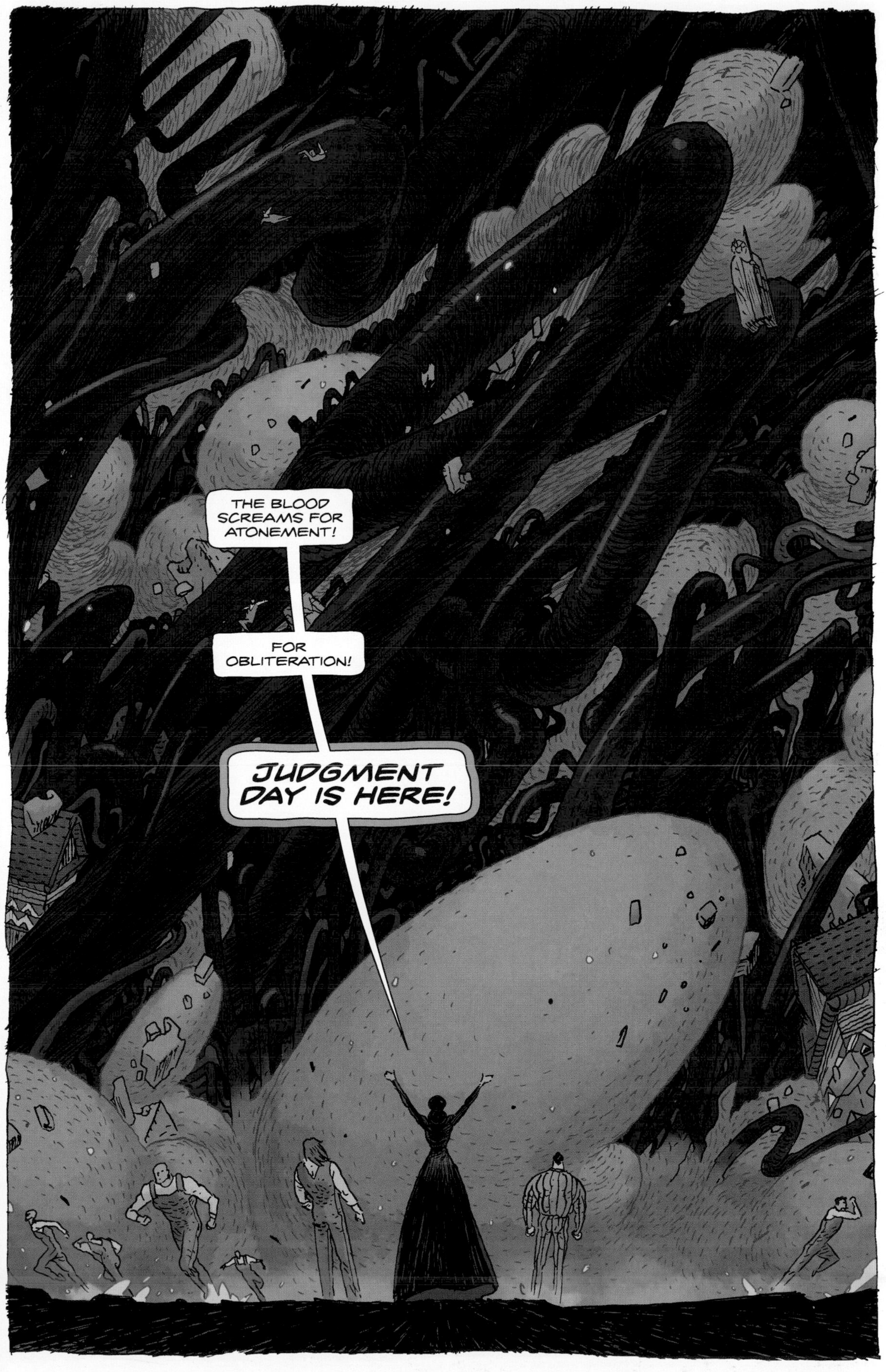
THE BLOOD SCREAMS FOR ATONEMENT!
FOR OBLITERATION!
JUDGMENT DAY IS HERE!

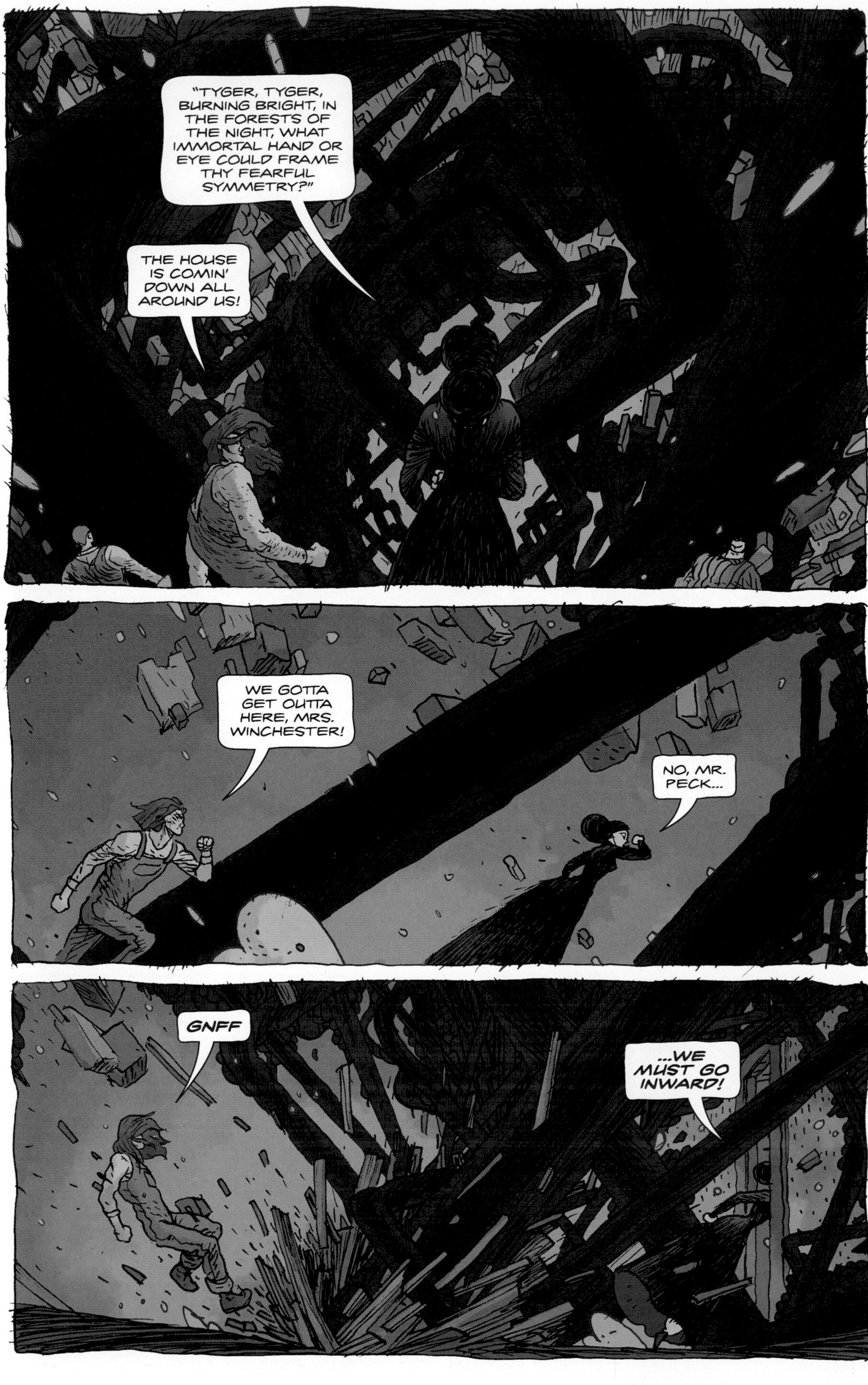
"TYGER, TYGER, BURNING BRIGHT, IN THE FORESTS OF THE NIGHT, WHAT IMMORTAL HAND OR EYE COULD FRAME THY FEARFUL SYMMETRY?"
THE HOUSE IS COMIN' DOWN ALL AROUND US!
WE GOTTA GET OUTTA HERE, MRS. WINCHESTER!
NO, MR. PECK...
GNFF
...WE MUST GO INWARD!

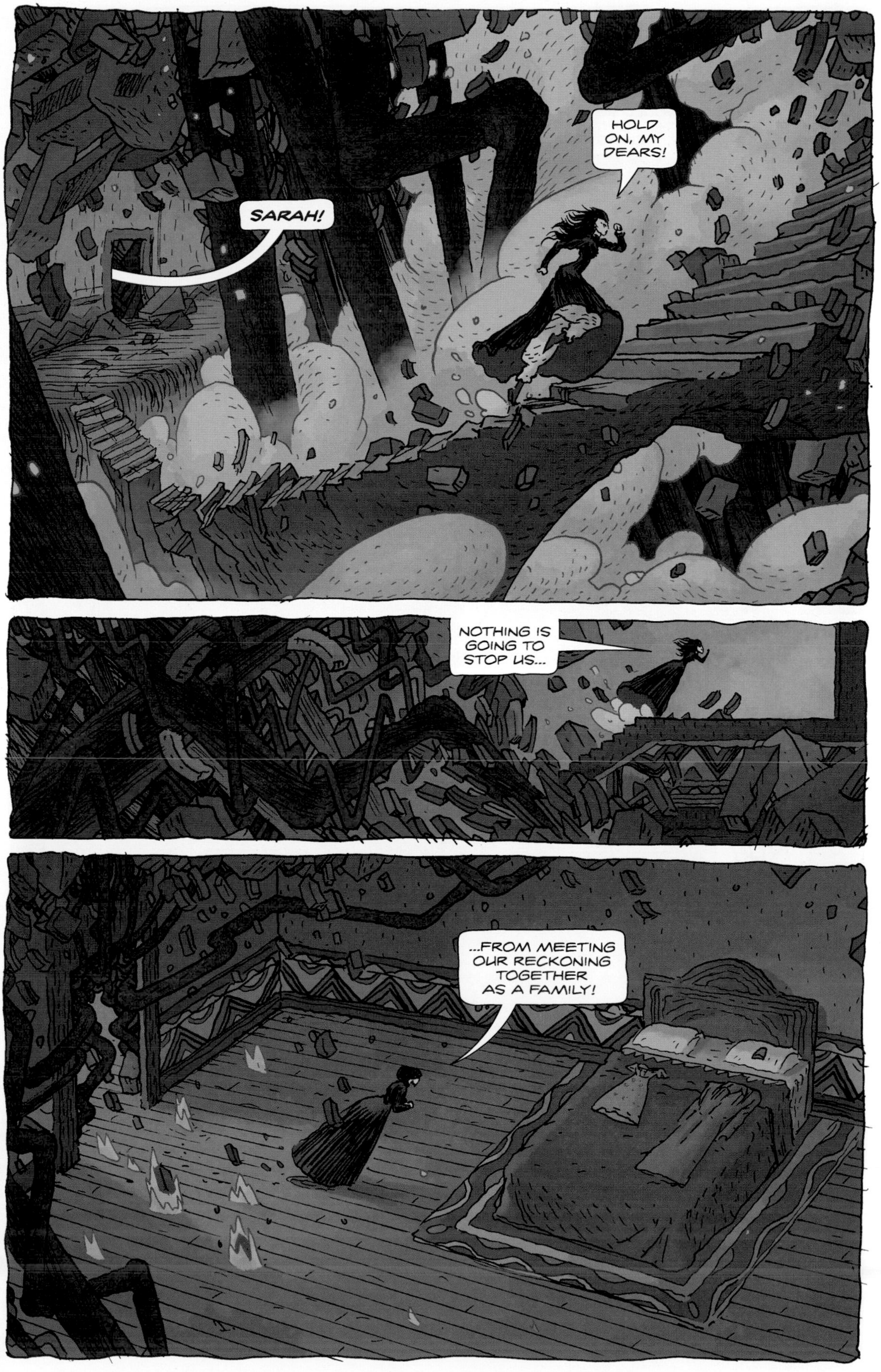
HOLD ON, MY DEARS!
SARAH!
NOTHING IS GOING TO STOP US...
...FROM MEETING OUR RECKONING TOGETHER AS A FAMILY!

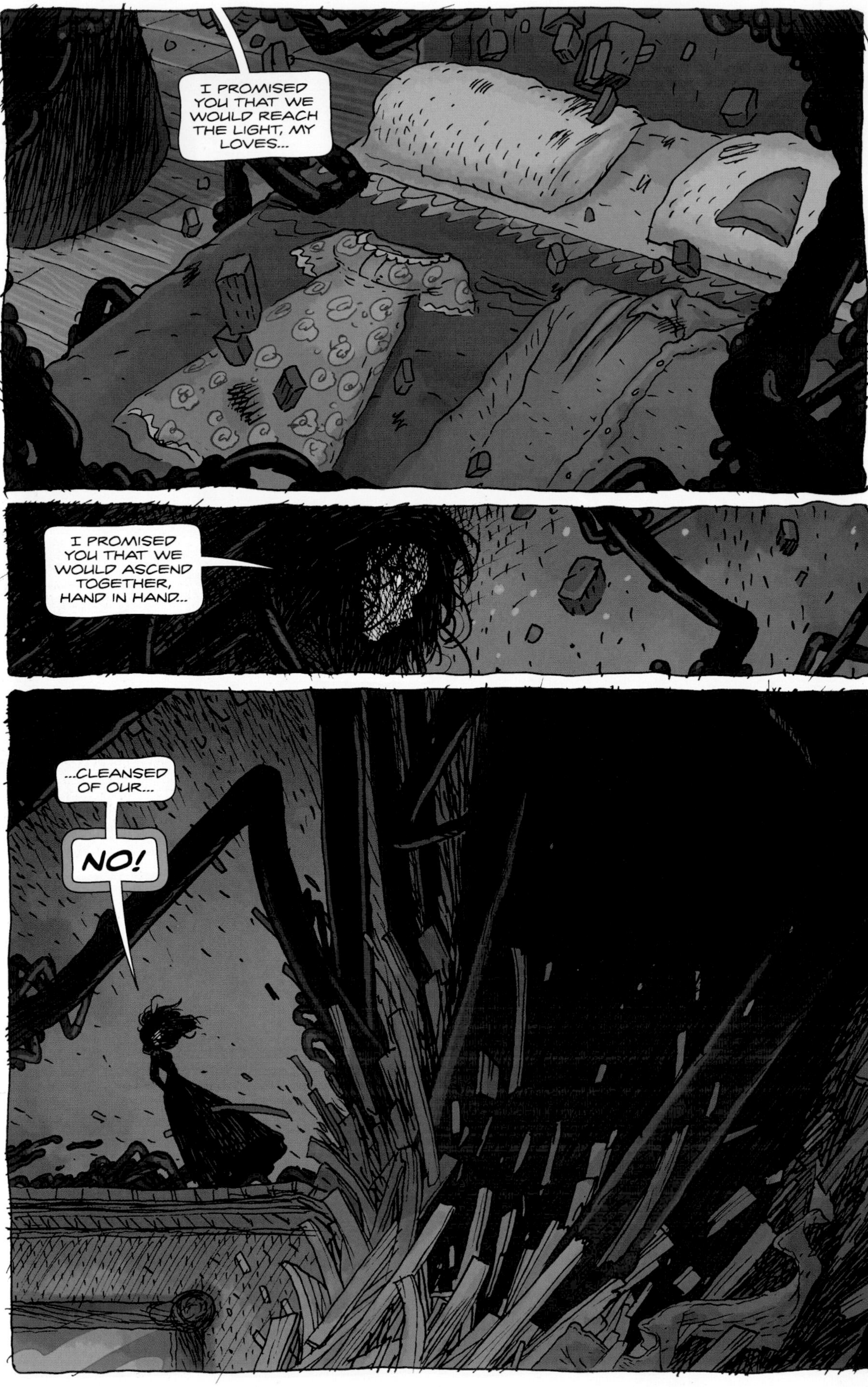
I PROMISED YOU THAT WE WOULD REACH THE LIGHT, MY LOVES...
I PROMISED YOU THAT WE WOULD ASCEND TOGETHER, HAND IN HAND...
...CLEANSED OF OUR...
NO!

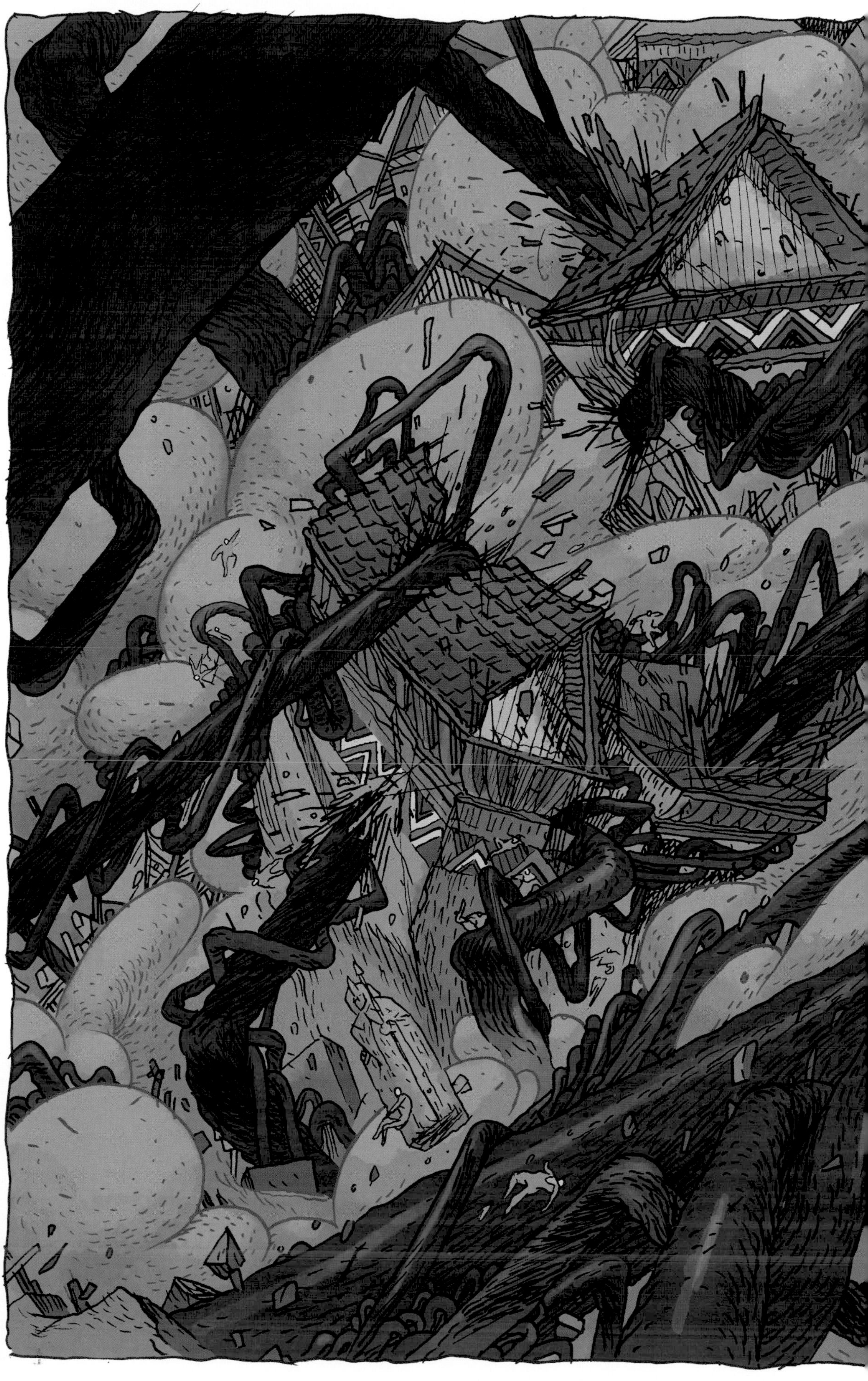

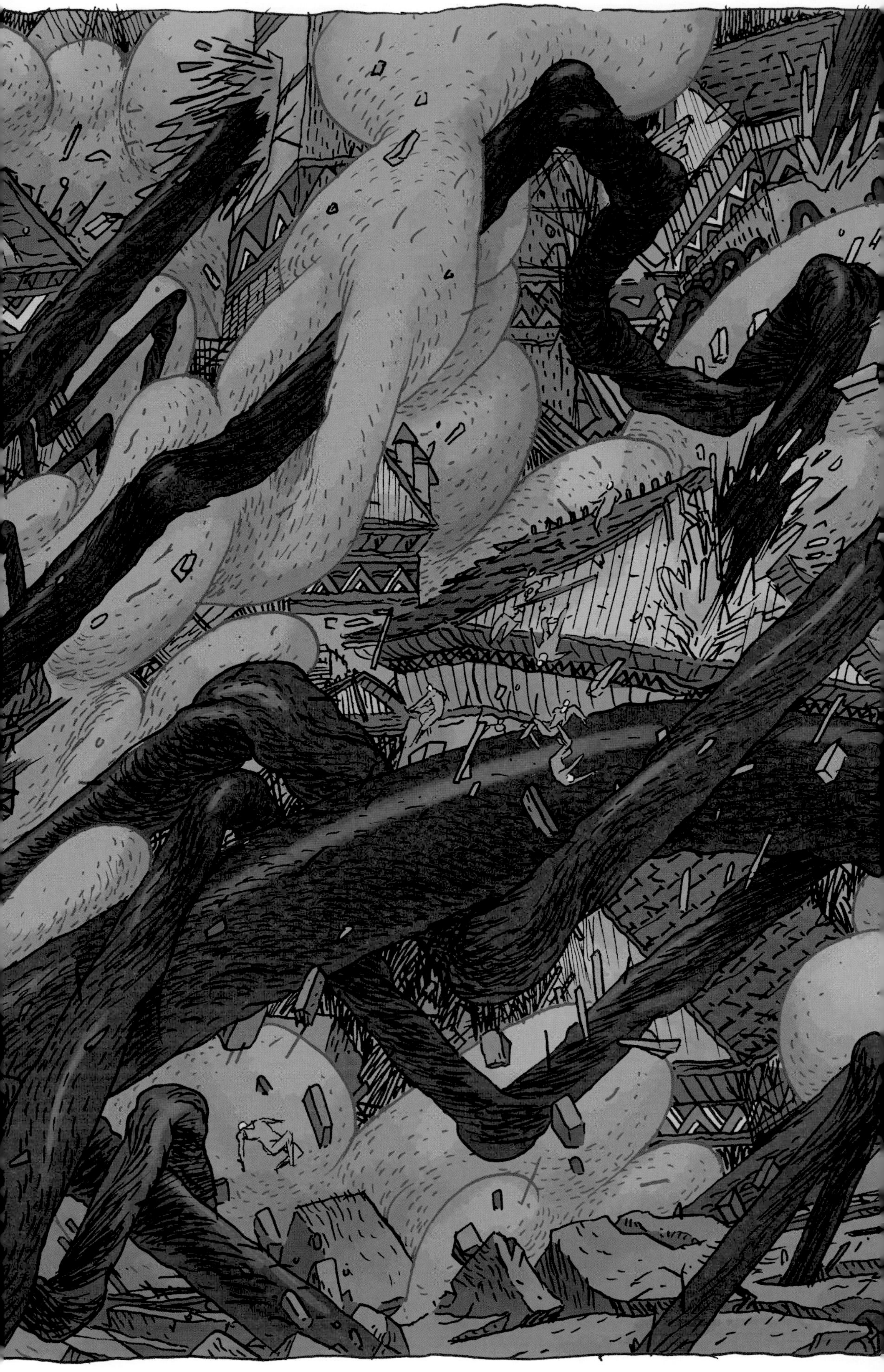

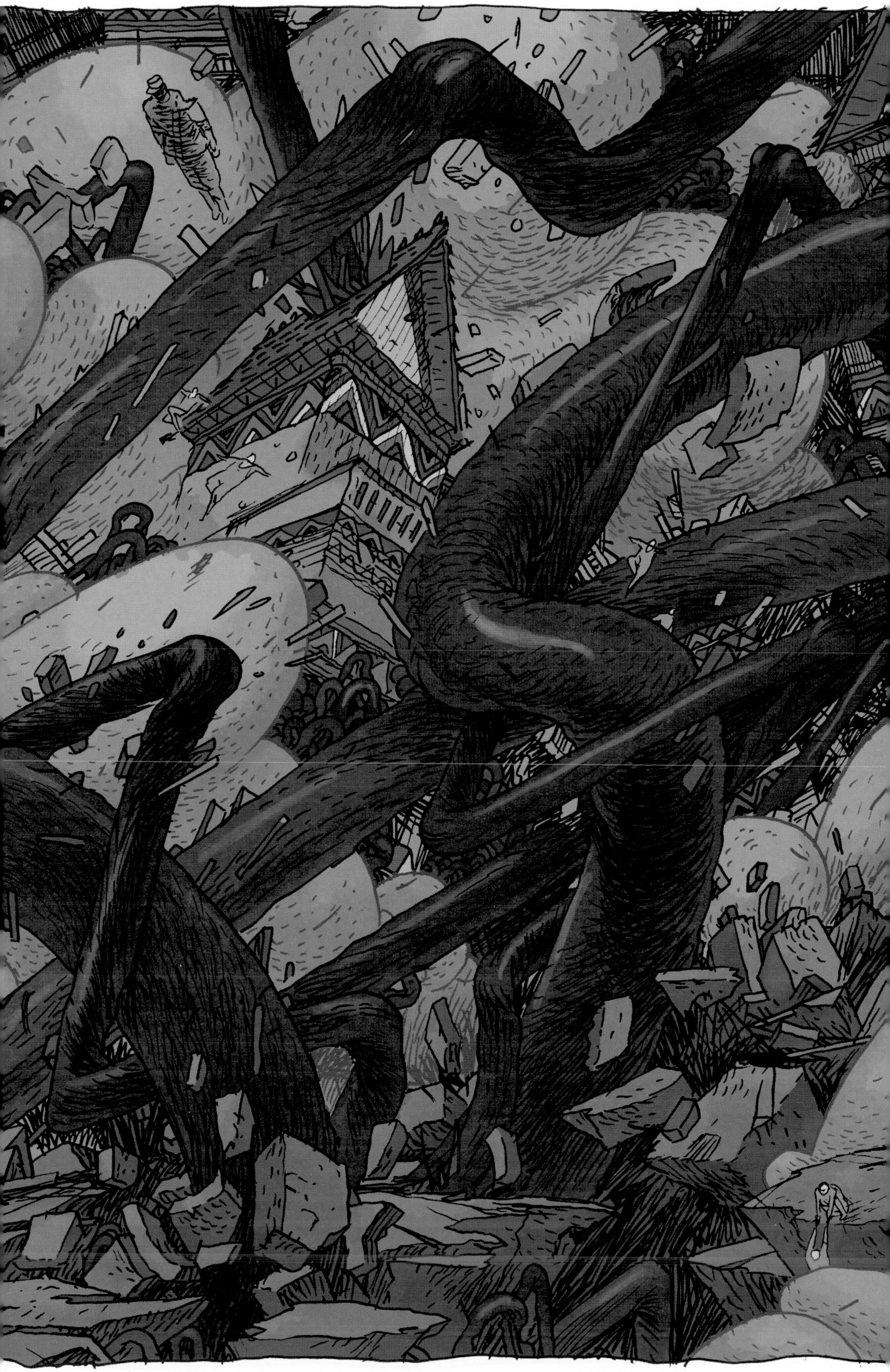

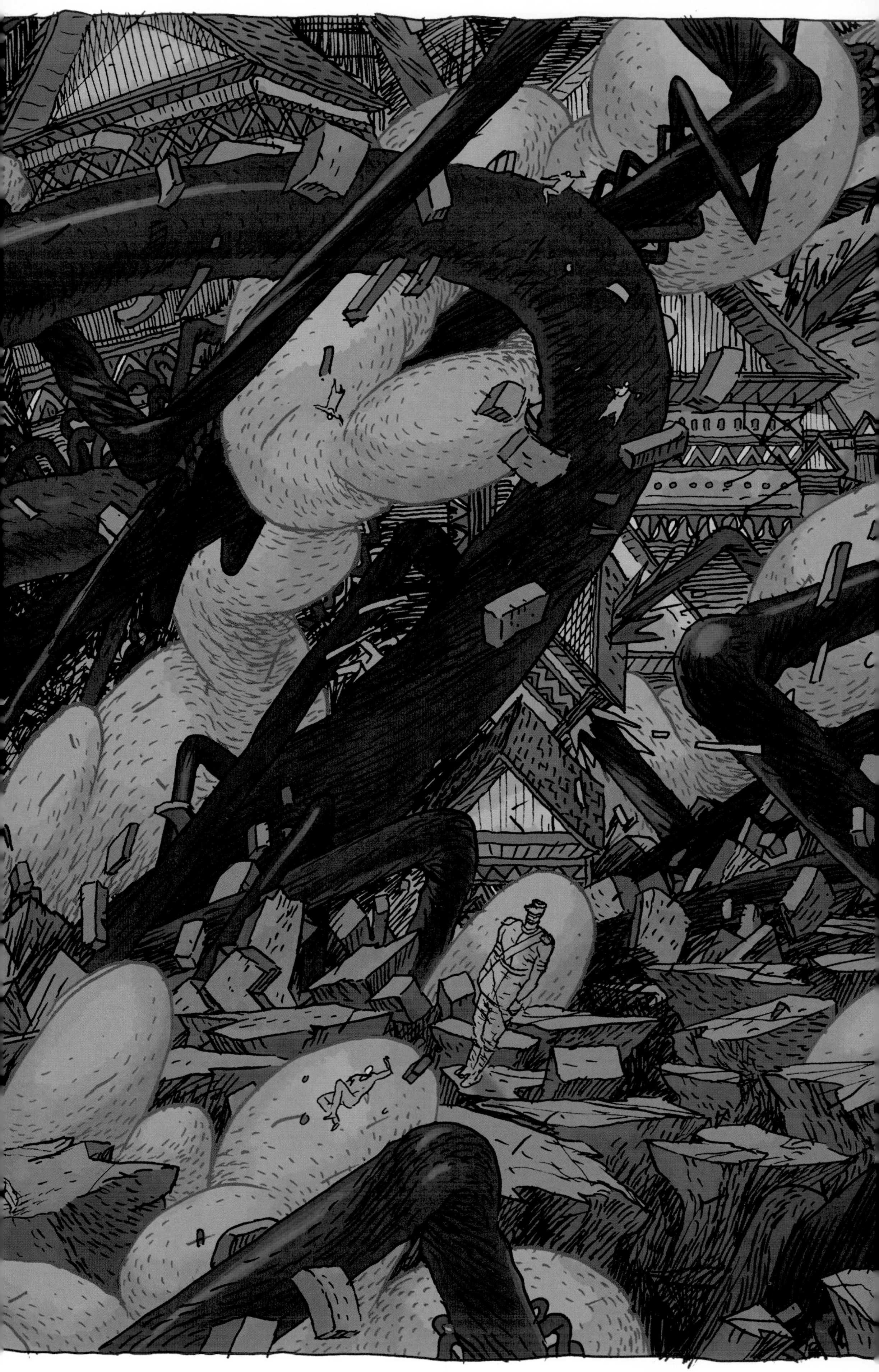

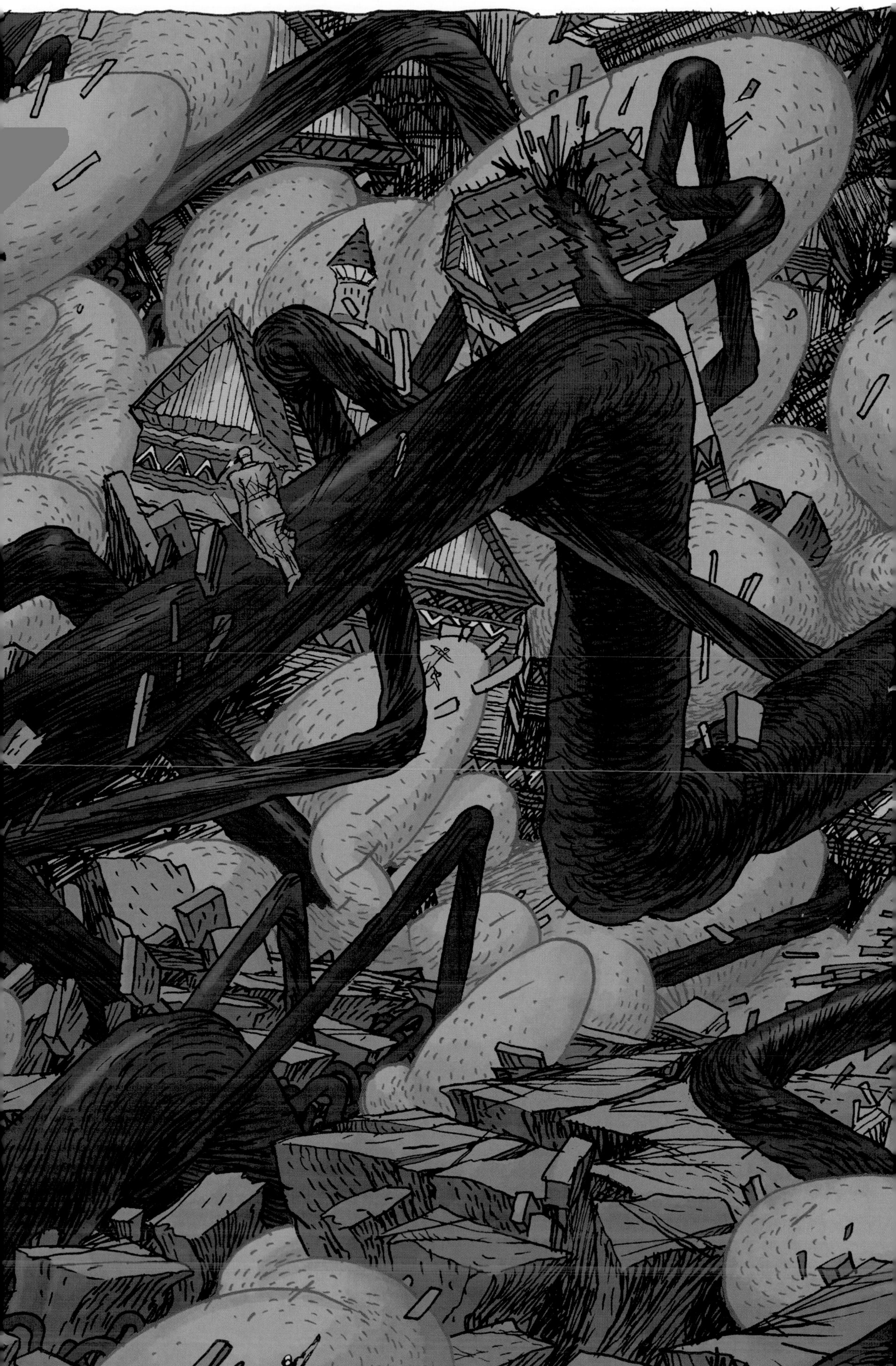

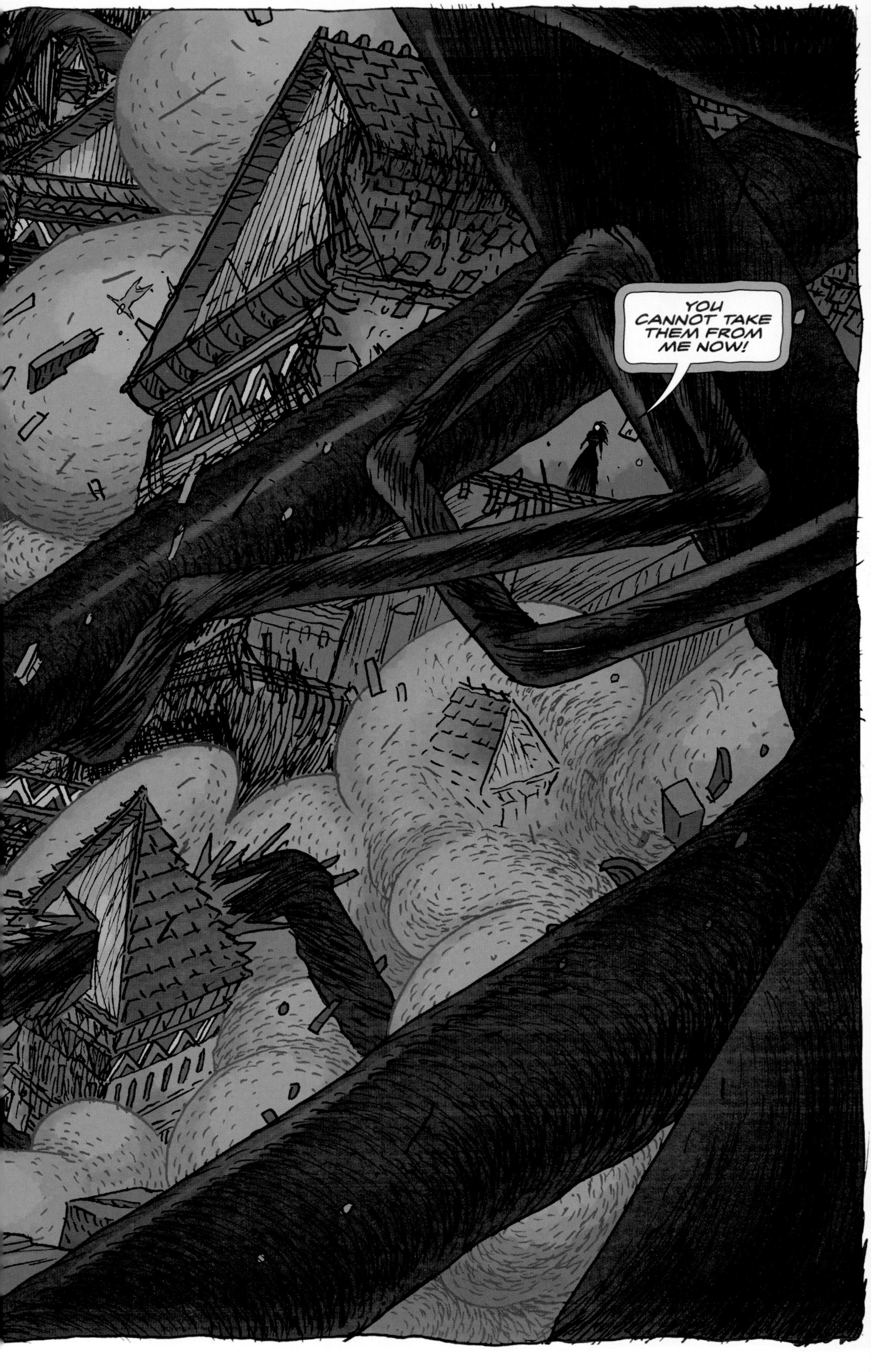
YOU CANNOT TAKE THEM FROM ME NOW!

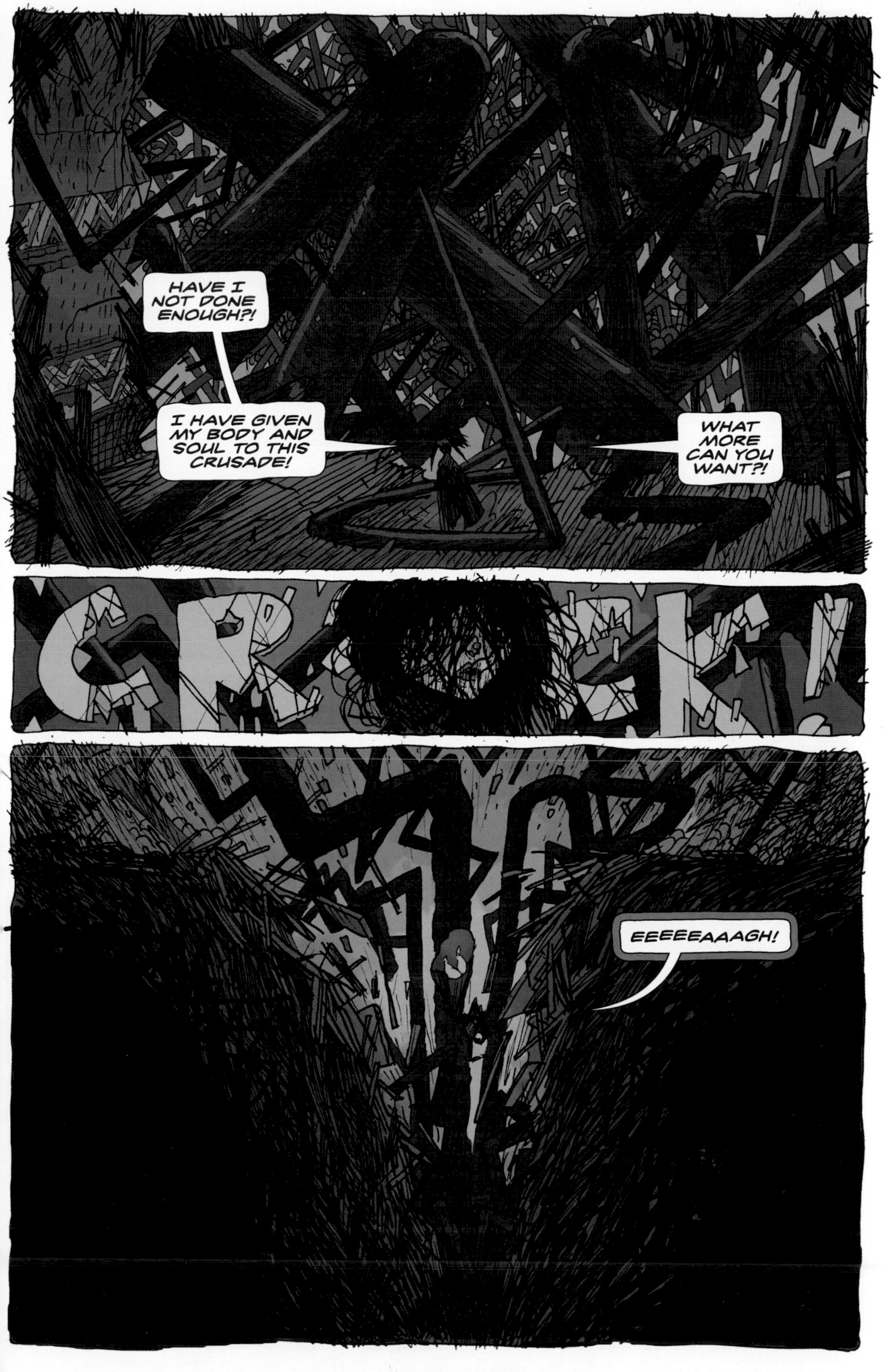
HAVE I NOT DONE ENOUGH?!
I HAVE GIVEN MY BODY AND SOUL TO THIS CRUSADE!
WHAT MORE CAN YOU WANT?!
EEEEEAAAGH!

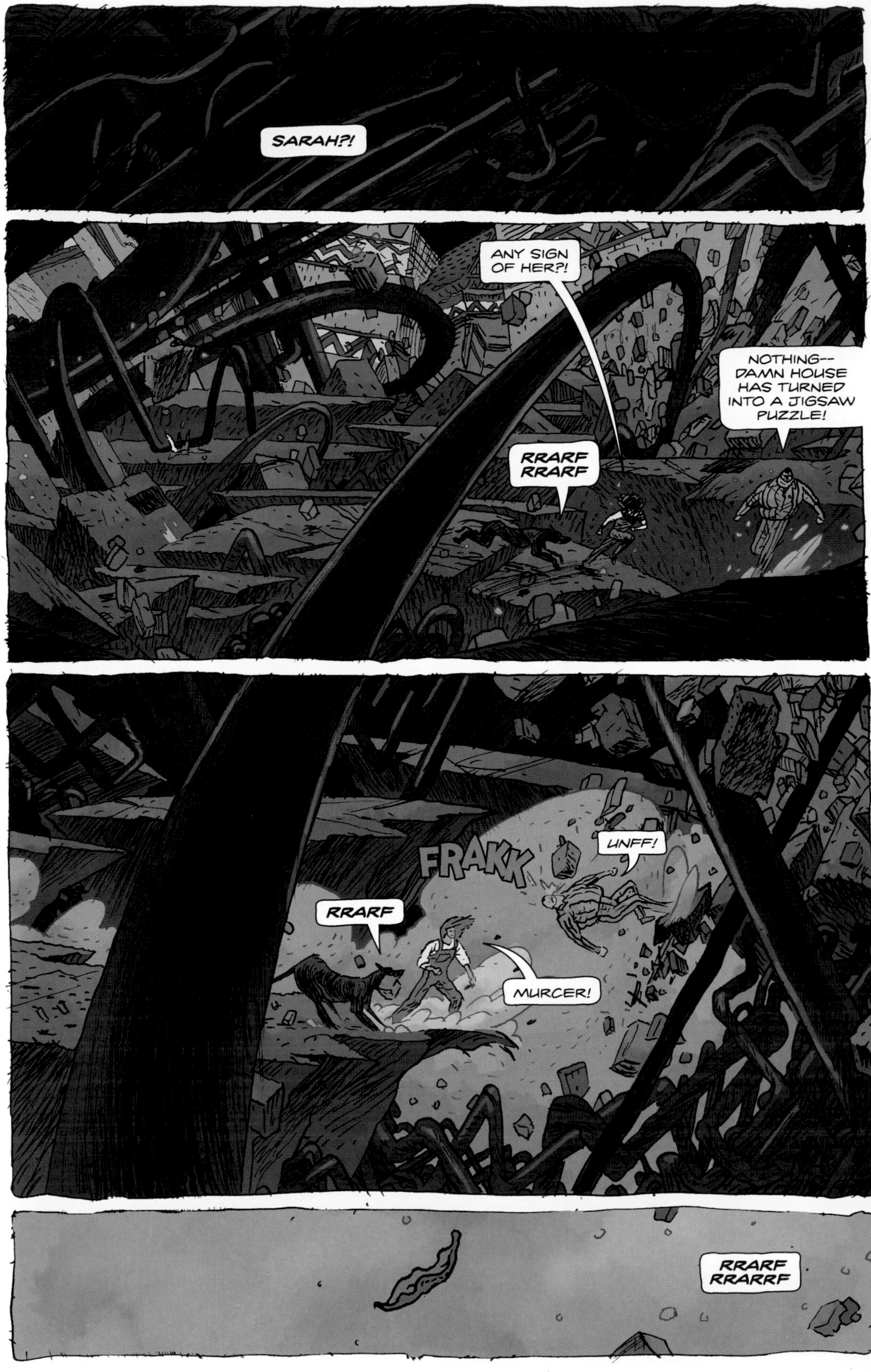
SARAH?!
ANY SIGN OF HER?!
NOTHING-- DAMN HOUSE HAS TURNED INTO A JIGSAW PUZZLE!
RRARF RRARF
FRAKK
UNFF!
RRARF
MURCER!
RRARF RRARRF

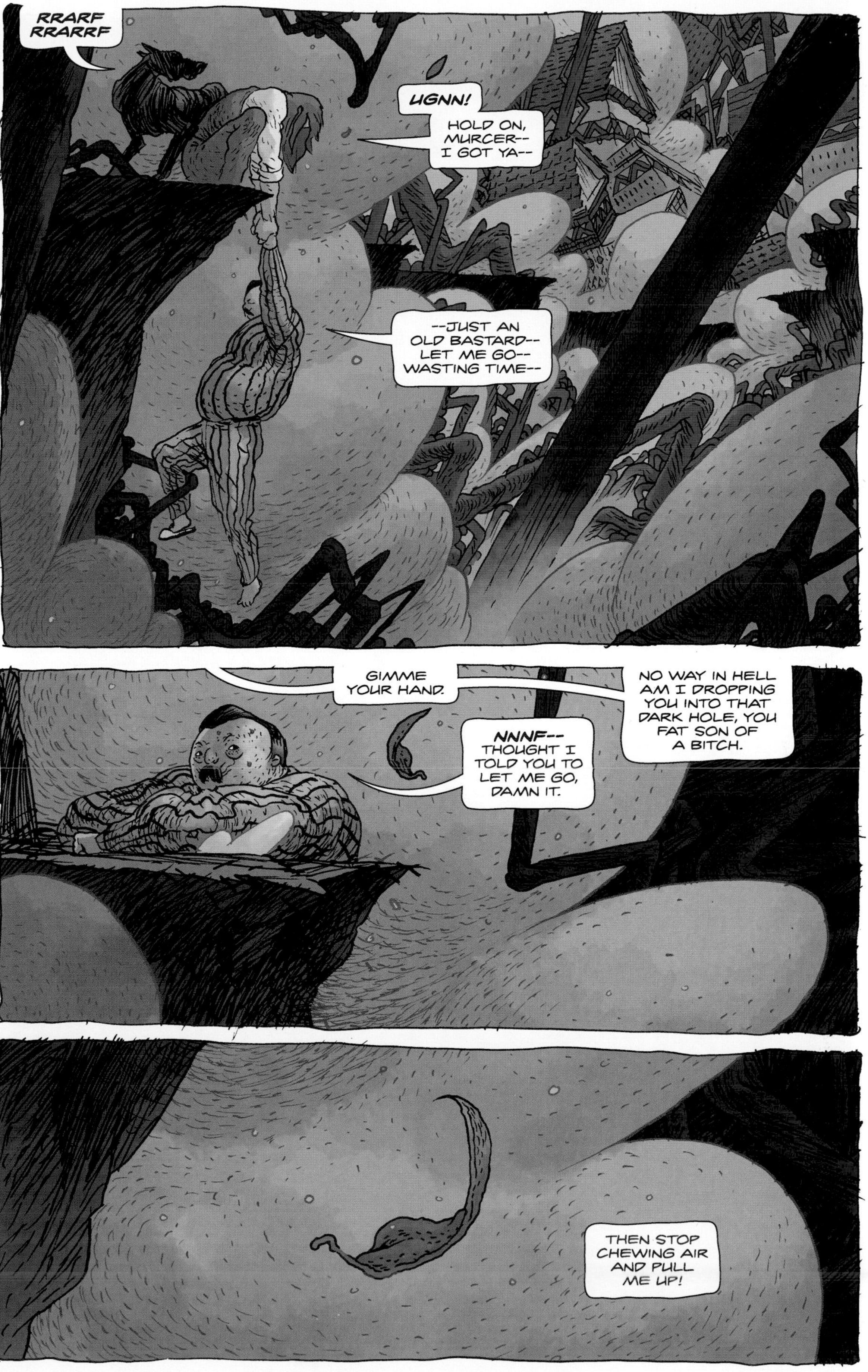
RRARF RRARRF
UGNN!
HOLD ON, MURCER-- I GOT YA--
--JUST AN OLD BASTARD-- LET ME GO-- WASTING TIME--
GIMME YOUR HAND.
NO WAY IN HELL AM I DROPPING YOU INTO THAT DARK HOLE, YOU FAT SON OF A BITCH.
NNNF-- THOUGHT I TOLD YOU TO LET ME GO, DAMN IT.
THEN STOP CHEWING AIR AND PULL ME UP!

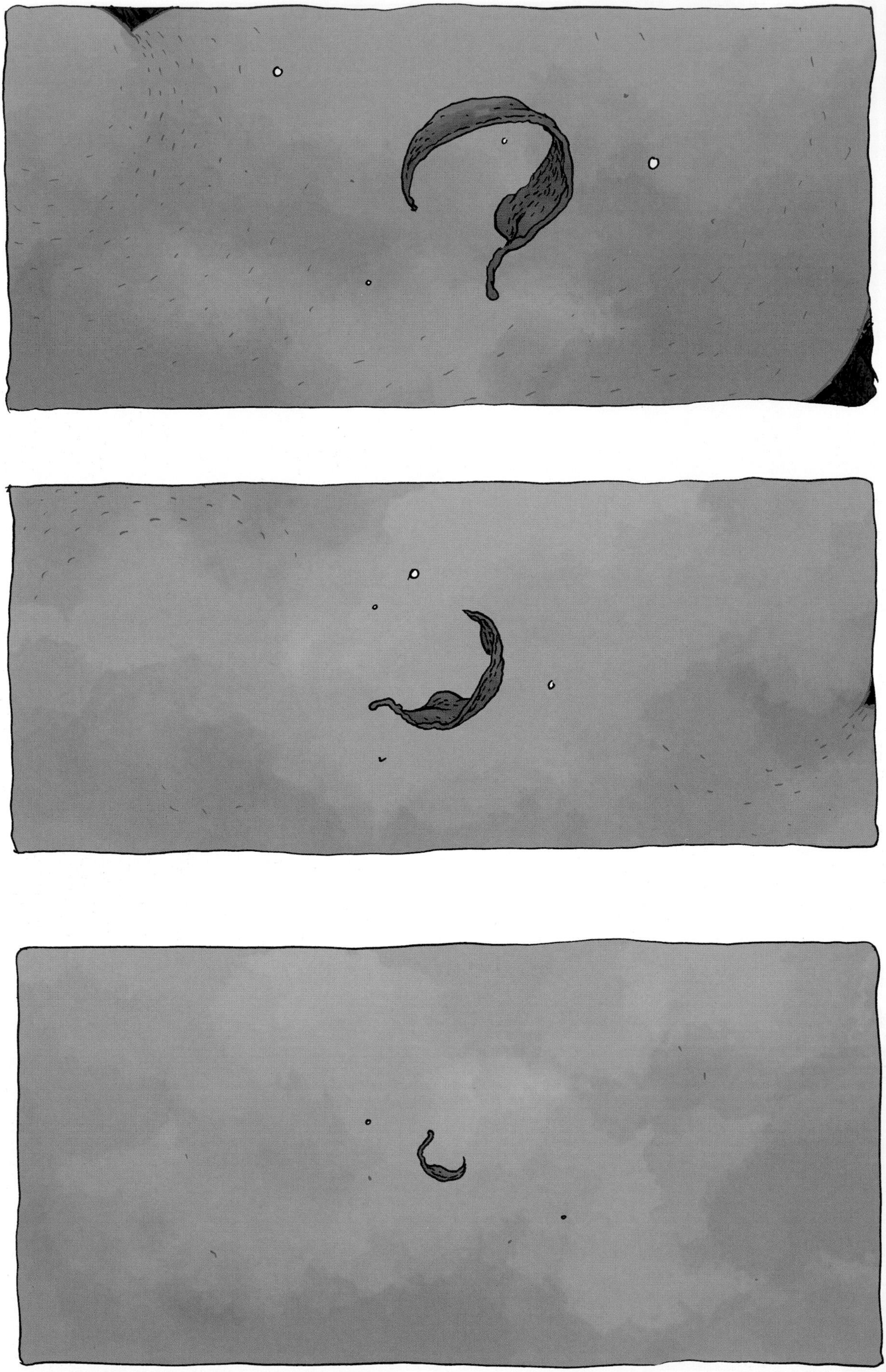

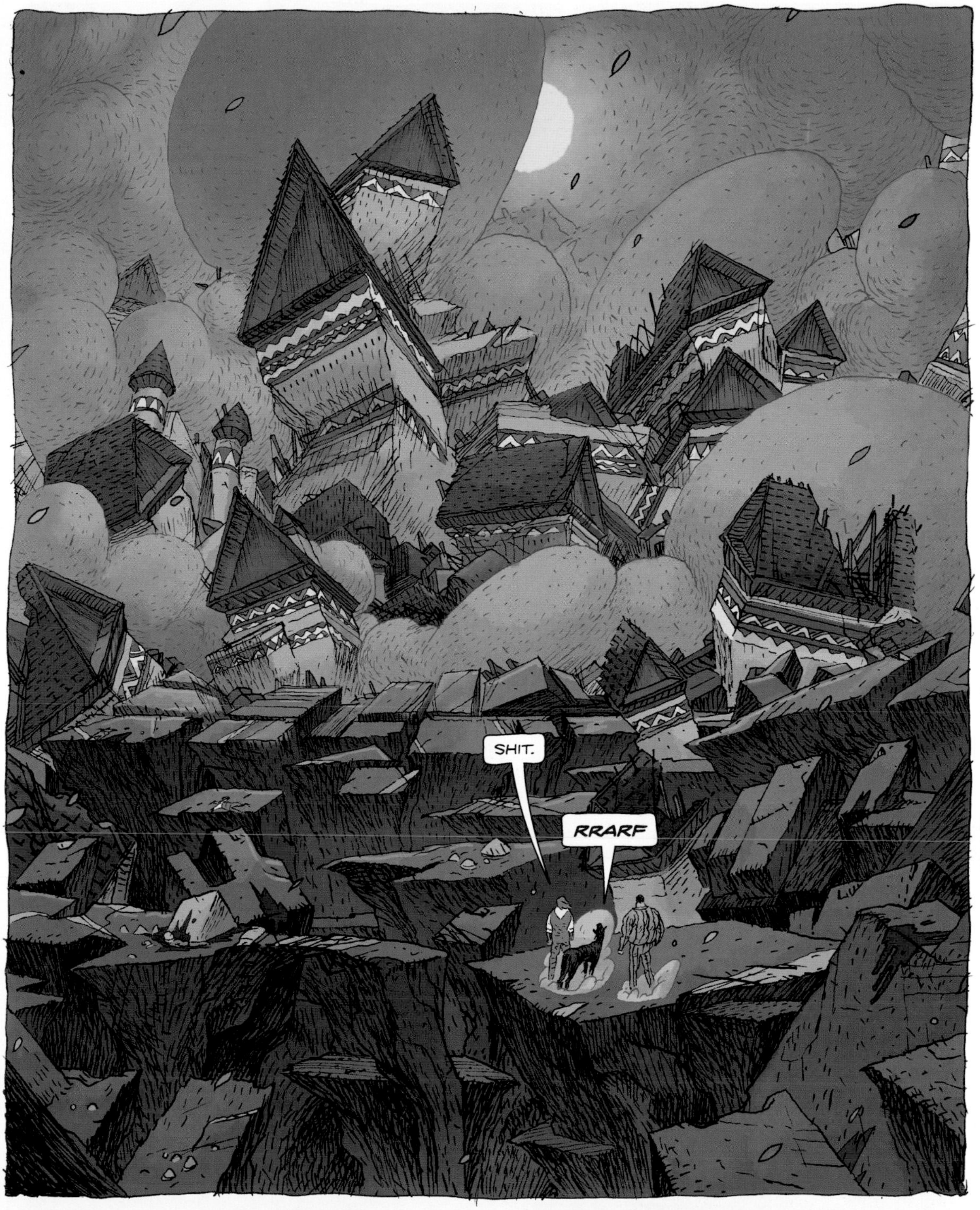
SHIT.
RRARF

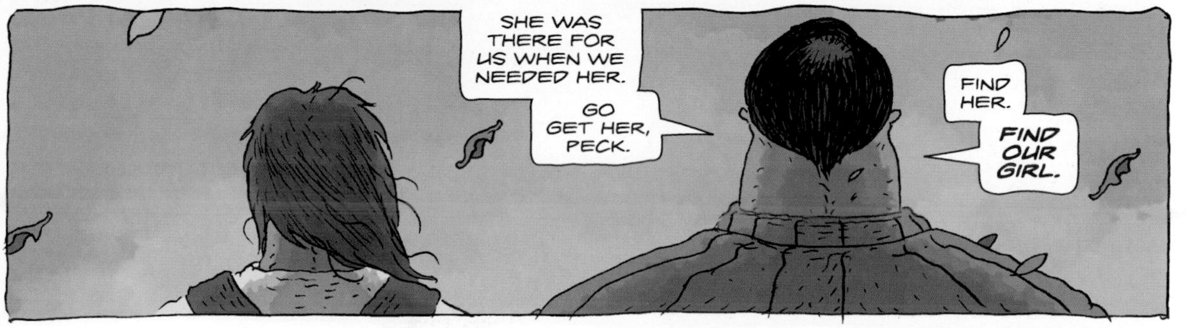
SHE WAS THERE FOR US WHEN WE NEEDED HER.
GO GET HER, PECK.
FIND HER.
FIND OUR GIRL.

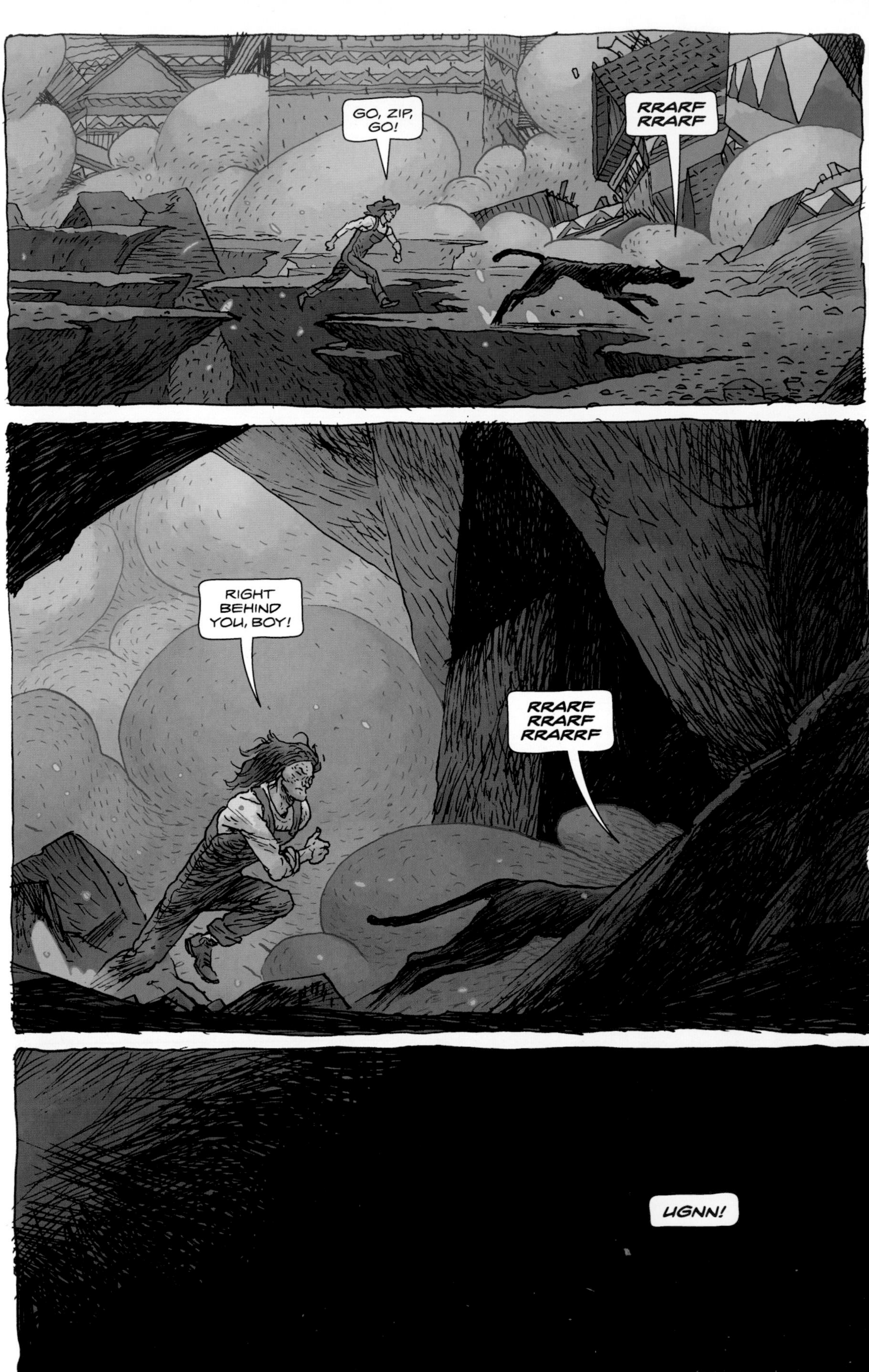
GO, ZIP, GO!
RRARF RRARF
RIGHT BEHIND YOU, BOY!
RRARF RRARF RRARRF
UGNN!

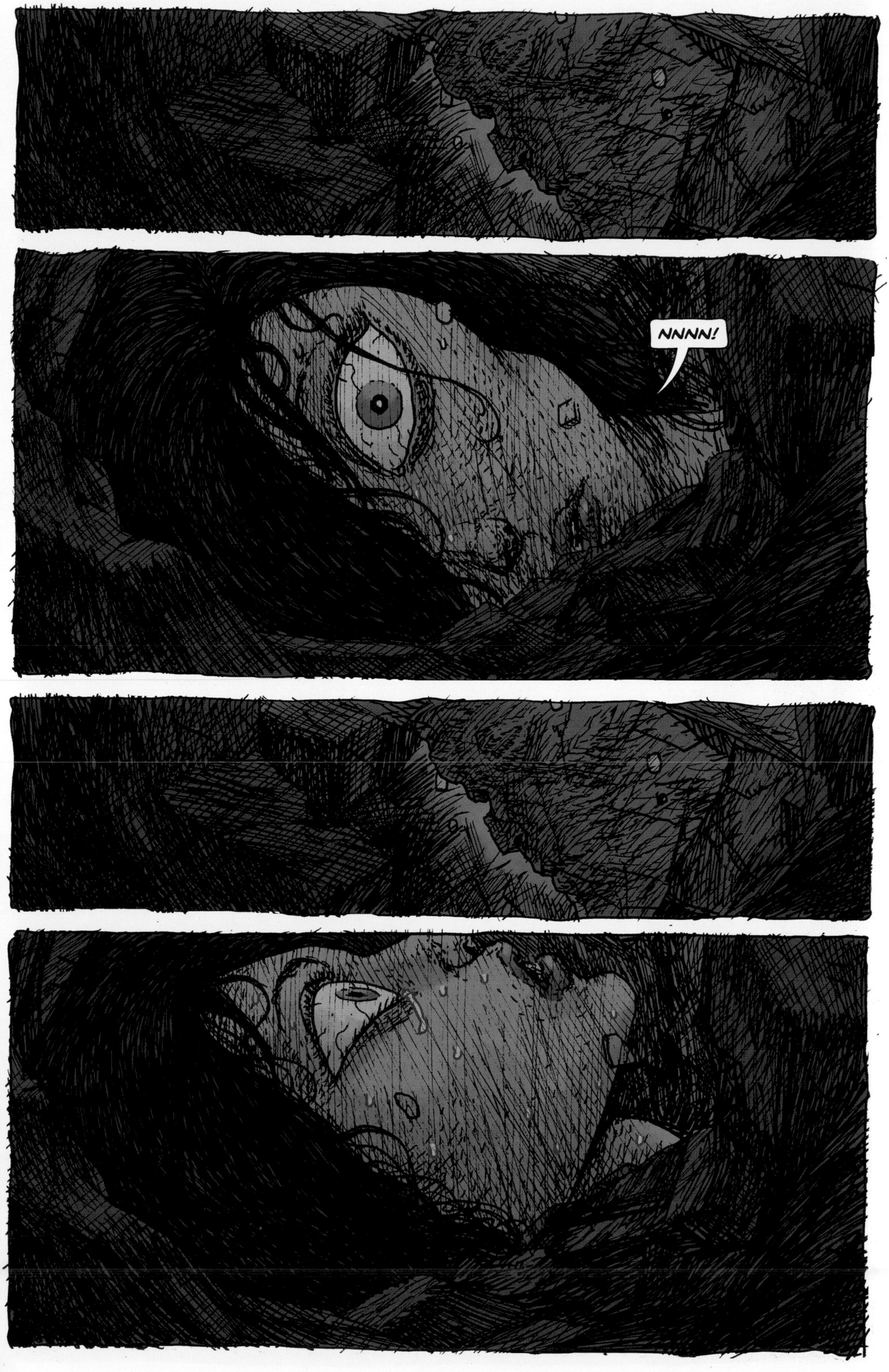
NNNN!

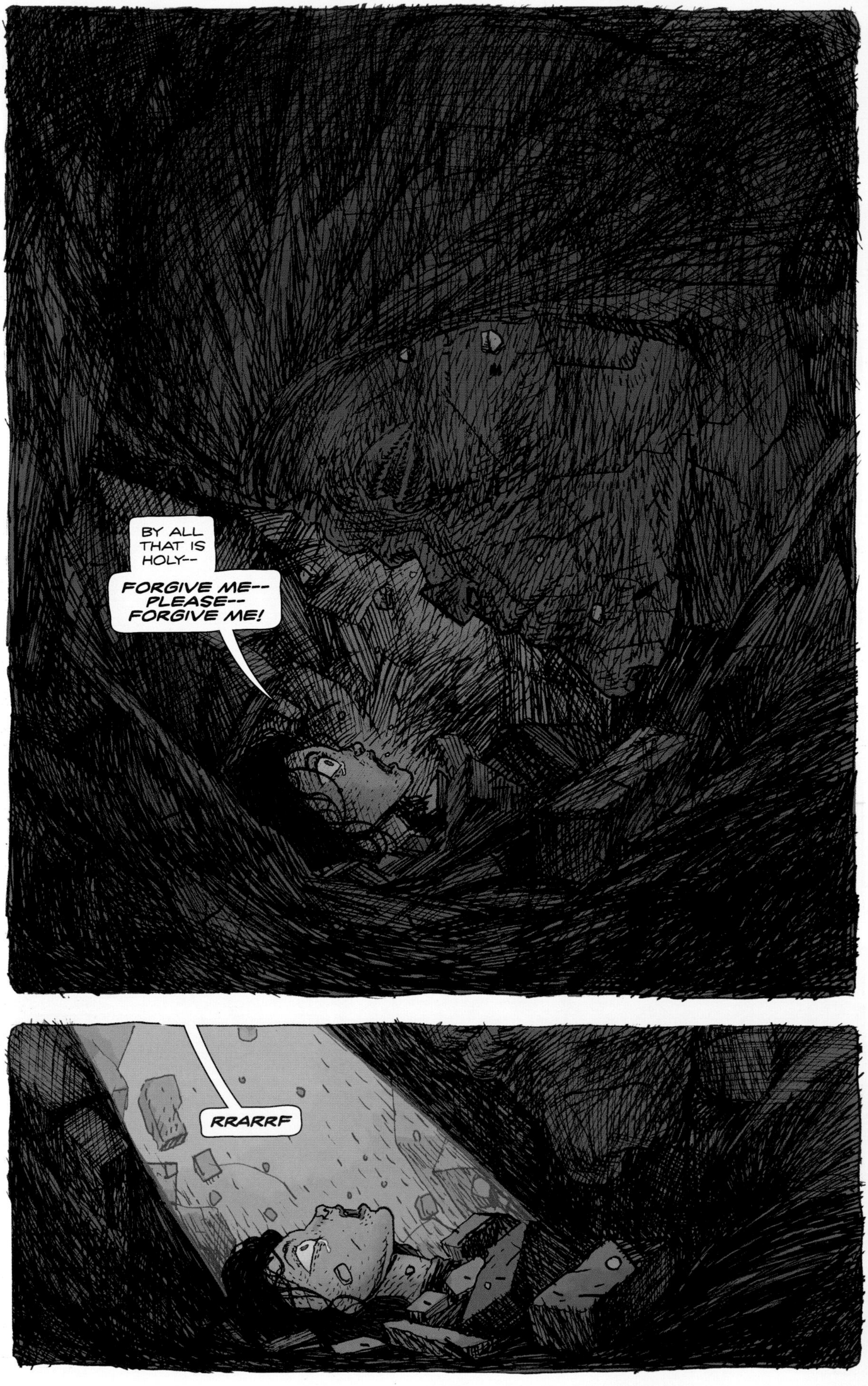
BY ALL THAT IS HOLY--
FORGIVE ME-- PLEASE-- FORGIVE ME!
RRARRF

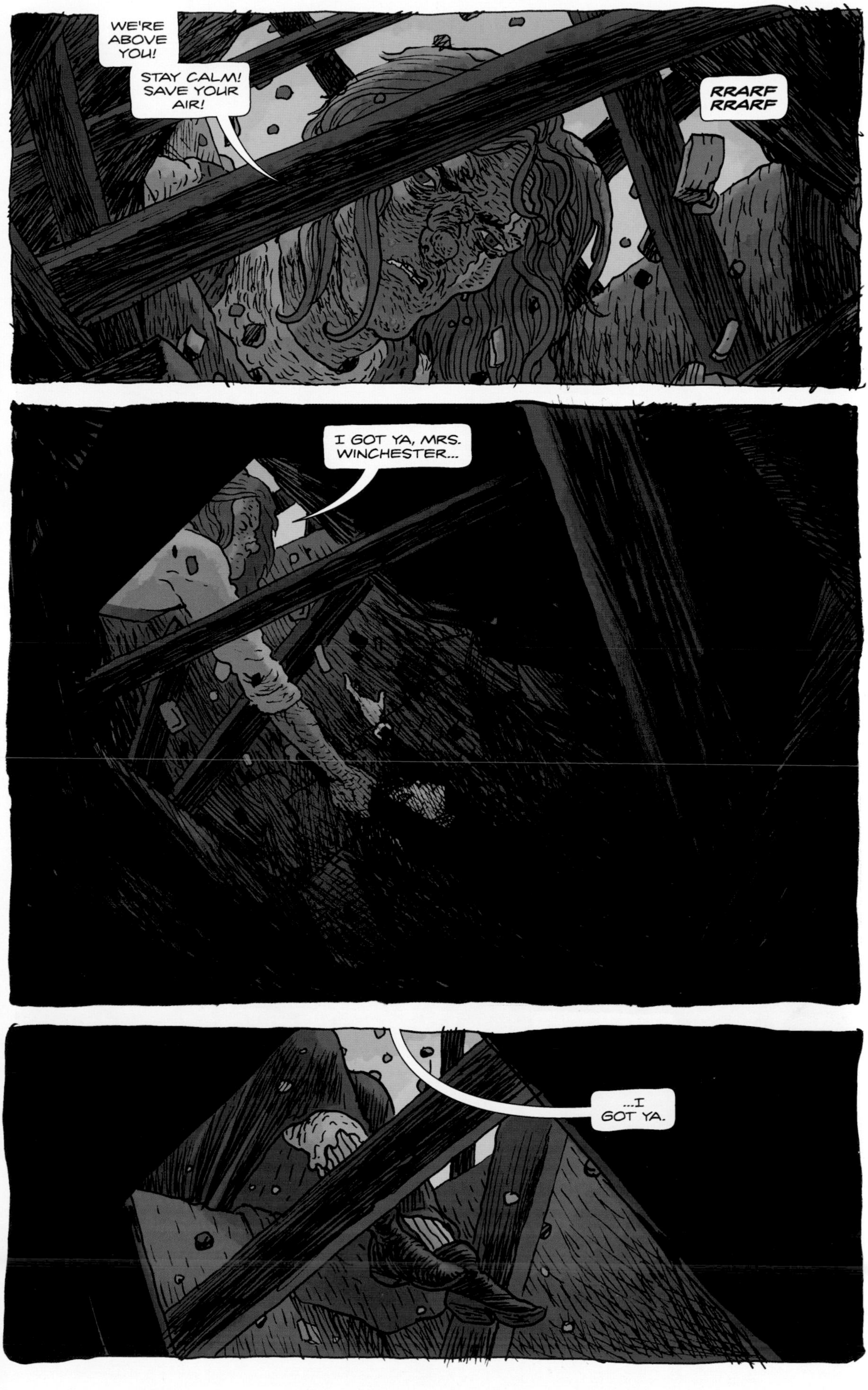
WE'RE ABOVE YOU!
STAY CALM! SAVE YOUR AIR!
RRARF RRARF
I GOT YA, MRS. WINCHESTER...
...I GOT YA.

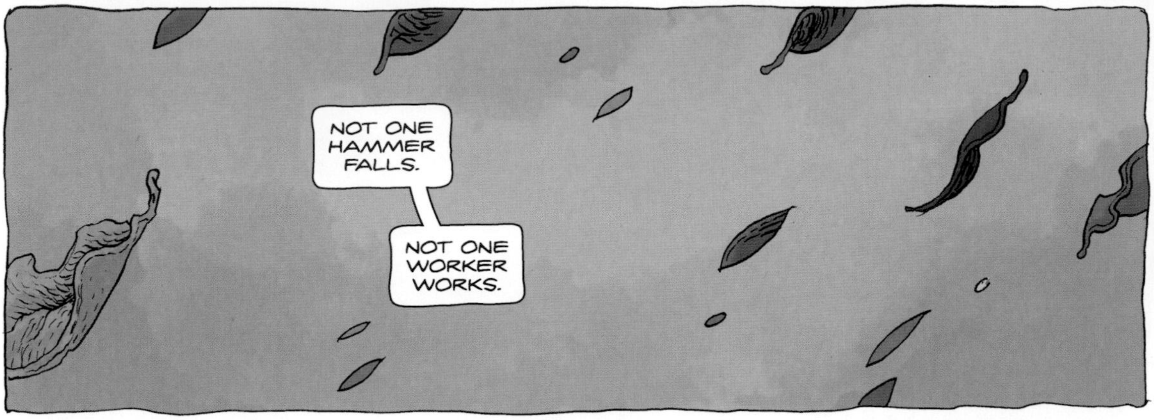
NOT ONE HAMMER FALLS.
NOT ONE WORKER WORKS.

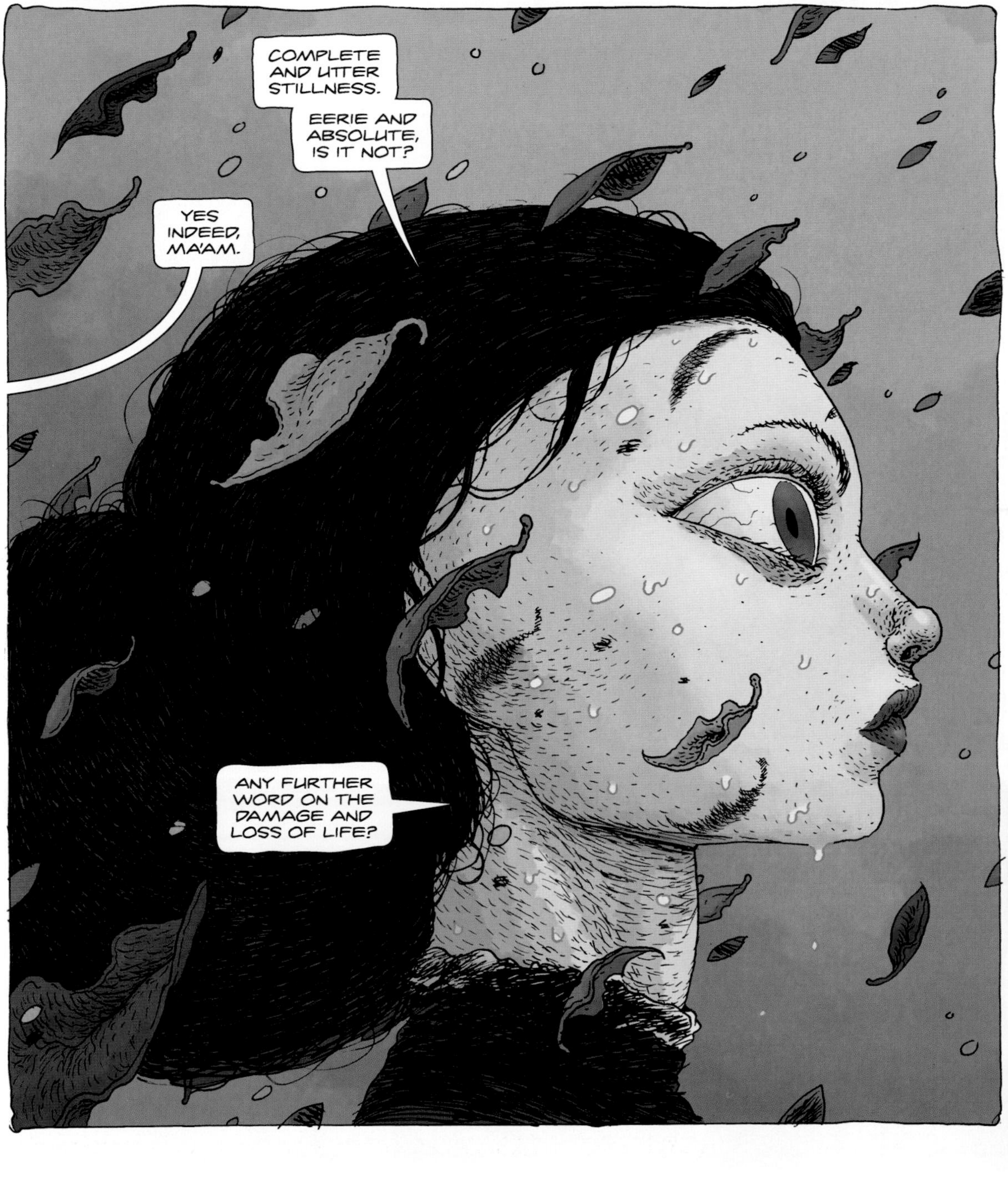
COMPLETE AND UTTER STILLNESS.
EERIE AND ABSOLUTE, IS IT NOT?
YES INDEED, MA'AM.
ANY FURTHER WORD ON THE DAMAGE AND LOSS OF LIFE?

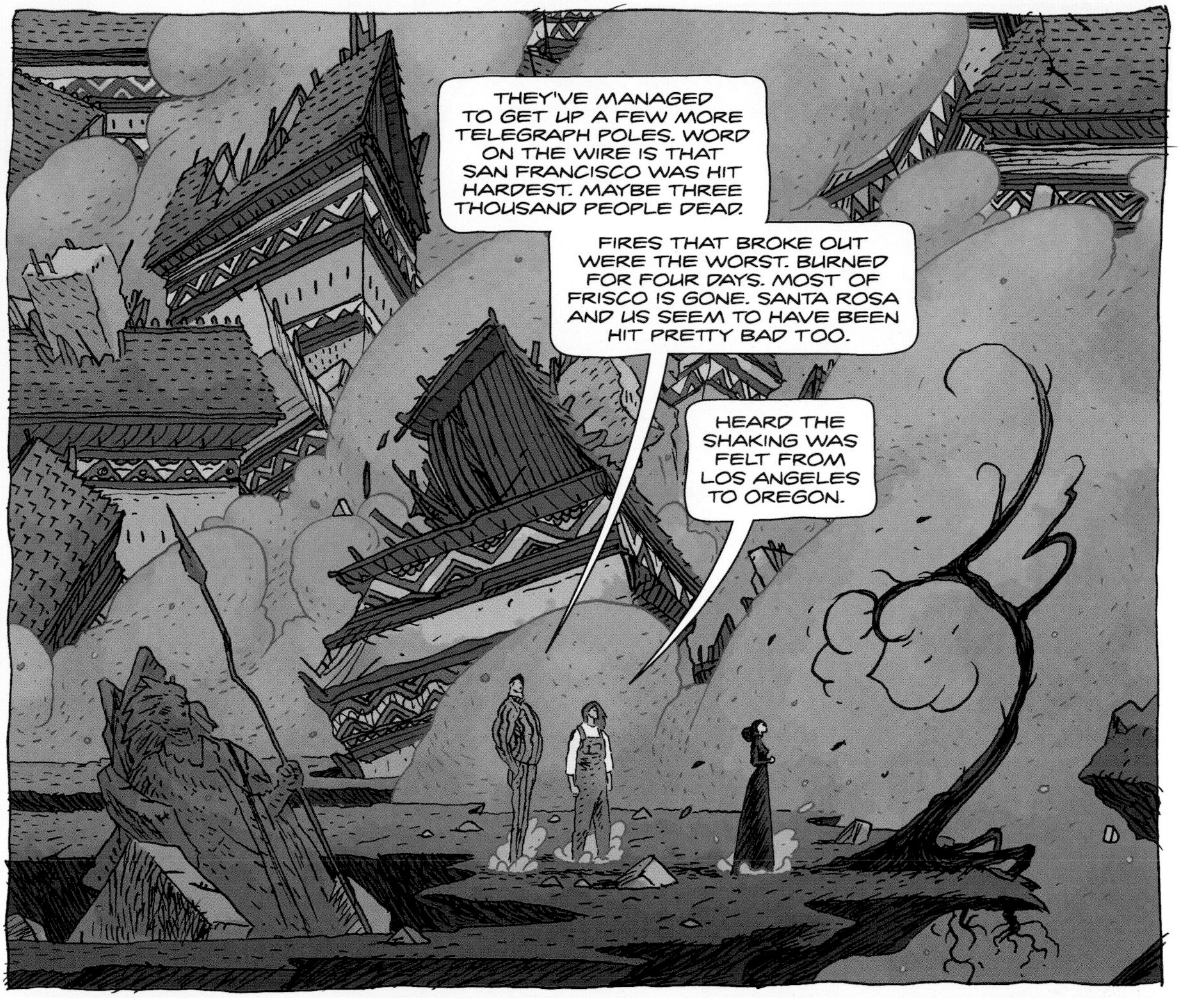
THEY'VE MANAGED TO GET UP A FEW MORE TELEGRAPH POLES. WORD ON THE WIRE IS THAT SAN FRANCISCO WAS HIT HARDEST. MAYBE THREE THOUSAND PEOPLE DEAD.
FIRES THAT BROKE OUT WERE THE WORST. BURNED FOR FOUR DAYS. MOST OF FRISCO IS GONE. SANTA ROSA AND US SEEM TO HAVE BEEN HIT PRETTY BAD TOO.
HEARD THE SHAKING WAS FELT FROM LOS ANGELES TO OREGON.

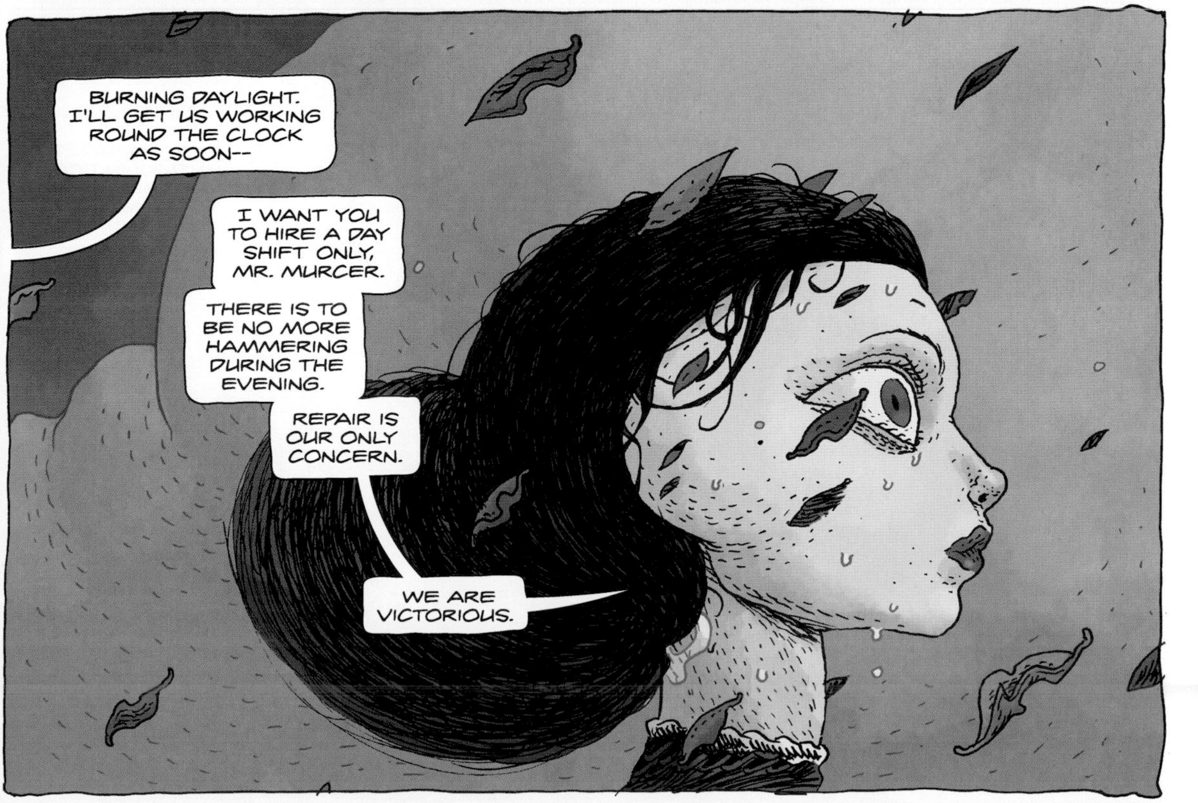
BURNING DAYLIGHT. I'LL GET US WORKING ROUND THE CLOCK AS SOON--
I WANT YOU TO HIRE A DAY SHIFT ONLY, MR. MURCER.
THERE IS TO BE NO MORE HAMMERING DURING THE EVENING.
REPAIR IS OUR ONLY CONCERN.
WE ARE VICTORIOUS.

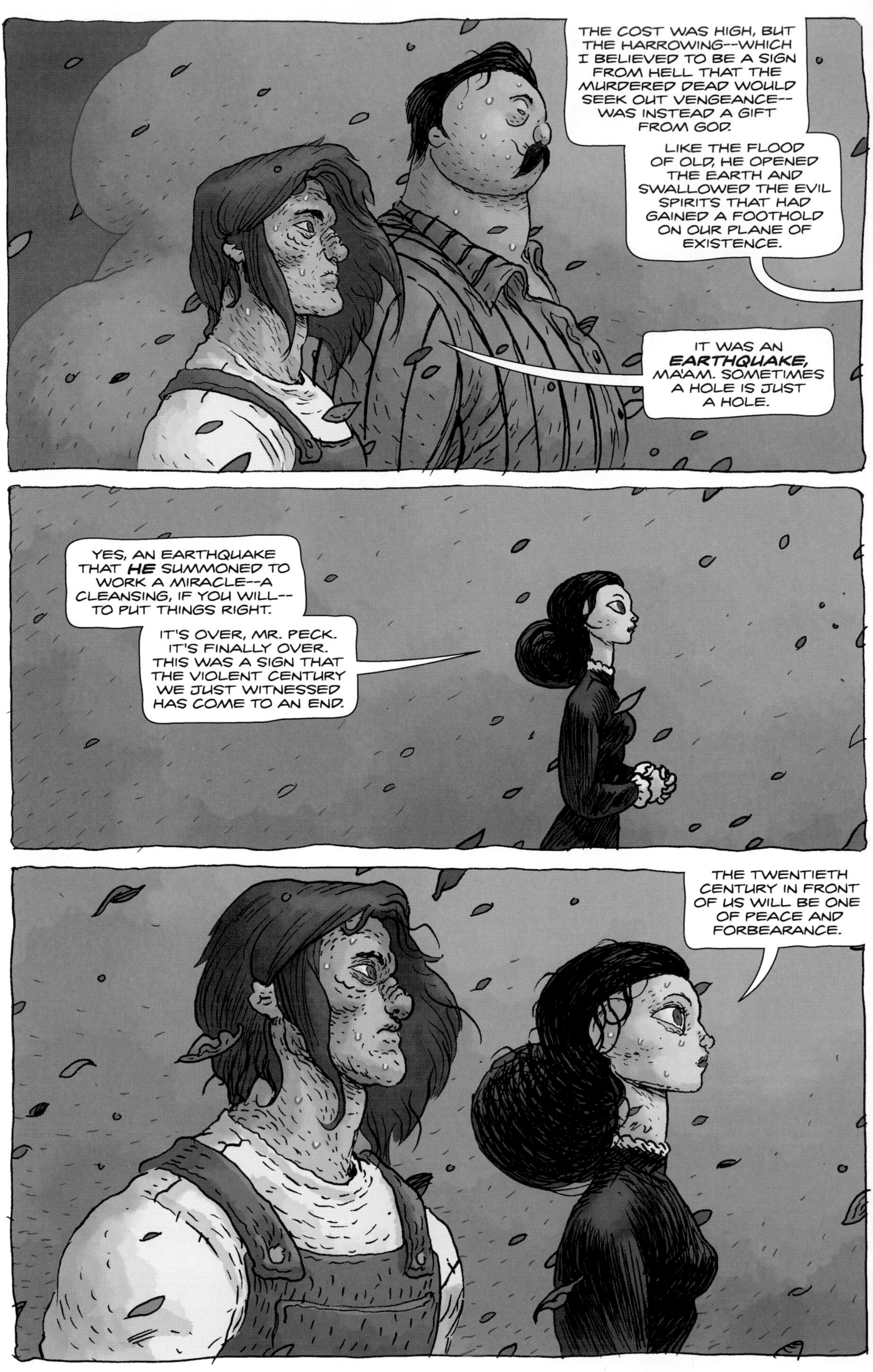
THE COST WAS HIGH, BUT THE HARROWING--WHICH I BELIEVED TO BE A SIGN FROM HELL THAT THE MURDERED DEAD WOULD SEEK OUT VENGEANCE--WAS INSTEAD A GIFT FROM GOD.
LIKE THE FLOOD OF OLD, HE OPENED THE EARTH AND SWALLOWED THE EVIL SPIRITS THAT HAD GAINED A FOOTHOLD ON OUR PLANE OF EXISTENCE.
IT WAS AN ***EARTHQUAKE,*** MA'AM. SOMETIMES A HOLE IS JUST A HOLE.
YES, AN EARTHQUAKE THAT ***HE*** SUMMONED TO WORK A MIRACLE--A CLEANSING, IF YOU WILL--TO PUT THINGS RIGHT.
IT'S OVER, MR. PECK. IT'S FINALLY OVER. THIS WAS A SIGN THAT THE VIOLENT CENTURY WE JUST WITNESSED HAS COME TO AN END.
THE TWENTIETH CENTURY IN FRONT OF US WILL BE ONE OF PEACE AND FORBEARANCE.

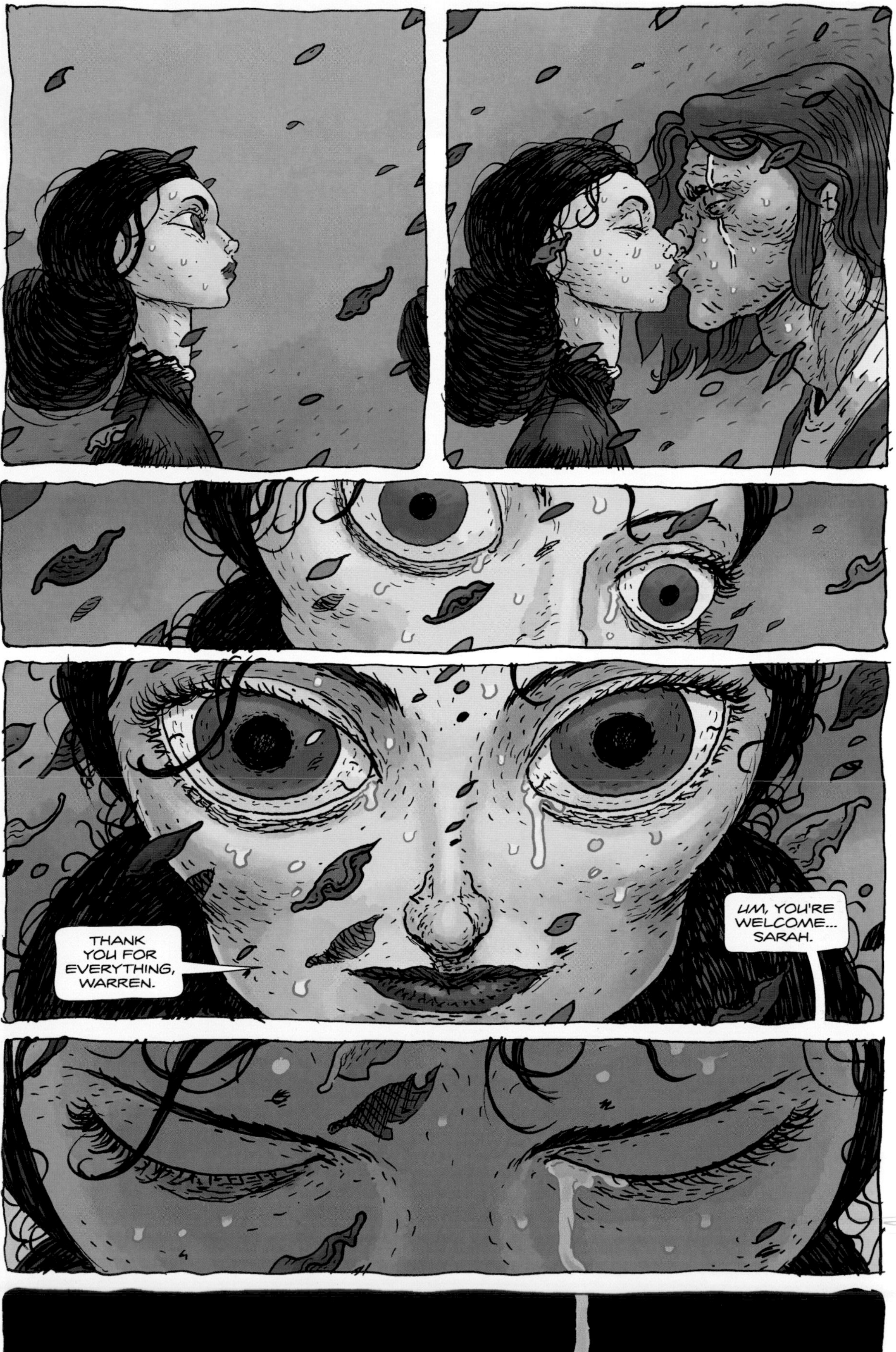
THANK YOU FOR EVERYTHING, WARREN.
UM, YOU'RE WELCOME... SARAH.

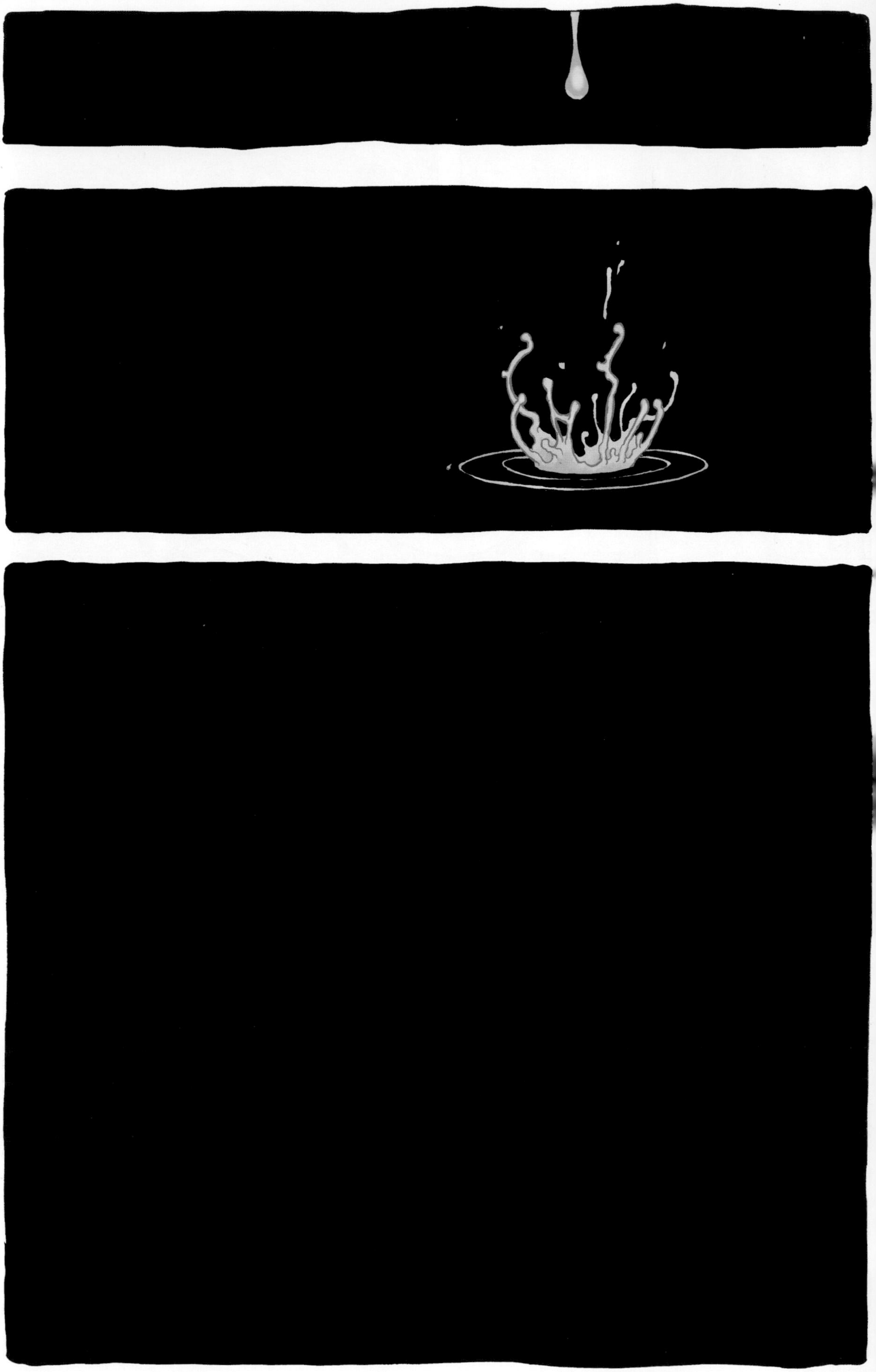

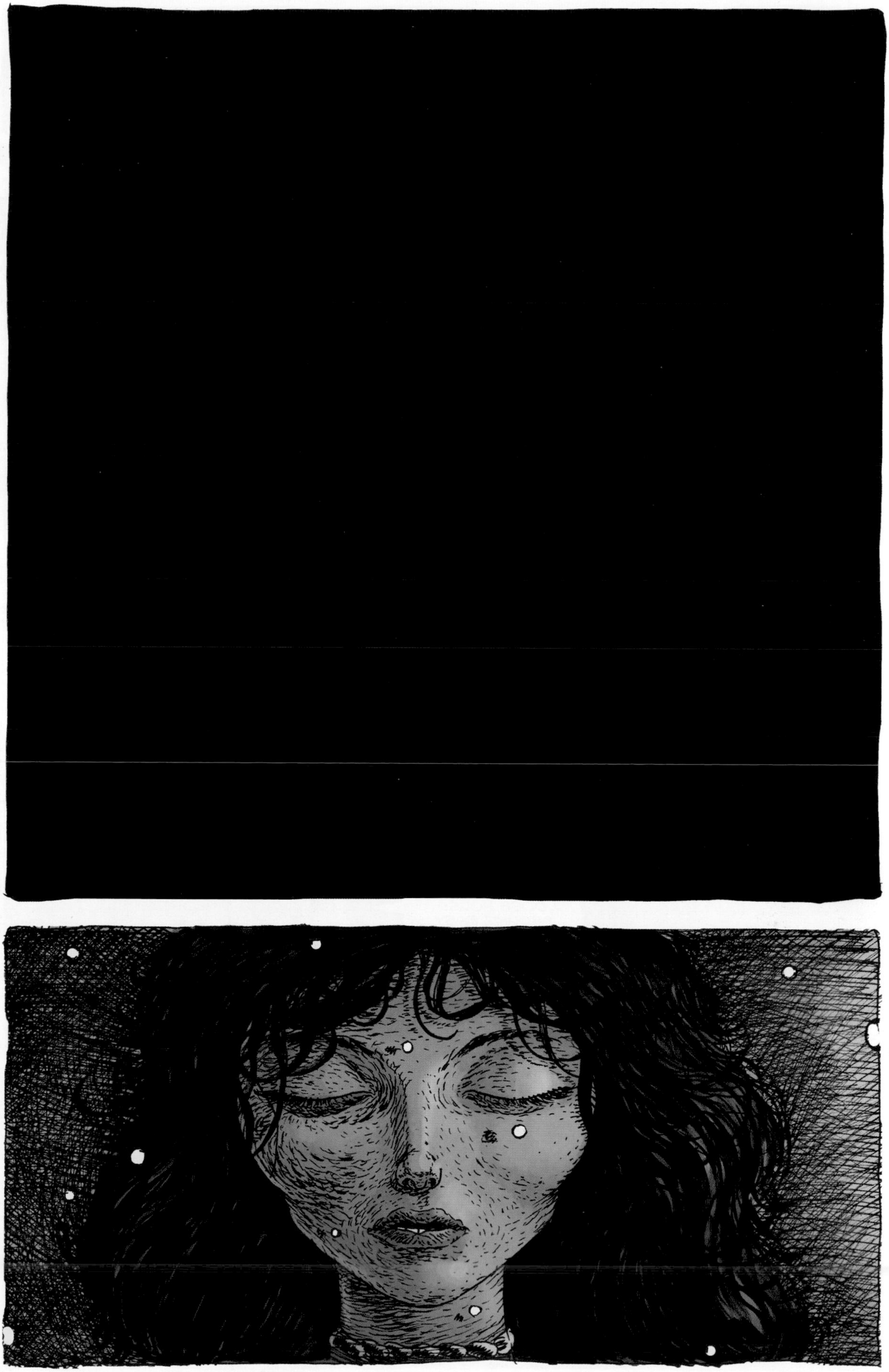

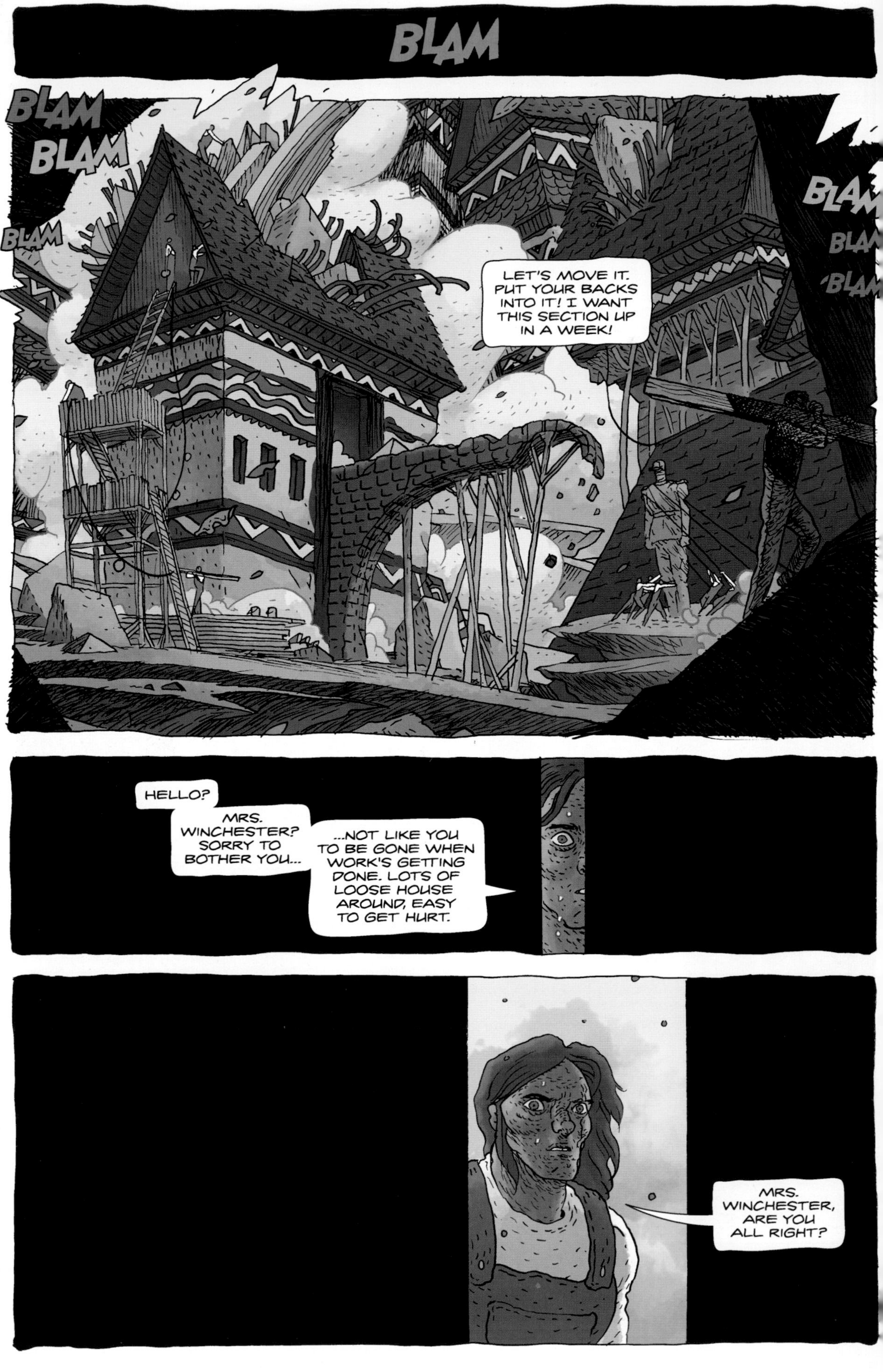
BLAM
BLAM
BLAM
BLAM
BLAM
BLAM
BLAM
LET'S MOVE IT. PUT YOUR BACKS INTO IT! I WANT THIS SECTION UP IN A WEEK!
HELLO?
MRS. WINCHESTER? SORRY TO BOTHER YOU...
...NOT LIKE YOU TO BE GONE WHEN WORK'S GETTING DONE. LOTS OF LOOSE HOUSE AROUND, EASY TO GET HURT.
MRS. WINCHESTER, ARE YOU ALL RIGHT?

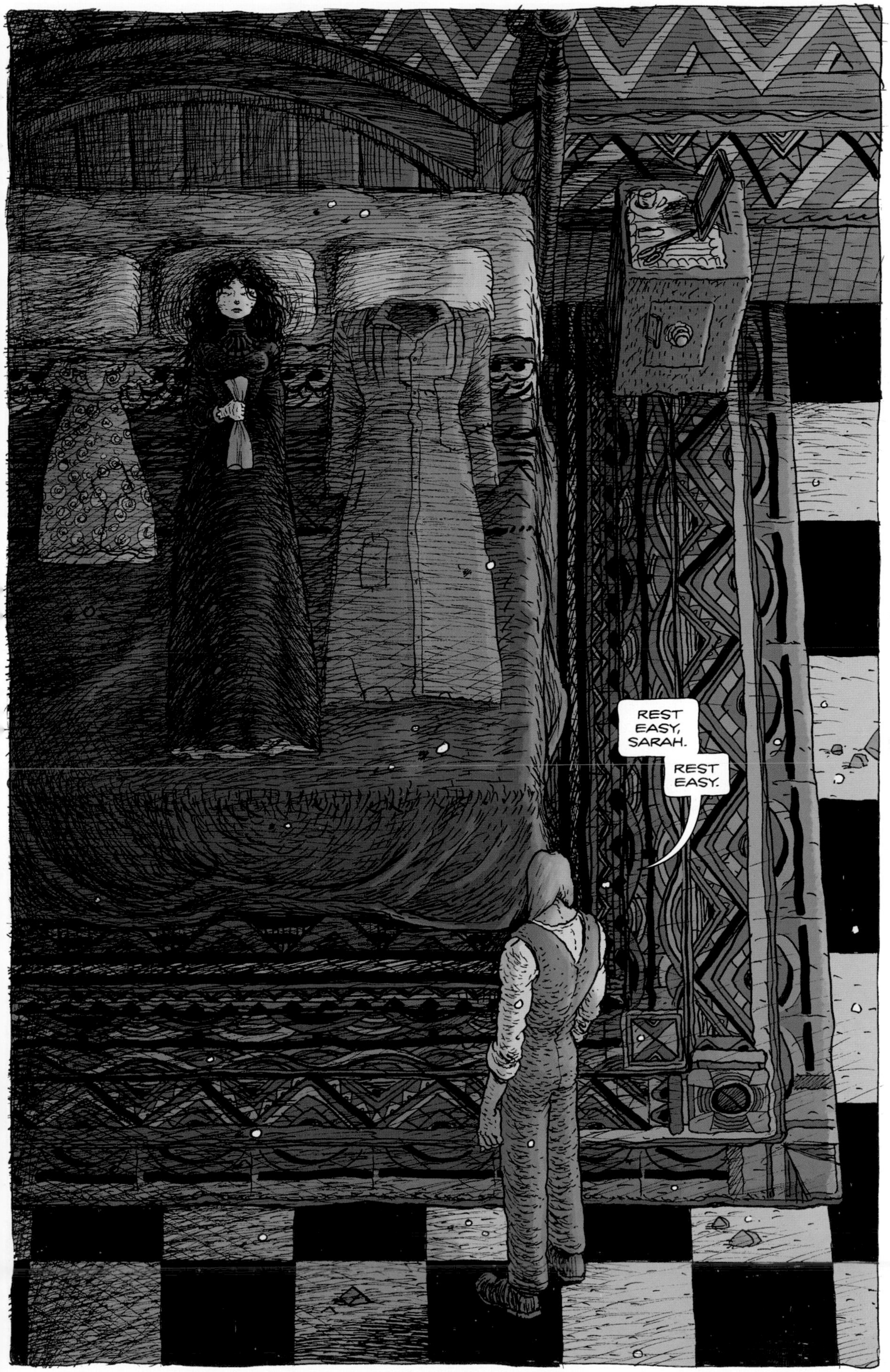
REST EASY, SARAH.
REST EASY.

For Warren

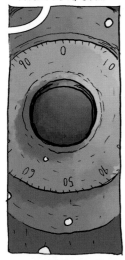

TWO, SIXTEEN,
THREE, SEVENTEEN,
NINETEEN, SIX...

CLANKK

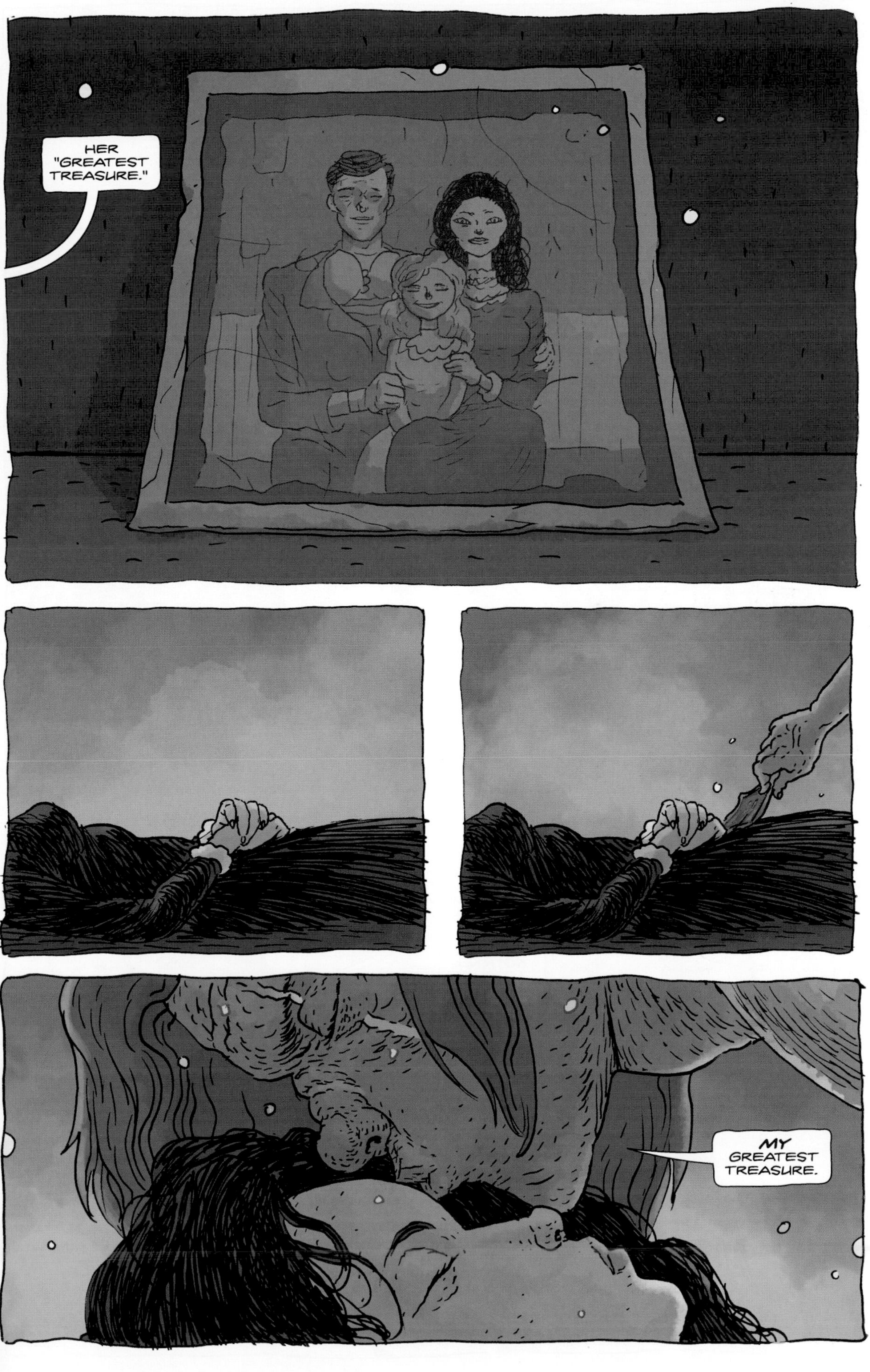
HER "GREATEST TREASURE."
MY GREATEST TREASURE.

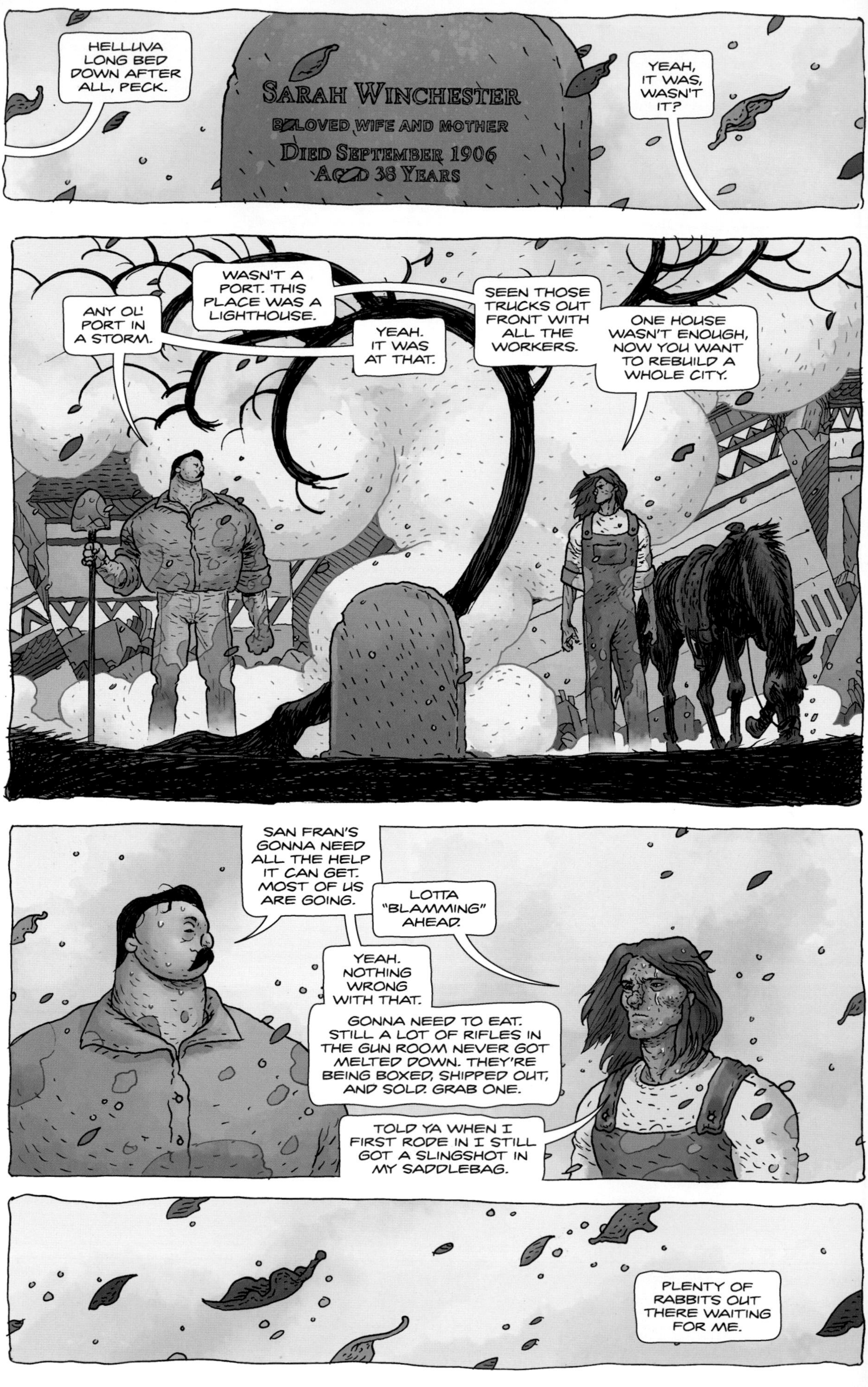
HELLUVA LONG BED DOWN AFTER ALL, PECK.
SARAH WINCHESTER
BELOVED WIFE AND MOTHER
DIED SEPTEMBER 1906
AGED 38 YEARS
YEAH, IT WAS, WASN'T IT?
ANY OL' PORT IN A STORM.
WASN'T A PORT. THIS PLACE WAS A LIGHTHOUSE.
YEAH. IT WAS AT THAT.
SEEN THOSE TRUCKS OUT FRONT WITH ALL THE WORKERS.
ONE HOUSE WASN'T ENOUGH, NOW YOU WANT TO REBUILD A WHOLE CITY.
SAN FRAN'S GONNA NEED ALL THE HELP IT CAN GET. MOST OF US ARE GOING.
LOTTA "BLAMMING" AHEAD.
YEAH. NOTHING WRONG WITH THAT.
GONNA NEED TO EAT. STILL A LOT OF RIFLES IN THE GUN ROOM NEVER GOT MELTED DOWN. THEY'RE BEING BOXED, SHIPPED OUT, AND SOLD. GRAB ONE.
TOLD YA WHEN I FIRST RODE IN I STILL GOT A SLINGSHOT IN MY SADDLEBAG.
PLENTY OF RABBITS OUT THERE WAITING FOR ME.

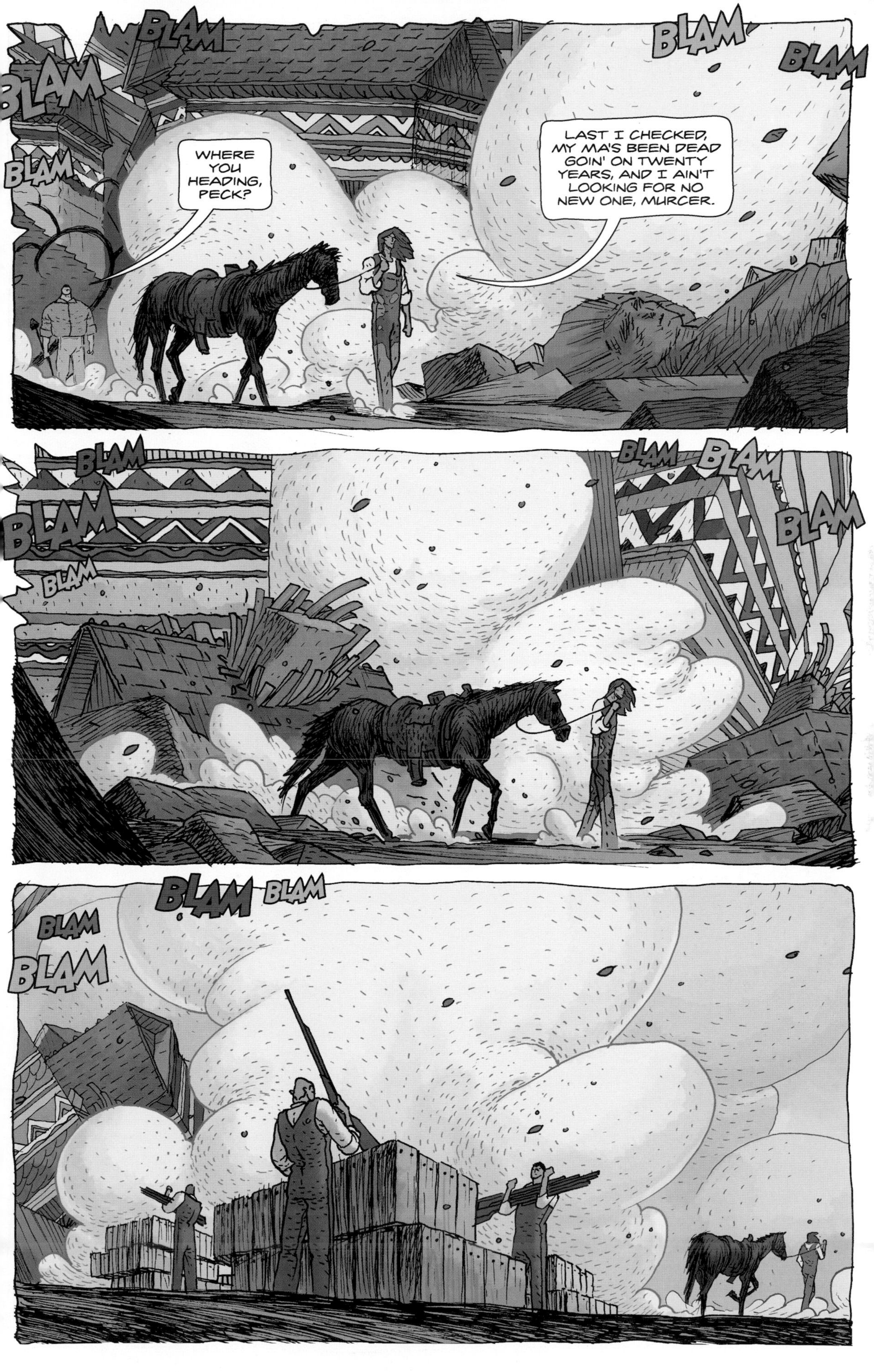
BLAM
BLAM
BLAM
BLAM
BLAM
WHERE YOU HEADING, PECK?
LAST I CHECKED, MY MA'S BEEN DEAD GOIN' ON TWENTY YEARS, AND I AIN'T LOOKING FOR NO NEW ONE, MURCER.
BLAM
BLAM
BLAM
BLAM
BLAM
BLAM
BLAM
BLAM
BLAM
BLAM

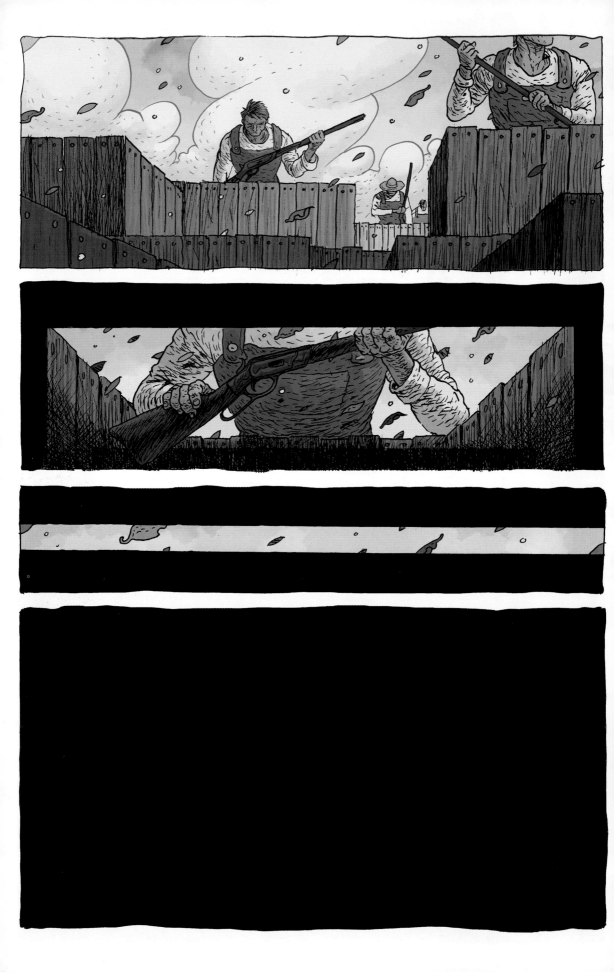

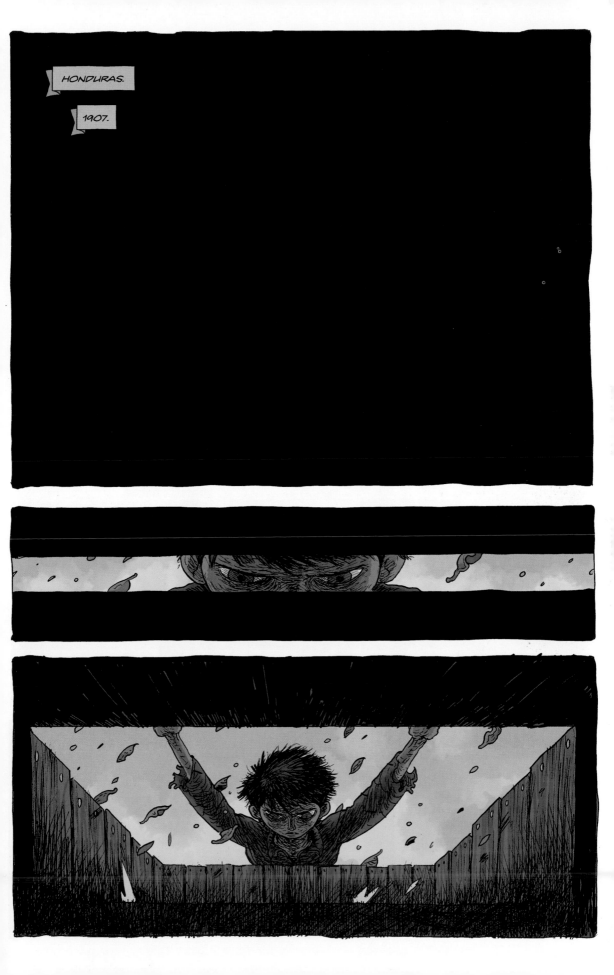

HONDURAS.

1907.

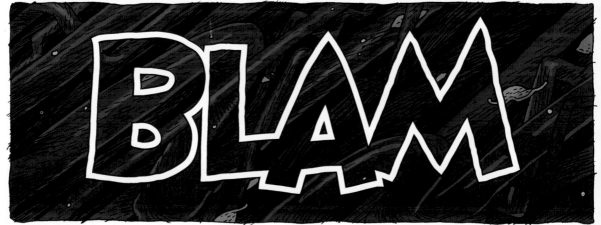

BLAM

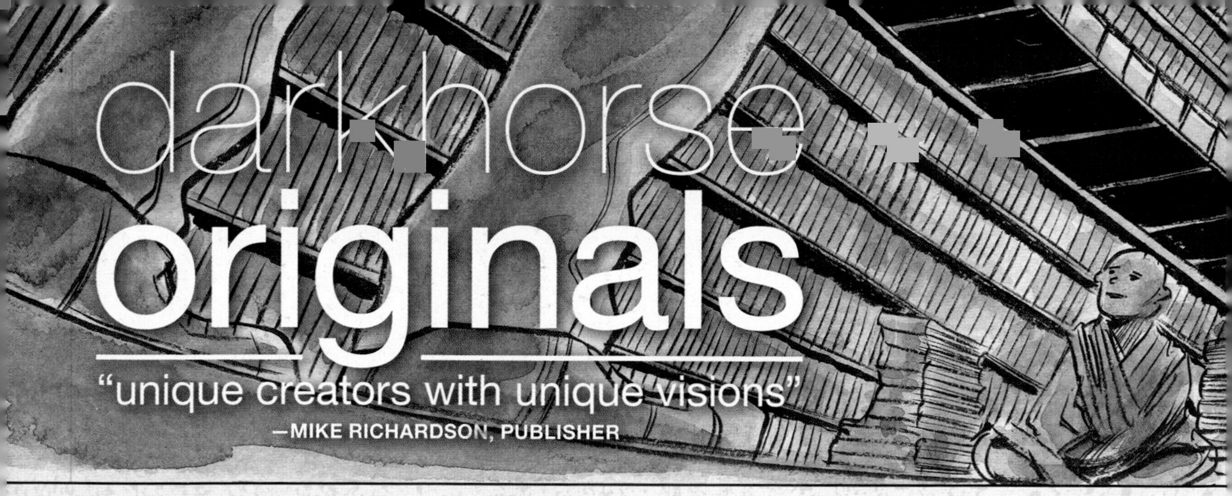
dark horse
originals
"unique creators with unique visions"
—MIKE RICHARDSON, PUBLISHER

3 STORY: THE SECRET HISTORY OF THE GIANT MAN
978-1-59582-356-4 | $19.99

365 SAMURAI AND A FEW BOWLS OF RICE
978-1-59582-412-7 | $16.99

THE ADVENTURES OF BLANCHE
978-1-59582-258-1 | $15.99

APOCALYPTIGIRL: AN ARIA FOR THE END TIMES
978-1-61655-566-5 | $9.99

BEANWORLD
Volume 1: Wahoolazuma!
978-1-59582-240-6 | $19.99
Volume 2: A Gift Comes!
978-1-59582-299-4 | $19.99
Volume 3: Remember Here When You Are There!
978-1-59582-355-7 | $19.99
Volume 3.5: Tales of the Beanworld
978-1-59582-897-2 | $14.99

BLACKSAD
978-1-59582-393-9 | $29.99

BLACKSAD: A SILENT HELL
978-1-59582-931-3 | $19.99

BLOOD SONG: A SILENT BALLAD
978-1-59582-389-2 | $19.99

THE BOOK OF GRICKLE
978-1-59582-430-1 | $17.99

BRODY'S GHOST COLLECTED EDITION
978-1-61655-901-4 | $24.99

BUCKO
978-1-59582-973-3 | $19.99

CHANNEL ZERO
978-1-59582-936-8 | $19.99

CHERUBS
978-1-59582-984-9 | $19.99

CHIMICHANGA
978-1-59582-755-5 | $14.99

CITIZEN REX
978-1-59582-556-8 | $19.99

THE COMPLETE PISTOLWHIP
978-1-61655-720-1 | $27.99

CROSSING THE EMPTY QUARTER AND OTHER STORIES
978-1-59582-388-5 | $24.99

DE:TALES
HC: 978-1-59582-557-5 | $19.99
TPB: 978-1-59307-485-2 | $14.99

EVERYBODY GETS IT WRONG! AND OTHER STORIES: DAVID CHELSEA'S 24-HOUR COMICS
978-1-61655-155-1 | $19.99

EXURBIA
978-1-59582-339-7 | $9.99

FLUFFY
978-1-59307-972-7 | $19.99

GREEN RIVER KILLER
978-1-61655-812-3 | $19.99

HEART IN A BOX
978-1-61655-694-5 | $14.99

INSOMNIA CAFÉ
978-1-59582-357-1 | $14.99

THE MIGHTY SKULLBOY ARMY
Volume 2
978-1-59582-872-9 | $14.99

MILK AND CHEESE: DAIRY PRODUCTS GONE BAD
978-1-59582-805-7 | $19.99

MIND MGMT
Volume 1: The Manager
978-1-59582-797-5 | $19.99
Volume 2: The Futurist
978-1-61655-198-8 | $19.99
Volume 3: The Home Maker
978-1-61655-390-6 | $19.99
Volume 4: The Magician
978-1-61655-391-3 | $19.99
Volume 5: The Eraser
978-1-61655-696-9 | $19.99
Volume 6: The Immortals
978-1-61655-798-0 | $19.99

MOTEL ART IMPROVEMENT SERVICE
978-1-59582-550-6 | $19.99

THE NIGHT OF YOUR LIFE
978-1-59582-183-6 | $15.99

NINGEN'S NIGHTMARES
978-1-59582-859-0 | $12.99

NOIR
978-1-59582-358-8 | $12.99

PIXU: THE MARK OF EVIL
978-1-61655-813-0 | $14.99

RESET
978-1-61655-003-5 | $15.99

SACRIFICE
978-1-59582-985-6 | $19.99

SINFEST: VIVA LA RESISTANCE
978-1-59582-424-0 | $14.99

SPEAK OF THE DEVIL
978-1-59582-193-5 | $19.99

UNCLE SILAS
978-1-59582-566-7 | $9.99

DARK HORSE BOOKS

AVAILABLE AT YOUR LOCAL COMICS SHOP OR BOOKSTORE!
To find a comics shop in your area, call 1-888-266-4226

For more information or to order direct:
On the web: DarkHorse.com
E-mail: mailorder@darkhorse.com
Phone: 1-800-862-0052 Mon.–Fri. 9 AM to 5 PM Pacific Time.

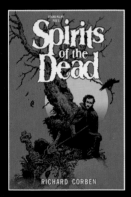

HELLBOY IN HELL VOLUME 1: THE DESCENT
Mike Mignola
ISBN 978-1-61655-444-6 | $17.99

THE AUTHENTIC ACCOUNTS OF BILLY THE KID'S OLD TIMEY ODDITIES
Eric Powell, Kyle Hotz
ISBN 978-1-61655-470-5 | $24.99

EDGAR ALLAN POE'S SPIRITS OF THE DEAD
Richard Corben
ISBN 978-1-61655-356-2 | $24.99

COLDER VOLUME 1
Paul Tobin, Juan Ferreyra
ISBN 978-1-61655-136-0 | $17.99

SIN TITULO
Cameron Stewart
ISBN 978-1-61655-248-0 | $19.99

GRINDHOUSE: DOORS OPEN AT MIDNIGHT DOUBLE FEATURE VOLUME 1
Alex de Campi, Chris Peterson, Simon Fraser
ISBN 978-1-61655-377-7 | $17.99

GUILLERMO DEL TORO AND CHUCK HOGAN'S THE STRAIN VOLUME 1
David Lapham, Mike Huddleston
ISBN 978-1-61655-032-5 | $19.99

HARROW COUNTY VOLUME 1: COUNTLESS HAINTS
Tyler Crook and Cullen Bunn
ISBN 978-1-61655-780-5 | $14.99

ALABASTER: WOLVES
Caitlín R. Kiernan and Steve Lieber
ISBN 978-1-61655-025-7 | $19.99

DEATH FOLLOWS
Cullen Bunn, A. C. Zamudio, and Carlos Nicolas Zamudio
ISBN 978-1-61655-951-9 | $17.99

HOUSE OF PENANCE
Peter J. Tomasi and Ian Bertram
ISBN 978-1-50670-033-5 | $19.99